ENGLISH CRITICAL TEXTS

ENGLISH
CRITICAL TEXTS
16th Century to 20th Century

Edited, with Notes
and an Appendix of Classical Extracts, by
D. J. ENRIGHT
and
ERNST DE CHICKERA

LONDON
OXFORD UNIVERSITY PRESS

Oxford University Press, Amen House, London E.C.4

GLASGOW NEW YORK TORONTO MELBOURNE WELLINGTON
BOMBAY CALCUTTA MADRAS KARACHI LAHORE DACCA
CAPE TOWN SALISBURY NAIROBI IBADAN ACCRA
KUALA LUMPUR HONG KONG

© Oxford University Press 1962

First published 1962
Reprinted 1963

Printed in Great Britain by
The Camelot Press Ltd., London and Southampton

Contents

NOTES

INTRODUCTION

Literary Criticism: An Approach

PERHAPS the best we can do by way of *approaching* a definition of literary criticism is to raise a number of questions, doubts, and suggestions, and hope that between them they will make up some kind of meaning. Procedure by negatives is often helpful, and we might begin with the proposition that literary criticism can never be a science. That proposition has been made often enough, by lazy readers and writers as well as by energetic ones: and obviously it lends itself conveniently to the exponents of 'One Opinion is as Good as Another'. Nevertheless, the fact remains that could criticism achieve the exactitude and absoluteness of science—of what one thinks of as science—then there would be only *one* opinion about any one work of literature. If there were any possible watertight system of rules then we should have no need of literary critics; nor should we need teachers of literature, except as what they sometimes are—the disc-jockeys of culture. We should simply apply the Golden Rules (whether ten or ten thousand), and the answer would automatically emerge: this is good, or this is bad, or this is so-so. In the case of a really complicated system an electronic brain might be employed. But indeed, if there were any such system, we should not need any more artists. If we knew all the rules, we could play the game ourselves: every man his own artist: you too can be a Shakespeare. For the creative artist is not precisely the man who breaks the rules but the man who makes new rules necessary: the man who incidentally and implicitly creates new rules. The critic then explicates these new rules—makes them as explicit as they can be made, that is. Logically, the work of art which allows itself to be judged—and judged fairly—by previously existent standards is dead, or at the best a skilful pastiche.

Now let us phrase our question as 'How can we—or how can

the critic—tell what is *good* literature?' In leaving aside the *nature* of this goodness, the kind of good which it is or which it does, it may seem that we are putting the cart before the horse. It may be objected that first of all we should say what literary goodness ultimately is—whether moral, religious, political, or physical—and then explore the means whereby we can ascertain whether or not that goodness is present in a particular specimen of literature. It is true that in assaying an ore, one would first define the 'truth' in question—the presence of gold, it might be —and then submit the object to an appropriate examination. But in art the procedure is different. We do not know in advance what the appropriate examination is—and so we must first decide whether the object is truthful, and then we can attempt to define the 'truth' about which it is being truthful. And it is, in fact, when we define 'truth' first and then go to the poem (say) to look for that truth that we fail to appreciate the poem for what it is. We are looking *for* something instead of *at* something: we are expecting confirmation of what we already know instead of preparing ourselves for illumination, and perhaps contradiction: we are telling the poet what's what when we should be asking him what precisely his 'what' is. Thus theosophical critics prove that the German poet Rilke was a theosophist, and Marxist critics demonstrate how *Wuthering Heights* is an epic of class warfare.

And this indicates the essential difficulty which critics face, in keeping an open, responsive mind—which of course is all the more necessary the more widely the poet departs from the currently accepted idea of poetry—and at the same time maintaining an actively critical, vigilant mind. The critic in action must always be hoping for something which is new, not amenable to direct comparison with anything which already exists, and genuine—and at the same time he must be on his guard against the factitiously new, the contrived façade of novelty. What is required of him is that he should be a man of eminently sceptical good will; and, especially in those who concern themselves with contemporary literature, the correct proportions of good will and scepticism are rarely achieved.

Criticism of art is based on the assumption that a successful work has an accessible meaning, in the sense that reasonably

normal persons approaching the work under appropriate conditions will derive fundamentally the same experience from
it. It is of course easy to argue against this, to point to the
diversity of our natural gifts and the variety of our past experience—with the result that the critic emerges as a kind of
small parasite on the body artistic, and indeed the artist
himself as merely a larger kind of parasite on the community.
Fortunately, common sense and common observation tell us
that we are all human, that we have much in common in the
shape of our mental and spiritual limbs as in that of our
physical members.

This being so, the critic has two functions. Firstly, he should
be concerned to see that the reader approaches the work under
conditions appropriate to it; and this involves drawing the
reader's attention to whatever is original or individual in
the writer's technique and demonstrating how this results in the
precise original or individual achievement. The point here is
that we are apt to think of art in terms of one particular school—
the Greek drama, to take an old example—and to assume that
a different kind of art—Elizabethan drama—is a more or less
unsuccessful attempt to reach a similar result by means of a
different technique. The critic's second function—and the two
are really inseparable and simultaneous—is to arrive at and
express a meaningful judgement of value. This is not to demand
a literary class-list, with poets or poems arranged in neat order
of priority. But none the less we do ask that the critic should
commit himself to some such personal judgement, and he
could hardly do this very clearly without referring to other
poets or poems. The word 'good' means nothing by itself, and—
unless the critic is prepared to dash continually into some other
world, into morals or politics or neurology, and is confident of
the usefulness of such excursions—he will most readily and
most accurately indicate his values in this way: by remaining
chiefly inside literature, that is, by a tactful ranging among
various literary works. For no work of real interest exists merely
in or for itself: in its terms of reference, it will be microcosmic.

There is a species of interpretative commentary from which
literary criticism (the regular contact with and pointing to
rhythm, imagery, music, the weight of the words, the taking

into account of the context, and reference to and fro within the complete work) is almost absent. The danger here is that the commentator, falling in love afresh with his own ideas and theories, will drift farther and farther away from the work which he is supposedly elucidating, and that the trusting reader who follows him will be unable to get back to that work. The reader is left with the immovable opaque block of the commentary, and what little he has received of the original work has been emasculated and pre-digested, instead of gained through personal effort. The usual critical procedure of fairly constant reference to the text is the only safeguard against this very human weakness—just as the comparative-critical judgements which the critic makes are the best preventive of that painful situation where we see the commentator, displaying all the signs of Jacob wrestling with the angel, injecting his own enthusiasms into the corpse of an inferior piece of writing.

A common answer to the question, 'How do we tell good literature from bad?' is: 'It's merely a question of taste.' It is true that it is a question of taste: but most people will agree that there are important—humanly important—differences between good taste and bad. The expression 'good taste' has fallen into disrepute: it denotes what you have if you use So-and-so's hair-oil; on another level it is associated with literary Clubland, up-to-date dilettantism. But for all that, it is a good word—*taste*—something in the mouth as well as in the mind, something which you enjoy and which nourishes at the same time. We use it here to mean the ability to distinguish between the genuine and the fake—and, more important, the habit of naturally and actively enjoying the former and rejecting the latter. The word *naturally* should be stressed, for there is nothing 'conscious' or pretentious about a formed good taste. But taste is as much the result of training and experience as of innate gifts. And where training is concerned, we must admit that it does not come from listening to talk about the Nature of the Goodness of Good Literature—except, perhaps, in as far as that talk happens to be aesthetically pleasing. It seems that little help can be expected from the shadowy abstractions of the so-called aesthetic philosopher, who too often might be described as the kind of person who knows all about Taste and

Beauty without possessing the one or being able to recognize the other. Basic training will rather take the form of close study of what are acknowledged as 'classics'. For if we have gone some way towards assimilating them, then we shall have realized forcibly the necessity for judging each work by rules which arise from within that work—by the particular, implicit, and ultimately indefinable laws which it invokes itself. Good work, we may suggest in parenthesis, extols itself and the critic's function is to make this process in some degree explicit, while bad work condemns itself and the critic must show where and how that condemnation is taking place.

Chaucer, Shakespeare, Milton, Jonson, Donne, 'Pope, Wordsworth, Keats—these are all great writers by common consent, and they are all in obvious ways *different*. They demonstrate that there cannot be any hard and fast laws of literature. They also provide us, as Arnold proposed, with something in the way of 'touchstones'. Naturally a mere acceptance of the classics will not produce a literary critic, or even a secular reader of taste. And naturally the note struck by one work will not be the same as that sounded by another equally good. The 'touchstone' has often been used as a brick-end to hurl at anything new or different: but, as Dryden showed of blank verse, there is no guarantee that even the most natural activity will not be done badly. Good will and common sense are prerequisites to reading as to other activities; and one can hardly learn how to read, how to detect the false ring of the counterfeit article, without reading a good deal.

Literary criticism, we have suggested, can never be a science. But it may at certain times wear the superficial appearance of one, in a certain place and within certain boundaries, and still be useful criticism. The beginning of D. H. Lawrence's essay on Galsworthy is very much to the point:

> Literary criticism can be no more than a reasoned account of the feeling produced upon the critic by the book he is criticizing. Criticism can never be a science: it is, in the first place, much too personal, and in the second, it is concerned with values that science ignores. . . . All the critical twiddle-twaddle about style and form, all this pseudo-scientific classifying and analysing of books in an imitation-botanical fashion, is mere impertinence and mostly dull

jargon. A critic must be able to *feel* the impact of a work of art in all its complexity and its force. To do so, he must be a man of force and complexity himself, which few critics are. A man with a paltry, impudent nature will never write anything but paltry, impudent criticism. And a man who is *emotionally* educated is rare as a phoenix. The more scholastically educated a man is generally, the more he is an emotional bore.

More than this, even an artistically and emotionally educated man must be a man of good faith. He must have the courage to admit what he feels, as well as the flexibility to *know* what he feels. So Sainte-Beuve remains, to me, a great critic. And a man like Macaulay, brilliant as he is, is unsatisfactory, because he is not honest. He is emotionally very alive, but he juggles his feelings. He prefers a fine effect to the sincere statement of his aesthetic and emotional reaction. . . . A critic must be emotionally alive in every fibre, intellectually capable and skilful in essential logic, and then morally very honest. Then it seems to me a good critic should give his reader a few standards to go by. He can change the standards for every new critical attempt, so long as he keeps good faith. But it is just as well to say: This and this is the standard we judge by. Sainte-Beuve, on the whole, set up the standard of the 'good man'. He sincerely believed that the great man was essentially the good man in the widest range of human sympathy. This remained his universal standard. Pater's standard was the lonely philosopher of pure thought and pure aesthetic truth. Macaulay's standard was tainted by a political or democratic bias, he must be on the side of the weak. Gibbon tried a purely moral standard, individual morality.

'Criticism can never be a science', Lawrence says—yet a little later he adds, 'a good critic should give his readers a few standards to go by'. He then mentions several critics and (roughly speaking) the standards they went by. Lawrence himself does not believe in absolute standards: in 'Why the Novel Matters' he demands, 'Once and for all and for ever, let us have done with the ugly imperialism of any absolute'. But, even taking into account the different societies in which these critics lived, we can see that some of the standards described are more useful than others. By Lawrence's account, Sainte-Beuve with his standard of 'human sympathy' is a critic of altogether wider range than Pater with his concern for the 'aesthetic' and Macaulay with his political bias.

Lawrence clearly has nothing large or exhaustive in mind when he speaks of 'a few standards'; and it seems likely that these standards will emerge from the critic's treatment of specific works. Sometimes—T. S. Eliot's 'Tradition and the Individual Talent' is an instance—the critic may present the reader with generalization or theory. But we think it will be agreed that Eliot's most important critical work, the part most likely to be of permanent interest, consists in his handling of particular pieces of literature, and it is from these essays, notably those on Marvell, Massinger, and the Metaphysical Poets, that we derive our clearest conception of his standards. Indeed, experience suggests that it becomes increasingly possible to reduce a critic's work to a set system as he shows an increasing interest in subject matter as something which exists apart from style and can be so discussed. Critics who are famous for their systems of criticism usually turn out to be primarily moralists, psychologists, philosophers, political theorists, or evangelists, and literature for them is the stone on which they grind their axes. From them one turns with relief to Keats's remarks on 'Negative Capability' and the 'chameleon poet' and his freedom from 'identity'.

Perhaps, then, we can interpret Lawrence's demand for 'a few standards' to mean a loosely framed scaffolding of preferences and antipathies, probably suggested by the critic implicitly in the course of his dealings with specific works or partially stated in an occasional generalization—a scaffolding which gives him plenty of room in which to manœuvre as he passes from one work to another. One cannot feel much sympathy for those people who demand that a critic should put all his cards on the table, should declare his rules and regulations in advance. Generally what they really want to know is whether he belongs to the same party or the same church as they. The 'bases' of his criticism surely should emerge from the literary judgements to which he commits himself in the course of his job. Only in that context can they define themselves at all adequately: only in that context are they of any interest to us.

Another aspect of the problem presents itself thus: 'Should we expect to agree with everything a good critic says? And can a critic of the past have any interest for a society whose life and tastes have changed considerably?' We are all aware of the suspicion which surrounds the curious activity of criticism.

True, the greater part of current criticism is niggling virtuosity: criticism for criticism's sake; a hundred opinionated flowers bloom every quarter from the smallest patch of literature. But more serious are the doubts inspired by (say) Johnson's comments on Shakespeare's tendency to 'sacrifice virtue to convenience'—or on *Lycidas*: 'In this poem there is no nature, for there is no truth; there is no art, for there is nothing new. Its form is that of a pastoral, easy, vulgar, and therefore disgusting.'

Is there no third alternative to accepting Pope's *Essay on Criticism* or Arnold's *Study of Poetry* wholesale as gospel truth or else dismissing them as mere and utterly invalidated 'period pieces'? Certainly we should not expect to agree with everything said by the best of critics, whether living or dead; the human factor (and literature is made for human beings, not human beings for literature) cannot be reduced to the point at which such concord would ensue. And in fact there will probably be much more to disagree with in the work of a good critic than in that of a poor one. We have only to think of Johnson: in spite of all the occasions where contemporary opinion differs radically from his, we know very well that he is one of the greatest of English critics. Whenever he said anything, he really *said* something; and his mistaken judgements (as they may seem to us) are yet illuminating, where the watery correctness of most critics leaves us in the dark. The comments on *Lycidas* at least tell us plainly enough how the poem struck one particular thinking man at a particular time. And, by presenting what under certain conditions was a feasible attitude, they help us in arriving at our own (and possibly very different) apprehension of the poem. A critic should be careful, but he should not hedge: he should have convictions and the courage of them. 'The opinions prevalent in one age, as truths above the reach of controversy, are confuted and rejected in another, and rise again to reception in remoter times', Johnson wrote in his *Preface to Shakespeare*. 'Thus the human mind is kept in motion without progress.' Perhaps without progress; but if it were not kept in motion, the human mind would certainly suffer regress. And in his essay on 'Johnson as Critic and Poet', Eliot proposes a helpful distinction between a limited sensibility and a defective sensibility. Johnson was bound by the limitations of his own age: then at least his judgements do not suffer from the limitations of our own age. And of how many men can it be said that their most notable limitations were merely those of the age in which they lived?

Much has been written of late regarding the critic's impartiality or 'objectivity', and the 'deflection' suffered by Christian or non-Christian critics as the case may be. The inquiry must of course extend to other religious beliefs as well as to beliefs of an extra-religious kind. It does not seem likely that a man who in his private life lacks any strong beliefs or antagonisms will be well equipped to write interestingly about literature. Nor that a man who holds such beliefs or antagonisms will be able to discard them completely when dealing with a literary work which engages him on his deepest levels. 'Negative Capability' is capable up to a point, but not so far that it prevents the critic from being (in Eliot's words from 'The Frontiers of Criticism') 'the whole man, a man with convictions and principles, and of knowledge and experience of life'. 'Deflection' of some sort and in some degree is surely inevitable from time to time. We may, if we will, term this a 'limitation'. But we can adjust ourselves to a revealed bias, and our real complaint against a critic is that he is deliberately attempting to conceal his bias or that he is pretending to an absolute impartiality which is the prerogative of the angel and of the ape. The critic, as Lawrence says, must 'keep good faith'.

In conclusion, here is a succinct account of the critic in action. It occurs in F. R. Leavis's 'Literary Criticism and Philosophy', a consideration of the difference in approach to literature between the literary critic and the philosopher:

The critic—the reader of poetry—is indeed concerned with evaluation, but to figure him as measuring with a norm which he brings up to the object and applies from the outside is to misrepresent the process. The critic's aim is, first, to realize as sensitively and completely as possible this or that which claims his attention; and a certain valuing is implicit in the realizing. As he matures in experience of the new thing he asks, explicitly and implicitly: 'Where does this come? How does it stand in relation to . . .? How relatively important does it seem?' And the organization into which it settles as a constituent in becoming 'placed' is an organization of similarly 'placed' things, things that have found their bearings with regard to one another, and not a theoretical system or a system determined by abstract considerations. . . .

The business of the literary critic is to attain a peculiar completeness of response and to observe a peculiarly strict relevance in developing his response into commentary; he must be on his guard against abstracting improperly from what is in front of him and against any premature or irrelevant generalizing—of it or from it. His first concern is to enter into possession of the given poem (let us say) in its concrete fulness, and his constant concern is never to lose his completeness of possession, but rather to increase it. In making value-judgments (and judgments as to significance), implicitly or explicitly, he does so out of that completeness of possession and with that fulness of response. He doesn't ask, 'How does this accord with these specifications of goodness in poetry?'; he aims to make fully conscious and articulate the immediate sense of value that 'places' the poem. . . .

     *   *   *   *   *

The present volume consists basically of those critical texts which, in our experience in various countries, are the most commonly studied, but which hitherto have only been available separately and thus at considerable expense. We are grateful to university teachers, more especially in India and Ceylon, for their advice as to the contents. Considerations of space have prevented us from including everything we should have desired. While we do not agree with those scholars who maintain that English literary criticism cannot be *understood* without a study of the classical critics, we have compromised to the extent of appending extracts from Aristotle, Horace, and Longinus.

All Shakespeare references are to the New Shakespeare (Cambridge) edition; all classical references are to the Loeb Classics (Heinemann), from which the English versions are taken except where otherwise indicated; and all Dante references are to the Temple Classics edition (Dent). Reference to an author without mention of a title pertains to the present collection; for example, 'Dryden, 24' indicates line 24 of Dryden's *Essay of Dramatic Poesy*. Our guiding principle in annotation has been to give a note only where it seemed necessary to clarify the sense of the passage; we have sought to avoid explanation for explanation's sake; but occasionally we have referred to other pronouncements by the same critic or to relevant pronouncements by other critics in order to indicate that continuity and diversity within criticism which an anthology of this size cannot cogently convey.

We wish to record our indebtedness to Isobel Andrews, of the Library of the University of Malaya in Singapore, and to Madeleine Enright for help in tracing references, and to Magdalene Tan Tai Wah and Jenny Choong Liew Kee who shared the burden of the typing.

Grateful acknowledgements are due to the following publishers for permission to use copyright material: Messrs. William Heinemann Ltd., Laurence Pollinger Ltd. and the Estate of the late Mrs. Frieda Lawrence (for 'Why the Novel Matters' and an extract from 'John Galsworthy' by D. H. Lawrence), Faber and Faber Ltd. (for 'Tradition and the Individual Talent', 'The Metaphysical Poets' and an extract from 'Andrew Marvell' by T. S. Eliot), Chatto and Windus Ltd. (for 'Keats' from *Revaluation* and an extract from 'Literary Criticism and Philosophy' by F. R. Leavis) and the Loeb Classical Library for the extracts from their translations of the texts by Aristotle, Longinus, Demetrius and Horace.

THE EDITORS

Department of English
University of Malaya in Singapore,
September, 1961

TEXTS

PHILIP SIDNEY

An Apology for Poetry

purpose of poetry = delightful teaching

WHEN the right virtuous Edward Wotton and I were at the
Emperor's court together, we gave ourselves to learn horsemanship of John Pietro Pugliano, one that with great commendation had the place of an esquire in his stable; and he,
according to the fertileness of the Italian wit, did not only 5
afford us the demonstration of his practice, but sought to
enrich our minds with the contemplations therein which he
thought most precious. But with none I remember mine ears
were at any time more laden, than when—either angered with
slow payment, or moved with our learner-like admiration—he 10
exercised his speech in the praise of his faculty. He said soldiers
were the noblest estate of mankind, and horsemen the noblest
of soldiers. He said they were the masters of war and ornaments
of peace, speedy goers and strong abiders, triumphers both in
camps and courts. Nay, to so unbelieved a point he proceeded, 15
as that no earthly thing bred such wonder to a prince as to
be a good horseman; skill of government was but a *pedanteria*
in comparison. Then would he add certain praises, by telling
what a peerless beast the horse was, the only serviceable
courtier without flattery, the beast of most beauty, faithfulness, 20
courage, and such more, that if I had not been a piece of a
logician before I came to him, I think he would have persuaded
me to have wished myself a horse. But thus much at least with
his no few words he drove into me, that self-love is better than
any gilding to make that seem gorgeous wherein ourselves be 25
parties.

Wherein if Pugliano's strong affection and weak arguments
will not satisfy you, I will give you a nearer example of myself,
who, I know not by what mischance, in these my not old years
and idlest times, having slipped into the title of a poet, am 30
provoked to say something unto you in the defence of that my

3

unelected vocation, which if I handle with more good will
than good reasons, bear with me, since the scholar is to be
pardoned that followeth the steps of his master.

35   And yet I must say that, as I have just cause to make a pitiful
defence of poor poetry, which from almost the highest estimation of learning is fallen to be the laughing-stock of children,
so have I need to bring some more available proofs, since the
former is by no man barred of his deserved credit, the silly
40 latter hath had even the names of philosophers used to the
defacing of it, with great danger of civil war among the Muses.
    And first, truly, to all them that, professing learning, inveigh
against poetry, may justly be objected that they go very near
to ungratefulness, to seek to deface that which, in the noblest
45 nations and languages that are known, hath been the first
light-giver to ignorance, and first nurse, whose milk by little
and little enabled them to feed afterwards of tougher knowledges. And will they now play the hedgehog, that, being
received into the den, drove out his host? Or rather the vipers,
50 that with their birth kill their parents? Let learned Greece in
any of her manifold sciences be able to show me one book
before Musaeus, Homer, and Hesiod, all three nothing else but
poets. Nay, let any history be brought that can say any writers
were there before them, if they were not men of the same skill,
55 as Orpheus, Linus, and some other are named, who, having
been the first of that country that made pens deliverers of their
knowledge to their posterity, may justly challenge to be called
their fathers in learning. For not only in time they had this
priority (although in itself antiquity be venerable) but went
60 before them as causes, to draw with their charming sweetness
the wild untamed wits to an admiration of knowledge. So as
Amphion was said to move stones with his poetry to build
Thebes, and Orpheus to be listened to by beasts, indeed stony
and beastly people. So among the Romans were Livius An-
65 dronicus and Ennius; so in the Italian language the first that
made it aspire to be a treasure-house of science were the poets
Dante, Boccaccio, and Petrarch; so in our English were Gower
and Chaucer, after whom, encouraged and delighted with their
excellent foregoing, others have followed to beautify our
70 mother-tongue, as well in the same kind as in other arts.

This did so notably show itself, that the philosophers of Greece durst not a long time appear to the world but under the masks of poets. So Thales, Empedocles, and Parmenides sang their natural philosophy in verses; so did Pythagoras and Phocylides their moral counsels; so did Tyrtaeus in war mat- 75 ters, and Solon in matters of policy; or rather they, being poets, did exercise their delightful vein in those points of highest knowledge which before them lay hid to the world. For that wise Solon was directly a poet it is manifest, having written in verse the notable fable of the Atlantic Island which was con- 80 tinued by Plato. And truly even Plato whosoever well considereth, shall find that in the body of his work, though the inside and strength were philosophy, the skin, as it were, and beauty depended most of poetry. For all standeth upon dialogues; wherein he feigneth many honest burgesses of Athens 85 to speak of such matters that, if they had been set on the rack, they would never have confessed them; besides his poetical describing the circumstances of their meetings, as the wellordering of a banquet, the delicacy of a walk, with interlacing mere tales, as Gyges' Ring and others, which who knoweth not 90 to be flowers of poetry did never walk into Apollo's garden.

And even historiographers, (although their lips sound of things done, and verity be written in their foreheads,) have been glad to borrow both fashion and perchance weight of poets. So Herodotus entitled his history by the name of the 95 nine Muses; and both he and all the rest that followed him either stole or usurped of poetry their passionate describing of passions, the many particularities of battles which no man could affirm, or, if that be denied me, long orations put in the mouths of great kings and captains, which it is certain they 100 never pronounced.

So that truly neither philosopher nor historiographer could, at the first, have entered into the gates of popular judgements, if they had not taken a great passport of poetry; which in all nations at this day, where learning flourisheth not, is plain to 105 be seen, in all which they have some feeling of poetry. In Turkey, besides their lawgiving divines they have no other writers but poets. In our neighbour-country Ireland, where truly learning goeth very bare, yet are their poets held in a

110 devout reverence. Even among the most barbarous and simple
Indians, where no writing is, yet have they their poets, who
make and sing songs (which they call *areytos*), both of their
ancestors' deeds and praises of their gods. A sufficient probability that, if ever learning come among them, it must be
115 by having their hard dull wits softened and sharpened with
the sweet delights of poetry; for until they find a pleasure in the
exercises of the mind, great promises of much knowledge will
little persuade them that know not the fruits of knowledge. In
Wales, the true remnant of the ancient Britons, as there are
120 good authorities to show the long time they had poets, which
they called bards, so through all the conquests of Romans,
Saxons, Danes, and Normans, some of whom did seek to ruin
all memory of learning from among them, yet do their poets
even to this day last; so as it is not more notable in soon
125 beginning, than in long continuing.

But since the authors of most of our sciences were the Romans,
and before them the Greeks, let us a little stand upon their
authorities, but even so far as to see what names they have
given unto this now scorned skill. Among the Romans a poet
130 was called *vates*, which is as much as a diviner, foreseer, or
prophet, as by his conjoined words, *vaticinium* and *vaticinari*, is
manifest; so heavenly a title did that excellent people bestow
upon this heart-ravishing knowledge. And so far were they
carried into the admiration thereof, that they thought in the
135 chanceable hitting upon any such verses great foretokens of
their following fortunes were placed; whereupon grew the
word of *Sortes Virgilianae*, when by sudden opening Virgil's book
they lighted upon any verse of his making; whereof the Histories of the Emperors' Lives are full: as of Albinus, the governor
140 of our island, who in his childhood met with this verse,

Arma amens capio, nec sat rationis in armis,

and in his age performed it; which although it were a very vain
and godless superstition, as also it was to think that spirits
were commanded by such verses—whereupon this word
145 charms, derived of *carmina*, cometh—so yet serveth it to show
the great reverence those wits were held in, and altogether not
without ground, since both the oracles of Delphos and Sibylla's

(margin note: Romans called poet "prophet" (vates))

prophecies were wholly delivered in verses; for that same exquisite observing of number and measure in words, and that high-flying liberty of conceit proper to the poet, did seem 150 to have some divine force in it.

And may not I presume a little further to show the reasonableness of this word *vates*, and say that the holy David's Psalms are a divine poem? If I do, I shall not do it without the testimony of great learned men, both ancient and modern. 155 But even the name Psalms will speak for me, which, being interpreted, is nothing but Songs; then, that it is fully written in metre, as all learned Hebricians agree, although the rules be not yet fully found; lastly and principally, his handling his prophecy, which is merely poetical. For what else is the awaking 160 his musical instruments, the often and free changing of persons, his notable *prosopopoeias*, when he maketh you, as it were, see God coming in His majesty, his telling of the beasts' joyfulness and hills' leaping, but a heavenly poesy, wherein almost he showeth himself a passionate lover of that unspeakable and 165 everlasting beauty to be seen by the eyes of the mind, only cleared by faith? But truly, now, having named him, I fear me I seem to profane that holy name, applying it to poetry, which is among us thrown down to so ridiculous an estimation. But they that with quiet judgements will look a little deeper into 170 it, shall find the end and working of it such as, being rightly applied, deserveth not to be scourged out of the church of God.

But now let us see how the Greeks named it and how they deemed of it. The Greeks called him a Poet, which name hath, as the most excellent, gone through other languages. It cometh 175 of this word *poiein*, which is 'to make'; wherein I know not whether by luck or wisdom we Englishmen have met with the Greeks in calling him a maker. Which name, how high and incomparable a title it is, I had rather were known by marking the scope of other sciences than by my partial allegation. 180

There is no art delivered unto mankind that hath not the works of nature for his principal object, without which they could not consist, and on which they so depend as they become actors and players, as it were, of what nature will have set forth. So doth the astronomer look upon the stars, and, by that he 185 seeth, set down what order nature hath taken therein. So do

the geometrician and arithmetician in their divers sorts of
quantities. So doth the musician in times tell you which by
nature agree, which not. The natural philosopher thereon hath
190 his name, and the moral philosopher standeth upon the natural
virtues, vices, and passions of man; and 'follow nature', saith
he, 'therein, and thou shalt not err.' The lawyer saith what
men have determined; the historian what men have done. The
grammarian speaketh only of the rules of speech, and the
195 rhetorician and logician, considering what in nature will
soonest prove and persuade, thereon give artificial rules, which
still are compassed within the circle of a question, according
to the proposed matter. The physician weigheth the nature of
man's body, and the nature of things helpful or hurtful unto it.
200 And the metaphysic, though it be in the second and abstract
notions, and therefore be counted supernatural, yet doth he,
indeed, build upon the depth of nature.

Only the poet, disdaining to be tied to any such subjection,
lifted up with the vigour of his own invention, doth grow, in
205 effect, into another nature, in making things either better than
nature bringeth forth, or, quite anew, forms such as never
were in nature, as the heroes, demi-gods, cyclops, chimeras,
furies, and such like; so as he goeth hand in hand with Nature,
not enclosed within the narrow warrant of her gifts, but freely
210 ranging only within the zodiac of his own wit. Nature never set
forth the earth in so rich tapestry as divers poets have done;
neither with pleasant rivers, fruitful trees, sweet-smelling
flowers, nor whatsoever else may make the too-much-loved
earth more lovely; her world is brazen, the poets only deliver
215 a golden.

But let those things alone, and go to man—for whom as the
other things are, so it seemeth in him her uttermost cunning is
employed—and know whether she have brought forth so true
a lover as Theagenes; so constant a friend as Pylades; so
220 valiant a man as Orlando; so right a prince as Xenophon's
Cyrus; so excellent a man every way as Virgil's Aeneas?
Neither let this be jestingly conceived, because the works of
the one be essential, the other in imitation or fiction; for any
understanding knoweth the skill of the artificer standeth in that
225 idea, or fore-conceit of the work, and not in the work itself.

And that the poet hath that idea is manifest, by delivering
them forth in such excellency as he hath imagined them. Which
delivering forth, also, is not wholly imaginative, as we are
wont to say by them that build castles in the air; but so far
substantially it worketh, not only to make a Cyrus, which had 230
been but a particular excellency, as nature might have done,
but to bestow a Cyrus upon the world to make many Cyruses, if
they will learn aright why and how that maker made him.
Neither let it be deemed too saucy a comparison to balance
the highest point of man's wit with the efficacy of nature; but 235
rather give right honour to the Heavenly Maker of that maker,
who, having made man to His own likeness, set him beyond
and over all the works of that second nature. Which in nothing
he showeth so much as in poetry, when, with the force of a
divine breath, he bringeth things forth far surpassing her doings, 240
with no small argument to the incredulous of that first accursed
fall of Adam,—since our erected wit maketh us know what
perfection is, and yet our infected will keepeth us from reaching
unto it. But these arguments will by few be understood, and by
fewer granted; thus much I hope will be given me, that the 245
Greeks, with some probability of reason, gave him the name
above all names of learning.

Now let us go to a more ordinary opening of him, that the
truth may be the more palpable; and so, I hope, though we
get not so unmatched a praise as the etymology of his names 250
will grant, yet his very description, which no man will deny,
shall not justly be barred from a principal commendation.

Poesy, therefore, is an art of imitation, for so Aristotle
termeth it in his word *Mimesis*, that is to say, a representing,
counterfeiting, or figuring forth; to speak metaphorically, a 255
speaking picture, with this end, to teach and delight.

Of this have been three several kinds. The chief, both in
antiquity and excellency, were they that did imitate the incon-
ceivable excellencies of God. Such were David in his Psalms;
Solomon in his Song of Songs, in his Ecclesiastes and Proverbs; 260
Moses and Deborah in their Hymns; and the writer of Job;
which, beside other, the learned Emanuel Tremellius and
Franciscus Junius do entitle the poetical part of the Scripture.
Against these none will speak that hath the Holy Ghost in due

265 holy reverence. In this kind, though in a full wrong divinity,
were Orpheus, Amphion, Homer in his Hymns, and many
other, both Greeks and Romans. And this poesy must be used by
whosoever will follow St. James's counsel in singing psalms when
they are merry; and I know is used with the fruit of comfort
270 by some, when, in sorrowful pangs of their death-bringing
sins, they find the consolation of the never-leaving goodness.

philosophy The second kind is of them that deal with matters philosophical: either moral, as Tyrtaeus, Phocylides, and Cato; or
natural, as Lucretius and Virgil's Georgics; or astronomical,
275 as Manilius and Pontanus; or historical, as Lucan; which who
mislike, the fault is in their judgement, quite out of taste, and
not in the sweet food of sweetly uttered knowledge.

But because this second sort is wrapped within the fold of
the proposed subject, and takes not the free course of his own
280 invention, whether they properly be poets or no let gram-
marians dispute, and go to the third, indeed right poets, of
whom chiefly this question ariseth. Betwixt whom and these
second is such a kind of difference as betwixt the meaner sort of
painters, who counterfeit only such faces as are set before them,
285 and the more excellent, who having no law but wit, bestow
that in colours upon you which is fittest for the eye to see; as
the constant though lamenting look of Lucretia, when she
punished in herself another's fault; wherein he painteth not
Lucretia, whom he never saw, but painteth the outward beauty
290 of such a virtue. For these third be they which most properly do
teach imitate to teach and delight; and to imitate borrow nothing
what of what is, hath been, or shall be; but range, only reined with
should learned discretion, into the divine consideration of what may
be be and should be. These be they that, as the first and most noble
295 sort, may justly be termed *vates*; so these are waited on in the
excellentest languages and best understandings with the fore-
described name of poets. For these, indeed, do merely make to
imitate, and imitate both to delight and teach, and delight to
move men to take that goodness in hand, which without
300 delight they would fly as from a stranger; and teach to make
them know that goodness whereunto they are moved; which
being the noblest scope to which ever any learning was directed,
yet want there not idle tongues to bark at them.

These be subdivided into sundry more special denomina- tions. The most notable be the heroic, lyric, tragic, comic, 305 satiric, iambic, elegiac, pastoral, and certain others, some of these being termed according to the matter they deal with, some by the sorts of verses they liked best to write in,—for indeed the greatest part of poets have apparelled their poetical inventions in that numberous kind of writing which is called 310 verse. Indeed but apparelled, verse being but an ornament and no cause to poetry, since there have been many most excellent poets that never versified, and now swarm many versifiers that need never answer to the name of poets. For Xenophon, who did imitate so excellently as to give us *effigiem justi imperii*—the 315 portraiture of a just empire, under the name of Cyrus (as Cicero says of him) made therein an absolute heroical poem; so did Heliodorus in his sugared invention of that picture of love in Theagenes and Chariclea; and yet both these writ in prose. Which I speak to show that it is not rhyming and 320 versing that maketh a poet (no more than a long gown maketh an advocate, who, though he pleaded in armour, should be an advocate and no soldier,) but it is that feigning notable images of virtues, vices, or what else, with that delightful teaching, which must be the right describing note to know a poet by. 325 Although indeed the Senate of Poets hath chosen verse as their fittest raiment, meaning, as in matter they passed all in all, so in manner to go beyond them; not speaking, (table-talk fashion, or like men in a dream,) words as they chanceably fall from the mouth, but peizing each syllable of each word by just 330 proportion, according to the dignity of the subject.

Now, therefore, it shall not be amiss, first to weigh this latter sort of poetry by his works, and then by his parts; and if in neither of these anatomies he be condemnable, I hope we shall obtain a more favourable sentence. This purifying of wit, this 335 enriching of memory, enabling of judgement, and enlarging of conceit, which commonly we call learning, under what name soever it come forth or to what immediate end soever it be directed, the final end is to lead and draw us to as high a perfection as our degenerate souls, made worse by their clayey lodgings, 340 can be capable of. This, according to the inclination of man, bred many-formed impressions. For some that thought this

felicity principally to be gotten by knowledge, and no knowledge
to be so high or heavenly as acquaintance with the stars, gave
345 themselves to astronomy; others, persuading themselves to be
demi-gods if they knew the causes of things, became natural and
supernatural philosophers. Some an admirable delight drew to
music, and some the certainty of demonstration to the mathe-
matics; but all, one and other, having this scope: to know, and
350 by knowledge to lift up the mind from the dungeon of the body
to the enjoying his own divine essence. But when by the balance
of experience it was found that the astronomer, looking to the
stars, might fall into a ditch, that the inquiring philosopher
might be blind in himself, and the mathematician might draw
355 forth a straight line with a crooked heart; then lo! did proof,
the overruler of opinions, make manifest, that all these are but
serving sciences, which, as they have each a private end in
themselves, so yet are they all directed to the highest end of
the mistress-knowledge, by the Greeks called *architektonikē*,
360 which stands, as I think, in the knowledge of a man's self, in
the ethic and politic consideration, with the end of well-doing,
and not of well-knowing only; even as the saddler's next end is
to make a good saddle, but his further end to serve a nobler
faculty, which is horsemanship; so the horseman's to soldiery;
365 and the soldier not only to have the skill, but to perform the
practice of a soldier. So that the ending end of all earthly
learning being virtuous action, those skills that most serve to
bring forth that have a most just title to be princes over all the
rest; wherein, if we can show, the poet is worthy to have it
370 before any other competitors.

poet's worthiness

Among whom as principal challengers step forth the moral
philosophers; whom, me thinketh, I see coming toward me
with a sullen gravity, (as though they could not abide vice by
daylight,) rudely clothed, for to witness outwardly their con-
375 tempt of outward things; with books in their hands against
glory, whereto they set their names; sophistically speaking
against subtlety; and angry with any man in whom they see
the foul fault of anger. These men, casting largess as they go of
Definitions, Divisions, and Distinctions, with a scornful inter-
380 rogative do soberly ask whether it be possible to find any path
so ready to lead a man to virtue, as that which teacheth what

virtue is, and teacheth it not only by delivering forth his very
being, his causes and effects, but also by making known his
enemy, Vice, which must be destroyed, and his cumbersome
servant, Passion, which must be mastered, by showing the 385
generalities that containeth it, and the specialities that are
derived from it; lastly, by plain setting down how it extendeth
itself out of the limits of a man's own little world, to the government of families, and maintaining of public societies?

The historian scarcely giveth leisure to the moralist to say 390
so much, but that he, laden with old mouse-eaten records,
authorizing himself for the most part upon other histories,
whose greatest authorities are built upon the notable foundation of hearsay; having much ado to accord differing writers,
and to pick truth out of partiality; better acquainted with a 395
thousand years ago than with the present age, and yet better
knowing how this word goeth than how his own wit runneth;
curious for antiquities and inquisitive of novelties, a wonder
to young folks and a tyrant in table-talk; denieth, in a great
chafe, that any man for teaching of virtue and virtuous actions 400
is comparable to him. 'I am *testis temporum, lux veritatis, vita
memoriae, magistra vitae, nuntia vetustatis,* etc. The philosopher,'
saith he, 'teacheth a disputative virtue, but I do an active.
His virtue is excellent in the dangerless Academy of Plato, but
mine showeth forth her honourable face in the battles of 405
Marathon, Pharsalia, Poitiers, and Agincourt. He teacheth
virtue by certain abstract considerations, but I only bid you
follow the footing of them that have gone before you. Old-aged
experience goeth beyond the fine-witted philosopher; but I give
the experience of many ages. Lastly, if he make the song-book, 410
I put the learner's hand to the lute; and if he be the guide,
I am the light.' Then would he allege you innumerable examples, conferring story by story, how much the wisest senators
and princes have been directed by the credit of history, as
Brutus, Alphonsus of Aragon (and who not, if need be?). At 415
length the long line of their disputation maketh a point in this,
that the one giveth the precept, and the other the example.

Now whom shall we find, since the question standeth for the
highest form in the school of learning, to be moderator? Truly,
as me seemeth, the poet; and if not a moderator, even the man 420

that ought to carry the title from them both, and much more
from all other serving sciences. Therefore compare we the poet
with the historian and with the moral philosopher; and if he
go beyond them both, no other human skill can match him.
425 For as for the divine, with all reverence it is ever to be excepted,
not only for having his scope as far beyond any of these as
eternity exceedeth a moment, but even for passing each of these
in themselves. And for the lawyer, though *Jus* be the daughter
of Justice, and Justice the chief of virtues, yet because he
430 seeketh to make men good rather *formidine poenae* than *virtutis
amore*; or, to say righter, doth not endeavour to make men good,
but that their evil hurt not others; having no care, so he be a
good citizen, how bad a man he be; therefore, as our wickedness maketh him necessary, and necessity maketh him honour-
435 able, so is he not in the deepest truth to stand in rank with
these, who all endeavour to take naughtiness away, and plant
goodness even in the secretest cabinet of our souls. And these
four are all that any way deal in that consideration of men's
manners, which being the supreme knowledge, they that best
440 breed it deserve the best commendation.

The philosopher therefore and the historian are they which
would win the goal, the one by precept, the other by example;
but both, not having both, do both halt. For the philosopher,
setting down with thorny argument the bare rule, is so hard of
445 utterance and so misty to be conceived, that one that hath no
other guide but him shall wade in him till he be old, before he
shall find sufficient cause to be honest. For his knowledge
standeth so upon the abstract and general, that happy is that
man who may understand him, and more happy that can apply
450 what he doth understand. On the other side, the historian,
wanting the precept, is so tied, not to what should be but to
what is, to the particular truth of things and not to the general
reason of things, that his example draweth no necessary consequence, and therefore a less fruitful doctrine.

455 Now doth the peerless poet perform both; for whatsoever
the philosopher saith should be done, he giveth a perfect picture
of it in some one by whom he presupposeth it was done, so as
he coupleth the general notion with the particular example.
A perfect picture, I say; for he yieldeth to the powers of the

mind an image of that whereof the philosopher bestoweth but a 460
wordish description, which doth neither strike, pierce, nor
possess the sight of the soul so much as that other doth. For as,
in outward things, to a man that had never seen an elephant
or a rhinoceros, who should tell him most exquisitely all their
shapes, colour, bigness, and particular marks; or of a gorgeous 465
palace, the architecture, with declaring the full beauties,
might well make the hearer able to repeat, as it were by rote,
all he had heard, yet should never satisfy his inward conceit
with being witness to itself of a true lively knowledge; but the
same man, as soon as he might see those beasts well painted, or 470
that house well in model, should straightways grow, without
need of any description, to a judicial comprehending of them:
so no doubt the philosopher, with his learned definitions, be it
of virtues or vices, matters of public policy or private government, replenisheth the memory with many infallible grounds 475
of wisdom, which notwithstanding lie dark before the imaginative and judging power, if they be not illuminated or figured
forth by the speaking picture of poesy.

Tully taketh much pains, and many times not without
poetical helps, to make us know the force love of our country 480
hath in us. Let us but hear old Anchises speaking in the midst
of Troy's flames, or see Ulysses, in the fullness of all Calypso's
delights, bewail his absence from barren and beggarly Ithaca.
Anger, the Stoics said, was a short madness. Let but Sophocles
bring you Ajax on a stage, killing or whipping sheep and oxen, 485
thinking them the army of Greeks, with their chieftains
Agamemnon and Menelaus, and tell me if you have not a
more familiar insight into anger, than finding in the schoolmen
his genus and difference. See whether wisdom and temperance
in Ulysses and Diomedes, valour in Achilles, friendship in 490
Nisus and Euryalus, even to an ignorant man carry not an
apparent shining. And, contrarily, the remorse of conscience
in Oedipus; the soon-repenting pride of Agamemnon; the self-
devouring cruelty in his father Atreus; the violence of ambition
in the two Theban brothers; the sour sweetness of revenge in 495
Medea; and, to fall lower, the Terentian Gnatho and our
Chaucer's Pandar, so expressed that we now use their names to
signify their trades; and finally, all virtues, vices, and passions

so in their own natural states laid to the view, that we seem
500 not to hear of them, but clearly to see through them.

But even in the most excellent determination of goodness,
what philosopher's counsel can so readily direct a prince, as
the feigned Cyrus in Xenophon? Or a virtuous man in all
fortunes, as Aeneas in Virgil? Or a whole commonwealth, as
505 the way of Sir Thomas More's Utopia? I say the way, because
where Sir Thomas More erred, it was the fault of the man, and
not of the poet; for that way of patterning a commonwealth
was most absolute, though he, perchance, hath not so absolutely
performed it. For the question is, whether the feigned image of
510 poesy, or the regular instruction of philosophy, hath the more
force in teaching. Wherein if the philosophers have more rightly
showed themselves philosophers than the poets have attained
to the high top of their profession, (as in truth,

Mediocribus esse poetis
515   Non Di, non homines, non concessere columnae,)

it is, I say again, not the fault of the art, but that by few men
that art can be accomplished.

Certainly, even our Saviour Christ could as well have given
the moral commonplaces of uncharitableness and humbleness
520 as the divine narration of Dives and Lazarus; or of disobedience
and mercy, as that heavenly discourse of the lost child and the
gracious father; but that his through-searching wisdom knew
the estate of Dives burning in hell, and of Lazarus in Abraham's
bosom, would more constantly, as it were, inhabit both the
525 memory and judgement. Truly, for myself, me seems I see before
mine eyes the lost child's disdainful prodigality turned to envy
a swine's dinner; which by the learned divines are thought not
historical acts, but instructing parables.

For conclusion, I say the philosopher teacheth, but he
530 teacheth obscurely, so as the learned only can understand him;
that is to say, he teacheth them that are already taught. But the
poet is the food for the tenderest stomachs; the poet is indeed
the right popular philosopher. Whereof Aesop's tales give good
proof; whose pretty allegories, stealing under the formal tales
535 of beasts, make many, more beastly than beasts, begin to hear
the sound of virtue from those dumb speakers.

But now may it be alleged that if this imagining of matters be so fit for the imagination, then must the historian needs surpass, who bringeth you images of true matters, such as indeed were done, and not such as fantastically or falsely may be 540 suggested to have been done. Truly, Aristotle himself, in his Discourse of Poesy, plainly determineth this question, saying that poetry is *philosophoteron* and *spoudaioteron*, that is to say, it is more philosophical and more studiously serious than history. His reason is, because poesy dealeth with *katholou*, that is to 545 say with the universal consideration, and the history with *kathekaston*, the particular. 'Now,' saith he, 'the universal weighs what is fit to be said or done, either in likelihood or necessity, which the poesy considereth in his imposed names; and the particular only marketh whether Alcibiades did, or 550 suffered, this or that': thus far Aristotle. Which reason of his, as all his, is most full of reason.

For, indeed, if the question were whether it were better to have a particular act truly or falsely set down, there is no doubt which is to be chosen, no more than whether you had 555 rather have Vespasian's picture right as he was, or, at the painter's pleasure, nothing resembling. But if the question be for your own use and learning, whether it be better to have it set down as it should be or as it was, then certainly is more doctrinable the feigned Cyrus of Xenophon than the true 560 Cyrus in Justin; and the feigned Aeneas in Virgil than the right Aeneas in Dares Phrygius; as to a lady that desired to fashion her countenance to the best grace, a painter should more benefit her to portrait a most sweet face, writing Canidia upon it, than to paint Canidia as she was, who, Horace 565 sweareth, was foul and ill-favoured.

If the poet do his part aright, he will show you in Tantalus, Atreus, and such like, nothing that is not to be shunned; in Cyrus, Aeneas, Ulysses, each thing to be followed. Where the historian, bound to tell things as things were, cannot be liberal 570 (without he will be poetical,) of a perfect pattern, but, as in Alexander, or Scipio himself, show doings, some to be liked, some to be misliked; and then how will you discern what to follow, but by your own discretion, which you had without reading Quintus Curtius? And whereas a man may say, though 575

in universal consideration of doctrine the poet prevaileth, yet
that the history, in his saying such a thing was done, doth
warrant a man more in that he shall follow, the answer is manifest: that if he stand upon that *was*, as if he should argue, be-
580 cause it rained yesterday therefore it should rain today, then
indeed it hath some advantage to a gross conceit. But if he
know an example only informs a conjectured likelihood, and
so go by reason, the poet doth so far exceed him as he is to
frame his example to that which is most reasonable, be it in
585 warlike, politic, or private matters; where the historian in his
bare *was* hath many times that which we call fortune to over-
rule the best wisdom. Many times he must tell events whereof
he can yield no cause; or if he do, it must be poetically.

For, that a feigned example hath as much force to teach as a
590 true example, (for as for to move, it is clear, since the feigned
may be tuned to the highest key of passion,) let us take one
example wherein a poet and a historian do concur. Herodotus
and Justin do both testify that Zopyrus, king Darius' faithful
servant, seeing his master long resisted by the rebellious Baby-
595 lonians, feigned himself in extreme disgrace of his king; for
verifying of which he caused his own nose and ears to be cut off,
and so flying to the Babylonians, was received, and for his
known valour so far credited, that he did find means to deliver
them over to Darius. Much like matter doth Livy record of
600 Tarquinius and his son. Xenophon excellently feigneth such
another strategem, performed by Abradates in Cyrus' behalf.
Now would I fain know, if occasion be presented unto you to
serve your prince by such an honest dissimulation, why do you
not as well learn it of Xenophon's fiction as of the other's
605 verity? and, truly, so much the better, as you shall save your
nose by the bargain; for Abradates did not counterfeit so
far.

So, then, the best of the historian is subject to the poet; for
whatsoever action or faction, whatsoever counsel, policy, or
610 war-stratagem the historian is bound to recite, that may the
poet, if he list, with his imitation make his own, beautifying it
both for further teaching and more delighting, as it pleaseth
him; having all, from Dante's Heaven to his Hell, under the
authority of his pen. Which if I be asked what poets have done

so? as I might well name some, yet say I, and say again, I 615
speak of the art, and not of the artificer.

Now, to that which commonly is attributed to the praise of
histories, in respect of the notable learning is gotten by marking
the success, as though therein a man should see virtue exalted
and vice punished, truly that commendation is peculiar to 620
poetry and far off from history. For, indeed, poetry ever setteth
virtue so out in her best colours, making Fortune her well-
waiting handmaid, that one must needs be enamoured of her.
Well may you see Ulysses in a storm, and in other hard plights;
but they are but exercises of patience and magnanimity, to 625
make them shine the more in the near following prosperity.
And, of the contrary part, if evil men come to the stage, they
ever go out, (as the tragedy writer answered to one that misliked the show of such persons) so manacled, as they little
animate folks to follow them. But the historian, being captived 630
to the truth of a foolish world, is many times a terror from well-
doing, and an encouragement to unbridled wickedness. For
see we not valiant Miltiades rot in his fetters? The just Phocion
and the accomplished Socrates put to death like traitors? The
cruel Severus live prosperously? The excellent Severus miser- 635
ably murdered? Sylla and Marius dying in their beds? Pompey
and Cicero slain then, when they would have thought exile a
happiness? See we not virtuous Cato driven to kill himself, and
rebel Caesar so advanced that his name yet, after sixteen
hundred years, lasteth in the highest honour? And mark but 640
even Caesar's own words of the forenamed Sylla, (who in that
only did honestly, to put down his dishonest tyranny), *literas
nescivit*: as if want of learning caused him to do well. He meant
it not by poetry, which, not content with earthly plagues,
deviseth new punishments in hell for tyrants; nor yet by philo- 645
sophy, which teacheth *occidendos esse*; but, no doubt, by skill
in history, for that indeed can afford you Cypselus, Periander,
Phalaris, Dionysius, and I know not how many more of the
same kennel, that speed well enough in their abominable in-
justice or usurpation. 650

I conclude, therefore, that he excelleth history, not only in
furnishing the mind with knowledge, but in setting it forward
to that which deserveth to be called and accounted good;

which setting forward, and moving to well-doing, indeed
655 setteth the laurel crown upon the poet as victorious, not only
of the historian, but over the philosopher, howsoever in teaching it may be questionable. For suppose it be granted, (that
which I suppose with great reason may be denied,) that the
philosopher, in respect of his methodical proceeding, doth
660 teach more perfectly than the poet, yet do I think that no man
is so much *philophilosophos* as to compare the philosopher in
moving with the poet. And that moving is of a higher degree
than teaching, it may by this appear, that it is well nigh both
the cause and the effect of teaching; for who will be taught, if
665 he be not moved with desire to be taught? And what so much
good doth that teaching bring forth (I speak still of moral
doctrine,) as that it moveth one to do that which it doth teach?
For, as Aristotle saith, it is not *gnosis* but *praxis* must be the fruit;
and how *praxis* can be, without being moved to practise, it is
670 no hard matter to consider. The philosopher showeth you the
way, he informeth you of the particularities, as well of the
tediousness of the way, as of the pleasant lodging you shall
have when your journey is ended, as of the many by-turnings
that may divert you from your way; but this is to no man but
675 to him that will read him, and read him with attentive, studious
painfulness; which constant desire whosoever hath in him, hath
already passed half the hardness of the way, and therefore is
beholding to the philosopher but for the other half. Nay, truly,
learned men have learnedly thought, that where once reason
680 hath so much overmastered passion as that the mind hath a
free desire to do well, the inward light each mind hath in itself
is as good as a philosopher's book; since in nature we know
it is well to do well, and what is well and what is evil, although
not in the words of art which philosophers bestow upon us; for
685 out of natural conceit the philosophers drew it. But to be moved
to do that which we know, or to be moved with desire to know,
hoc opus, hic labor est.

Now therein of all sciences, (I speak still of human, and
according to the human conceit,) is our poet the monarch.
690 For he doth not only show the way, but giveth so sweet a prospect into the way as will entice any man to enter into it. Nay,
he doth, as if your journey should lie through a fair vineyard,

at the very first give you a cluster of grapes, that full of that taste
you may long to pass further. He beginneth not with obscure
definitions, which must blur the margin with interpretations, 695
and load the memory with doubtfulness. But he cometh to
you with words set in delightful proportion, either accompanied
with, or prepared for, the well-enchanting skill of music; and
with a tale, forsooth, he cometh unto you, with a tale which
holdeth children from play, and old men from the chimney- 700
corner; and, pretending no more, doth intend the winning of
the mind from wickedness to virtue; even as the child is often
brought to take most wholesome things, by hiding them in such
other as have a pleasant taste,—which, if one should begin to
tell them the nature of the aloes or rhubarb they should receive, 705
would sooner take their physic at their ears than at their mouth.
So is it in men, (most of which are childish in the best things,
till they be cradled in their graves,) glad they will be to hear
the tales of Hercules, Achilles, Cyrus, Aeneas; and, hearing
them, must needs hear the right description of wisdom, valour, 710
and justice; which, if they had been barely, (that is to say
philosophically,) set out, they would swear they be brought to
school again.

That imitation whereof poetry is, hath the most conveniency
to nature of all other; insomuch that, as Aristotle saith, those 715
things which in themselves are horrible, as cruel battles,
unnatural monsters, are made in poetical imitation delightful.
Truly, I have known men, that even with reading Amadis de
Gaule, (which, God knoweth, wanteth much of a perfect poesy,)
have found their hearts moved to the exercise of courtesy, 720
liberality, and especially courage. Who readeth Aeneas carrying
old Anchises on his back, that wisheth not it were his fortune to
perform so excellent an act? Whom do not those words of
Turnus move, the tale of Turnus having planted his image in
the imagination? 725

Fugientem haec terra videbit?
Usque adeone mori miserum est?

Where the philosophers, as they scorn to delight, so must they
be content little to move, saving wrangling whether virtue be
the chief or the only good, whether the contemplative or the 730

active life do excel, which Plato and Boethius well knew, and
therefore made Mistress Philosophy very often borrow the
masking raiment of Poesy. For even those hard-hearted evil men
who think virtue a school-name, and know no other good but
735 *indulgere genio*, and therefore despise the austere admonitions of
the philosopher, and feel not the inward reason they stand upon,
yet will be content to be delighted, which is all the good-fellow
poet seemeth to promise; and so steal to see the form of goodness (which seen, they cannot but love) ere themselves be
740 aware, as if they took a medicine of cherries.

Infinite proofs of the strange effects of this poetical invention
might be alleged; only two shall serve, which are so often
remembered as I think all men know them. The one of Menenius Agrippa, who, when the whole people of Rome had
745 resolutely divided themselves from the senate, with apparent
show of utter ruin, though he were, for that time, an excellent
orator, came not among them upon trust either of figurative
speeches or cunning insinuations, and much less with far-
fetched maxims of philosophy, which, (especially if they were
750 Platonic,) they must have learned geometry before they could
well have conceived; but, forsooth, he behaves himself like a
homely and familiar poet. He telleth them a tale, that there
was a time when all the parts of the body made a mutinous
conspiracy against the belly, which they thought devoured the
755 fruits of each other's labour; they concluded they would let so
unprofitable a spender starve. In the end, to be short—for the
tale is notorious, and as notorious that it was a tale—with
punishing the belly they plagued themselves. This, applied by
him, wrought such effect in the people, as I never read that
760 ever words brought forth but then so sudden and so good an
alteration; for upon reasonable conditions a perfect reconcilement ensued.

The other is of Nathan the prophet, who, when the holy
David had so far forsaken God as to confirm adultery with
765 murder, when he was to do the tenderest office of a friend, in
laying his own shame before his eyes, (sent by God to call again
so chosen a servant,) how doth he it but by telling of a man
whose beloved lamb was ungratefully taken from his bosom?
The application most divinely true, but the discourse itself

feigned; which made David (I speak of the second and in- 770
strumental cause) as in a glass to see his own filthiness, as that
heavenly Psalm of Mercy well testifieth.

By these, therefore, examples and reasons, I think it may be
manifest that the poet, with that same hand of delight, doth
draw the mind more effectually than any other art doth. And 775
so a conclusion not unfitly ensueth: that as virtue is the most
excellent resting-place for all worldly learning to make his end
of, so poetry, being the most familiar to teach it, and most
princely to move towards it, in the most excellent work is the
most excellent workman.   780

But I am content not only to decipher him by his works,
(although works in commendation or dispraise must ever hold
a high authority,) but more narrowly will examine his parts;
so that, as in a man, though all together may carry a presence
full of majesty and beauty, perchance in some one defectious 785
piece we may find a blemish.

Now in his parts, kinds, or species, (as you list to term them,)
it is to be noted that some poesies have coupled together two or
three kinds, as tragical and comical, whereupon is risen the
tragi-comical; some, in the like manner, have mingled prose 790
and verse, as Sannazzaro and Boethius; some have mingled *types of*
matters heroical and pastoral; but that cometh all to one in this *poetry*
question, for, if severed they be good, the conjunction cannot
be hurtful. Therefore, perchance forgetting some, and leaving
some as needless to be remembered, it shall not be amiss in a 795
word to cite the special kinds, to see what faults may be found
in the right use of them.

Is it then the pastoral poem which is misliked?—for per- *pastoral*
chance where the hedge is lowest they will soonest leap over.
Is the poor pipe disdained, which sometimes out of Meliboeus' 800
mouth can show the misery of people under hard lords and
ravening soldiers, and again, by Tityrus, what blessedness is
derived to them that lie lowest from the goodness of them that
sit highest? sometimes, under the pretty tales of wolves and
sheep, can include the whole considerations of wrong-doing 805
and patience; sometimes show that contention for trifles can
get but a trifling victory; where perchance a man may see that
even Alexander and Darius, when they strove who should be

cock of this world's dunghill, the benefit they got was that the
810 after-livers may say:

> Haec memini et victum frustra contendere Thyrsim;
> Ex illo Corydon, Corydon est tempore nobis.

Or is it the lamenting elegiac, which in a kind heart would
move rather pity than blame; who bewaileth, with the great
815 philosopher Heraclitus, the weakness of mankind and the
wretchedness of the world; who surely is to be praised, either
for compassionate accompanying just causes of lamentation, or
for rightly painting out how weak be the passions of woefulness?

Is it the bitter but wholesome iambic, who rubs the galled
820 mind, in making shame the trumpet of villainy with bold and
open crying out against naughtiness?

Or the satiric? who

> Omne vafer vitium ridenti tangit amico;

who sportingly never leaveth till he make a man laugh at folly,
825 and at length ashamed to laugh at himself, which he cannot
avoid without avoiding the folly; who, while *circum praecordia
ludit*, giveth us to feel how many headaches a passionate life
bringeth us to,—how, when all is done,

> Est Ulubris, animus si nos non deficit aequus.

830 No, perchance it is the comic; whom naughty play-makers
and stage-keepers have justly made odious. To the argument
of abuse I will answer after. Only thus much now is to be said,
that the comedy is an imitation of the common errors of our
life, which he representeth in the most ridiculous and scornful
835 sort that may be, so as it is impossible that any beholder can be
content to be such a one. Now, as in geometry the oblique must
be known as well as the right and in arithmetic the odd as well
as the even; so in the actions of our life who seeth not the
filthiness of evil, wanteth a great foil to perceive the beauty of
840 virtue. This doth the comedy handle so, in our private and
domestical matters, as with hearing it we get, as it were, an
experience what is to be looked for of a niggardly Demea, of a
crafty Davus, of a flattering Gnatho, of a vain-glorious Thraso;
and not only to know what effects are to be expected, but to

know who be such, by the signifying badge given them by the 845
comedian. And little reason hath any man to say that men
learn evil by seeing it so set out, since, as I said before, there is
no man living, but by the force truth hath in nature, no sooner
seeth these men play their parts, but wisheth them *in pistrinum*,
although perchance the sack of his own faults lie so behind his 850
back, that he seeth not himself to dance the same measure,—
whereto yet nothing can more open his eyes than to find his
own actions contemptibly set forth.

So that the right use of comedy will, I think, by nobody be
blamed, and much less of the high and excellent tragedy, that 855
openeth the greatest wounds, and showeth forth the ulcers that
are covered with tissue; that maketh kings fear to be tyrants,
and tyrants manifest their tyrannical humours; that with
stirring the effects of admiration and commiseration teacheth
the uncertainty of this world, and upon how weak foundations 860
gilden roofs are builded; that maketh us know:

> Qui sceptra saevus duro imperio regit,
> Timet timentes, metus in auctorem redit.

But how much it can move, Plutarch yieldeth a notable testimony of the abominable tyrant Alexander Pheraeus; from 865
whose eyes a tragedy, well made and represented, drew
abundance of tears, who without all pity had murdered infinite numbers, and some of his own blood; so as he that was
not ashamed to make matters for tragedies, yet could not resist
the sweet violence of a tragedy. And if it wrought no further 870
good in him, it was that he, in despite of himself, withdrew
himself from hearkening to that which might mollify his hardened heart. But it is not the tragedy they do mislike, for it
were too absurd to cast out so excellent a representation of
whatsoever is most worthy to be learned. 875

Is it the lyric that most displeaseth, who with his tuned lyre
and well-accorded voice, giveth praise, the reward of virtue, to
virtuous acts; who giveth moral precepts and natural problems;
who sometimes raiseth up his voice to the height of the heavens,
in singing the lauds of the immortal God? Certainly I must 880
confess mine own barbarousness; I never heard the old song
of Percy and Douglas that I found not my heart moved more

than with a trumpet; and yet it is sung but by some blind crowder, with no rougher voice than rude style; which being so evil
885 apparalled in the dust and cobwebs of that uncivil age, what
would it work, trimmed in the gorgeous eloquence of Pindar?
In Hungary I have seen it the manner at all feasts, and other
such meetings, to have songs of their ancestors' valour, which
that right soldier-like nation think the chiefest kindlers of brave
890 courage. The incomparable Lacedaemonians did not only
carry that kind of music ever with them to the field, but even at
home, as such songs were made, so were they all content to be
singers of them; when the lusty men were to tell what they did,
the old men what they had done, and the young men what
895 they would do. And where a man may say that Pindar many
times praiseth highly victories of small moment, matters rather
of sport than virtue; as it may be answered, it was the fault of
the poet, and not of the poetry, so indeed the chief fault was in
the time and custom of the Greeks, who set those toys at so
900 high a price that Philip of Macedon reckoned a horserace won
at Olympus among his three fearful felicities. But as the
inimitable Pindar often did, so is that kind most capable and
most fit to awake the thoughts from the sleep of idleness, to
embrace honourable enterprises.
905   There rests the heroical, whose very name, I think, should
daunt all backbiters. For by what conceit can a tongue be
directed to speak evil of that which draweth with it no less
champions than Achilles, Cyrus, Aeneas, Turnus, Tydeus,
Rinaldo? who doth not only teach and move to a truth, but
910 teacheth and moveth to the most high and excellent truth; who
maketh magnanimity and justice shine through all misty fear-
fulness and foggy desires; who, if the saying of Plato and Tully
be true, that who could see virtue would be wonderfully
ravished with the love of her beauty, this man setteth her out
915 to make her more lovely, in her holiday apparel, to the eye of
any that will deign not to disdain until they understand. But
if anything be already said in the defence of sweet poetry, all
concurreth to the maintaining the heroical, which is not only
a kind, but the best and most accomplished kind of poetry.
920 For, as the image of each action stirreth and instructeth the
mind, so the lofty image of such worthies most inflameth the

mind with desire to be worthy, and informs with counsel how to be worthy. Only let Aeneas be worn in the tablet of your memory, how he governeth himself in the ruin of his country; in the preserving his old father, and carrying away his religious 925 ceremonies; in obeying the gods' commandment to leave Dido, though not only all passionate kindness, but even the human consideration of virtuous gratefulness, would have craved other of him; how in storms, how in sports, how in war, how in peace, how a fugitive, how victorious, how besieged, how besieging, 930 how to strangers, how to allies, how to enemies, how to his own; lastly, how in his inward self, and how in his outward government; and I think, in a mind not prejudiced with a prejudicating humour, he will be found in excellency fruitful. Yea, even as Horace saith, *melius Chrysippo et Crantore*. But, truly, 935 I imagine it falleth out with these poet-whippers as with some good women who often are sick, but in faith they cannot tell where. So the name of poetry is odious to them, but neither his cause nor effects, neither the sum that contains him nor the particularities descending from him, give any fast handle to 940 their carping dispraise.

Since, then, poetry is of all human learnings the most ancient and of most fatherly antiquity, as from whence other learnings have taken their beginnings; since it is so universal that no learned nation doth despise it, nor no barbarous nation is 945 without it; since both Roman and Greek gave divine names unto it, the one of prophesying, the other of making, and that indeed that name of making is fit for him, considering that whereas other arts retain themselves within their subject, and receive, as it were, their being from it, the poet only, bringeth 950 his own stuff, and doth not learn a conceit out of a matter, but maketh matter for a conceit; since neither his description nor his end containeth any evil, the thing described cannot be evil; since his effects be so good as to teach goodness, and delight the learners of it; since therein (namely in moral doctrine, the 955 chief of all knowledges,) he doth not only far pass the historian, but for instructing is well nigh comparable to the philosopher, and for moving leaveth him behind him; since the Holy Scripture, (wherein there is no uncleanness,) hath whole parts in it poetical, and that even our Saviour Christ vouchsafed to use 960 the flowers of it; since all his kinds are not only in their united forms, but in their several dissections fully commendable; I think, and think I think rightly, the laurel crown appointed for triumphing captains doth worthily, of all other learnings, 965 honour the poet's triumph.

But because we have ears as well as tongues, and that the lightest reasons that may be will seem to weigh greatly, if nothing be put in the counter-balance, let us hear, and, as well as we can, ponder, what objections be made against this art, 970 which may be worthy either of yielding or answering.

First, truly, I note not only in these *misomousoi*, poet-haters, but in all that kind of people who seek a praise by dispraising others, that they do prodigally spend a great many wandering words in quips and scoffs, carping and taunting at each thing 975 which, by stirring the spleen, may stay the brain from a through-beholding the worthiness of the subject. Those kind of objections, as they are full of a very idle easiness (since there is nothing of so sacred a majesty but that an itching tongue may rub itself upon it), so deserve they no other answer, but, instead 980 of laughing at the jest, to laugh at the jester. We know a playing wit can praise the discretion of an ass, the comfortableness of being in debt, and the jolly commodity of being sick of the plague. So of the contrary side, if we will turn Ovid's verse,

Ut lateat virtus proximitate mali,

985 'that good lie hid in nearness of the evil,' Agrippa will be as merry in showing the vanity of science, as Erasmus was in commending of folly; neither shall any man or matter escape some touch of these smiling railers. But for Erasmus and Agrippa, they had another foundation than the superficial part 990 would promise. Marry, these other pleasant fault-finders, who will correct the verb before they understand the noun, and confute others' knowledge before they confirm their own, I would have them only remember that scoffing cometh not of wisdom; so as the best title in true English they get with their 995 merriments is to be called good fools, for so have our grave forefathers ever termed that humorous kind of jesters.

But that which giveth greatest scope to their scorning humours is rhyming and versing. It is already said, (and as I think truly said,) it is not rhyming and versing that maketh poesy. One may be a poet without versing, and a versifier without poetry. But yet presuppose it were inseparable (as indeed it seemeth Scaliger judgeth,) truly it were an inseparable commendation. For if *oratio* next to *ratio*, speech next to reason, be the greatest gift bestowed upon mortality, that cannot be praiseless which doth most polish that blessing of speech; which considereth each word, not only, (as a man may say,) by his forcible quality, but by his best-measured quantity; carrying even in themselves a harmony, without, perchance, number, measure, order, proportion be in our time grown odious.

But lay aside the just praise it hath by being the only fit speech for music (music, I say, the most divine striker of the senses,) thus much is undoubtedly true, that if reading be foolish without remembering, memory being the only treasurer of knowledge, those words which are fittest for memory are likewise most convenient for knowledge. Now that verse far exceedeth prose in the knitting up of the memory, the reason is manifest; the words, (besides their delight, which hath a great affinity to memory,) being so set, as one cannot be lost but the whole work fails; which, accusing itself, calleth the remembrance back to itself, and so most strongly confirmeth it. Besides, one word so, as it were, begetting another, as, be it in rhyme or measured verse, by the former a man shall have a near guess to the follower. Lastly, even they that have taught the art of memory have showed nothing so apt for it as a certain room divided into many places, well and throughly known; now that hath the verse in effect perfectly, every word having his natural seat, which seat must needs make the word remembered. But what needeth more in a thing so known to all men? Who is it that ever was a scholar that doth not carry away some verses of Virgil, Horace, or Cato, which in his youth he learned, and even to his old age serve him for hourly lessons? as:

Percontatorem fugito, nam garrulus idem est.

Dum sibi quisque placet, credula turba sumus.

But the fitness it hath for memory is notably proved by all delivery of arts, wherein, for the most part, from grammar to

logic, mathematic, physic, and the rest, the rules chiefly necessary to be borne away are compiled in verses. So that verse
being in itself sweet and orderly, and being best for memory,
the only handle of knowledge, it must be in jest that any man
1040 can speak against it.

Now, then, go we to the most important imputations laid to
the poor poets: for aught I can yet learn they are these.
/ First, that there being many other more fruitful knowledges,
a man might better spend his time in them than in this.
1045 ₂ Secondly, that it is the mother of lies.

₃ Thirdly, that it is the nurse of abuse, infecting us with many
pestilent desires, with a siren's sweetness drawing the mind
to the serpent's tail of sinful fancies, and herein especially
comedies give the largest field to ear, as Chaucer saith; how,
1050 both in other nations and in ours, before poets did soften us, we
were full of courage, given to martial exercises, the pillars of
manlike liberty, and not lulled asleep in shady idleness with
poets' pastimes.

₄ And, lastly and chiefly, they cry out with an open mouth,
1055 as if they had overshot Robin Hood, that Plato banished them
out of his Commonwealth. Truly this is much, if there be much
truth in it.

First, to the first: that a man might better spend his time is a
reason indeed; but it doth, (as they say,) but *petere principium*.
1060 For if it be, as I affirm, that no learning is so good as that which
teacheth and moveth to virtue, and that none can both teach
and move thereto so much as poesy, then is the conclusion
manifest that ink and paper cannot be to a more profitable
purpose employed. And certainly, though a man should grant
1065 their first assumption, it should follow, (me thinks,) very un-
willingly, that good is not good because better is better. But
I still and utterly deny that there is sprung out of earth a more
fruitful knowledge.

To the second, therefore, that they should be the principal
1070 liars, I answer paradoxically, but truly, I think truly, that of all
writers under the sun the poet is the least liar, and though he
would, as a poet, can scarcely be a liar. The astronomer, with
his cousin the geometrician, can hardly escape when they take
upon them to measure the height of the stars. How often, think

you, do the physicians lie, when they aver things good for sick- 1075
nesses, which afterwards send Charon a great number of souls
drowned in a potion before they come to his ferry? And no less
of the rest which take upon them to affirm. Now, for the poet,
he nothing affirmeth, and therefore never lieth. For, as I take
it, to lie is to affirm that to be true which is false; so as the 1080
other artists, and especially the historian, affirming many
things, can, in the cloudy knowledge of mankind, hardly escape
from many lies. But the poet, as I said before, never affirmeth.
The poet never maketh any circles about your imagination, to
conjure you to believe for true what he writeth. He citeth not 1085
authorities of other histories, but even for his entry calleth the
sweet Muses to inspire into him a good invention; in troth, not
labouring to tell you what is or is not, but what should or
should not be. And therefore, though he recount things not
true, yet because he telleth them not for true, he lieth not; 1090
without we will say that Nathan lied in his speech, before
alleged, to David; which, as a wicked man durst scarce say, so
think I none so simple would say that Aesop lied in the tales of
his beasts; for who thinketh that Aesop wrote it for actually
true, were well worthy to have his name chronicled among 1095
the beasts he writeth of. What child is there that, coming to a
play, and seeing Thebes written in great letters upon an old
door, doth believe that it is Thebes? If then a man can arrive,
at that child's-age, to know that the poet's persons and doings
are but pictures what should be, and not stories what have 1100
been, they will never give the lie to things not affirmatively, but
allegorically and figuratively written. And therefore, as in
history looking for truth, they may go away full-fraught with
falsehood, so in poesy looking for fiction, they shall use the
narration but as an imaginative ground-plot of a profitable 1105
invention. But hereto is replied that the poets give names to
men they write of, which argueth a conceit of an actual truth,
and so, not being true, proveth a falsehood. And doth the
lawyer lie then, when, under the names of John a Stile, and
John a Noakes, he putteth his case? But that is easily answered. 1110
Their naming of men is but to make their picture the more
lively, and not to build any history. Painting men, they cannot
leave men nameless. We see we cannot play at chess but that

we must give names to our chess-men; and yet, me thinks, he
1115 were a very partial champion of truth that would say we lied
for giving a piece of wood the reverend title of a bishop. The
poet nameth Cyrus and Aeneas no other way than to show
what men of their fames, fortunes, and estates should do.

(3) Their third is, how much it abuseth men's wit, training it to
1120 wanton sinfulness and lustful love. For indeed that is the
principal, if not the only, abuse I can hear alleged. They say
the comedies rather teach than reprehend amorous conceits.
They say the lyric is larded with passionate sonnets, the
elegiac weeps the want of his mistress, and that even to the
1125 heroical Cupid hath ambitiously climbed. Alas! Love, I would
thou couldst as well defend thyself as thou canst offend
others! I would those on whom thou dost attend could either
put thee away, or yield good reason why they keep thee! But
grant love of beauty to be a beastly fault, (although it be very
1130 hard, since only man, and no beast, hath that gift to discern
beauty); grant that lovely name of Love to deserve all hateful
reproaches, (although even some of my masters the philosophers
spent a good deal of their lamp-oil in setting forth the excellency
of it): grant, I say, whatsoever they will have granted,—that
1135 not only love, but lust, but vanity, but, (if they list,) scurrility,
possesseth many leaves of the poets' books; yet think I, when this
is granted, they will find their sentence may with good manners
put the last words foremost, and not say that poetry abuseth
man's wit, but that man's wit abuseth poetry. For I will not
1140 deny, but that man's wit may make poesy, (which should be
eikastikē, which some learned have defined, figuring forth good
things), to be *phantastikē*, which doth contrariwise infect the
fancy with unworthy objects; as the painter that should give
to the eye either some excellent perspective, or some fine picture
1145 fit for building or fortification, or containing in it some notable
example, as Abraham sacrificing his son Isaac, Judith killing
Holofernes, David fighting with Goliath, may leave those, and
please an ill-pleased eye with wanton shows of better-hidden
matters. But what! shall the abuse of a thing make the right
1150 use odious? Nay, truly, though I yield that poesy may not only
be abused, but that being abused, by the reason of his sweet
charming force, it can do more hurt than any other army of

words, yet shall it be so far from concluding that the abuse should give reproach to the abused, that contrariwise it is a good reason, that whatsoever, being abused, doth most harm, 1155 being rightly used—and upon the right use each thing receiveth his title—doth most good. Do we not see the skill of physic, (the best rampire to our often-assaulted bodies,) being abused, teach poison, the most violent destroyer? Doth not knowledge of law, whose end is to even and right all things, being abused, grow 1160 the crooked fosterer of horrible injuries? Doth not, (to go to the highest,) God's word abused, breed heresy; and his Name abused, become blasphemy? Truly a needle cannot do much hurt, and as truly (with leave of ladies be it spoken,) it cannot do much good. With a sword thou mayst kill thy father, and 1165 with a sword thou mayst defend thy prince and country. So that, as in their calling poets the fathers of lies they say nothing, so in this their argument of abuse they prove the commendation.

They allege herewith, that before poets began to be in price 1170 our nation hath set their hearts' delight upon action, and not upon imagination; rather doing things worthy to be written, than writing things fit to be done. What that before-time was, I think scarcely Sphinx can tell; since no memory is so ancient that hath the precedence of poetry. And certain it is that, in 1175 our plainest homeliness, yet never was the Albion nation without poetry. Marry, this argument, though it be levelled against poetry, yet is it indeed a chain-shot against all learning, or bookishness, as they commonly term it. Of such mind were certain Goths, of whom it is written that, having in the spoil of 1180 a famous city taken a fair library, one hangman (belike fit to execute the fruits of their wits) who had murdered a great number of bodies, would have set fire on it. 'No,' said another very gravely, 'take heed what you do; for while they are busy about these toys, we shall with more leisure conquer their 1185 countries.' This, indeed, is the ordinary doctrine of ignorance, and many words sometimes I have heard spent in it; but because this reason is generally against all learning, as well as poetry, or rather all learning but poetry; because it were too large a digression to handle, or at least too superfluous, (since 1190 it is manifest that all government of action is to be gotten by knowledge, and knowledge best by gathering many knowledges, which is reading;) I only, with Horace, to him that is of that opinion

1195   Jubeo stultum esse libenter;

for as for poetry itself, it is the freest from this objection, for poetry is the companion of the camps. I dare undertake, Orlando Furioso or honest King Arthur will never displease a soldier; but the quiddity of *ens*, and *prima materia*, will hardly 1200 agree with a corselet. And therefore, as I said in the beginning, even Turks and Tartars are delighted with poets. Homer, a Greek, flourished before Greece flourished; and if to a slight conjecture a conjecture may be opposed, truly it may seem, that as by him their learned men took almost their first light 1205 of knowledge, so their active men received their first motions of courage. Only Alexander's example may serve, who by Plutarch is accounted of such virtue, that Fortune was not his guide but his footstool; whose acts speak for him, though Plutarch did not; indeed the phoenix of warlike princes. This 1210 Alexander left his schoolmaster, living Aristotle, behind him, but took dead Homer with him. He put the philosopher Callisthenes to death, for his seeming philosophical, indeed mutinous, stubbornness; but the chief thing he was ever heard to wish for was that Homer had been alive. He well found he received 1215 more bravery of mind by the pattern of Achilles, than by hearing the definition of fortitude. And therefore if Cato misliked Fulvius for carrying Ennius with him to the field, it may be answered that if Cato misliked it, the noble Fulvius liked it, or else he had not done it. For it was not the excellent Cato 1220 Uticensis, (whose authority I would much more have reverenced;) but it was the former, in truth a bitter punisher of faults, but else a man that had never well sacrificed to the Graces. He misliked and cried out upon all Greek learning; and yet, being fourscore years old, began to learn it, belike 1225 fearing that Pluto understood not Latin. Indeed, the Roman laws allowed no person to be carried to the wars but he that was in the soldiers' roll. And therefore though Cato misliked his unmustered person, he misliked not his work. And if he had, Scipio Nasica, judged by common consent the best Roman,

loved him. Both the other Scipio brothers, who had by their 1230
virtues no less surnames than of Asia and Afric, so loved him
that they caused his body to be buried in their sepulchre. So
as Cato's authority being but against his person, and that
answered with so far greater than himself, is herein of no
validity. 1235

But now, indeed, my burden is great, that Plato's name is ⟨4⟩
laid upon me, whom, I must confess, of all philosophers I have
ever esteemed most worthy of reverence; and with great reason,
since of all philosophers he is the most poetical. Yet if he will
defile the fountain out of which his flowing streams have pro- 1240
ceeded, let us boldly examine with what reasons he did it.

First, truly, a man might maliciously object that Plato, being
a philosopher, was a natural enemy of poets. For, indeed, after
the philosophers had picked out of the sweet mysteries of poetry
the right discerning true points of knowledge, they forthwith, 1245
putting it in method, and making a school-art of that which
the poets did only teach by a divine delightfulness, beginning to
spurn at their guides, like ungrateful prentices were not content
to set up shops for themselves, but sought by all means to discredit their masters; which by the force of delight being barred 1250
them, the less they could overthrow them the more they hated
them. For, indeed, they found for Homer seven cities strove
who should have him for their citizen; where many cities
banished philosophers, as not fit members to live among them.
For only repeating certain of Euripides' verses, many Athenians 1255
had their lives saved of the Syracusans, when the Athenians
themselves thought many philosophers unworthy to live.
Certain poets as Simonides and Pindar, had so prevailed with
Hiero the First, that of a tyrant they made him a just king;
where Plato could do so little with Dionysius, that he himself of 1260
a philosopher was made a slave. But who should do thus, I confess,
should requite the objections made against poets with like
cavillations against philosophers; as likewise one should do that
should bid one read Phaedrus or Symposium in Plato, or the
Discourse of Love in Plutarch, and see whether any poet do 1265
authorize abominable filthiness, as they do.

Again, a man might ask out of what commonwealth Plato
did banish them. In sooth, thence where he himself alloweth

community of women. So as belike this banishment grew not for
1270 effeminate wantonness, since little should poetical sonnets be
hurtful when a man might have what woman he listed. But
I honour philosophical instructions, and bless the wits which
bred them, so as they be not abused, which is likewise stretched
to poetry. Saint Paul himself, who yet, for the credit of poets,
1275 allegeth twice two poets, and one of them by the name of a
prophet, setteth a watchword upon philosophy,—indeed upon
the abuse. So doth Plato upon the abuse, not upon poetry.
Plato found fault that the poets of his time filled the world with
wrong opinions of the gods, making light tales of that unspotted
1280 essence, and therefore would not have the youth depraved with
such opinions. Herein may much be said; let this suffice: the
poets did not induce such opinions, but did imitate those
opinions already induced. For all the Greek stories can well
testify that the very religion of that time stood upon many and
1285 many-fashioned gods; not taught so by the poets, but followed
according to their nature of imitation. Who list may read in
Plutarch the discourses of Isis and Osiris, of the cause why
Oracles ceased, of the Divine Providence, and see whether the
theology of that nation stood not upon such dreams, which the
1290 poets indeed superstitiously observed; and truly, (since they
had not the light of Christ,) did much better in it than the
philosophers, who, shaking off superstition, brought in atheism.
    Plato therefore, (whose authority I had much rather justly
construe than unjustly resist,) meant not in general of poets, in
1295 those words of which Julius Scaliger saith, *Qua authoritate barbari
quidam atque hispidi abuti velint ad poetas e republica exigendos*; but
only meant to drive out those wrong opinions of the Deity,
(whereof now, without further law, Christianity hath taken
away all the hurtful belief,) perchance, (as he thought,)
1300 nourished by the then esteemed poets. And a man need go no
further than to Plato himself to know his meaning; who, in his
dialogue called *Ion*, giveth high and rightly divine commendation unto poetry. So as Plato, banishing the abuse, not the thing,
not banishing it, but giving due honour unto it, shall be our
1305 patron and not our adversary. For, indeed, I had much rather,
(since truly I may do it,) show their mistaking of Plato, under
whose lion's skin they would make an ass-like braying against

poesy, than go about to overthrow his authority; whom, the wiser a man is, the more just cause he shall find to have in admiration; especially since he attributeth unto poesy more 1310 than myself do, namely to be a very inspiring of a divine force, far above man's wit as in the aforenamed dialogue is apparent.

Of the other side, who would show the honours have been by the best sort of judgements granted them, a whole sea of examples would present themselves: Alexanders, Caesars, 1315 Scipios, all favourers of poets; Laelius, called the Roman Socrates, himself a poet, so as part of *Heautontimoroumenos* in Terence was supposed to be made by him. And even the Greek Socrates, whom Apollo confirmed to be the only wise man, is said to have spent part of his old time in putting Aesop's 1320 Fables into verses; and therefore full evil should it become his scholar, Plato, to put such words in his master's mouth against poets. But what needs more? Aristotle writes the Art of Poesy; and why, if it should not be written? Plutarch teacheth the use to be gathered of them; and how, if they should not be read? 1325 And who reads Plutarch's either history or philosophy, shall find he trimmeth both their garments with guards of poesy. But I list not to defend poesy with the help of her underling historiography. Let it suffice that it is a fit soil for praise to dwell upon; and what dispraise may set upon it, is either easily 1330 overcome, or transformed into just commendation.

So that, since the excellencies of it may be so easily and so justly confirmed, and the low-creeping objections so soon trodden down: it not being an art of lies, but of true doctrine; not of effeminateness, but of notable stirring of courage; not of 1335 abusing man's wit, but of strengthening man's wit; not banished, but honoured by Plato; let us rather plant more laurels for to engarland our poets' heads (which honour of being laureate, as besides them only triumphant captains were, is a sufficient authority to show the price they ought to be held in) 1340 than suffer the ill-savoured breath of such wrong speakers once to blow upon the clear springs of poesy.

But since I have run so long a career in this matter, me thinks, before I give my pen a full stop, it shall be but a little more lost time to inquire why England, the mother of excellent minds, 1345 should be grown so hard a stepmother to poets, who certainly in wit ought to pass all others, since all only proceedeth from their wit, being indeed makers of themselves, not takers of others. How can I but exclaim,

1350   Musa, mihi causas memora, quo numine laeso?

Sweet poesy! that hath anciently had kings, emperors, senators, great captains, such as, besides a thousand others, David, Adrian, Sophocles, Germanicus, not only to favour poets, but to be poets; and of our nearer times can present for
1355 her patrons a Robert, King of Sicily; the great King Francis of France; King James of Scotland; such cardinals as Bembus and Bibbiena; such famous preachers and teachers as Beza and Melancthon; so learned philosophers as Fracastorius and Scaliger; so great orators as Pontanus and Muretus; so piercing
1360 wits as George Buchanan; so grave counsellors as, besides many, but before all, that Hospital of France, than whom, I think, that realm never brought forth a more accomplished judgement more firmly builded upon virtue; I say these, with numbers of others, not only to read others' poesies but to
1365 poetize for others' reading. That poesy, thus embraced in all other places, should only find in our time a hard welcome in England, I think the very earth lamenteth it, and therefore decketh our soil with fewer laurels than it was accustomed. For heretofore poets have in England also flourished; and, which is
1370 to be noted, even in those times when the trumpet of Mars did sound loudest. And now that an over-faint quietness should seem to strew the house for poets, they are almost in as good reputation as the mountebanks at Venice. Truly even that, as of the one side it giveth great praise to poesy, which, like Venus
1375 (but to better purpose,) hath rather be troubled in the net with Mars, than enjoy the homely quiet of Vulcan; so serves it for a piece of a reason why they are less grateful to idle England, which now can scarce endure the pain of a pen. Upon this necessarily followeth, that base men with servile wits undertake
1380 it, who think it enough if they can be rewarded of the printer. And so as Epaminondas is said, with the honour of his virtue to have made an office, by his exercising it, which before was contemptible, to become highly respected; so these men, no more but setting their names to it, by their own disgracefulness

disgrace the most graceful poesy. For now, without any com- 1385
mission, they do post over the banks of Helicon, till they make
the readers more weary than post-horses; while, in the mean
time, they,

Queis meliore luto finxit praecordia Titan,

are better content to suppress the outflowing of their wit than, 1390
by publishing them, to be accounted knights of the same order.

But I that, before ever I durst aspire unto the dignity, am
admitted into the company of the paper-blurrers, do find the
very true cause of our wanting estimation is want of desert,
taking upon us to be poets in despite of Pallas. Now wherein 1395
we want desert were a thankworthy labour to express; but if I
knew, I should have mended myself. But I, as I never desired
the title, so have I neglected the means to come by it; only,
overmastered by some thoughts, I yielded an inky tribute unto
them. Marry, they that delight in poesy itself should seek to 1400
know what they do and how they do; and especially look themselves in an unflattering glass of reason, if they be inclinable
unto it. For poesy must not be drawn by the ears, it must be
gently led, or rather it must lead; which was partly the cause
that made the ancient learned affirm it was a divine gift, and no 1405
human skill, since all other knowledges lie ready for any that
hath strength of wit; a poet no industry can make if his own
genius be not carried unto it. And therefore is it an old proverb:
Orator fit, poeta nascitur. Yet confess I always that, as the fertilest
ground must be manured, so must the highest-flying wit have a 1410
Daedalus to guide him. That Daedalus, they say, both in this
and in other, hath three wings to bear itself up into the air of
due commendation: that is, art, imitation, and exercise. But
these, neither artificial rules nor imitative patterns, we much
cumber ourselves withal. Exercise indeed we do, but that very 1415
fore-backwardly, for where we should exercise to know, we
exercise as having known; and so is our brain delivered of much
matter which never was begotten by knowledge. For, there
being two principal parts, matter to be expressed by words,
and words to express the matter, in neither we use art or imita- 1420
tion rightly. Our matter is *quodlibet* indeed, though wrongly
performing Ovid's verse,

Quicquid conabar dicere, versus erat;

never marshalling it into any assured rank, that almost the
1425 readers cannot tell where to find themselves.

Chaucer, undoubtedly, did excellently in his *Troilus and
Criseyde*; of whom, truly, I know not whether to marvel more,
either that he in that misty time could see so clearly, or that
we in this clear age walk so stumblingly after him. Yet had he
1430 great wants, fit to be forgiven in so reverend antiquity. I account the *Mirror for Magistrates* meetly furnished of beautiful
parts; and in the Earl of Surrey's *Lyrics* many things tasting of a
noble birth, and worthy of a noble mind. The *Shepheardes
Calender* hath much poetry in his eclogues, indeed worthy the
1435 reading, if I be not deceived. That same framing of his style to
an old rustic language I dare not allow, since neither Theocritus in Greek, Virgil in Latin, nor Sannazzaro in Italian did
affect it. Besides these, I do not remember to have seen but
few (to speak boldly) printed, that have poetical sinews in
1440 them; for proof whereof, let but most of the verses be put in
prose, and then ask the meaning, and it will be found that one
verse did but beget another, without ordering at the first what
should be at the last; which becomes a confused mass of words,
with a tinkling sound of rime, barely accompanied with reason.
1445 Our tragedies and comedies not without cause cried out
against, observing rules neither of honest civility nor of skilful
poetry: excepting *Gorboduc*, (again I say of those that I have
seen,) which notwithstanding as it is full of stately speeches and
well-sounding phrases, climbing to the height of Seneca's style,
1450 and as full of notable morality, which it doth most delightfully
teach, and so obtain the very end of poesy; yet in truth it is
very defectious in the circumstances; which grieveth me,
because it might not remain as an exact model of all tragedies.
For it is faulty both in place and time, the two necessary com-
1455 panions of all corporal actions. For where the stage should
always represent but one place, and the uttermost time pre-
supposed in it should be, both by Aristotle's precept and common reason, but one day, there is both many days and many
places inartificially imagined.
1460 But if it be so in *Gorboduc*, how much more in all the rest?

where you shall have Asia of the one side, and Afric of the other, and so many other under-kingdoms, that the player, when he cometh in, must ever begin with telling where he is, or else the tale will not be conceived. Now ye shall have three ladies walk to gather flowers, and then we must believe the 1465 stage to be a garden. By and by we hear news of shipwreck in the same place, and then we are to blame if we accept it not for a rock. Upon the back of that comes out a hideous monster with fire and smoke, and then the miserable beholders are bound to take it for a cave. While in the mean time two armies 1470 fly in, represented with four swords and bucklers, and then what hard heart will not receive it for a pitched field?

Now of time they are much more liberal. For ordinary it is that two young princes fall in love; after many traverses she is got with child, delivered of a fair boy, he is lost, groweth a man, 1475 falleth in love, and is ready to get another child, and all this in two hours' space; which how absurd it is in sense even sense may imagine, and art hath taught, and all ancient examples justified, and at this day the ordinary players in Italy will not err in. Yet will some bring in an example of Eunuchus in 1480 Terence, that containeth matter of two days, yet far short of twenty years. True it is, and so was it to be played in two days, and so fitted to the time it set forth. And though Plautus have in one place done amiss, let us hit with him, and not miss with him. But they will say, How then shall we set forth a story 1485 which containeth both many places and many times? And do they not know that a tragedy is tied to the laws of poesy, and not of history; not bound to follow the story, but having liberty either to feign a quite new matter, or to frame the history to the most tragical conveniency? Again, many things may be 1490 told which cannot be showed, if they know the difference betwixt reporting and representing. As for example I may speak, (though I am here,) of Peru, and in speech digress from that to the description of Calicut; but in action I cannot represent it without Pacolet's horse. And so was the manner the 1495 ancients took, by some *Nuntius* to recount things done in former time or other place.

Lastly, if they will represent an history, they must not, (as Horace saith,) begin *ab ovo*, but they must come to the principal

1500 point of that one action which they will represent. By example
this will be best expressed. I have a story of young Polydorus,
delivered for safety's sake, with great riches, by his father
Priamus to Polymnestor, King of Thrace, in the Trojan war
time. He, after some years, hearing the overthrow of Priamus,
1505 for to make the treasure his own murdereth the child; the body
of the child is taken up; Hecuba, she, the same day, findeth a
sleight to be revenged most cruelly of the tyrant. Where now
would one of our tragedy-writers begin, but with the delivery
of the child? Then should he sail over into Thrace, and so
1510 spend I know not how many years, and travel numbers of
places. But where doth Euripides? Even with the finding of
the body, leaving the rest to be told by the spirit of Polydorus.
This needs no further to be enlarged; the dullest wit may
conceive it.

1515   But, besides these gross absurdities, how all their plays be
neither right tragedies nor right comedies, mingling kings and
clowns, not because the matter so carrieth it, but thrust in the
clown by head and shoulders to play a part in majestical
matters, with neither decency nor discretion; so as neither the
1520 admiration and commiseration, nor the right sportfulness, is
by their mongrel tragi-comedy obtained. I know Apuleius did
somewhat so, but that is a thing recounted with space of time,
not represented in one moment; and I know the ancients
have one or two examples of tragi-comedies, as Plautus hath
1525 *Amphitryo*. But, if we mark them well, we shall find that they
never, or very daintily, match hornpipes and funerals. So falleth
it out that, having indeed no right comedy in that comical
part of our tragedy, we have nothing but scurrility, unworthy
of any chaste ears, or some extreme show of doltishness, indeed
1530 fit to lift up a loud laughter, and nothing else; where the whole
tract of a comedy should be full of delight, as the tragedy
should be still maintained in a well-raised admiration.

    But our comedians think there is no delight without laughter,
which is very wrong; for though laughter may come with
1535 delight, yet cometh it not of delight, as though delight should
be the cause of laughter; but well may one thing breed both
together. Nay, rather in themselves they have, as it were, a
kind of contrariety. For delight we scarcely do, but in things

that have a conveniency to ourselves, or to the general nature; laughter almost ever cometh of things most disproportioned to 1540 ourselves and nature. Delight hath a joy in it either permanent or present; laughter hath only a scornful tickling. For example, we are ravished with delight to see a fair woman, and yet are far from being moved to laughter. We laugh at deformed creatures, wherein certainly we cannot delight. We delight in 1545 good chances, we laugh at mischances. We delight to hear the happiness of our friends and country, at which he were worthy to be laughed at that would laugh. We shall, contrarily, laugh sometimes to find a matter quite mistaken and go down the hill against the bias, in the mouth of some such men, as for the 1550 respect of them one shall be heartily sorry, yet he cannot choose but laugh, and so is rather pained than delighted with laughter. Yet deny I not but that they may go well together. For as in Alexander's picture well set out we delight without laughter, and in twenty mad antics we laugh without delight; so in 1555 Hercules, painted, with his great beard and furious countenance, in woman's attire, spinning at Omphale's commandment, it breedeth both delight and laughter; for the representing of so strange a power in love procureth delight, and the scornfulness of the action stirreth laughter.   1560

But I speak to this purpose, that all the end of the comical part be not upon such scornful matters as stir laughter only, but mixed with it that delightful teaching which is the end of poesy. And the great fault, even in that point of laughter, and forbidden plainly by Aristotle, is that they stir laughter in 1565 sinful things, which are rather execrable than ridiculous; or in miserable, which are rather to be pitied than scorned. For what is it to make folks gape at a wretched beggar or a beggarly clown, or, against law of hospitality, to jest at strangers because they speak not English as well as we do? what do we learn? 1570 since it is certain:

> Nil habet infelix paupertas durius in se,
> Quam quod ridiculos homines facit.

But rather a busy loving courtier; a heartless threatening Thraso; a self-wise-seeming schoolmaster; a wry-transformed 1575 traveller: these if we saw walk in stage-names, which we play naturally, therein were delightful laughter and teaching delightfulness, as in the other, the tragedies of Buchanan do justly bring forth a divine admiration.

1580   But I have lavished out too many words of this play-matter. I do it, because, as they are excelling parts of poesy, so is there none so much used in England, and none can be more pitifully abused; which, like an unmannerly daughter, showing a bad education, causeth her mother Poesy's honesty to be called in 1585 question.

Other sorts of poetry almost have we none, but that lyrical kind of songs and sonnets, which, Lord, if he gave us so good minds, how well it might be employed, and with how heavenly fruit both private and public, in singing the praises of the 1590 immortal beauty, the immortal goodness of that God who giveth us hands to write, and wits to conceive!—of which we might well want words, but never matter; of which we could turn our eyes to nothing, but we should ever have new-budding occasions.

But truly, many of such writings as come under the banner 1595 of unresistible love, if I were a mistress would never persuade me they were in love; so coldly they apply fiery speeches, as men that had rather read lovers' writings, (and so caught up certain swelling phrases, which hang together like a man which once told me the wind was at north-west and by south, because 1600 he would be sure to name winds enough) than that in truth they feel those passions; which easily, as I think, may be be- wrayed by that same forcibleness, or *energeia* (as the Greeks call it) of the writer. But let this be a sufficient, though short note, that we miss the right use of the material point of poesy.

1605   Now for the outside of it, which is words, or (as I may term it) diction, it is even well worse; so is that honey-flowing matron, Eloquence, apparelled, or rather disguised, in a courtesan-like painted affection: one time with so far-fetched words, they may seem monsters, but must seem strangers, to 1610 any poor Englishman; another time with coursing of a letter, as if they were bound to follow the method of a dictionary; another time with figures and flowers extremely winter-starved.

But I would this fault were only peculiar to versifiers, and had not as large possession among prose-printers, and, (which is 1615 to be marvelled,) among many scholars, and, (which is to be

pitied,) among some preachers. Truly I could wish—if at least
I might be so bold to wish in a thing beyond the reach of my
capacity—the diligent imitators of Tully and Demosthenes
(most worthy to be imitated) did not so much keep Nizolian
paper-books of their figures and phrases, as by attentive trans- 1620
lation, as it were, devour them whole, and make them wholly
theirs. For now they cast sugar and spice upon every dish that
is served to the table; like those Indians, not content to wear
ear-rings at the fit and natural place of the ears, but they will
thrust jewels through their nose and lips, because they will be 1625
sure to be fine. Tully, when he was to drive out Catiline as it
were with a thunderbolt of eloquence, often used that figure of
repetition, as *Vivit. Vivit? Immo in senatum venit*, etc. Indeed,
inflamed with a well-grounded rage, he would have his words,
as it were, double out of his mouth; and so do that artificially, 1630
which we see men in choler do naturally. And we, having noted
the grace of those words, hale them in sometime to a familiar
epistle, when it were too much choler to be choleric. How well
store of *similiter cadences* doth sound with the gravity of the
pulpit, I would but invoke Demosthenes' soul to tell, who with 1635
a rare daintiness useth them. Truly they have made me think
of the sophister that with too much subtlety would prove two
eggs three, and though he might be counted a sophister, had
none for his labour. So these men bringing in such a kind of
eloquence, well may they obtain an opinion of a seeming 1640
fineness, but persuade few, which should be the end of their
fineness.

Now for similitudes, in certain printed discourses, I think all
herbarists, all stories of beasts, fowls, and fishes are rifled up,
that they may come in multitudes to wait upon any of our 1645
conceits, which certainly is as absurd a surfeit to the ears as is
possible. For the force of a similitude not being to prove any
thing to a contrary disputer, but only to explain to a willing
hearer; when that is done, the rest is a most tedious prattling,
rather overswaying the memory from the purpose whereto 1650
they were applied, than any whit informing the judgement,
already either satisfied or by similitudes not to be satisfied.

For my part, I do not doubt, when Antonius and Crassus,
the great forefathers of Cicero in eloquence, the one (as Cicero

1655 testifieth of them) pretended not to know art, the other not to set by it, because with a plain sensibleness they might win credit of popular ears, which credit is the nearest step to persuasion, which persuasion is the chief mark of oratory,—I do not doubt, I say, but that they used these knacks very sparingly;

1660 which who doth generally use, any man may see doth dance to his own music, and so be noted by the audience more careful to speak curiously than to speak truly. Undoubtedly (at least to my opinion undoubtedly) I have found in divers smalllearned courtiers a more sound style than in some professors of

1665 learning; of which I can guess no other cause, but that the courtier following that which by practice he findeth fittest to nature, therein, though he know it not, doth according to art, though not by art; where the other, using art to show art and not to hide art (as in these cases he should do) flieth from nature,

1670 and indeed abuseth art.

But what! me thinks I deserve to be pounded for straying from poetry to oratory. But both have such an affinity in this wordish consideration, that I think this digression will make my meaning receive the fuller understanding: which is not to

1675 take upon me to teach poets how they should do, but only, finding myself sick among the rest, to show some one or two spots of the common infection grown among the most part of writers; that, acknowledging ourselves somewhat awry, we may bend to the right use both of matter and manner: whereto

1680 our language giveth us great occasion, being, indeed, capable of any excellent exercising of it.

I know some will say it is a mingled language. And why not so much the better, taking the best of both the other? Another will say it wanteth grammar. Nay, truly, it hath that praise

1685 that it wanteth not grammar: for grammar it might have, but it needs it not; being so easy in itself, and so void of those cumbersome differences of cases, genders, moods, and tenses, which, I think, was a piece of the Tower of Babylon's curse, that a man should be put to school to learn his mother-tongue. But

1690 for the uttering sweetly and properly the conceits of the mind, which is the end of speech, that hath it equally with any other tongue in the world; and is particularly happy in compositions of two or three words together,—near the Greek, far beyond the

Latin, which is one of the greatest beauties can be in a language.

Now of versifying there are two sorts, the one ancient, the *1695* other modern. The ancient marked the quantity of each syllable, and according to that framed his verse; the modern observing only number, with some regard of the accent, the chief life of it standeth in that like sounding of the words, which we call rhyme. Whether of these be the more excellent would *1700* bear many speeches; the ancient no doubt more fit for music, both words and tune observing quantity; and more fit lively to express divers passions, by the low or lofty sound of the well-weighed syllable. The latter likewise with his rhyme striketh a certain music to the ear; and, in fine, since it doth delight, *1705* though by another way, it obtaineth the same purpose; there being in either, sweetness, and wanting in neither, majesty. Truly the English, before any other vulgar language I know, is fit for both sorts. For, for the ancient, the Italian is so full of vowels that it must ever be cumbered with elisions; the Dutch *1710* so, of the other side, with consonants, that they cannot yield the sweet sliding fit for a verse. The French in his whole language hath not one word that hath his accent in the last syllable saving two, called antepenultima, and little more hath the Spanish; and therefore very gracelessly may they use *1715* dactyls. The English is subject to none of these defects. Now for rhyme, though we do not observe quantity, yet we observe the accent very precisely, which other languages either cannot do, or will not do so absolutely. That caesura, or breathing-place in the midst of the verse, neither Italian nor Spanish have, the *1720* French and we never almost fail of.

Lastly, even the very rhyme itself the Italian cannot put in the last syllable, by the French named the masculine rhyme, but still in the next to the last, which the French call the female, or the next before that, which the Italians term *sdruc-* *1725* *ciola*. The example of the former is *buono*, *suono*; of the *sdrucciola* is *femina*, *semina*. The French, of the other side, hath both the male as *bon*, *son*; and the female, as *plaise*, *taise*; but the *sdrucciola* he hath not. Where the English hath all three, as *due*, *true*; *father*, *rather*; *motion*, *potion*; with much more which might be *1730* said, but that already I find the triflingness of this discourse is much too much enlarged.

CECT

So that since the ever praiseworthy poesy is full of virtue-
breeding delightfulness, and void of no gift that ought to be in
1735 the noble name of learning; since the blames laid against it are
either false or feeble; since the cause why it is not esteemed in
England is the fault of poet-apes, not poets; since, lastly, our
tongue is most fit to honour poesy, and to be honoured by
poesy; I conjure you all that have had the evil luck to read
1740 this ink-wasting toy of mine, even in the name of the Nine
Muses, no more to scorn the sacred mysteries of poesy; no more
to laugh at the name of Poets, as though they were next inheritors to Fools; no more to jest at the reverend title of 'a rhymer';
but to believe, with Aristotle, that they were the ancient
1745 treasurers of the Grecians' divinity; to believe, with Bembus,
that they were first bringers-in of all civility; to believe, with
Scaliger, that no philosopher's precepts can sooner make you
an honest man than the reading of Virgil; to believe, with
Clauserus, the translator of Cornutus, that it pleased the
1750 Heavenly Deity by Hesiod and Homer, under the veil of
fables, to give us all knowledge, logic, rhetoric, philosophy
natural and moral, and *quid non*? to believe, with me, that
there are many mysteries contained in poetry which of purpose
were written darkly, lest by profane wits it should be abused;
1755 to believe, with Landino, that they are so beloved of the gods,
that whatsoever they write proceeds of a divine fury; lastly, to
believe themselves, when they tell you they will make you
immortal by their verses.

Thus doing, your name shall flourish in the printers' shops.
1760 Thus doing, you shall be of kin to many a poetical preface.
Thus doing, you shall be most fair, most rich, most wise, most
all; you shall dwell upon superlatives. Thus doing, though you
be *libertino patre natus*, you shall suddenly grow *Herculea proles*.

Si quid mea carmina possunt.

1765 Thus doing, your soul shall be placed with Dante's Beatrice or
Virgil's Anchises.

But if—fie of such a but!—you be born so near the dull-
making cataract of Nilus, that you cannot bear the planet-like
music of poetry; if you have so earth-creeping a mind that it
1770 cannot lift itself up to look to the sky of poetry, or rather, by a

certain rustical disdain, will become such a mome as to be a Momus of Poetry; then, though I will not wish unto you the ass's ears of Midas, nor to be driven by a poet's verses, as Bubonax was, to hang himself; nor to be rhymed to death, as is said to be done in Ireland; yet thus much curse I must send you 1775 in the behalf of all poets: that while you live, you live in love, and never get favour, for lacking skill of a sonnet; and when you die, your memory die from the earth, for want of an epitaph.

JOHN DRYDEN

An Essay of Dramatic Poesy

IT was that memorable day, in the first summer of the late war,
when our navy engaged the Dutch; a day wherein the two most
mighty and best appointed fleets which any age had ever seen,
disputed the command of the greater half of the globe, the
5 commerce of nations, and the riches of the universe: while
these vast floating bodies, on either side, moved against each
other in parallel lines, and our countrymen, under the happy
conduct of his Royal Highness, went breaking, by little and
little, into the line of the enemies; the noise of the cannon from
10 both navies reached our ears about the city, so that all men
being alarmed with it, and in a dreadful suspense of the event,
which they knew was then deciding, every one went following
the sound as his fancy led him; and leaving the town almost
empty, some took towards the park, some cross the river,
15 others down it; all seeking the noise in the depth of silence.
Among the rest, it was the fortune of Eugenius, Crites,
Lisideius, and Neander, to be in company together; three of
them persons whom their wit and quality have made known to
all the town; and whom I have chosen to hide under these
20 borrowed names, that they may not suffer by so ill a relation
as I am going to make of their discourse.
Taking then a barge, which a servant of Lisideius had provided for them, they made haste to shoot the bridge, and left
behind them that great fall of waters which hindered them from
25 hearing what they desired: after which, having disengaged
themselves from many vessels which rode at anchor in the
Thames, and almost blocked up the passage towards Green-
wich, they ordered the watermen to let fall their oars more
gently; and then, every one favouring his own curiosity with a
30 strict silence, it was not long ere they perceived the air to break
about them like the noise of distant thunder, or of swallows in

a chimney: those little undulations of sound, though almost
vanishing before they reached them, yet still seeming to retain
somewhat of their first horror, which they had betwixt the
fleets. After they had attentively listened till such time as the 35
sound by little and little went from them, Eugenius, lifting up
his head, and taking notice of it, was the first who congratulated
to the rest that happy omen of our nation's victory: adding,
that we had but this to desire in confirmation of it, that we
might hear no more of that noise, which was now leaving the 40
English coast. When the rest had concurred in the same
opinion, Crites, a person of a sharp judgement, and somewhat
too delicate a taste in wit, which the world have mistaken in
him for ill-nature, said, smiling to us, that if the concernment of
this battle had not been so exceeding great, he could scarce 45
have wished the victory at the price he knew he must pay for it,
in being subject to the reading and hearing of so many ill
verses as he was sure would be made on that subject. Adding,
that no argument could scape some of those eternal rhymers,
who watch a battle with more diligence than the ravens and 50
birds of prey; and the worst of them surest to be first in upon
the quarry: while the better able, either out of modesty writ
not at all, or set that due value upon their poems, as to let them
be often desired and long expected. 'There are some of those
impertinent people of whom you speak,' answered Lisideius, 55
'who to my knowledge are already so provided, either way,
that they can produce not only a panegyric upon the victory,
but, if need be, a funeral elegy on the duke; wherein, after
they have crowned his valour with many laurels, they will at
last deplore the odds under which he fell, concluding that his 60
courage deserved a better destiny.' All the company smiled at
the conceit of Lisideius; but Crites, more eager than before,
began to make particular exceptions against some writers, and
said, the public magistrate ought to send betimes to forbid
them; and that it concerned the peace and quiet of all honest 65
people, that ill poets should be as well silenced as seditious
preachers. 'In my opinion,' replied Eugenius, 'you pursue your
point too far; for as to my own particular, I am so great a
lover of poesy, that I could wish them all rewarded, who
attempt but to do well; at least, I would not have them worse 70

used than one of their brethren was by Sylla the Dictator:—
Quem in concione vidimus (says Tully,) *cum ei libellum malus poeta
de populo subjecisset, quod epigramma in eum fecisset tantummodo
alternis versibus longiusculis, statim ex iis rebus quas tunc vendebat
75 jubere ei praemium tribui, sub ea conditione ne quid postea scriberet.*
'I could wish with all my heart,' replied Crites, 'that many
whom we know were as bountifully thanked upon the same
condition,—that they would never trouble us again. For
amongst others, I have a mortal apprehension of two poets,
80 whom this victory, with the help of both her wings, will never
be able to escape.' ''Tis easy to guess whom you intend,' said
Lisideius; 'and without naming them, I ask you, if one of them
does not perpetually pay us with clenches upon words, and a
certain clownish kind of raillery? if now and then he does not
85 offer at a catachresis or Clevelandism, wresting and torturing a
word into another meaning: in fine, if he be not one of those
whom the French would call *un mauvais bouffon*; one who is so
much a well-willer to the satire, that he intends at least to
spare no man; and though he cannot strike a blow to hurt
90 any, yet he ought to be punished for the malice of the action,
as our witches are justly hanged, because they think themselves
to be such; and suffer deservedly for believing they did mischief,
because they meant it.' 'You have described him,' said Crites,
'so exactly, that I am afraid to come after you with my other
95 extremity of poetry. He is one of those who, having had some
advantage of education and converse, knows better than the
other what a poet should be, but puts it into practice more un-
luckily than any man; his style and matter are everywhere
alike: he is the most calm, peaceable writer you ever read: he
100 never disquiets your passions with the least concernment, but
still leaves you in as even a temper as he found you; he is a
very Leveller in poetry: he creeps along with ten little words
in every line, and helps out his numbers with *For to*, and *Unto*,
and all the pretty expletives he can find, till he drags them to
105 the end of another line; while the sense is left tired half way
behind it: he doubly starves all his verses, first for want of
thought, and then of expression; his poetry neither has wit in
it, nor seems to have it; like him in Martial:
    Pauper videri *Cinna* vult, et est pauper.

'He affects plainness, to cover his want of imagination: when 110
he writes the serious way, the highest flight of his fancy is some
miserable antithesis, or seeming contradiction; and in the
comic he is still reaching at some thin conceit, the ghost of a
jest, and that too flies before him, never to be caught; these
swallows which we see before us on the Thames are the just 115
resemblance of his wit: you may observe how near the water
they stoop, how many proffers they make to dip, and yet how
seldom they touch it; and when they do, it is but the surface:
they skim over it but to catch a gnat, and then mount into the
air and leave it.'   120

'Well, gentlemen,' said Eugenius, 'you may speak your
pleasure of these authors; but though I and some few more
about the town may give you a peaceable hearing, yet assure
yourselves, there are multitudes who would think you malicious
and them injured: especially him whom you first described; 125
he is the very Withers of the city: they have bought more
editions of his works than would serve to lay under all their
pies at the Lord Mayor's Christmas. When his famous poem
first came out in the year 1660, I have seen them reading it in
the midst of 'Change time; nay so vehement they were at it, 130
that they lost their bargain by the candles' ends; but what will
you say, if he has been received amongst great persons? I can
assure you he is, this day, the envy of one who is lord in the art
of quibbling; and who does not take it well, that any man
should intrude so far into his province.' 'All I would wish,' 135
replied Crites, 'is, that they who love his writings, may still
admire him, and his fellow poet: *Qui Bavium non odit, &c.*, is
curse sufficient.' 'And farther,' added Lisideius, 'I believe there
is no man who writes well, but would think he had hard
measure, if their admirers should praise anything of his: *Nam* 140
quos contemnimus, eorum quoque laudes contemnimus.' 'There are so
few who write well in this age,' says Crites, 'that methinks any
praises should be welcome; they neither rise to the dignity of
the last age, nor to any of the ancients: and we may cry out
of the writers of this time, with more reason than Petronius of 145
his, *Pace vestra liceat dixisse, primi omnium eloquentium perdidistis:*
you have debauched the true old poetry so far, that Nature,
which is the soul of it, is not in any of your writings.'

'If your quarrel,' said Eugenius, 'to those who now write, be
150 grounded only on your reverence to antiquity, there is no man
more rez dy to adore those great Greeks and Romans than I am:
but on the other side, I cannot think so contemptibly of the
age in which I live, or so dishonourably of my own country,
as not to judge we equal the ancients in most kinds of poesy,
155 and in some surpass them; neither know I any reason why I
may not be as zealous for the reputation of our age, as we find
the ancients themselves were in reference to those who lived
before them. For you hear your Horace saying,

Indignor quidquam reprehendi, non quia crasse
160   Compositum, illepideve putetur, sed quia nuper.

And after:

Si meliora dies, ut vina, poemata reddit,
Scire velim, pretim chartis quotus arroget annus?

'But I see I am engaging in a wide dispute, where the argu-
165 ments are not like to reach close on either side; for poesy is of
so large an extent, and so many both of the ancients and
moderns have done well in all kinds of it, that in citing one
against the other, we shall take up more time this evening than
each man's occasions will allow him: therefore I would ask
170 Crites to what part of poesy he would confine his arguments,
and whether he would defend the general cause of the ancients
against the moderns, or oppose any age of the moderns against
this of ours?'

Crites, a little while considering upon this demand, told
175 Eugenius, that if he pleased, he would limit their dispute to
Dramatic Poesy; in which he thought it not difficult to prove,
either that the ancients were superior to the moderns, or the
last age to this of ours.

Eugenius was somewhat surprised, when he heard Crites
180 make choice of that subject. 'For ought I see,' said he, 'I have
undertaken a harder province than I imagined; for though I
never judged the plays of the Greek or Roman poets comparable to ours, yet, on the other side, those we now see acted
come short of many which were written in the last age: but my
185 comfort is, if we are overcome, it will be only by our own
countrymen: and if we yield to them in this one part of poesy,

we more surpass them in all the other: for in the epic or lyric
way, it will be hard for them to show us one such amongst
them, as we have many now living, or who lately were: they
can produce nothing so courtly writ, or which expresses so 190
much the conversation of a gentleman, as Sir John Suckling;
nothing so even, sweet, and flowing, as Mr. Waller; nothing so
majestic, so correct, as Sir John Denham; nothing so elevated,
so copious, and full of spirit, as Mr. Cowley; as for the Italian,
French, and Spanish plays, I can make it evident, that those 195
who now write surpass them; and that the drama is wholly
ours.'

All of them were thus far of Eugenius's opinion, that the
sweetness of English verse was never understood or practised
by our fathers; even Crites himself did not much oppose it; and 200
every one was willing to acknowledge how much our poesy is
improved by the happiness of some writers yet living; who
first taught us to mould our thoughts into easy and significant
words,—to retrench the superfluities of expression,—and to
make our rhyme so properly a part of the verse, that it should 205
never mislead the sense, but itself be led and governed by it.

Eugenius was going to continue this discourse, when Lisideius
told him that it was necessary, before they proceeded further,
to take a standing measure of their controversy; for how was
it possible to be decided who writ the best plays, before we 210
know what a play should be? But, this once agreed on by both
parties, each might have recourse to it, either to prove his own
advantages, or to discover the failings of his adversary.

He had no sooner said this, but all desired the favour of
him to give the definition of a play; and they were the more 215
importunate, because neither Aristotle, nor Horace, nor any
other, who had writ of that subject, had ever done it.

Lisideius, after some modest denials, at last confessed he had
a rude notion of it; indeed, rather a description than a definition; but which served to guide him in his private thoughts, 220
when he was to make a judgement of what others writ: that he
conceived a play ought to be, *A just and lively image of human
nature, representing its passions and humours, and the changes of
fortune to which it is subject, for the delight and instruction of mankind.*

This definition, though Crites raised a logical objection 225 against it—that it was only *genere et fine*, and so not altogether perfect, was yet well received by the rest; and after they had given order to the watermen to turn their barge, and row softly, that they might take the cool of the evening in their return,

230 Crites, being desired by the company to begin, spoke on behalf of the ancients, in this manner:—

'If confidence presage a victory, Eugenius, in his own opinion, has already triumphed over the ancients: nothing seems more easy to him, than to overcome those whom it is

235 our greatest praise to have imitated well; for we do not only build upon their foundations, but by their models. Dramatic Poesy had time enough, reckoning from Thespis (who first invented it) to Aristophanes, to be born, to grow up, and to flourish in maturity. It has been observed of arts and sciences,

240 that in one and the same century they have arrived to great perfection; and no wonder, since every age has a kind of universal genius, which inclines those that live in it to some particular studies: the work then, being pushed on by many hands, must of necessity go forward.

245 'Is it not evident, in these last hundred years, when the study of philosophy has been the business of all the Virtuosi in Christendom, that almost a new nature has been revealed to us? That more errors of the school have been detected, more useful experiments in philosophy have been made, more noble

250 secrets in optics, medicine, anatomy, astronomy, discovered, than in all those credulous and doting ages from Aristotle to us?—so true it is, that nothing spreads more fast than science, when rightly and generally cultivated.

'Add to this, the more than common emulation that was in

255 those times of writing well; which though it be found in all ages and all persons that pretend to the same reputation, yet poesy, being then in more esteem than now it is, had greater honours decreed to the professors of it, and consequently the rivalship was more high between them; they had judges or-

260 dained to decide their merit, and prizes to reward it; and historians have been diligent to record of Aeschylus, Euripides, Sophocles, Lycophron, and the rest of them, both who they were that vanquished in these wars of the theatre, and how often they were crowned: while the Asian kings and Grecian

commonwealths scarce afforded them a nobler subject than the 265
unmanly luxuries of a debauched court, or giddy intrigues of a
factious city:—*Alit aemulatio ingenia*, (says Paterculus,) *et nunc
invidia, nunc admiratio incitationem accendit*: Emulation is the spur
of wit; and sometimes envy, sometimes admiration, quickens
our endeavours. 270

'But now, since the rewards of honour are taken away, that
virtuous emulation is turned into direct malice; yet so slothful,
that it contents itself to condemn and cry down others, without attempting to do better: it is a reputation too unprofitable,
to take the necessary pains for it; yet, wishing they had it, that 275
desire is incitement enough to hinder others from it. And this,
in short, Eugenius, is the reason why you have now so few
good poets, and so many severe judges. Certainly, to imitate
the ancients well, much labour and long study is required;
which pains, I have already shown, our poets would want 280
encouragement to take, if yet they had ability to go through
the work. Those ancients have been faithful imitators and wise
observers of that nature which is so torn and ill represented in
our plays; they have handed down to us a perfect resemblance
of her; which we, like ill copiers, neglecting to look on, have 285
rendered monstrous, and disfigured. But, that you may know
how much you are indebted to those your masters, and be
ashamed to have so ill requited them, I must remember you,
that all the rules by which we practise the drama at this day,
(either such as relate to the justness and symmetry of the plot, or 290
the episodical ornaments, such as descriptions, narrations, and
other beauties, which are not essential to the play,) were
delivered to us from the observations which Aristotle made, of
those poets, who either lived before him, or were his contemporaries: we have added nothing of our own, except we have 295
the confidence to say our wit is better; of which, none boast in
this our age, but such as understand not theirs. Of that book
which Aristotle has left us, περὶ τῆς Ποιητικῆς, Horace's *Art of
Poetry* is an excellent comment, and, I believe, restores to us
that Second Book of his concerning Comedy, which is wanting 300
in him.

'Out of these two have been extracted the famous Rules,
which the French call *Des Trois Unités*, or, The Three Unities,

which ought to be observed in every regular play; namely, of
305 Time, Place, and Action.

'The unity of time they comprehend in twenty-four hours,
the compass of a natural day, or as near as it can be contrived;
and the reason of it is obvious to every one,—that the time of
the feigned action, or fable of the play, should be proportioned
310 as near as can be to the duration of that time in which it is
represented: since therefore, all plays are acted on the theatre
in the space of time much within the compass of twenty-four
hours, that play is to be thought the nearest imitation of nature,
whose plot or action is confined within that time; and, by the
315 same rule which concludes this general proportion of time, it
follows, that all the parts of it are (as near as may be) to be
equally subdivided; namely, that one act take not up the supposed time of half a day, which is out of proportion to the rest;
since the other four are then to be straitened within the com-
320 pass of the remaining half: for it is unnatural that one act,
which being spoke or written is not longer than the rest, should
be supposed longer by the audience; it is therefore the poet's
duty, to take care that no act should be imagined to exceed
the time in which it is represented on the stage; and that the
325 intervals and inequalities of time be supposed to fall out
between the acts.

'This rule of time, how well it has been observed by the
ancients, most of their plays will witness; you see them in their
tragedies, (wherein to follow this rule, is certainly most diffi-
330 cult,) from the very beginning of their plays, falling close into
that part of the story which they intend for the action or
principal object of it, leaving the former part to be delivered
by narration: so that they set the audience, as it were, at the
post where the race is to be concluded; and, saving them
335 the tedious expectation of seeing the poet set out and ride the
beginning of the course, they suffer you not to behold him, till
he is in sight of the goal, and just upon you.

'For the second unity, which is that of Place, the ancients
meant by it, that the scene ought to be continued through the
340 play, in the same place where it was laid in the beginning: for,
the stage on which it is represented being but one and the same
place, it is unnatural to conceive it many,—and those far

distant from one another. I will not deny but, by the variation
of painted scenes, the fancy, which in these cases will contribute
to its own deceit, may sometimes imagine it several places, 345
with some appearance of probability; yet it still carries the
greater likelihood of truth, if those places be supposed so near
each other, as in the same town or city; which may all be
comprehended under the larger denomination of one place; for
a greater distance will bear no proportion to the shortness of 350
time which is allotted, in the acting, to pass from one of them
to another; for the observation of this, next to the ancients, the
French are to be most commended. They tie themselves so
strictly to the unity of place, that you never see in any of their
plays, a scene changed in the middle of an act: if the act begins 355
in a garden, a street, or chamber, 'tis ended in the same place;
and that you may know it to be the same, the stage is so
supplied with persons, that it is never empty all the time: he
who enters second, has business with him who was on before;
and before the second quits the stage, a third appears who has 360
business with him. This Corneille calls *la liaison des scènes*, the
continuity or joining of the scenes; and 'tis a good mark of a
well-contrived play, when all the persons are known to each
other, and every one of them has some affairs with all the rest.

'As for the third unity, which is that of Action, the ancients 365
meant no other by it than what the logicians do by their *finis*,
the end or scope of any action; that which is the first in intention, and last in execution: now the poet is to aim at one great
and complete action, to the carrying on of which all things in
his play, even the very obstacles, are to be subservient; and the 370
reason of this is as evident as any of the former. For two actions,
equally laboured and driven on by the writer, would destroy
the unity of the poem; it would be no longer one play, but two:
not but that there may be many actions in a play, as Ben
Jonson has observed in his *Discoveries*; but they must be all 375
subservient to the great one, which our language happily
expresses in the name of *under-plots*: such as in Terence's
Eunuch is the difference and reconcilement of Thais and Phaedria, which is not the chief business of the play, but promotes
the marriage of Chaerea and Chremes's sister, principally in- 380
tended by the poet. There ought to be but one action, says

Corneille, that is, one complete action, which leaves the mind
of the audience in a full repose; but this cannot be brought to
pass but by many other imperfect actions, which conduce to
385 it, and hold the audience in a delightful suspense of what will be.

'If by these rules (to omit many other drawn from the precepts and practice of the ancients) we should judge our modern
plays, 'tis probable that few of them would endure the trial:
that which should be the business of a day, takes up in some of
390 them an age; instead of one action, they are the epitomes of a
man's life; and for one spot of ground, which the stage should
represent, we are sometimes in more countries than the map
can show us.

'But if we allow the Ancients to have contrived well, we must
395 acknowledge them to have written better. Questionless we
are deprived of a great stock of wit in the loss of Menander
among the Greek poets, and of Caecilius, Afranius, and Varius,
among the Romans; we may guess at Menander's excellency
by the plays of Terence, who translated some of his; and yet
400 wanted so much of him, that he was called by C. Caesar the
half-Menander; and may judge of Varius, by the testimonies
of Horace, Martial, and Velleius Paterculus. 'Tis probable that
these, could they be recovered, would decide the controversy;
but so long as Aristophanes and Plautus are extant, while the
405 tragedies of Euripides, Sophocles, and Seneca, are in our hands,
I can never see one of those plays which are now written, but
it increases my admiration of the ancients. And yet I must
acknowledge further, that to admire them as we ought, we
should understand them better than we do. Doubtless many
410 things appear flat to us, the wit of which depended on some
custom or story, which never came to our knowledge; or perhaps on some criticism in their language, which being so long
dead, and only remaining in their books, 'tis not possible they
should make us understand perfectly. To read Macrobius, ex-
415 plaining the propriety and elegancy of many words in Virgil,
which I had before passed over without consideration as common things, is enough to assure me that I ought to think the
same of Terence; and that in the purity of his style (which Tully
so much valued that he ever carried his works about him) there
420 is yet left in him great room for admiration, if I knew but

where to place it. In the mean time I must desire you to take notice, that the greatest man of the last age, Ben Jonson, was willing to give place to them in all things: he was not only a professed imitator of Horace, but a learned plagiary of all the others; you track him everywhere in their snow: if Horace, 425 Lucan, Petronius Arbiter, Seneca, and Juvenal, had their own from him, there are few serious thoughts which are new in him: you will pardon me, therefore, if I presume he loved their fashion, when he wore their clothes. But since I have otherwise a great veneration for him, and you, Eugenius, prefer him 430 above all other poets, I will use no further argument to you than his example: I will produce before you Father Ben, dressed in all the ornaments and colours of the ancients; you will need no other guide to our party, if you follow him; and whether you consider the bad plays of our age, or regard the 435 good plays of the last, both the best and worst of the modern poets will equally instruct you to admire the ancients.'

Crites had no sooner left speaking, but Eugenius, who had waited with some impatience for it, thus began:

'I have observed in your speech, that the former part of it is 440 convincing as to what the moderns have profited by the rules of the ancients; but in the latter you are careful to conceal how much they have excelled them; we own all the helps we have from them, and want neither veneration nor gratitude, while we acknowledge that, to overcome them, we must make use 445 of the advantages we have received from them: but to these assistances we have joined our own industry; for, had we sat down with a dull imitation of them, we might then have lost somewhat of the old perfection, but never acquired any that was new. We draw not therefore after their lines, but those of 450 nature; and having the life before us, besides the experience of all they knew, it is no wonder if we hit some airs and features which they have missed. I deny not what you urge of arts and sciences, that they have flourished in some ages more than others; but your instance in philosophy makes for me: for if 455 natural causes be more known now than in the time of Aristotle, because more studied, it follows that poesy and other arts may, with the same pains, arrive still nearer to perfection; and, that granted, it will rest for you to prove that they wrought more

460 perfect images of human life than we; which seeing in your
discourse you have avoided to make good, it shall now be my
task to show you some part of their defects, and some few
excellencies of the moderns. And I think there is none among us
can imagine I do it enviously, or with purpose to detract from
465 them; for what interest of fame or profit can the living lose by
the reputation of the dead? On the other side, it is a great truth
which Velleius Paterculus affirms: *Audita visis libentius laudamus*;
*et praesentia invidia praeterita admiratione prosequimur; et his nos
obrui, illis instrui credimus:* that praise or censure is certainly the
470 most sincere, which unbribed posterity shall give us.

'Be pleased then in the first place to take notice, that the
Greek poesy, which Crites has affirmed to have arrived to perfection in the reign of the old comedy, was so far from it, that
the distinction of it into acts was not known to them; or if it
475 were, it is yet so darkly delivered to us that we cannot make
it out.

'All we know of it is, from the singing of their Chorus; and
that too is so uncertain, that in some of their plays we have
reason to conjecture they sung more than five times. Aristotle
480 indeed divides the integral parts of a play into four. First, the
Protasis, or entrance, which gives light only to the characters
of the persons, and proceeds very little into any part of the
action. Secondly, the *Epitasis*, or working up of the plot; where
the play grows warmer, the design or action of it is drawing on,
485 and you see something promising that it will come to pass.
Thirdly, the *Catastasis*, called by the Romans, *Status*, the height
and full growth of the play: we may call it properly the
counter-turn, which destroys that expectation, embroils the
action in new difficulties, and leaves you far distant from that
490 hope in which it found you; as you may have observed in a violent stream resisted by a narrow passage,—it runs round to an
eddy, and carries back the waters with more swiftness than it
brought them on. Lastly, the *Catastrophe*, which the Grecians
called λύσις, the French *le dénouement*, and we the discovery,
495 or unravelling of the plot: there you see all things settling again
upon their first foundations; and, the obstacles which hindered
the design or action of the play once removed, it ends with that
resemblance of truth and nature, that the audience are satisfied

with the conduct of it. Thus this great man delivered to us the image of a play; and I must confess it is so lively, that from 500 thence much light has been derived to the forming it more perfectly into acts and scenes: but what poet first limited to five the number of the acts, I know not; only we see it so firmly established in the time of Horace, that he gives it for a rule in comedy,—*Neu brevior quinto, neu sit productior actu.* So that you see 505 the Grecians cannot be said to have consummated this art; writing rather by entrances, than by acts, and having rather a general indigested notion of a play, than knowing how and where to bestow the particular graces of it.

'But since the Spaniards at this day allow but three acts, 510 which they call *Jornadas*, to a play, and the Italians in many of theirs follow them, when I condemn the ancients, I declare it is not altogether because they have not five acts to every play, but because they have not confined themselves to one certain number: it is building a house without a model; and when 515 they succeeded in such undertakings, they ought to have sacrificed to Fortune, not to the Muses.

'Next, for the plot, which Aristotle called τὸ μῦθος, and often τῶν πραγμάτων σύνθεσις, and from him the Romans *Fabula*; it has already been judiciously observed by a late 520 writer, that in their tragedies it was only some tale derived from Thebes or Troy, or at least something that happened in those two ages; which was worn so threadbare by the pens of all the epic poets, and even by tradition itself of the talkative Greeklings, (as Ben Jonson calls them,) that before it came upon the 525 stage, it was already known to all the audience: and the people, so soon as ever they heard the name of Oedipus, knew as well as the poet, that he had killed his father by a mistake, and committed incest with his mother, before the play; that they were now to hear of a great plague, an oracle, and the 530 ghost of Laius: so that they sat with a yawning kind of expectation, till he was to come with his eyes pulled out, and speak a hundred or more verses in a tragic tone, in complaint of his misfortunes. But one Oedipus, Hercules, or Medea, had been tolerable: poor people, they escaped not so good cheap; they 535 had still the *chapon bouillé* set before them, till their appetites were cloyed with the same dish, and, the novelty being gone,

the pleasure vanished; so that one main end of Dramatic Poesy in its definition, which was to cause delight, was of consequence
540 destroyed.

'In their comedies, the Romans generally borrowed their plots from the Greek poets; and theirs was commonly a little girl stolen or wandered from her parents, brought back unknown to the city, there got with child by some lewd young
545 fellow; who, by the help of his servant, cheats his father; and when her time comes to cry,—*Juno Lucina, fer opem,*—one or other sees a little box or cabinet which was carried away with her, and so discovers her to her friends, if some god do not prevent it, by coming down in a machine, and taking the thanks
550 of it to himself.

'By the plot you may guess much of the characters of the persons. An old father, who would willingly, before he dies, see his son well married; his debauched son, kind in his nature to his mistress, but miserably in want of money; a servant or slave,
555 who has so much wit to strike in with him, and help to dupe his father; a braggadocio captain, a parasite, and a lady of pleasure.

'As for the poor honest maid, on whom the story is built, and who ought to be one of the principal actors in the play, she is
560 commonly a mute in it: she has the breeding of the old Elizabeth way, which was for maids to be seen and not to be heard; and it is enough you know she is willing to be married, when the fifth act requires it.

'These are plots built after the Italian mode of houses,—you
565 see through them all at once: the characters are indeed the imitation of nature, but so narrow, as if they had imitated only an eye or a hand, and did not dare to venture on the lines of a face, or the proportion of a body.

'But in how strait a compass soever they have bounded
570 their plots and characters, we will pass it by, if they have regularly pursued them, and perfectly observed those three unities of time, place, and action; the knowledge of which you say is derived to us from them. But in the first place give me leave to tell you, that the unity of place, however it might be prac-
575 tised by them, was never any of their rules: we neither find it in Aristotle, Horace, or any who have written of it, till in our age

the French poets first made it a precept of the stage. The unity
of time, even Terence himself, who was the best and most
regular of them, has neglected: his *Heautontimorumenos*, or Self-
Punisher, takes up visibly two days, says Scaliger; the two first 580
acts concluding the first day, the three last the day ensuing; and
Euripides, in tying himself to one day, has committed an
absurdity never to be forgiven him; for in one of his tragedies
he has made Theseus go from Athens to Thebes, which was
about forty English miles, under the walls of it to give battle, 585
and appear victorious in the next act; and yet, from the time of
his departure to the return of the Nuntius, who gives the relation of his victory, Aethra and the Chorus have but thirty-six
verses; which is not for every mile a verse.

'The like error is as evident in Terence's *Eunuch*, when 590
Laches, the old man, enters by mistake into the house of
Thais; where, betwixt his exit and the entrance of Pythias,
who comes to give ample relation of the disorders he has raised
within, Parmeno, who was left upon the stage, has not above five
lines to speak. *C'est bien employer un temps si court*, says the French 595
poet, who furnished me with one of the observations: and almost
all their tragedies will afford us examples of the like nature.

'It is true, they have kept the continuity, or, as you called it,
liaison des scènes, somewhat better: two do not perpetually come
in together, talk, and go out together; and other two succeed 600
them, and do the same throughout the act, which the English
call by the name of single scenes; but the reason is, because they
have seldom above two or three scenes, properly so called, in
every act; for it is to be accounted a new scene, not only every
time the stage is empty; but every person who enters, though 605
to others, makes it so; because he introduces a new business.
Now the plots of their plays being narrow, and the persons few,
one of their acts was written in a less compass than one of our
well-wrought scenes; and yet they are often deficient even in
this. To go no farther than Terence; you find in the *Eunuch*, 610
Antipho entering single in the midst of the third act, after
Chremes and Pythias were gone off; in the same play you have
likewise Dorias beginning the fourth act alone; and after she
had made a relation of what was done at the Soldier's entertainment, (which by the way was very inartificial, because she 615

was presumed to speak directly to the audience, and to acquaint
them with what was necessary to be known, but yet should
have been so contrived by the poet as to have been told by
persons of the drama to one another, and so by them to have
620 come to the knowledge of the people,) she quits the stage,
and Phaedria enters next, alone likewise: he also gives you an
account of himself, and of his returning from the country, in
monologue; to which unnatural way of narration Terence is
subject in all his plays. In his *Adelphi*, or Brothers, Syrus and
625 Demea enter after the scene was broken by the departure of
Sostrata, Geta, and Canthara; and indeed you can scarce look
into any of his comedies, where you will not presently discover
the same interruption.

'But as they have failed both in laying of their plots, and in
630 the management, swerving from the rules of their own art by
misrepresenting nature to us, in which they have ill satisfied
one intention of a play, which was delight; so in the instructive
part they have erred worse: instead of punishing vice and
rewarding virtue, they have often shown a prosperous wicked-
635 ness, and an unhappy piety: they have set before us a bloody
image of revenge in Medea, and given her dragons to convey
her safe from punishment; a Priam and Astyanax murdered,
and Cassandra ravished, and the lust and murder ending in
the victory of him who acted them: in short, there is no in-
640 decorum in any of our modern plays, which if I would excuse,
I could not shadow with some authority from the ancients.

'And one further note of them let me leave you: tragedies
and comedies were not writ then as they are now, promiscu-
ously, by the same person; but he who found his genius bending
645 to the one, never attempted the other way. This is so plain,
that I need not instance to you, that Aristophanes, Plautus,
Terence, never any of them writ a tragedy; Aeschylus, Euripides, Sophocles, and Seneca, never meddled with comedy:
the sock and buskin were not worn by the same poet. Having
650 then so much care to excel in one kind, very little is to be pardoned them, if they miscarried in it; and this would lead me to
the consideration of their wit, had not Crites given me sufficient
warning not to be too bold in my judgement of it; because, the
languages being dead, and many of the customs and little

accidents on which it depended lost to us, we are not competent 655
judges of it. But though I grant that here and there we may miss
the application of a proverb or a custom, yet a thing well said
will be wit in all languages; and though it may lose something
in the translation, yet to him who reads it in the original, 'tis
still the same: he has an idea of its excellency, though it cannot 660
pass from his mind into any other expression or words than
those in which he finds it. When Phaedria, in the *Eunuch*, had a
command from his mistress to be absent two days, and, encour-
aging himself to go through with it, said, *Tandem ego non illa
caream, si sit opus, vel totum triduum*?—Parmeno, to mock the 665
softness of his master, lifting up his hands and eyes, cries out,
as it were in admiration, *Hui! universum triduum!* the elegancy of
which *universum*, though it cannot be rendered in our language,
yet leaves an impression on our souls: but this happens seldom
in him; in Plautus oftener, who is infinitely too bold in his 670
metaphors and coining words, out of which many times his wit
is nothing; which questionless was one reason why Horace
falls upon him so severely in those verses:

> Sed proavi nostri Plautinos et numeros et
> Laudavere sales, nimium patienter utrumque,   675
> Ne dicam stolide.

For Horace himself was cautious to obtrude a new word on his
readers, and makes custom and common use the best measure
of receiving it into our writings:

> Multa renascentur quae nunc cecidere, cadentque   680
> Quae nunc sunt in honore vocabula, si volet usus,
> Quem penes arbitrium est, et jus, et norma loquendi.

The not observing this rule is that which the world has
blamed in our satirist, Cleveland: to express a thing hard and
unnaturally, is his new way of elocution. 'Tis true, no poet 685
but may sometimes use a catachresis: Virgil does it—

> Mistaque ridenti colocasia fundet acantho—

in his eclogue of Pollio; and in his seventh *Aeneid*

> —mirantur et undae,
> Miratur nemus insuetum fulgentia longe   690
> Scuta virum fluvio pictasque innare carinas.

And Ovid once so modestly, that he asks leave to do it:

> —quem, si verbo audacia detur,
> Haud metuam summi dixisse Palatia caeli:

695 calling the court of Jupiter by the name of Augustus's palace;
though in another place he is more bold, where he says,—*et
longas visent Capitolia pompas.* But to do this always, and never
be able to write a line without it, though it may be admired
by some few pedants, will not pass upon those who know that
700 wit is best conveyed to us in the most easy language; and is
most to be admired when a great thought comes dressed in
words so commonly received, that it is understood by the
meanest apprehensions, as the best meat is the most easily
digested: but we cannot read a verse of Cleveland's without
705 making a face at it, as if every word were a pill to swallow: he
gives us many times a hard nut to break our teeth, without a
kernel for our pains. So that there is this difference betwixt his
Satires and doctor Donne's; that the one gives us deep thoughts
in common language, though rough cadence; the other gives
710 us common thoughts in abstruse words: 'tis true, in some
places his wit is independent of his words, as in that of the rebel
Scot:

> Had Cain been Scot, God would have chang'd his doom;
> Not forc'd him wander, but confin'd him home.

715 *Si sic omnia dixisset!* This is wit in all languages: it is like
Mercury, never to be lost or killed:—and so that other—

> For beauty, like white powder, makes no noise,
> And yet the silent hypocrite destroys.

You see the last line is highly metaphorical, but it is so soft
720 and gentle, that it does not shock us as we read it.

'But, to return from whence I have digressed, to the consideration of the ancients' writing, and their wit (of which by
this time you will grant us in some measure to be fit judges).
Though I see many excellent thoughts in Seneca, yet he of
725 them who had a genius most proper for the stage, was Ovid; he
had a way of writing so fit to stir up a pleasing admiration and
concernment, which are the objects of a tragedy, and to show
the various movements of a soul combating betwixt two different passions, that, had he lived in our age, or in his own could

have writ with our advantages, no man but must have yielded 730
to him; and therefore I am confident the *Medea* is none of his:
for, though I esteem it for the gravity and sententiousness of it,
which he himself concludes to be suitable to a tragedy,—
Omne genus scripti gravitate tragaedia vincit,—yet it moves not my
soul enough to judge that he, who in the epic way wrote things 735
so near the drama as the story of Myrrha, of Caunus and Biblis,
and the rest, should stir up no more concernment where he
most endeavoured it. The master-piece of Seneca I hold to
be that scene in the *Troades,* where Ulysses is seeking for
Astyanax to kill him: there you see the tenderness of a mother 740
so represented in Andromache, that it raises compassion to a
high degree in the reader, and bears the nearest resemblance
of any thing in the tragedies of the ancients to the excellent
scenes of passion in Shakespeare, or in Fletcher: for love-scenes,
you will find few among them; their tragic poets dealt not with 745
that soft passion, but with lust, cruelty, revenge, ambition, and
those bloody actions they produced; which were more capable
of raising horror than compassion in an audience: leaving
love untouched, whose gentleness would have tempered them;
which is the most frequent of all the passions, and which, being 750
the private concernment of every person, is soothed by viewing
its own image in a public entertainment.

'Among their comedies, we find a scene or two of tenderness,
and that where you would least expect it, in Plautus; but to
speak generally, their lovers say little, when they see each other, 755
but *anima mea vita mea*; Ζωὴ καὶ ψυχή, as the women in Juvenal's
time used to cry out in the fury of their kindness. Any sudden
gust of passion (as an ecstasy of love in an unexpected meeting)
cannot better be expressed than in a word and a sigh, breaking
one another. Nature is dumb on such occasions; and to make 760
her speak, would be to represent her unlike herself. But there
are a thousand other concernments of lovers, as jealousies,
complaints, contrivances, and the like, where not to open
their minds at large to each other, were to be wanting to their
own love, and to the expectation of the audience; who watch 765
the movements of their minds, as much as the changes of their
fortunes. For the imaging of the first is properly the work of a
poet; the latter he borrows from the historian.'

Eugenius was proceeding in that part of his discourse, when
770 Crites interrupted him. 'I see,' said he, 'Eugenius and I are
never like to have this question decided betwixt us; for he
maintains, the moderns have acquired a new perfection in
writing; I can only grant they have altered the mode of it.
Homer described his heroes men of great appetites, lovers of
775 beef broiled upon the coals, and good fellows; contrary to the
practice of the French Romances, whose heroes neither eat,
nor drink, nor sleep, for love. Virgil makes Aeneas a bold
avower of his own virtues:

Sum pius Aeneas, fama super aethera notus;

780 which, in the civility of our poets, is the character of a fanfaron or Hector: for with us the knight takes occasion to walk
out, or sleep, to avoid the vanity of telling his own story, which
the trusty 'squire is ever to perform for him. So in their love-
scenes, of which Eugenius spoke last, the ancients were more
785 hearty, we more talkative: they writ love as it was then the
mode to make it; and I will grant thus much to Eugenius, that
perhaps one of their poets, had he lived in our age, *si foret hoc
nostrum fato delapsus in aevum*, (as Horace says of Lucilius) he
had altered many things; not that they were not natural
790 before, but that he might accommodate himself to the age in
which he lived. Yet in the mean time, we are not to conclude
any thing rashly against those great men, but preserve to them
the dignity of masters, and give that honour to their memories,
quos Libitina sacravit, part of which we expect may be paid to us
795 in future times.'

This moderation of Crites, as it was pleasing to all the
company, so it put an end to that dispute; which Eugenius,
who seemed to have the better of the argument, would urge no
farther: but Lisideius, after he had acknowledged himself of
800 Eugenius's opinion concerning the ancients, yet told him, he
had forborne, till his discourse were ended, to ask him why he
preferred the English plays above those of other nations? and
whether we ought not to submit our stage to the exactness of
our next neighbours?
805   'Though,' said Eugenius, 'I am at all times ready to defend
the honour of my country against the French, and to maintain,

we are as well able to vanquish them with our pens, as our
ancestors have been with their swords; yet, if you please,'
added he, looking upon Neander, 'I will commit this cause to
my friend's management; his opinion of our plays is the same 810
with mine: and besides, there is no reason, that Crites and I,
who have now left the stage, should re-enter so suddenly upon
it; which is against the laws of comedy.'

'If the question had been stated,' replied Lisideius, 'who had
writ best, the French or English, forty years ago, I should have 815
been of your opinion, and adjudged the honour to our own
nation; but since that time,' (said he, turning towards Neander,) 'we have been so long together bad Englishmen, that we
had not leisure to be good poets. Beaumont, Fletcher, and
Jonson, (who were only capable of bringing us to that degree 820
of perfection which we have,) were just then leaving the world;
as if in an age of so much horror, wit and those milder studies
of humanity, had no farther business among us. But the Muses,
who ever follow peace, went to plant in another country: it
was then, that the great Cardinal of Richelieu began to take 825
them into his protection; and that, by his encouragement,
Corneille, and some other Frenchmen, reformed their theatre
(which before was as much below ours, as it now surpasses it
and the rest of Europe). But because Crites in his discourse for
the ancients has prevented me, by observing many rules of 830
the stage which the moderns have borrowed from them, I shall
only, in short, demand of you, whether you are not convinced
that of all nations the French have best observed them? In
the unity of time you find them so scrupulous, that it yet
remains a dispute among their poets, whether the artificial 835
day of twelve hours, more or less, be not meant by Aristotle,
rather than the natural one of twenty-four; and consequently,
whether all plays ought not to be reduced into that compass.
This I can testify, that in all their dramas writ within these
last twenty years and upwards, I have not observed any that 840
have extended the time to thirty hours: in the unity of place
they are full as scrupulous; for many of their critics limit it
to that very spot of ground where the play is supposed to begin;
none of them exceed the compass of the same town or city.
The unity of action in all plays is yet more conspicuous; for 845

they do not burden them with under-plots, as the English do: which is the reason why many scenes of our tragi-comedies carry on a design that is nothing of kin to the main plot; and that we see two distinct webs in a play, like those in ill-wrought 850 stuffs; and two actions, that is, two plays, carried on together, to the confounding of the audience; who, before they are warm in their concernments for one part, are diverted to another; and by that means espouse the interest of neither. From hence likewise it arises, that the one half of our actors are not known 855 to the other. They keep their distances, as if they were Montagues and Capulets, and seldom begin an acquaintance till the last scene of the fifth act, when they are all to meet upon the stage. There is no theatre in the world has anything so absurd as the English tragi-comedy; 'tis a drama of our own invention, 860 and the fashion of it is enough to proclaim it so; here a course of mirth, there another of sadness and passion, and a third of honour and a duel: thus, in two hours and a half, we run through all the fits of Bedlam. The French affords you as much variety on the same day, but they do it not so unseasonably, or 865 *mal à propos*, as we: our poets present you the play and the farce together; and our stages still retain somewhat of the original civility of the Red Bull:

Atque ursum et pugiles media inter carmina poscunt.

The end of tragedies or serious plays, says Aristotle, is to 870 beget admiration, compassion, or concernment; but are not mirth and compassion things incompatible? and is it not evident that the poet must of necessity destroy the former by intermingling of the latter? that is, he must ruin the sole end and object of his tragedy, to introduce somewhat that is forced 875 into it, and is not of the body of it. Would you not think that physician mad, who, having prescribed a purge, should immediately order you to take restringents?

'But to leave our plays, and return to theirs. I have noted one great advantage they have had in the plotting of their 880 tragedies; that is, they are always grounded upon some known history: according to that of Horace, *Ex noto fictum carmen sequar*; and in that they have so imitated the ancients, that they have surpassed them. For the ancients, as was observed before, took for the foundation of their plays some poetical fiction, such as under that consideration could move but little concern- 885 ment in the audience, because they already knew the event of it. But the French goes farther:

Atque ita mentitur, sic veris falsa remiscet,
Primo ne medium, medio ne discrepet imum.

He so interweaves truth with probable fiction, that he puts a 890 pleasing fallacy upon us; mends the intrigues of fate, and dispenses with the severity of history, to reward that virtue which has been rendered to us there unfortunate. Sometimes the story has left the success so doubtful, that the writer is free, by the privilege of a poet, to take that which of two or more relations 895 will best suit with his design: as for example, in the death of Cyrus, whom Justin and some others report to have perished in the Scythian war, but Xenophon affirms to have died in his bed of extreme old age. Nay more, when the event is past dispute, even then we are willing to be deceived, and the poet, 900 if he contrives it with appearance of truth, has all the audience of his party; at least during the time his play is acting: so naturally we are kind to virtue, when our own interest is not in question, that we take it up as the general concernment of mankind. On the other side, if you consider the historical 905 plays of Shakespeare, they are rather so many chronicles of kings, or the business many times of thirty or forty years, cramped into a representation of two hours and a half; which is not to imitate or paint nature, but rather to draw her in miniature, to take her in little; to look upon her through the 910 wrong end of a perspective, and receive her images not only much less, but infinitely more imperfect than the life: this, instead of making a play delightful, renders it ridiculous:

Quodcunque ostendis mihi sic, incredulus odi.

For the spirit of man cannot be satisfied but with truth, or 915 at least verisimility; and a poem is to contain, if not τὰ ἔτυμα, yet ἐτύμοισιν ὁμοῖα, as one of the Greek poets has expressed it.

'Another thing in which the French differ from us and from the Spaniards, is that they do not embarrass, or cumber themselves with too much plot; they only represent so much of a 920 story as will constitute one whole and great action sufficient

for a play; we, who undertake more, do but multiply adventures; which, not being produced from one another, as effects
from causes, but barely following, constitute many actions in
925 the drama, and consequently make it many plays.

'But by pursuing closely one argument, which is not cloyed
with many turns, the French have gained more liberty for
verse, in which they write; they have leisure to dwell on a
subject which deserves it; and to represent the passions, (which
930 we have acknowledged to be the poet's work,) without being
hurried from one thing to another, as we are in the plays of
Calderon, which we have seen lately upon our theatres, under
the name of Spanish plots. I have taken notice but of one
tragedy of ours, whose plot has that uniformity and unity of
935 design in it, which I have commended in the French; and that
is *Rollo*, or rather, under the name of Rollo, the story of Bas-
sianus and Geta in Herodian: there indeed the plot is neither
large nor intricate, but just enough to fill the minds of the audience, not to cloy them. Besides, you see it founded upon the
940 truth of history,—only the time of the action is not reducible
to the strictness of the rules; and you see in some places a little
farce mingled, which is below the dignity of the other parts;
and in this all our poets are extremely peccant: even Ben
Jonson himself, in *Sejanus* and *Catiline*, has given us this olio of a
945 play, this unnatural mixture of comedy and tragedy; which to
me sounds just as ridiculously as the history of David with the
merry humours of Golias. In *Sejanus* you may take notice of the
scene betwixt Livia and the physician, which is a pleasant
satire upon the artificial helps of beauty: in *Catiline* you may
950 see the parliament of women; the little envies of them to one
another; and all that passes betwixt Curio and Fulvia: scenes
admirable in their kind, but of an ill mingle with the rest.

'But I return again to the French writers, who, as I have said,
do not burden themselves too much with plot, which has been
955 reproached to them by an ingenious person of our nation as a
fault; for, he says, they commonly make but one person considerable in a play; they dwell on him, and his concernments,
while the rest of the persons are only subservient to set him off.
If he intends this by it,—that there is one person in the play
960 who is of greater dignity than the rest, he must tax, not only

theirs, but those of the ancients, and which he would be loth
to do, the best of ours; for it is impossible but that one person
must be more conspicuous in it than any other, and consequently the greatest share in the action must devolve on him.
We see it so in the management of all affairs; even in the most 965
equal aristocracy, the balance cannot be so justly poised, but
some one will be superior to the rest, either in parts, fortune,
interest, or the consideration of some glorious exploit; which
will reduce the greatest part of business into his hands.

'But, if he would have us to imagine, that in exalting one 970
character the rest of them are neglected, and that all of them
have not some share or other in the action of the play, I desire
him to produce any of Corneille's tragedies, wherein every
person, like so many servants in a well-governed family, has not
some employment, and who is not necessary to the carrying 975
on of the plot, or at least to your understanding it.

'There are indeed some protatic persons in the ancients,
whom they make use of in their plays, either to hear or give the
relation: but the French avoid this with great address, making
their narrations only to, or by such, who are some way inter- 980
ested in the main design. And now I am speaking of relations,
I cannot take a fitter opportunity to add this in favour of the
French, that they often use them with better judgement and
more à propos than the English do. Not that I commend narrations in general,—but there are two sorts of them. One, of 985
those things which are antecedent to the play, and are related
to make the conduct of it more clear to us. But 'tis a fault
to choose such subjects for the stage as will force us on that
rock, because we see they are seldom listened to by the audience, and that is many times the ruin of the play; for, being 990
once let pass without attention, the audience can never recover
themselves to understand the plot: and indeed it is somewhat
unreasonable that they should be put to so much trouble, as
that, to comprehend what passes in their sight, they must have
recourse to what was done, perhaps, ten or twenty years ago.   995

'But there is another sort of relations, that is, of things happening in the action of the play, and supposed to be done
behind the scenes; and this is many times both convenient and
beautiful; for by it the French avoid the tumult to which we

1000 are subject in England, by representing duels, battles, and the like; which renders our stage too like the theatres where they fight prizes. For what is more ridiculous than to represent an army with a drum and five men behind it; all which the hero of the other side is to drive in before him; or to see a duel

1005 fought, and one slain with two or three thrusts of the foils, which we know are so blunted, that we might give a man an hour to kill another in good earnest with them.

'I have observed that in all our tragedies, the audience cannot forbear laughing when the actors are to die; it is the most

1010 comic part of the whole play. All *passions* may be lively represented on the stage, if to the well-writing of them the actor supplies a good commanded voice, and limbs that move easily, and without stiffness; but there are many *actions* which can never be imitated to a just height: dying especially is a thing

1015 which none but a Roman gladiator could naturally perform on the stage, when he did not imitate or represent, but do it; and therefore it is better to omit the representation of it.

'The words of a good writer, which describe it lively, will make a deeper impression of belief in us than all the actor can

1020 insinuate into us, when he seems to fall dead before us; as a poet in the description of a beautiful garden, or a meadow, will please our imagination more than the place itself can please our sight. When we see death represented, we are convinced it is but fiction; but when we hear it related, our eyes, the

1025 strongest witnesses, are wanting, which might have undeceived us; and we are all willing to favour the sleight, when the poet does not too grossly impose on us. They therefore who imagine these relations would make no concernment in the audience, are deceived, by confounding them with the other, which are

1030 of things antecedent to the play: those are made often in cold blood, as I may say, to the audience; but these are warmed with our concernments, which were before awakened in the play. What the philosophers say of motion, that, when it is once begun, it continues of itself, and will do so to eternity,

1035 without some stop put to it, is clearly true on this occasion: the soul, being already moved with the characters and fortunes of those imaginary persons, continues going of its own accord; and we are no more weary to hear what becomes of them when

they are not on the stage, than we are to listen to the news of
an absent mistress. But it is objected, that if one part of the 1040
play may be related, then why not all? I answer, some parts of
the action are more fit to be represented, some to be related.
Corneille says judiciously, that the poet is not obliged to expose
to view all particular actions which conduce to the principal:
he ought to select such of them to be seen, which will appear 1045
with the greatest beauty, either by the magnificence of the
show, or the vehemence of passions which they produce, or
some other charm which they have in them; and let the rest
arrive to the audience by narration. 'Tis a great mistake in us
to believe the French present no part of the action on the stage; 1050
every alteration or crossing of a design, every new-sprung
passion, and turn of it, is a part of the action, and much the
noblest, except we conceive nothing to be action till the players
come to blows; as if the painting of the hero's mind were not
more properly the poet's work than the strength of his body. 1055
Nor does this anything contradict the opinion of Horace,
where he tells us,

> Segnius irritant animos demissa per aurem,
> Quam quae sunt oculis subjecta fidelibus.

For he says immediately after,   1060

> —Non tamen intus
> Digna geri promes in scenam; multaque tolles
> Ex oculis, quae mox narret facundia praesens.

Among which many he recounts some:

> Nec pueros coram populo Medea trucidet,   1065
> Aut in avem Progne mutetur, Cadmus in anguem; &c.

That is, those actions which by reason of their cruelty will
cause aversion in us, or by reason of their impossibility, unbe-
lief, ought either wholly to be avoided by a poet, or only
delivered by narration. To which we may have leave to add, 1070
such as, to avoid tumult, (as was before hinted,) or to reduce
the plot into a more reasonable compass of time, or for defect
of beauty in them, are rather to be related than presented to
the eye. Examples of all these kinds are frequent, not only
among all the ancients, but in the best received of our English 1075
poets. We find Ben Jonson using them in his *Magnetic Lady*,

where one comes out from dinner, and relates the quarrels
and disorders of it, to save the undecent appearance of them
on the stage, and to abbreviate the story; and this in express
1080 imitation of Terence, who had done the same before him in his
Eunuch, where Pythias makes the like relation of what had
happened within at the Soldier's entertainment. The relations
likewise of Sejanus's death, and the prodigies before it, are
remarkable; the one of which was hid from sight, to avoid the
1085 horror and tumult of the representation; the other, to shun
the introducing of things impossible to be believed. In that
excellent play, *The King and No King*, Fletcher goes yet farther;
for the whole unravelling of the plot is done by narration in
the fifth act, after the manner of the ancients; and it moves
1090 great concernment in the audience, though it be only a relation
of what was done many years before the play. I could multiply
other instances, but these are sufficient to prove that there is
no error in choosing a subject which requires this sort of
narrations; in the ill management of them, there may.

1095   'But I find I have been too long in this discourse, since the
French have many other excellences not common to us; as
that you never see any of their plays end with a conversion,
or simple change of will, which is the ordinary way which our
poets use to end theirs. It shows little art in the conclusion
1100 of a dramatic poem, when they who have hindered the felicity
during the four acts, desist from it in the fifth, without some
powerful cause to take them off their design; and though I deny
not but such reasons may be found, yet it is a path that is
cautiously to be trod, and the poet is to be sure he convinces
1105 the audience that the motive is strong enough. As for example,
the conversion of the Usurer in *The Scornful Lady*, seems to me a
little forced; for, being a Usurer, which implies a lover of money
to the highest degree of covetousness,—and such the poet has
represented him,—the account he gives for the sudden change
1110 is, that he has been duped by the wild young fellow; which in
reason might render him more wary another time, and make
him punish himself with harder fare and coarser clothes, to get
up again what he had lost: but that he should look on it as a
judgement, and so repent, we may expect to hear in a sermon,
1115 but I should never endure it in a play.

'I pass by this; neither will I insist on the care they take, that no person after his first entrance shall ever appear, but the business which brings him upon the stage shall be evident; which rule, if observed, must needs render all the events in the play more natural; for there you see the probability of every 1120 accident, in the cause that produced it; and that which appears chance in the play, will seem so reasonable to you, that you will there find it almost necessary: so that in the exit of the actor you have a clear account of his purpose and design in the next entrance; (though, if the scene be well wrought, the event 1125 will commonly deceive you;) for there is nothing so absurd, says Corneille, as for an actor to leave the stage, only because he has no more to say.

'I should now speak of the beauty of their rhyme, and the just reason I have to prefer that way of writing in tragedies 1130 before ours in blank verse; but because it is partly received by us, and therefore not altogether peculiar to them, I will say no more of it in relation to their plays. For our own, I doubt not but it will exceedingly beautify them; and I can see but one reason why it should not generally obtain, that is, because our 1135 poets write so ill in it. This indeed may prove a more prevailing argument than all others which are used to destroy it, and therefore I am only troubled when great and judicious poets, and those who are acknowledged such, have writ or spoke against it: as for others, they are to be answered by that one sentence of 1140 an ancient author:—*Sed ut primo ad consequendos eos quos priores ducimus, accendimur, ita ubi aut proeteriri, aut aequari eos posse desperavimus, studium cum spe senescit: quod, scilicet, assequi non potest, sequi desinit; . . . praeteritoque eo in quo eminere non possumus, aliquid in quo nitamur, conquirimus.'* 1145

Lisideius concluded in this manner; and Neander, after a little pause, thus answered him:

'I shall grant Lisideius, without much dispute, a great part of what he has urged against us; for I acknowledge that the French contrive their plots more regularly, and observe the 1150 laws of comedy, and decorum of the stage, (to speak generally,) with more exactness than the English. Further, I deny not but he has taxed us justly in some irregularities of ours, which he has mentioned; yet, after all, I am of opinion that neither our

DECT

1155 faults nor their virtues are considerable enough to place them above us.

'For the lively imitation of nature being in the definition of a play, those which best fulfil that law ought to be esteemed superior to the others. 'Tis true, those beauties of the French 1160 poesy are such as will raise perfection higher where it is, but are not sufficient to give it where it is not: they are indeed the beauties of a statue, but not of a man, because not animated with the soul of poesy, which is imitation of humour and passions: and this Lisideius himself, or any other, however biassed 1165 to their party, cannot but acknowledge, if he will either compare the humours of our comedies, or the characters of our serious plays, with theirs. He who will look upon theirs which have been written till these last ten years, or thereabouts, will find it a hard matter to pick out two or three passable humours 1170 amongst them. Corneille himself, their arch-poet, what has he produced except *The Liar*, and you know how it was cried up in France; but when it came upon the English stage, though well translated, and that part of Dorant acted to so much advantage as I am confident it never received in its own country, the most 1175 favourable to it would not put it in competition with many of Fletcher's or Ben Jonson's. In the rest of Corneille's comedies you have little humour; he tells you himself, his way is, first to show two lovers in good intelligence with each other; in the working up of the play to embroil them by some mistake, and 1180 in the latter end to clear it, and reconcile them.

'But of late years Molière, the younger Corneille, Quinault, and some others, have been imitating afar off the quick turns and graces of the English stage. They have mixed their serious plays with mirth, like our tragi-comedies, since the death of 1185 Cardinal Richelieu; which Lisideius and many others not observing, have commended that in them for a virtue which they themselves no longer practise. Most of their new plays are, like some of ours, derived from the Spanish novels. There is scarce one of them without a veil, and a trusty Diego, who 1190 drolls much after the rate of *The Adventures*. But their humours, if I may grace them with that name, are so thin-sown, that never above one of them comes up in any play. I dare take upon me to find more variety of them in some one play of Ben

Jonson's, than in all theirs together; as he who has seen *The Alchemist*, *The Silent Woman*, or *Bartholomew Fair*, cannot 1195 but acknowledge with me.

'I grant the French have performed what was possible on the ground-work of the Spanish plays; what was pleasant before, they have made regular: but there is not above one good play to be writ on all those plots; they are too much alike to please 1200 often; which we need not the experience of our own stage to justify. As for their new way of mingling mirth with serious plot, I do not, with Lisideius, condemn the thing, though I cannot approve their manner of doing it. He tells us, we cannot so speedily recollect ourselves after a scene of great 1205 passion and concernment, as to pass to another of mirth and humour, and to enjoy it with any relish: but why should he imagine the soul of man more heavy than his senses? Does not the eye pass from an unpleasant object to a pleasant in a much shorter time than is required to this? and does not the un- 1210 pleasantness of the first commend the beauty of the latter? The old rule of logic might have convinced him, that contraries, when placed near, set off each other. A continued gravity keeps the spirit too much bent; we must refresh it sometimes, as we bait in a journey that we may go on with greater ease. A scene of 1215 mirth, mixed with tragedy, has the same effect upon us which our music has betwixt the acts; which we find a relief to us from the best plots and language of the stage, if the discourses have been long. I must therefore have stronger arguments, ere I am convinced that compassion and mirth in the same subject 1220 destroy each other; and in the mean time cannot but conclude, to the honour of our nation, that we have invented, increased, and perfected a more pleasant way of writing for the stage, than was ever known to the ancients or moderns of any nation, which is tragi-comedy. 1225

'And this leads me to wonder why Lisideius and many others should cry up the barrenness of the French plots, above the variety and copiousness of the English. Their plots are single; they carry on one design, which is pushed forward by all the actors, every scene in the play contributing and moving towards 1230 it. Our plays, besides the main design, have under-plots or by-concernments, of less considerable persons and intrigues, which are carried on with the motion of the main plot: as they say the orb of the fixed stars, and those of the planets, though 1235 they have motions of their own, are whirled about by the motion of the *primum mobile*, in which they are contained. That similitude expresses much of the English stage; for if contrary motions may be found in nature to agree; if a planet can go east and west at the same time;—one way by virtue of his own 1240 motion, the other by the force of the first mover;—it will not be difficult to imagine how the under-plot, which is only different, not contrary to the great design, may naturally be conducted along with it.

'Eugenius has already shown us, from the confession of the 1245 French poets, that the unity of action is sufficiently preserved, if all the imperfect actions of the play are conducing to the main design; but when those petty intrigues of a play are so ill ordered, that they have no coherence with the other, I must grant that Lisideius has reason to tax that want of due connec-1250 tion; for co-ordination in a play is as dangerous and unnatural as in a state. In the mean time he must acknowledge, our variety, if well ordered, will afford a greater pleasure to the audience.

'As for his other argument, that by pursuing one single 1255 theme they gain an advantage to express and work up the passions, I wish any example he could bring from them would make it good; for I confess their verses are to me the coldest I have ever read. Neither, indeed, is it possible for them, in the way they take, so to express passion, as that the effects of it 1260 should appear in the concernment of an audience, their speeches being so many declamations, which tire us with the length; so that instead of persuading us to grieve for their imaginary heroes, we are concerned for our own trouble, as we are in tedious visits of bad company; we are in pain till they are gone. 1265 When the French stage came to be reformed by Cardinal Richelieu, those long harangues were introduced to comply with the gravity of a churchman. Look upon the *Cinna* and the *Pompey*; they are not so properly to be called plays, as long discourses of reason of state; and *Polyeucte* in matters of religion 1270 is as solemn as the long stops upon our organs. Since that time it is grown into a custom, and their actors speak by the hour-

glass, like our parsons; nay, they account it the grace of their
parts, and think themselves disparaged by the poet, if they may
not twice or thrice in a play entertain the audience with a
speech of a hundred lines. I deny not but this may suit well 1275
enough with the French; for as we, who are a more sullen
people, come to be diverted at our plays, so they, who are of an
airy and gay temper, come thither to make themselves more
serious: and this I conceive to be one reason why comedies are
more pleasing to us, and tragedies to them. But to speak generally: 1280
it cannot be denied that short speeches and replies are more
apt to move the passions and beget concernment in us, than the
other; for it is unnatural for any one in a gust of passion to speak
long together, or for another in the same condition to suffer
him, without interruption. Grief and passion are like floods 1285
raised in little brooks by a sudden rain; they are quickly up;
and if the concernment be poured unexpectedly in upon us,
it overflows us: but a long sober shower gives them leisure to
run out as they came in, without troubling the ordinary current.
As for comedy, repartee is one of its chiefest graces; the greatest 1290
pleasure of the audience is a chase of wit, kept up on both sides,
and swiftly managed. And this our forefathers, if not we, have
had in Fletcher's plays, to a much higher degree of perfection
than the French poets can reasonably hope to reach.

'There is another part of Lisideius's discourse, in which 1295
he rather excused our neighbours, than commended them; that
is, for aiming only to make one person considerable in their
plays. 'Tis very true what he has urged, that one character in
all plays, even without the poet's care, will have advantage of
all the others; and that the design of the whole drama will 1300
chiefly depend on it. But this hinders not that there may be
more shining characters in the play: many persons of a second
magnitude, nay, some so very near, so almost equal to the first,
that greatness may be opposed to greatness, and all the persons
be made considerable, not only by their quality, but their 1305
action. 'Tis evident that the more the persons are, the greater
will be the variety of the plot. If then the parts are managed
so regularly, that the beauty of the whole be kept entire, and
that the variety become not a perplexed and confused mass of
accidents, you will find it infinitely pleasing to be led in a 1310

labyrinth of design, where you see some of your way before you, yet discern not the end till you arrive at it. And that all this is practicable, I can produce for examples many of our English plays: as *The Maid's Tragedy*, *The Alchemist*, *The Silent Woman*: I
1315 was going to have named *The Fox*, but that the unity of design seems not exactly observed in it; for there appear two actions in the play; the first naturally ending with the fourth act; the second forced from it in the fifth: which yet is the less to be condemned in him, because the disguise of Volpone, though it
1320 suited not with his character as a crafty or covetous person, agreed well enough with that of a voluptuary; and by it the poet gained the end at which he aimed, the punishment of vice, and the reward of virtue, both which that disguise produced. So that to judge equally of it, it was an excellent fifth act,
1325 but not so naturally proceeding from the former.

'But to leave this, and pass to the latter part of Lisideius's discourse, which concerns relations: I must acknowledge with him, that the French have reason to hide that part of the action which would occasion too much tumult on the stage,
1330 and to choose rather to have it made known by narration to the audience. Farther, I think it very convenient, for the reasons he has given, that all incredible actions were removed; but whether custom has so insinuated itself into our countrymen, or nature has so formed them to fierceness, I know not; but
1335 they will scarcely suffer combats and other objects of horror to be taken from them. And indeed, the indecency of tumults is all which can be objected against fighting: for why may not our imagination as well suffer itself to be deluded with the probability of it, as with any other thing in the play? For my
1340 part, I can with as great ease persuade myself that the blows are given in good earnest, as I can, that they who strike them are kings or princes, or those persons which they represent. For objects of incredibility,—I would be satisfied from Lisideius, whether we have any so removed from all appearance of truth,
1345 as are those of Corneille's *Andromède*; a play which has been frequented the most of any he has writ. If the Perseus, or the son of a heathen god, the Pegasus, and the Monster, were not capable to choke a strong belief, let him blame any representation of ours hereafter. Those indeed were objects of delight; yet

the reason is the same as to the probability: for he makes it 1350
not a Ballette or masque, but a play, which is to resemble
truth. But for death, that it ought not to be represented, I
have, besides the arguments alleged by Lisideius, the authority
of Ben Jonson, who has forborne it in his tragedies; for both the
death of Sejanus and Catiline are related: though in the latter 1355
I cannot but observe one irregularity of that great poet; he
has removed the scene in the same act from Rome to Catiline's
army, and from thence again to Rome; and besides, has
allowed a very inconsiderable time, after Catiline's speech,
for the striking of the battle, and the return of Petreius, who is 1360
to relate the event of it to the senate: which I should not
animadvert on him, who was otherwise a painful observer of
τὸ πρέπον, or the *decorum* of the stage, if he had not used
extreme severity in his judgement on the incomparable Shakespeare for the same fault.—To conclude on this subject of 1365
relations; if we are to be blamed for showing too much of the
action, the French are as faulty for discovering too little of it: a
mean betwixt both should be observed by every judicious
writer, so as the audience may neither be left unsatisfied by not
seeing what is beautiful, or shocked by beholding what is either 1370
incredible or undecent.

'I hope I have already proved in this discourse, that though
we are not altogether so punctual as the French, in observing
the laws of comedy, yet our errors are so few, and little, and
those things wherein we excel them so considerable, that we 1375
ought of right to be preferred before them. But what will
Lisideius say, if they themselves acknowledge they are too
strictly bounded by those laws, for breaking which he has
blamed the English? I will allege Corneille's words, as I find
them in the end of his Discourse of the three Unities:—*Il est* 1380
facile aux spéculatifs d'être sévères, *&c.* "'Tis easy for speculative
persons to judge severely; but if they would produce to public
view ten or twelve pieces of this nature, they would perhaps give
more latitude to the rules than I have done, when by experience, they had known how much we are limited and con- 1385
strained by them, and how many beauties of the stage they
banished from it." To illustrate a little what he has said:—
By their servile observations of the unities of time and place,

and integrity of scenes, they have brought on themselves that
1390 dearth of plot, and narrowness of imagination, which may be
observed in all their plays. How many beautiful accidents
might naturally happen in two or three days, which cannot
arrive with any probability in the compass of twenty-four
hours? There is time to be allowed also for maturity of design,
1395 which, amongst great and prudent persons, such as are often
represented in tragedy, cannot, with any likelihood of truth, be
brought to pass at so short a warning. Further; by tying themselves strictly to the unity of place, and unbroken scenes, they
are forced many times to omit some beauties which cannot be
1400 shown where the act began; but might, if the scene were interrupted, and the stage cleared for the persons to enter in another
place; and therefore the French poets are often forced upon
absurdities; for if the act begins in a chamber, all the persons
in the play must have some business or other to come thither,
1405 or else they are not to be shown that act; and sometimes their
characters are very unfitting to appear there: as, suppose it
were the king's bed-chamber; yet the meanest man in the
tragedy must come and dispatch his business there, rather than
in the lobby or courtyard, (which is fitter for him,) for fear
1410 the stage should be cleared, and the scenes broken. Many
times they fall by it in a greater inconvenience; for they keep
their scenes unbroken, and yet change the place; as in one of
their newest plays, where the act begins in the street. There a
gentleman is to meet his friend; he sees him with his man,
1415 coming out from his father's house; they talk together, and the
first goes out: the second, who is a lover, has made an appointment with his mistress; she appears at the window, and then
we are to imagine the scene lies under it. This gentleman is
called away, and leaves his servant with his mistress; presently
1420 her father is heard from within; the young lady is afraid the
servingman should be discovered, and thrusts him into a place
of safety, which is supposed to be her closet. After this, the father
enters to the daughter, and now the scene is in a house; for
he is seeking from one room to another for this poor Philipin,
1425 or French Diego, who is heard from within, drolling and breaking many a miserable conceit on the subject of his sad condition.
In this ridiculous manner the play goes forward, the stage

being never empty all the while: so that the street, the window, the houses, and the closet, are made to walk about, and the persons to stand still. Now what, I beseech you, is more easy than 1430 to write a regular French play, or more difficult than to write an irregular English one, like those of Fletcher, or of Shakespeare?

'If they content themselves, as Corneille did, with some flat design, which, like an ill riddle, is found out ere it be half proposed, such plots we can make every way regular, as easily 1435 as they; but whenever they endeavour to rise to any quick turns and counterturns of plot, as some of them have attempted, since Corneille's plays have been less in vogue, you see they write as irregularly as we, though they cover it more speciously. Hence the reason is perspicuous, why no French plays, when 1440 translated, have, or ever can succeed on the English stage. For, if you consider the plots, our own are fuller of variety; if the writing, ours are more quick and fuller of spirit; and therefore 'tis a strange mistake in those who decry the way of writing plays in verse, as if the English therein imitated the 1445 French. We have borrowed nothing from them; our plots are weaved in English looms: we endeavour therein to follow the variety and greatness of characters which are derived to us from Shakespeare and Fletcher; the copiousness and well-knitting of the intrigues we have from Jonson; and for the verse itself 1450 we have English precedents of elder date than any of Corneille's plays. Not to name our old comedies before Shakespeare, which were all writ in verse of six feet, or Alexandrines, such as the French now use,—I can show in Shakespeare, many scenes of rhyme together, and the like in Ben Jonson's tragedies: in 1455 *Catiline* and *Sejanus* sometimes thirty or forty lines,—I mean besides the Chorus, or the monologues; which, by the way, showed Ben no enemy to this way of writing, especially if you read his *Sad Shepherd*, which goes sometimes on rhyme, some- times on blank verse, like a horse who eases himself on trot 1460 and amble. You find him likewise commending Fletcher's pastoral of *The Faithful Shepherdess*, which is for the most part rhyme, though not refined to that purity to which it hath since been brought. And these examples are enough to clear us from a servile imitation of the French. 1465

'But to return whence I have digressed: I dare boldly affirm

these two things of the English drama;—First, that we have
many plays of ours as regular as any of theirs, and which,
besides, have more variety of plot and characters; and secondly,
1470 that in most of the irregular plays of Shakespeare or Fletcher,
(for Ben Jonson's are for the most part regular,) there is a
more masculine fancy and greater spirit in the writing, than
there is in any of the French. I could produce, even in Shakespeare's and Fletcher's works, some plays which are almost
1475 exactly formed; as *The Merry Wives of Windsor*, and *The Scornful
Lady*: but because (generally speaking) Shakespeare, who writ
first, did not perfectly observe the laws of comedy, and Fletcher,
who came nearer to perfection, yet through carelessness made
many faults; I will take the pattern of a perfect play from Ben
1480 Jonson, who was a careful and learned observer of the dramatic
laws, and from all his comedies I shall select *The Silent Woman*;
of which I will make a short examen, according to those rules
which the French observe.'

    As Neander was beginning to examine *The Silent Woman*,
1485 Eugenius, earnestly regarding him; 'I beseech you, Neander,'
said he, 'gratify the company, and me in particular, so far, as
before you speak of the play, to give us a character of the
author; and tell us frankly your opinion, whether you do not
think all writers, both French and English, ought to give place
1490 to him.'

    'I fear,' replied Neander, 'that in obeying your commands I
shall draw some envy on myself. Besides, in performing them,
it will be first necessary to speak somewhat of Shakespeare and
Fletcher, his rivals in poesy; and one of them, in my opinion, at
1495 least his equal, perhaps his superior.

    'To begin, then, with Shakespeare. He was the man who of
all modern, and perhaps ancient poets, had the largest and most
comprehensive soul. All the images of nature were still present
to him, and he drew them, not laboriously, but luckily; when
1500 he describes any thing, you more than see it, you feel it too.
Those who accuse him to have wanted learning, give him the
greater commendation: he was naturally learned; he needed
not the spectacles of books to read nature; he looked inwards,
and found her there. I cannot say he is every where alike;
1505 were he so, I should do him injury to compare him with the

greatest of mankind. He is many times flat, insipid; his comic wit
degenerating into clenches, his serious swelling into bombast.
But he is always great, when some great occasion is presented
to him; no man can say he ever had a fit subject for his wit,
and did not then raise himself as high above the rest of poets,   1510

Quantum lenta solent inter viburna cupressi.

The consideration of this made Mr. Hales of Eton say, that
there was no subject of which any poet ever writ, but he would
produce it much better done in Shakespeare; and however
others are now generally preferred before him, yet the age 1515
wherein he lived, which had contemporaries with him Fletcher
and Jonson, never equalled them to him in their esteem: and in
the last king's court, when Ben's reputation was at highest,
Sir John Suckling, and with him the greater part of the courtiers, set our Shakespeare far above him.   1520

'Beaumont and Fletcher, of whom I am next to speak, had,
with the advantage of Shakespeare's wit, which was their
precedent, great natural gifts, improved by study: Beaumont
especially being so accurate a judge of plays, that Ben Jonson,
while he lived, submitted all his writings to his censure, and, 1525
'tis thought, used his judgement in correcting, if not contriving,
all his plots. What value he had for him, appears by the verses
he writ to him: and therefore I need speak no further of it.
The first play that brought Fletcher and him in esteem was
their *Philaster*: for before that, they had written two or three 1530
very unsuccessfully, as the like is reported of Ben Jonson,
before he writ *Every Man in His Humour*. Their plots were generally more regular than Shakespeare's, especially those which
were made before Beaumont's death; and they understood and
imitated the conversation of gentlemen much better; whose 1535
wild debaucheries, and quickness of wit in repartees, no poet
before them could paint as they have done. Humour, which
Ben Jonson derived from particular persons, they made it not
their business to describe: they represented all the passions
very lively, but above all, love. I am apt to believe the English 1540
language in them arrived to its highest perfection: what words
have since been taken in, are rather superfluous than ornamental. Their plays are now the most pleasant and frequent

entertainments of the stage; two of theirs being acted through
1545 the year for one of Shakespeare's or Jonson's: the reason is,
because there is a certain gaiety in their comedies, and pathos
in their more serious plays, which suit generally with all men's
humours. Shakespeare's language is likewise a little obsolete,
and Ben Jonson's wit comes short of theirs.

1550   'As for Jonson, to whose character I am now arrived, if we
look upon him while he was himself, (for his last plays were but
his dotages) I think him the most learned and judicious writer
which any theatre ever had. He was a most severe judge of
himself, as well as others. One cannot say he wanted wit, but
1555 rather that he was frugal of it. In his works you find little to
retrench or alter. Wit, and language, and humour also in
some measure, we had before him; but something of art was
wanting to the drama, till he came. He managed his strength to
more advantage than any who preceded him. You seldom find
1560 him making love in any of his scenes, or endeavouring to move
the passions; his genius was too sullen and saturnine to do it
gracefully, especially when he knew he came after those who
had performed both to such a height. Humour was his proper
sphere; and in that he delighted most to represent mechanic
1565 people. He was deeply conversant in the ancients, both Greek
and Latin, and he borrowed boldly from them: there is scarce
a poet or historian among the Roman authors of those times
whom he has not translated in *Sejanus* and *Catiline*. But he has
done his robberies so openly, that one may see he fears not
1570 to be taxed by any law. He invades authors like a monarch;
and what would be theft in other poets, is only victory in him.
With the spoils of these writers he so represents old Rome to
us, in its rites, ceremonies, and customs, that if one of their
poets had written either of his tragedies, we had seen less of
1575 it than in him. If there was any fault in his language, 'twas
that he weaved it too closely and laboriously, in his comedies
especially: perhaps too, he did a little too much Romanize our
tongue, leaving the words which he translated almost as much
Latin as he found them: wherein, though he learnedly fol-
1580 lowed their language, he did not enough comply with the
idiom of ours. If I would compare him with Shakespeare, I
must acknowledge him the more correct poet, but Shakespeare

the greater wit. Shakespeare was the Homer, or father of our dramatic poets; Jonson was the Virgil, the pattern of elaborate writing; I admire him, but I love Shakespeare. To conclude of him; as he has given us the most correct plays, so in the precepts which he has laid down in his *Discoveries*, we have as many and profitable rules for perfecting the stage, as any wherewith the French can furnish us. 1585

'Having thus spoken of the author, I proceed to the examina- 1590 tion of his comedy, *The Silent Woman*.

Examen of the Silent Woman

'To begin first with the length of the action; it is so far from exceeding the compass of a natural day, that it takes not up an artificial one. 'Tis all included in the limits of three hours 1595 and a half, which is no more than is required for the present- ment on the stage: a beauty perhaps not much observed; if it had, we should not have looked on the Spanish translation of *Five Hours* with so much wonder. The scene of it is laid in London; the latitude of place is almost as little as you can 1600 imagine; for it lies all within the compass of two houses, and after the first act, in one. The continuity of scenes is observed more than in any of our plays, except his own *Fox* and *Alchemist*. They are not broken above twice or thrice at most in the whole comedy; and in the two best of Corneille's plays, the *Cid* and 1605 *Cinna*, they are interrupted once. The action of the play is entirely one; the end or aim of which is the settling Morose's estate on Dauphine. The intrigue of it is the greatest and most noble of any pure unmixed comedy in any language; you see in it many persons of various characters and humours, and all 1610 delightful. As first, Morose, or an old man, to whom all noise but his own talking is offensive. Some who would be thought critics, say this humour of his is forced: but to remove that objection, we may consider him first to be naturally of a delicate hearing, as many are, to whom all sharp sounds are unpleasant; 1615 and secondly, we may attribute much of it to the peevishness of his age, or the wayward authority of an old man in his own house, where he may make himself obeyed; and to this the poet seems to allude in his name Morose. Besides this, I am assured from divers persons, that Ben Jonson was actually 1620

acquainted with such a man, one altogether as ridiculous as he
is here represented. Others say, it is not enough to find one
man of such a humour; it must be common to more, and the
more common the more natural. To prove this, they instance
1625 in the best of comical characters, Falstaff. There are many
men resembling him; old, fat, merry, cowardly, drunken,
amorous, vain, and lying. But to convince these people, I need
but tell them, that humour is the ridiculous extravagance of
conversation, wherein one man differs from all others. If then
1630 it be common, or communicated to many, how differs it from
other men's? or what indeed causes it to be ridiculous so much
as the singularity of it? As for Falstaff, he is not properly one
humour, but a miscellany of humours or images, drawn from so
many several men: that wherein he is singular is his wit, or
1635 those things he says *praeter expectatum*, unexpected by the audience; his quick evasions, when you imagine him surprised,
which, as they are extremely diverting of themselves, so receive a great addition from the person; for the very sight of
such an unwieldy old debauched fellow is a comedy alone.
1640 And here, having a place so proper for it, I cannot but enlarge
somewhat upon this subject of humour into which I am fallen.
The ancients had little of it in their comedies; for the τὸ
γελοῖον of the old comedy, of which Aristophanes was chief, was
not so much to imitate a man, as to make the people laugh at
1645 some odd conceit, which had commonly somewhat of unnatural
or obscene in it. Thus, when you see Socrates brought upon the
stage, you are not to imagine him made ridiculous by the
imitation of his actions, but rather by making him perform
something very unlike himself; something so childish and
1650 absurd, as by comparing it with the gravity of the true Socrates,
makes a ridiculous object for the spectators. In their new
comedy which succeeded, the poets sought indeed to express
the ἦθος, as in their tragedies the πάθος of mankind. But
this ἦθος contained only the general characters of men and
1655 manners; as old men, lovers, serving-men, courtezans, para-
sites, and such other persons as we see in their comedies; all
which they made alike: that is, one old man or father, one
lover, one courtezan, so like another, as if the first of them had
begot the rest of every sort: *Ex homine hunc natum dicas.* The

same custom they observed likewise in their tragedies. As for 1660
the French, though they have the word *humeur* among them, yet
they have small use of it in their comedies or farces; they being
but ill imitations of the *ridiculum*, or that which stirred up
laughter in the old comedy. But among the English 'tis otherwise: where by humour is meant some extravagant habit, 1665
passion, or affection, particular (as I said before) to some one
person, by the oddness of which, he is immediately distinguished
from the rest of men; which being lively and naturally represented, most frequently begets that malicious pleasure in the
audience which is testified by laughter; as all things which are 1670
deviations from customs are ever the aptest to produce it:
though by the way this laughter is only accidental, as the person
represented is fantastic or bizarre; but pleasure is essential to
it, as the imitation of what is natural. The description of these
humours, drawn from the knowledge and observation of parti- 1675
cular persons, was the peculiar genius and talent of Ben Jonson;
to whose play I now return.

'Besides Morose, there are at least nine or ten different
characters and humours in *The Silent Woman*; all which persons
have several concernments of their own, yet are all used by the 1680
poet, to the conducting of the main design to perfection. I shall
not waste time in commending the writing of this play; but
I will give you my opinion, that there is more wit and acuteness of fancy in it than in any of Ben Jonson's. Besides that he
has here described the conversation of gentlemen in the persons 1685
of True-Wit, and his friends, with more gaiety, air, and
freedom, than in the rest of his comedies. For the contrivance
of the plot, 'tis extreme elaborate, and yet withal easy; for
the λύσις, or untying of it, 'tis so admirable, that when it is
done, no one of the audience would think the poet could have 1690
missed it; and yet it was concealed so much before the last
scene, that any other way would sooner have entered into your
thoughts. But I dare not take upon me to commend the fabric
of it, because it is altogether so full of art, that I must unravel
every scene in it to commend it as I ought. And this excellent 1695
contrivance is still the more to be admired, because 'tis comedy,
where the persons are only of common rank, and their business
private, not elevated by passions or high concernments, as in

serious plays. Here every one is a proper judge of all he sees,
1700 nothing is represented but that with which he daily converses:
so that by consequence all faults lie open to discovery, and few
are pardonable. 'Tis this which Horace has judiciously
observed:

> Creditur, ex medio quia res arcessit, habere
> 1705   Sudoris minimum; sed habet Comedia tanto
> Plus oneris, quanto veniae minus.

But our poet who was not ignorant of these difficulties, has made
use of all advantages; as he who designs a large leap takes his rise
from the highest ground. One of these advantages is that which
1710 Corneille has laid down as the greatest which can arrive to
any poem, and which he himself could never compass above
thrice in all his plays; viz. the making choice of some signal and
long-expected day, whereon the action of the play is to depend.
This day was that designed by Dauphine for the settling of his
1715 uncle's estate upon him; which to compass, he contrives to
marry him. That the marriage had been plotted by him long
beforehand, is made evident by what he tells True-wit in the
second act, that in one moment he had destroyed what he had
been raising many months.

1720   'There is another artifice of the poet, which I cannot here
omit, because by the frequent practice of it in his comedies
he has left it to us almost as a rule; that is, when he has any
character or humour wherein he would show a *coup de Maître*,
or his highest skill, he recommends it to your observation by a
1725 pleasant description of it before the person first appears. Thus,
in *Bartholomew Fair* he gives you the pictures of Numps and
Cokes, and in this those of Daw, Lafoole, Morose, and the
Collegiate Ladies; all which you hear described before you see
them. So that before they come upon the stage, you have a
1730 longing expectation of them, which prepares you to receive
them favourably; and when they are there, even from their
first appearance you are so far acquainted with them, that
nothing of their humour is lost to you.

    'I will observe yet one thing further of this admirable plot;
1735 the business of it rises in every act. The second is greater than
the first; the third than the second; and so forward to the fifth.
There too you see, till the very last scene, new difficulties

arising to obstruct the action of the play; and when the
audience is brought into despair that the business can naturally
be effected, then, and not before, the discovery is made. But 1740
that the poet might entertain you with more variety all this
while, he reserves some new characters to show you, which he
opens not till the second and third act; in the second Morose,
Daw, the Barber, and Otter; in the third the Collegiate Ladies:
all which he moves afterwards in by-walks, or under-plots, as 1745
diversions to the main design, lest it should grow tedious,
though they are still naturally joined with it, and somewhere or
other subservient to it. Thus, like a skilful chess-player, by
little and little he draws out his men, and makes his pawns of
use to his greater persons.   1750

'If this comedy and some others of his, were translated into
French prose, (which would now be no wonder to them, since
Molière has lately given them plays out of verse, which have
not displeased them,) I believe the controversy would soon be
decided betwixt the two nations, even making them the judges. 1755
But we need not call our heroes to our aid. Be it spoken to the
honour of the English, our nation can never want in any age
such who are able to dispute the empire of wit with any people
in the universe. And though the fury of a civil war, and power
for twenty years together abandoned to a barbarous race of 1760
men, enemies of all good learning, had buried the muses under
the ruins of monarchy; yet, with the restoration of our happiness, we see revived poesy lifting up its head, and already
shaking off the rubbish which lay so heavy on it. We have seen
since his Majesty's return, many dramatic poems which yield 1765
not to those of any foreign nation, and which deserve all laurels
but the English. I will set aside flattery and envy: it cannot be
denied but we have had some little blemish either in the plot
or writing of all those plays which have been made within
these seven years; (and perhaps there is no nation in the world 1770
so quick to discern them, or so difficult to pardon them, as ours:)
yet if we can persuade ourselves to use the candour of that poet,
who, though the most severe of critics, has left us this caution
by which to moderate our censures—

      —ubi plura nitent in carmine, non ego paucis   1775
      Offendar maculis;—

if, in consideration of their many and great beauties, we can
wink at some slight and little imperfections, if we, I say, can
be thus equal to ourselves, I ask no favour from the French.
1780 And if I do not venture upon any particular judgement of our
late plays, 'tis out of the consideration which an ancient
writer gives me: *vivorum, ut magna admiratio, ita censura difficilis*:
betwixt the extremes of admiration and malice, 'tis hard to
judge uprightly of the living. Only I think it may be permitted
1785 me to say, that as it is no lessening to us to yield to some plays,
and those not many, of our own nation in the last age, so can
it be no addition to pronounce of our present poets, that they
have far surpassed all the ancients, and the modern writers of
other countries.'
1790   This was the substance of what was then spoke on that
occasion; and Lisideius, I think, was going to reply, when he
was prevented thus by Crites: 'I am confident,' said he, 'that
the most material things that can be said have been already
urged on either side; if they have not, I must beg of Lisideius
1795 that he will defer his answer till another time: for I confess
I have a joint quarrel to you both, because you have concluded, without any reason given for it, that rhyme is proper
for the stage. I will not dispute how ancient it hath been
among us to write this way; perhaps our ancestors knew no
1800 better till Shakespeare's time. I will grant it was not altogether
left by him, and that Fletcher and Ben Jonson used it frequently
in their Pastorals, and sometimes in other plays. Further,—
I will not argue whether we received it originally from our own
countrymen, or from the French; for that is an inquiry of as
1805 little benefit, as theirs who, in the midst of the great plague, were
not so solicitous to provide against it, as to know whether we
had it from the malignity of our own air, or by transportation
from Holland. I have therefore only to affirm, that it is not
allowable in serious plays; for comedies, I find you already con-
1810 cluding with me. To prove this, I might satisfy myself to tell
you, how much in vain it is for you to strive against the stream
of the people's inclination; the greatest part of which are
prepossessed so much with those excellent plays of Shakespeare, Fletcher, and Ben Jonson, which have been written out
1815 of rhyme, that except you could bring them such as were

written better in it, and those too by persons of equal reputation
with them, it will be impossible for you to gain your cause with
them, who will still be judges. This it is to which, in fine, all
your reasons must submit. The unanimous consent of an
audience is so powerful, that even Julius Caesar (as Macrobius 1820
reports of him,) when he was perpetual dictator, was not able to
balance it on the other side; but when Laberius, a Roman
Knight, at his request contended in the *Mime* with another
poet, he was forced to cry out, *Etiam favente me victus es, Laberi.*
But I will not on this occasion take the advantage of the greater 1825
number, but only urge such reasons against rhyme, as I find
in the writings of those who have argued for the other way.
First then, I am of opinion, that rhyme is unnatural in a play,
because dialogue there is presented as the effect of sudden
thought: for a play is the imitation of nature; and since no 1830
man, without premeditation, speaks in rhyme, neither ought
he to do it on the stage. This hinders not but the fancy may be
there elevated to a higher pitch of thought than it is in ordinary
discourse; for there is a probability that men of excellent and
quick parts may speak noble things *extempore*: but those thoughts 1835
are never fettered with the numbers or sound of verse without
study, and therefore it cannot be but unnatural to present the
most free way of speaking in that which is the most constrained.
For this reason, says Aristotle, 'tis best to write tragedy in that
kind of verse which is the least such, or which is nearest prose: 1840
and this amongst the ancients was the Iambic, and with us is
blank verse, or the measure of verse kept exactly without
rhyme. These numbers therefore are fittest for a play; the
others for a paper of verses, or a poem; blank verse being as
much below them, as rhyme is improper for the drama. And if 1845
it be objected that neither are blank verses made *extempore*, yet,
as nearest nature, they are still to be preferred.—But there are
two particular exceptions, which many besides myself have
had to verse; by which it will appear yet more plainly how
improper it is in plays. And the first of them is grounded on 1850
that very reason for which some have commended rhyme; they
say, the quickness of repartees in argumentative scenes receives
an ornament from verse. Now what is more unreasonable than
to imagine that a man should not only light upon the wit, but

1855 the rhyme too, upon the sudden? This nicking of him who spoke before both in sound and measure, is so great a happiness, that you must at least suppose the persons of your play to be born poets: *Arcades omnes, et cantare pares, et respondere parati*: they must have arrived to the degree of *quicquid conabar dicere*;—
1860 to make verses almost whether they will or no. If they are any thing below this, it will look rather like the design of two, than the answer of one: it will appear that your actors hold intelligence together; that they perform their tricks like fortune-tellers, by confederacy. The hand of art will be too
1865 visible in it, against that maxim of all professions—*Ars est celare artem*; that it is the greatest perfection of art to keep itself undiscovered. Nor will it serve you to object, that however you manage it, 'tis still known to be a play; and, consequently, the dialogue of two persons understood to be the labour
1870 of one poet. For a play is still an imitation of nature; we know we are to be deceived, and we desire to be so; but no man ever was deceived but with a probability of truth; for who will suffer a gross lie to be fastened on him? Thus we sufficiently understand, that the scenes which represent cities and countries
1875 to us are not really such, but only painted on boards and canvas; but shall that excuse the ill painture or designment of them? Nay, rather ought they not be laboured with so much the more diligence and exactness, to help the imagination? since the mind of man does naturally tend to truth; and therefore
1880 the nearer any thing comes to the imitation of it, the more it pleases.

'Thus, you see, your rhyme is incapable of expressing the greatest thoughts naturally, and the lowest it cannot with any grace: for what is more unbefitting the majesty of verse,
1885 than to call a servant, or bid a door be shut in rhyme? and yet you are often forced on this miserable necessity. But verse, you say, circumscribes a quick and luxuriant fancy, which would extend itself too far on every subject, did not the labour which is required to well-turned and polished rhyme, set bounds
1890 to it. Yet this argument, if granted, would only prove that we may write better in verse, but not more naturally. Neither is it able to evince that; for he who wants judgement to confine his fancy in blank verse, may want it as much in rhyme: and he

who has it will avoid errors in both kinds. Latin verse was as great a confinement to the imagination of those poets, as 1895 rhyme to ours; and yet you find Ovid saying too much on every subject. *Nescivit* (says Seneca) *quod bene cessit relinquere*: of which he gives you one famous instance in his description of the deluge:

> Omnia pontus erat, deerant quoque litora ponto.   1900
> Now all was sea, nor had that sea a shore.

Thus Ovid's fancy was not limited by verse, and Virgil needed not verse to have bounded his.

'In our own language we see Ben Jonson confining himself to what ought to be said, even in the liberty of blank verse; 1905 and yet Corneille, the most judicious of the French poets, is still varying the same sense a hundred ways, and dwelling eternally on the same subject, though confined by rhyme. Some other exceptions I have to verse; but since these I have named are for the most part already public, I conceive it reasonable 1910 they should first be answered.'

'It concerns me less than any,' said Neander, (seeing he had ended,) 'to reply to this discourse; because when I should have proved that verse may be natural in plays, yet I should always be ready to confess, that those which I have written in this kind 1915 come short of that perfection which is required. Yet since you are pleased I should undertake this province, I will do it, though with all imaginable respect and deference, both to that person from whom you have borrowed your strongest arguments, and to whose judgement, when I have said all, I finally 1920 submit. But before I proceed to answer your objections, I must first remember you, that I exclude all comedy from my defence; and next that I deny not but blank verse may be also used; and content myself only to assert, that in serious plays where the subject and characters are great, and the plot unmixed with 1925 mirth, which might allay or divert these concernments which are produced, rhyme is there as natural and more effectual than blank verse.

'And now having laid down this as a foundation,—to begin with Crites,—I must crave leave to tell him, that some of his 1930 arguments against rhyme reach no farther than, from the faults

or defects of ill rhyme, to conclude against the use of it in
general. May not I conclude against blank verse by the same
reason? If the words of some poets who write in it, are either
1935 ill chosen, or ill placed, which makes not only rhyme, but all
kind of verse in any language unnatural, shall I, for their
vicious affectation, condemn those excellent lines of Fletcher,
which are written in that kind? Is there any thing in rhyme
more constrained than this line in blank verse?—*I heaven*
1940 *invoke, and strong resistance make*; where you see both the clauses
are placed unnaturally, that is, contrary to the common way
of speaking, and that without the excuse of a rhyme to cause it:
yet you would think me very ridiculous, if I should accuse the
stubbornness of blank verse for this, and not rather the stiffness
1945 of the poet. Therefore, Crites, you must either prove that words,
though well chosen, and duly placed, yet render not rhyme
natural in itself; or that, however natural and easy the rhyme
may be, yet it is not proper for a play. If you insist on the
former part, I would ask you, what other conditions are re-
1950 quired to make rhyme natural in itself, besides an election of
apt words, and a right disposition of them? For the due choice
of your words expresses your sense naturally, and the due
placing them adapts the rhyme to it. If you object that one
verse may be made for the sake of another, though both the
1955 words and rhyme be apt, I answer, it cannot possibly so fall
out; for either there is a dependence of sense betwixt the first
line and the second, or there is none: if there be that connection,
then in the natural position of the words the latter line must of
necessity flow from the former; if there be no dependence, yet
1960 still the due ordering of words makes the last line as natural in
itself as the other: so that the necessity of a rhyme never forces
any but bad or lazy writers to say what they would not otherwise. 'Tis true, there is both care and art required to write in
verse. A good poet never establishes the first line, till he has
1965 sought out such a rhyme as may fit the sense, already prepared
to heighten the second: many times the close of the sense falls
into the middle of the next verse, or farther off, and he may
often prevail himself of the same advantages in English which
Virgil had in Latin,—he may break off in the hemistich, and
1970 begin another line. Indeed, the not observing these two last

things, makes plays which are writ in verse, so tedious: for
though, most commonly, the sense is to be confined to the
couplet, yet nothing that does *perpetuo tenore fluere*, run in the
same channel, can please always. 'Tis like the murmuring of a
stream, which not varying in the fall, causes at first attention, 1975
at last drowsiness. Variety of cadences is the best rule; the
greatest help to the actors, and refreshment to the audience.

'If then verse may be made natural in itself, how becomes
it unnatural in a play? You say the stage is the representation
of nature, and no man in ordinary conversation speaks in 1980
rhyme. But you foresaw when you said this, that it might be
answered—neither does any man speak in blank verse, or in
measure without rhyme. Therefore you concluded, that which
is nearest nature is still to be preferred. But you took no notice
that rhyme might be made as natural as blank verse, by the well 1985
placing of the words, &c. All the difference between them, when
they are both correct, is, the sound in one, which the other
wants; and if so, the sweetness of it, and all the advantage
resulting from it, which are handled in the Preface to *The Rival
Ladies*, will yet stand good. As for that place of Aristotle, where 1990
he says, plays should be writ in that kind of verse which is
nearest prose, it makes little for you; blank verse being properly
but measured prose. Now measure alone, in any modern
language, does not constitute verse; those of the ancients in
Greek and Latin consisted in quantity of words, and a deter- 1995
minate number of feet. But when, by the inundation of the
Goths and Vandals into Italy, new languages were introduced,
and barbarously mingled with the Latin, of which the Italian,
Spanish, French, and ours, (made out of them and the Teutonic,) are dialects, a new way of poesy was practised; new, I 2000
say, in those countries, for in all probability it was that of the
conquerors in their own nations: at least we are able to prove,
that the eastern people have used it from all antiquity. *Vide
Daniel's Defence of Rhyme*. This new way consisted in measure
or number of feet, and rhyme; the sweetness of rhyme, and 2005
observation of accent, supplying the place of quantity in words,
which could neither exactly be observed by those barbarians,
who knew not the rules of it, neither was it suitable to their
tongues, as it had been to the Greek and Latin. No man is tied

2010 in modern poesy to observe any further rule in the feet of his verse, but that they be dissyllables; whether Spondee, Trochee, or Iambic, it matters not; only he is obliged to rhyme: neither do the Spanish, French, Italian, or Germans, acknowledge at all, or very rarely, any such kind of poesy as blank verse 2015 amongst them. Therefore, at most 'tis but a poetic prose, a *sermo pedestris*; and as such, most fit for comedies, where I acknowledge rhyme to be improper.—Further; as to that quotation of Aristotle, our couplet verses may be rendered as near prose as blank verse itself, by using those advantages I lately 2020 named,—as breaks in a hemistich, or running the sense into another line,—thereby making art and order appear as loose and free as nature: or not tying ourselves to couplets strictly, we may use the benefit of the Pindaric way practised in *The Siege of Rhodes*; where the numbers vary, and the rhyme is dis- 2025 posed carelessly, and far from often chiming. Neither is that other advantage of the ancients to be despised, of changing the kind of verse when they please, with the change of the scene, or some new entrance; for they confine not themselves always to iambics, but extend their liberty to all lyric numbers, and 2030 sometimes even to hexameter. But I need not go so far to prove that rhyme, as it succeeds to all other offices of Greek and Latin verse, so especially to this of plays, since the custom of nations at this day confirms it; the French, Italian, and Spanish tragedies are generally writ in it; and sure the universal consent 2035 of the most civilized parts of the world, ought in this, as it doth in other customs, to include the rest.

'But perhaps you may tell me, I have proposed such a way to make rhyme natural, and consequently proper to plays, as is unpracticable; and that I shall scarce find six or eight lines 2040 together in any play, where the words are so placed and chosen as is required to make it natural. I answer, no poet need constrain himself at all times to it. It is enough he makes it his general rule; for I deny not but sometimes there may be a greatness in placing the words otherwise; and sometimes they 2045 may sound better; sometimes also the variety itself is excuse enough. But if, for the most part, the words be placed as they are in the negligence of prose, it is sufficient to denominate the way practicable; for we esteem that to be such, which in the

trial oftener succeeds than misses. And thus far you may find
the practice made good in many plays: where you do not, 2050
remember still, that if you cannot find six natural rhymes together, it will be as hard for you to produce as many lines in
blank verse, even among the greatest of our poets, against
which I cannot make some reasonable exception.

'And this, Sir, calls to my remembrance the beginning of 2055
your discourse, where you told us we should never find the
audience favourable to this kind of writing, till we could
produce as good plays in rhyme, as Ben Jonson, Fletcher, and
Shakespeare, had writ out of it. But it is to raise envy to the
living, to compare them with the dead. They are honoured, 2060
and almost adored by us, as they deserve; neither do I know
any so presumptuous of themselves as to contend with them.
Yet give me leave to say thus much, without injury to their
ashes; that not only we shall never equal them, but they could
never equal themselves, were they to rise and write again. We 2065
acknowledge them our fathers in wit; but they have ruined
their estates themselves, before they came to their children's
hands. There is scarce a humour, a character, or any kind of
plot, which they have not used. All comes sullied or wasted
to us: and were they to entertain this age, they could not now 2070
make so plenteous treatments out of such decayed fortunes.
This therefore will be a good argument to us, either not to
write at all, or to attempt some other way. There is no bays
to be expected in their walks: *tentanda via est, qua me quoque*
possum tollere humo.   2075

'This way of writing in verse they have only left free to us;
our age is arrived to a perfection in it, which they never
knew; and which (if we may guess by what of theirs we have
seen in verse, as *The Faithful Shepherdess*, and *Sad Shepherd*) 'tis
probable they never could have reached. For the genius of 2080
every age is different; and though ours excel in this, I deny
not but to imitate nature in that perfection which they did in
prose, is a greater commendation than to write in verse
exactly. As for what you have added—that the people are not
generally inclined to like this way,—if it were true, it would 2085
be no wonder, that betwixt the shaking off an old habit, and
the introducing of a new, there should be difficulty. Do we

not see them stick to Hopkins' and Sternhold's psalms, and
forsake those of David, I mean Sandys' translation of them?
2090 If by the people you understand the multitude, the οἱ πολλοί,
'tis no matter what they think; they are sometimes in the right,
sometimes in the wrong: their judgement is a mere lottery.
Est ubi plebs recte putat, est ubi peccat. Horace says it of the vulgar,
judging poesy. But if you mean the mixed audience of the
2095 populace and the noblesse, I dare confidently affirm that a
great part of the latter sort are already favourable to verse; and
that no serious plays written since the King's return have been
more kindly received by them, than *The Siege of Rhodes*, the
Mustapha, *The Indian Queen*, and *Indian Emperor*.
2100   'But I come now to the inference of your first argument.
You said that the dialogue of plays is presented as the effect
of sudden thought, but no man speaks suddenly, or *extempore*,
in rhyme; and you inferred from thence, that rhyme, which
you acknowledge to be proper to epic poesy, cannot equally be
2105 proper to dramatic, unless we could suppose all men born so
much more than poets, that verses should be made in them,
not by them.
    'It has been formerly urged by you, and confessed by me,
that since no man spoke any kind of verse *extempore*, that which
2110 was nearest nature was to be preferred. I answer you, therefore,
by distinguishing betwixt what is nearest to the nature of
comedy, which is the imitation of common persons and ordinary
speaking, and what is nearest the nature of a serious play: this
last is indeed the representation of nature, but 'tis nature
2115 wrought up to a higher pitch. The plot, the characters, the wit,
the passions, the descriptions, are all exalted above the level of
common converse, as high as the imagination of the poet can
carry them, with proportion to verisimility. Tragedy, we know,
is wont to image to us the minds and fortunes of noble persons,
2120 and to portray these exactly; heroic rhyme is nearest nature,
as being the noblest kind of modern verse.

> Indignatur enim privatis et prope socco
> Dignis carminibus narrari cena Thyestae—

says Horace: and in another place,

2125   Effutire leves indigna tragoedia versus—.

Blank verse is acknowledged to be too low for a poem, nay more, for a paper of verses; but if too low for an ordinary sonnet, how much more for tragedy, which is by Aristotle, in the dispute betwixt the epic poesy and the dramatic, for many reasons he there alleges, ranked above it?   2130

'But setting this defence aside, your argument is almost as strong against the use of rhyme in poems as in plays; for the epic way is every where interlaced with dialogue, or discoursive scenes; and therefore you must either grant rhyme to be improper there, which is contrary to your assertion, or admit it 2135 into plays by the same title which you have given it to poems. For though tragedy be justly preferred above the other, yet there is a great affinity between them, as may easily be discovered in that definition of a play which Lisideius gave us. The *genus* of them is the same,—a just and lively image of 2140 human nature, in its actions, passions, and traverses of fortune: so is the end,—namely, for the delight and benefit of mankind. The characters and persons are still the same, viz. the greatest of both sorts; only the manner of acquainting us with those actions, passions, and fortunes, is different. Tragedy performs 2145 it *viva voce*, or by action, in dialogue; wherein it excels the epic poem, which does it chiefly by narration, and therefore is not so lively an image of human nature. However, the agreement betwixt them is such, that if rhyme be proper for one, it must be for the other. Verse, 'tis true, is not the effect of sudden 2150 thought; but this hinders not that sudden thought may be represented in verse, since those thoughts are such as must be higher than nature can raise them without premeditation, especially to a continuance of them, even out of verse; and consequently you cannot imagine them to have been sudden 2155 either in the poet or in the actors. A play, as I have said, to be like nature, is to be set above it; as statues which are placed on high are made greater than the life, that they may descend to the sight in their just proportion.

'Perhaps I have insisted too long on this objection; but the 2160 clearing of it will make my stay shorter on the rest. You tell us, Crites, that rhyme appears most unnatural in repartees, or short replies: when he who answers, (it being presumed he knew not what the other would say, yet) makes up that part

2165 of the verse which was left incomplete, and supplies both the sound and measure of it. This, you say, looks rather like the confederacy of two, than the answer of one.

'This, I confess, is an objection which is in every man's mouth, who loves not rhyme: but suppose, I beseech you, the 2170 repartee were made only in blank verse, might not part of the same argument be turned against you? for the measure is as often supplied there, as it is in rhyme; the latter half of the hemistich as commonly made up, or a second line subjoined as a reply to the former; which any one leaf in Jonson's plays will 2175 sufficiently clear to you. You will often find in the Greek tragedians, and in Seneca, that when a scene grows up into the warmth of repartees, which is the close fighting of it, the latter part of the trimeter is supplied by him who answers; and yet it was never observed as a fault in them by any of the 2180 ancient or modern critics. The case is the same in our verse, as it was in theirs; rhyme to us being in lieu of quantity to them. But if no latitude is to be allowed a poet, you take from him not only his licence of *quidlibet audendi*, but you tie him up in a straiter compass than you would a philosopher. This is 2185 indeed *Musas colere severiores*. You would have him follow nature, but he must follow her on foot: you have dismounted him from his Pegasus. But you tell us, this supplying the last half of a verse, or adjoining a whole second to the former, looks more like the design of two, than the answer of one. Suppose we 2190 acknowledge it: how comes this confederacy to be more displeasing to you, than in a dance which is well contrived? You see there the united design of many persons to make up one figure: after they have separated themselves in many petty divisions, they rejoin one by one into a gross: the confederacy 2195 is plain amongst them, for chance could never produce any thing so beautiful; and yet there is nothing in it, that shocks your sight. I acknowledge the hand of art appears in repartee, as of necessity it must in all kind of verse. But there is also the quick and poignant brevity of it (which is a high imitation of 2200 nature in those sudden gusts of passion) to mingle with it; and this, joined with the cadency and sweetness of the rhyme, leaves nothing in the soul of the hearer to desire. 'Tis an art which appears; but it appears only like the shadowings of painture, which being to cause the rounding of it, cannot be absent; but while that is considered, they are lost: so while we 2205 attend to the other beauties of the matter, the care and labour of the rhyme is carried from us, or at least drowned in its own sweetness, as bees are sometimes buried in their honey. When a poet has found the repartee, the last perfection he can add to it, is to put it into verse. However good the thought may be, how- 2210 ever apt the words in which 'tis couched, yet he finds himself at a little unrest, while rhyme is wanting: he cannot leave it till that comes naturally, and then is at ease, and sits down contented.

'From replies, which are the most elevated thoughts of verse, you pass to those which are most mean, and which are 2215 common with the lowest of household conversation. In these, you say, the majesty of verse suffers. You instance in the calling of a servant, or commanding a door to be shut, in rhyme. This, Crites, is a good observation of yours, but no argument: for it proves no more but that such thoughts should 2220 be waived, as often as may be, by the address of the poet. But suppose they are necessary in the places where he uses them, yet there is no need to put them into rhyme. He may place them in the beginning of a verse, and break it off, as unfit, when so debased, for any other use; or granting the worst,—that 2225 they require more room than the hemistich will allow, yet still there is a choice to be made of the best words, and least vulgar, (provided they be apt,) to express such thoughts. Many have blamed rhyme in general, for this fault, when the poet with a little care might have redressed it. But they do it with no more 2230 justice, than if English poesy should be made ridiculous for the sake of the Water-poet's rhymes. Our language is noble, full, and significant; and I know not why he who is master of it may not clothe ordinary things in it as decently as the Latin, if he use the same diligence in his choice of words: *delectus ver-* 2235 *borum origo est eloquentiae*. It was the saying of Julius Caesar, one so curious in his, that none of them can be changed but for a worse. One would think, *unlock the door*, was a thing as vulgar as could be spoken; and yet Seneca could make it sound high and lofty in his Latin: 2240

Reserate clusos regii postes laris.
Set wide the palace gates.

'But I turn from this exception, both because it happens not above twice or thrice in any play that those vulgar thoughts 2245 are used; and then too, (were there no other apology to be made, yet,) the necessity of them, which is alike in all kind of writing, may excuse them. For if they are little and mean in rhyme, they are of consequence such in blank verse. Besides that the great eagerness and precipitation with which they are 2250 spoken, makes us rather mind the substance than the dress; that for which they are spoken, rather than what is spoke. For they are always the effect of some hasty concernment, and something of consequence depends on them.

'Thus, Crites, I have endeavoured to answer your objections; 2255 it remains only that I should vindicate an argument for verse, which you have gone about to overthrow. It had formerly been said, that the easiness of blank verse renders the poet too luxuriant, but that the labour of rhyme bounds and circumscribes an over-fruitful fancy; the sense there being commonly 2260 confined to the couplet, and the words so ordered that the rhyme naturally follows them, not they the rhyme. To this you answered, that it was no argument to the question in hand; for the dispute was not which way a man may write best, but which is most proper for the subject on which he writes.

2265 'First, give me leave, Sir, to remember you, that the argument against which you raised this objection, was only secondary: it was built on this hypothesis,—that to write in verse was proper for serious plays. Which supposition being granted, (as it was briefly made out in that discourse, by showing how 2270 verse might be made natural,) it asserted, that this way of writing was a help to the poet's judgement, by putting bounds to a wild overflowing fancy. I think, therefore, it will not be hard for me to make good what it was to prove on that supposition. But you add, that were this let pass, yet he who wants 2275 judgement in the liberty of his fancy, may as well show the defect of it when he is confined to verse; for he who has judgement will avoid errors, and he who has it not, will commit them in all kinds of writing.

'This argument, as you have taken it from a most acute 2280 person, so I confess it carries much weight in it: but by using the word judgement here indefinitely, you seem to have put a fallacy upon us. I grant, he who has judgement, that is, so profound, so strong, or rather so infallible a judgement, that he needs no helps to keep it always poised and upright, will commit no faults either in rhyme or out of it. And on the other 2285 extreme, he who has a judgement so weak and crazed that no helps can correct or amend it, shall write scurvily out of rhyme, and worse in it. But the first of these judgements is no where to be found, and the latter is not fit to write at all. To speak therefore of judgement as it is in the best poets; they who 2290 have the greatest proportion of it, want other helps than from it, within. As for example, you would be loth to say, that he who is endued with a sound judgement has no need of history, geography, or moral philosophy, to write correctly. Judgement is indeed the master-workman in a play; but he requires many 2295 subordinate hands, many tools to his assistance. And verse I affirm to be one of these; 'tis a rule and line by which he keeps his building compact and even, which otherwise lawless imagination would raise either irregularly or loosely; at least, if the poet commits errors with this help, he would make greater 2300 and more without it:—'tis, in short, a slow and painful, but the surest kind of working. Ovid, whom you accuse for luxuriancy in verse, had perhaps been farther guilty of it, had he writ in prose. And for your instance of Ben Jonson, who, you say, writ exactly without the help of rhyme; you are to remember, 'tis 2305 only an aid to a luxuriant fancy, which his was not: as he did not want imagination, so none ever said he had much to spare. Neither was verse then refined so much, to be a help to that age, as it is to ours. Thus then the second thoughts being usually the best, as receiving the maturest digestion from judgement, and 2310 the last and most mature product of those thoughts being artful and laboured verse, it may well be inferred, that verse is a great help to a luxuriant fancy; and this is what that argument which you opposed was to evince.'

Neander was pursuing this discourse so eagerly, that Euge- 2315 nius had called to him twice or thrice, ere he took notice that the barge stood still, and that they were at the foot of Somerset-stairs, where they had appointed it to land. The company were all sorry to separate so soon, though a great part of the evening was already spent; and stood a-while looking back on 2320

the water, upon which the moon-beams played, and made it
appear like floating quicksilver: at last they went up through a
crowd of French people, who were merrily dancing in the open
air, and nothing concerned for the noise of guns which had
2325 alarmed the town that afternoon. Walking thence together
to the Piazze, they parted there; Eugenius and Lisideius to
some pleasant appointment they had made, and Crites and
Neander to their several lodgings.

ALEXANDER POPE

An Essay on Criticism

'Tis hard to say, if greater want of skill
Appear in writing or in judging ill;
But, of the two, less dang'rous is th' offence
To tire our patience, than mislead our sense.
Some few in that, but numbers err in this,   5
Ten censure wrong for one who writes amiss;
A fool might once himself alone expose,
Now one in verse makes many more in prose.
    'Tis with our judgments as our watches, none
Go just alike, yet each believes his own.   10
In Poets as true genius is but rare,
True Taste as seldom is the Critic's share;
Both must alike from Heav'n derive their light,
These born to judge, as well as those to write.
Let such teach others who themselves excel,   15
And censure freely who have written well.
Authors are partial to their wit, 'tis true,
But are not Critics to their judgment too?
    Yet if we look more closely, we shall find
Most have the seeds of judgment in their mind: 20
Nature affords at least a glimm'ring light;
The lines, tho' touch'd but faintly, are drawn right.
But as the slightest sketch, if justly trac'd,
Is by ill-colouring but the more disgrac'd,
So by false learning is good sense defac'd: 25
Some are bewilder'd in the maze of schools,
And some made coxcombs Nature meant but fools.
In search of wit these lose their common sense,
And then turn Critics in their own defence:
Each burns alike, who can, or cannot write,   30
Or with a Rival's, or an Eunuch's spite.

All fools have still an itching to deride,
And fain would be upon the laughing side.
If Maevius scribble in Apollo's spite,
35 There are who judge still worse than he can write.
Some have at first for Wits, then Poets pass'd,
Turn'd Critics next, and prov'd plain fools at last.
Some neither can for Wits nor Critics pass,
As heavy mules are neither horse nor ass.
40 Those half-learn'd witlings, num'rous in our isle,
As half-form'd insects on the banks of Nile;
Unfinish'd things, one knows not what to call,
Their generation's so equivocal:
To tell 'em, would a hundred tongues require,
45 Or one vain wit's, that might a hundred tire.
But you who seek to give and merit fame,
And justly bear a Critic's noble name,
Be sure yourself and your own reach to know,
How far your genius, taste, and learning go;
50 Launch not beyond your depth, but be discreet,
And mark that point where sense and dulness meet.
Nature to all things fix'd the limits fit,
And wisely curb'd proud man's pretending wit.
As on the land while here the ocean gains,
55 In other parts it leaves wide sandy plains;
Thus in the soul while memory prevails,
The solid pow'r of understanding fails;
Where beams of warm imagination play,
The memory's soft figures melt away.
60 One science only will one genius fit;
So vast is art, so narrow human wit:
Not only bounded to peculiar arts,
But oft in those confin'd to single parts.
Like kings we lose the conquests gain'd before,
65 By vain ambition still to make them more;
Each might his sev'ral province well command,
Would all but stoop to what they understand.
First follow Nature, and your judgment frame
By her just standard, which is still the same:
70 Unerring NATURE, still divinely bright,

One clear, unchang'd, and universal light,
Life, force, and beauty, must to all impart,
At once the source, and end, and test of Art.
Art from that fund each just supply provides,
Works without show, and without pomp presides: 75
In some fair body thus th' informing soul
With spirits feeds, with vigour fills the whole,
Each motion guides, and ev'ry nerve sustains;
Itself unseen, but in th' effects, remains.
Some, to whom Heav'n in wit has been profuse,   80
Want as much more, to turn it to its use;
For wit and judgment often are at strife,
Tho' meant each other's aid, like man and wife.
'Tis more to guide, than spur the Muse's steed;
Restrain his fury, than provoke his speed;   85
The winged courser, like a gen'rous horse,
Shows most true mettle when you check his course.
    Those RULES of old discovered, not devis'd,
Are Nature still, but Nature methodiz'd;
Nature, like liberty, is but restrain'd   90
By the same laws which first herself ordain'd.
    Hear how learn'd Greece her useful rules indites,
When to repress, and when indulge our flights:
High on Parnassus' top her sons she show'd,
And pointed out those arduous paths they trod;   95
Held from afar, aloft, th' immortal prize,
And urg'd the rest by equal steps to rise.
Just precepts thus from great examples giv'n,
She drew from them what they deriv'd from Heav'n.
The gen'rous Critic fann'd the Poet's fire,   100
And taught the world with reason to admire.
Then Criticism the Muse's handmaid prov'd,
To dress her charms, and make her more belov'd:
But following wits from that intention stray'd,
Who could not win the mistress, woo'd the maid;   105
Against the Poets their own arms they turn'd,
Sure to hate most the men from whom they learn'd.
So modern 'Pothecaries, taught the art
By Doctor's bills to play the Doctor's part,

110   Bold in the practice of mistaken rules,
      Prescribe, apply, and call their masters fools.
      Some on the leaves of ancient authors prey,
      Nor time nor moths e'er spoil'd so much as they.
      Some drily plain, without invention's aid,
115   Write dull receipts how poems may be made.
      These leave the sense, their learning to display,
      And those explain the meaning quite away.
         You then whose judgment the right course would steer,
      Know well each ANCIENT's proper character;
120   His fable, subject, scope in ev'ry page;
      Religion, Country, genius of his Age:
      Without all these at once before your eyes,
      Cavil you may, but never criticize.
      Be Homer's works your study and delight,
125   Read them by day, and meditate by night;
      Thence form your judgment, thence your maxims bring,
      And trace the Muses upward to their spring.
      Still with itself compar'd, his text peruse;
      And let your comment be the Mantuan Muse.
130   When first young Maro in his boundless mind
      A work t'outlast immortal Rome design'd,
      Perhaps he seem'd above the critic's law,
      And but from Nature's fountains scorn'd to draw:
      But when t'examine ev'ry part he came,
135   Nature and Homer were, he found, the same.
      Convinc'd, amaz'd, he checks the bold design;
      And rules as strict his labour'd work confine,
      As if the Stagirite o'erlook'd each line.
      Learn hence for ancient rules a just esteem;
140   To copy nature is to copy them.
         Some beauties yet no Precepts can declare,
      For there's a happiness as well as care.
      Music resembles Poetry, in each
      Are nameless graces which no methods teach,
145   And which a master-hand alone can reach.
      If, where the rules not far enough extend,
      (Since rules were made but to promote their end)
         Some lucky Licence answer to the full

Th' intent propos'd, that Licence is a rule.
Thus Pegasus, a nearer way to take,   150
May boldly deviate from the common track;
From vulgar bounds with brave disorder part,
And snatch a grace beyond the reach of art,
Which without passing thro' the judgment, gains
The heart, and all its end at once attains.   155
In prospects thus, some objects please our eyes,
Which out of nature's common order rise,
The shapeless rock, or hanging precipice.
Great wits sometimes may gloriously offend,
And rise to faults true Critics dare not mend.   160
But tho' the Ancients thus their rules invade,
(As Kings dispense with laws themselves have made)
Moderns, beware! or if you must offend
Against the precept, ne'er transgress its End;
Let it be seldom, and compell'd by need;   165
And have, at least, their precedent to plead.
The Critic else proceeds without remorse,
Seizes your fame, and puts his laws in force.
      I know there are, to whose presumptuous thoughts
Those freer beauties, ev'n in them, seem faults.   170
Some figures monstrous and mis-shap'd appear,
Consider'd singly, or beheld too near,
Which, but proportion'd to their light, or place,
Due distance reconciles to form and grace.
A prudent chief not always must display   175
His pow'rs in equal ranks, and fair array.
But with th' occasion and the place comply,
Conceal his force, nay seem sometimes to fly.
Those oft are stratagems which error seem,
Nor is it Homer nods, but we that dream.   180
      Still green with bays each ancient Altar stands,
Above the reach of sacrilegious hands;
Secure from Flames, from Envy's fiercer rage,
Destructive War, and all-involving Age.
See, from each clime the learn'd their incense bring!   185
Hear, in all tongues consenting Paeans ring!
In praise so just let ev'ry voice be join'd,

And fill the gen'ral chorus of mankind.
Hail, Bards triumphant! born in happier days;
190 Immortal heirs of universal praise!
Whose honours with increase of ages grow,
As streams roll down, enlarging as they flow;
Nations unborn your mighty names shall sound,
And worlds applaud that must not yet be found!
195 Oh may some spark of your celestial fire,
The last, the meanest of your sons inspire,
(That on weak wings, from far, pursues your flights;
Glows while he reads, but trembles as he writes)
To teach vain Wits a science little known,
200 T' admire superior sense, and doubt their own!

Of all the Causes which conspire to blind
Man's erring judgment, and misguide the mind,
What the weak head with strongest bias rules,
Is *Pride*, the never-failing vice of fools.
205 Whatever nature has in worth denied,
She gives in large recruits of needful pride;
For as in bodies, thus in souls, we find
What wants in blood and spirits, swell'd with wind:
Pride, where wit fails, steps in to our defence,
210 And fills up all the mighty Void of sense.
If once right reason drives that cloud away,
Truth breaks upon us with resistless day.
Trust not yourself; but your defects to know,
Make use of ev'ry friend—and ev'ry foe.
215 A *little learning* is a dang'rous thing;
Drink deep, or taste not the Pierian spring:
There shallow draughts intoxicate the brain,
And drinking largely sobers us again.
Fir'd at first sight with what the Muse imparts,
220 In fearless youth we tempt the heights of Arts,
While from the bounded level of our mind
Short views we take, nor see the lengths behind;
But more advanc'd, behold with strange surprise
New distant scenes of endless science rise!
225 So pleas'd at first the tow'ring Alps we try,

Mount o'er the vales, and seem to tread the sky,
Th' eternal snows appear already past,
And the first clouds and mountains seem the last;
But, those attain'd, we tremble to survey
The growing labours of the lengthen'd way,   230
Th' increasing prospect tires our wand'ring eyes,
Hills peep o'er hills, and Alps on Alps arise!
   A perfect Judge will read each work of Wit
With the same spirit that its author writ:
Survey the WHOLE, nor seek slight faults to find   235
Where nature moves, and rapture warms the mind;
Nor lose, for that malignant dull delight,
The gen'rous pleasure to be charm'd with Wit.
But in such lays as neither ebb, nor flow,
Correctly cold, and regularly low,   240
That shunning faults, one quiet tenor keep;
We cannot blame indeed—but we may sleep.
In wit, as nature, what affects our hearts
Is not th' exactness of peculiar parts;
'Tis not a lip, or eye, we beauty call,   245
But the joint force and full result of all.
Thus when we view some well-proportion'd dome,
(The world's just wonder, and ev'n thine, O Rome!)
No single parts unequally surprise,
All comes united to th' admiring eyes;   250
No monstrous height, or breadth, or length appear;
The Whole at once is bold, and regular.
   Whoever thinks a faultless piece to see,
Thinks what ne'er was, nor is, nor e'er shall be.
In every work regard the writer's End,   255
Since none can compass more than they intend;
And if the means be just, the conduct true,
Applause, in spite of trivial faults, is due;
As men of breeding, sometimes men of wit,
T' avoid great errors, must the less commit: 260
Neglect the rules each verbal Critic lays,
For not to know some trifles, is a praise.
Most Critics, fond of some subservient art,
Still make the Whole depend upon a Part:

265 They talk of principles, but notions prize,
And all to one lov'd Folly sacrifice.
Once on a time, La Mancha's Knight, they say,
A certain bard encount'ring on the way,
Discours'd in terms as just, with looks as sage,
270 As e'er could Dennis of the Grecian stage;
Concluding all were desp'rate sots and fools,
Who durst depart from Aristotle's rules.
Our Author, happy in a judge so nice,
Produc'd his Play, and begg'd the Knight's advice,
275 Made him observe the subject, and the plot,
The manners, passions, unities; what not?
All which, exact to rule, were brought about,
Were but a Combat in the lists left out.
'What! leave the Combat out?' exclaims the Knight;
280 Yes, or we must renounce the Stagirite.
'Not so by Heav'n' (he answers in a rage),
'Knights, squires, and steeds, must enter on the stage.'
So vast a throng the stage can ne'er contain.
'Then build a new, or act it in a plain.'
285 Thus Critics, of less judgment than caprice,
Curious not knowing, not exact but nice,
Form short Ideas; and offend in arts
(As most in manners) by a love to parts.
Some to *Conceit* alone their taste confine,
290 And glitt'ring thoughts struck out at ev'ry line;
Pleas'd with a work where nothing's just or fit;
One glaring Chaos and wild heap of wit.
Poets like painters, thus, unskill'd to trace
The naked nature and the living grace,
295 With gold and jewels cover ev'ry part,
And hide with ornaments their want of art.
True Wit is Nature to advantage dress'd,
What oft was thought, but ne'er so well express'd;
Something, whose truth convinc'd at sight we find,
300 That gives us back the image of our mind.
As shades more sweetly recommend the light,
So modest plainness sets off sprightly wit.
For works may have more wit than does 'em good,

As bodies perish thro' excess of blood.

Others for *Language* all their care express,   305
And value books, as women men, for Dress:
Their praise is still,—the Style is excellent:
The Sense, they humbly take upon content.
Words are like leaves; and where they most abound,
Much fruit of sense beneath is rarely found,   310
False Eloquence, like the prismatic glass,
Its gaudy colours spreads on ev'ry place;
The face of Nature we no more survey,
All glares alike, without distinction gay:
But true expression, like th' unchanging Sun,   315
Clears and improves whate'er it shines upon,
It gilds all objects, but it alters none.
Expression is the dress of thought, and still
Appears more decent, as more suitable;
A vile conceit in pompous words express'd,   320
Is like a clown in regal purple dress'd:
For diff'rent styles with diff'rent subjects sort,
As several garbs with country, town, and court.
Some by old words to fame have made pretence,
Ancients in phrase, mere moderns in their sense;   325
Such labour'd nothings, in so strange a style,
Amaze th' unlearn'd, and make the learned smile.
Unlucky, as Fungoso in the play,
These sparks with awkward vanity display
What the fine gentleman wore yesterday;   330
And but so mimic ancient wits at best,
As apes our grandsires, in their doublets drest.
In words, as fashions, the same rule will hold;
Alike fantastic, if too new, or old:
Be not the first by whom the new are try'd,   335
Nor yet the last to lay the old aside.

But most by Numbers judge a Poet's song;
And smooth or rough, with them is right or wrong:
In the bright Muse though thousand charms conspire,
Her voice is all these tuneful fools admire;   340
Who haunt Parnassus but to please their ear,
Not mend their minds; as some to Church repair,

Not for the doctrine, but the music there.
These equal syllables alone require,
345   Tho' oft the ear the open vowels tire;
While expletives their feeble aid do join;
And ten low words oft creep in one dull line:
While they ring round the same unvary'd chimes,
With sure returns of still expected rhymes;
350   Where-e'er you find 'the cooling western breeze,'
In the next line, it 'whispers through the trees';
If crystal streams 'with pleasing murmurs creep,'
The reader's threaten'd (not in vain) with 'sleep':
Then, at the last and only couplet fraught
355   With some unmeaning thing they call a thought,
A needless Alexandrine ends the song
That, like a wounded snake, drags its slow length along.
Leave such to tune their own dull rhymes, and know
What's roundly smooth or languishingly slow;
360   And praise the easy vigour of a line,
Where Denham's strength, and Waller's sweetness join.
True ease in writing comes from art, not chance,
As those move easiest who have learn'd to dance.
'Tis not enough no harshness gives offence,
365   The sound must seem an Echo to the sense:
Soft is the strain when Zephyr gently blows,
And the smooth stream in smoother numbers flows;
But when loud surges lash the sounding shore,
The hoarse, rough verse should like the torrent roar:
370   When Ajax strives some rock's vast weight to throw,
The line too labours, and the words move slow;
Not so, when swift Camilla scours the plain,
Flies o'er th' unbending corn, and skims along the main.
Hear how Timotheus' varied lays surprise,
375   And bid alternate passions fall and rise!
While, at each change, the son of Libyan Jove
Now burns with glory, and then melts with love,
Now his fierce eyes with sparkling fury glow,
Now sighs steal out, and tears begin to flow:
380   Persians and Greeks like turns of nature found,
And the world's victor stood subdu'd by Sound!

The pow'r of Music all our hearts allow,
And what Timotheus was, is DRYDEN now.
  Avoid Extremes; and shun the fault of such,
Who still are pleas'd too little or too much.   385
At ev'ry trifle scorn to take offence,
That always shows great pride, or little sense;
Those heads, as stomachs, are not sure the best,
Which nauseate all, and nothing can digest.
Yet let not each gay Turn thy rapture move;   390
For fools admire, but men of sense approve:
As things seem large which we thro' mists descry,
Dulness is ever apt to magnify.
  Some foreign writers, some our own despise;
The Ancients only, or the Moderns prize.   395
Thus Wit, like Faith, by each man is apply'd
To one small sect, and all are damn'd beside.
Meanly they seek the blessing to confine,
And force that sun but on a part to shine,
Which not alone the southern wit sublimes,   400
But ripens spirits in cold northern climes;
Which from the first has shone on ages past,
Enlights the present, and shall warm the last;
Tho' each may feel increases and decays,
And see now clearer and now darker days.   405
Regard not then if Wit be old or new,
But blame the false, and value still the true.
  Some ne'er advance a Judgment of their own,
But catch the spreading notion of the Town;
They reason and conclude by precedent,   410
And own stale nonsense which they ne'er invent.
Some judge of authors' names, not works, and then
Nor praise nor blame the writings, but the men.
Of all this servile herd the worst is he
That in proud dulness joins with Quality.   415
A constant Critic at the great man's board,
To fetch and carry nonsense for my Lord.
What woful stuff this madrigal would be,
In some starv'd hackney sonneteer, or me?
But let a Lord once own the happy lines,   420

How the wit brightens! how the style refines!
Before his sacred name flies ev'ry fault,
And each exalted stanza teems with thought!
   The Vulgar thus through Imitation err;
425   As oft the Learn'd by being singular;
So much they scorn the crowd, that if the throng
By chance go right, they purposely go wrong;
So Schismatics the plain believers quit,
And are but damn'd for having too much wit.
430   Some praise at morning what they blame at night;
But always think the last opinion right.
A Muse by these is like a mistress us'd,
This hour she's idoliz'd, the next abus'd;
While their weak heads like towns unfortify'd,
435   'Twixt sense and nonsense daily change their side.
Ask them the cause; they're wiser still, they say;
And still to-morrow's wiser than to-day.
We think our fathers fools, so wise we grow,
Our wiser sons, no doubt, will think us so.
440   Once School-divines this zealous isle o'er-spread;
Who knew most Sentences, was deepest read;
Faith, Gospel, all, seem'd made to be disputed,
And none had sense enough to be confuted:
Scotists and Thomists, now, in peace remain,
445   Amidst their kindred cobwebs in Duck-lane.
If Faith itself has different dresses worn,
What wonder modes in Wit should take their turn?
Oft, leaving what is natural and fit,
The current folly proves the ready wit;
450   And authors think their reputation safe,
Which lives as long as fools are pleas'd to laugh.
   Some valuing those of their own side or mind,
Still make themselves the measure of mankind:
Fondly we think we honour merit then,
455   When we but praise ourselves in other men.
Parties in Wit attend on those of State,
And public faction doubles private hate.
Pride, Malice, Folly, against Dryden rose,
In various shapes of Parsons, Critics, Beaux;

But sense surviv'd, when merry jests were past;   460
For rising merit will buoy up at last.
Might he return, and bless once more our eyes,
New Blackmores and new Milbourns must arise:
Nay should great Homer lift his awful head,
Zoilus again would start up from the dead.   465
Envy will merit, as its shade, pursue;
But like a shadow, proves the substance true;
For envy'd Wit, like Sol eclips'd, makes known
Th' opposing body's grossness, not its own,
When first that sun too pow'rful beams displays,   470
It draws up vapours which obscure its rays;
But ev'n those clouds at last adorn its way,
Reflect new glories, and augment the day.
　　Be thou the first true merit to befriend;
His praise is lost, who stays, till all commend.   475
Short is the date, alas, of modern rhymes,
And 'tis but just to let them live betimes.
No longer now that golden age appears,
When Patriarch-wits surviv'd a thousand years:
Now length of Fame (our second life) is lost,   480
And bare threescore is all ev'n that can boast;
Our sons their fathers' failing language see,
And such as Chaucer is, shall Dryden be.
So when the faithful pencil has design'd
Some bright Idea of the master's mind,   485
Where a new world leaps out at his command,
And ready Nature waits upon his hand;
When the ripe colours soften and unite,
And sweetly melt into just shade and light;
When mellowing years their full perfection give,   490
And each bold figure just begins to live,
The treach'rous colours the fair art betray,
And all the bright creation fades away!
　　Unhappy Wit, like most mistaken things,
Atones not for that envy which it brings.   495
In youth alone its empty praise we boast,
But soon the short-liv'd vanity is lost:
Like some fair flow'r the early spring supplies,

That gaily blooms, but ev'n in blooming dies.
500   What is this Wit, which must our cares employ?
The owner's wife, that other men enjoy;
Then most our trouble still when most admir'd,
And still the more we give, the more requir'd;
Whose fame with pains we guard, but lose with ease,
505   Sure some to vex, but never all to please;
'Tis what the vicious fear, the virtuous shun,
By fools 'tis hated, and by knaves undone!
    If Wit so much from Ign'rance undergo,
Ah let not Learning too commence its foe!
510   Of old, those met rewards who could excel,
And such were prais'd who but endeavour'd well:
Tho' triumphs were to gen'rals only due,
Crowns were reserv'd to grace the soldiers too.
Now, they who reach Parnassus' lofty crown,
515   Employ their pains to spurn some others down;
And while self-love each jealous writer rules,
Contending wits become the sport of fools:
But still the worst with most regret commend,
For each ill Author is as bad a Friend.
520   To what base ends, and by what abject ways,
Are mortals urg'd thro' sacred lust of praise!
Ah ne'er so dire a thirst of glory boast,
Nor in the Critic let the Man be lost.
Good-nature and good-sense must ever join;
525   To err is human, to forgive, divine.
    But if in noble minds some dregs remain
Not yet purg'd off, of spleen and sour disdain;
Discharge that rage on more provoking crimes,
Nor fear a dearth in these flagitious times.
530   No pardon vile Obscenity should find,
Tho' wit and art conspire to move your mind;
But Dulness with Obscenity must prove
As shameful sure as Impotence in love.
In the fat age of pleasure, wealth and ease,
535   Sprung the rank weed, and thriv'd with large increase:
When love was all an easy Monarch's care;
Seldom at council, never in a war:

Jilts rul'd the state, and statesmen farces writ;
Nay wits had pensions, and young Lords had wit:
The Fair sate panting at a Courtier's play,   540
And not a Mask went unimprov'd away:
The modest fan was lifted up no more,
And Virgins smil'd at what they blush'd before.
The following licence of a Foreign reign
Did all the dregs of bold Socinus drain;   545
Then unbelieving priests reform'd the nation,
And taught more pleasant methods of salvation;
Where Heav'n's free subjects might their rights dispute,
Lest God himself should seem too absolute:
Pulpits their sacred satire learn'd to spare,   550
And Vice admir'd to find a flatt'rer there!
Encourag'd thus, Wit's Titans brav'd the skies,
And the press groan'd with licens'd blasphemies.
These monsters, Critics! with your darts engage,
Here point your thunder, and exhaust your rage!   555
Yet shun their fault, who, scandalously nice,
Will needs mistake an author into vice;
All seems infected that th' infected spy,
As all looks yellow to the jaundic'd eye.

LEARN then what MORALS Critics ought to show,   560
For 'tis but half a Judge's task, to know.
'Tis not enough, taste, judgment, learning, join;
In all you speak, let truth and candour shine:
That not alone what to your sense is due
All may allow; but seek your friendship too.   565
Be silent always when you doubt your sense;
And speak, tho' sure, with seeming diffidence:
Some positive, persisting fops we know,
Who, if once wrong, will needs be always so;
But you, with pleasure own your errors past,   570
And make each day a Critic on the last.
'Tis not enough, your counsel still be true;
Blunt truths more mischief than nice falsehoods do;
Men must be taught as if you taught them not,
And things unknown propos'd as things forgot.   575

Without Good Breeding, truth is disapprov'd;
That only makes superior sense belov'd.
   Be niggards of advice on no pretence;
For the worst avarice is that of sense.
580   With mean complacence ne'er betray your trust,
Nor be so civil as to prove unjust.
Fear not the anger of the wise to raise;
Those best can bear reproof, who merit praise.
   'Twere well might critics still this freedom take,
585   But Appius reddens at each word you speak,
And stares, tremendous, with a threat'ning eye,
Like some fierce tyrant in old tapestry.
Fear most to tax an Honourable fool,
Whose right it is, uncensur'd, to be dull;
590   Such, without wit, are Poets when they please,
As without learning they can take Degrees.
Leave dang'rous truths to unsuccessful Satires,
And flattery to fulsome Dedicators,
Whom, when they praise, the world believes no more,
595   Than when they promise to give scribbling o'er.
'Tis best sometimes your censure to restrain,
And charitably let the dull be vain:
Your silence there is better than your spite,
For who can rail so long as they can write?
600   Still humming on, their drowsy course they keep,
And lash'd so long, like tops, are lash'd asleep.
False steps but help them to renew the race,
As, after stumbling, Jades will mend their pace.
What crowds of these, impenitently bold,
605   In sounds and jingling syllables grown old,
Still run on Poets, in a raging vein,
Ev'n to the dregs and squeezings of the brain,
Strain out the last dull droppings of their sense,
And rhyme with all the rage of Impotence.
610   Such shameless Bards we have; and yet 'tis true,
There are as mad abandon'd Critics too.
The bookful blockhead, ignorantly read,
With loads of learned lumber in his head,
With his own tongue still edifies his ears,

And always list'ning to himself appears.   615
All books he reads, and all he reads assails,
From Dryden's Fables down to Durfey's Tales.
With him, most authors steal their works, or buy;
Garth did not write his own Dispensary.
Name a new Play, and he's the Poet's friend,   620
Nay show'd his faults—but when would Poets mend?
No place so sacred from such fops is barr'd,
Nor is Paul's church more safe than Paul's churchyard:
Nay, fly to Altars; there they'll talk you dead:
For Fools rush in where Angels fear to tread.   625
Distrustful sense with modest caution speaks,
It still looks home, and short excursions makes;
But rattling nonsense in full volleys breaks,
And never shock'd, and never turn'd aside,
Bursts out, resistless, with a thund'ring tide.   630
  But where's the man, who counsel can bestow,
Still pleas'd to teach, and yet not proud to know?
Unbiass'd, or by favour, or by spite;
Not dully prepossess'd, nor blindly right;
Tho' learn'd, well-bred; and tho' well-bred, sincere,   635
Modestly bold, and humanly severe:
Who to a friend his faults can freely show,
And gladly praise the merit of a foe?
Blest with a taste exact, yet unconfin'd;
A knowledge both of books and human kind: 640
Gen'rous converse; a soul exempt from pride;
And love to praise, with reason on his side?
  Such once were Critics; such the happy few,
Athens and Rome in better ages knew.
The mighty Stagirite first left the shore,   645
Spread all his sails, and durst the deeps explore:
He steer'd securely, and discover'd far,
Led by the light of the Maeonian Star.
Poets, a race long unconfin'd, and free,
Still fond and proud of savage liberty,   650
Receiv'd his laws; and stood convinc'd 'twas fit,
Who conquer'd Nature, should preside o'er Wit.
  Horace still charms with graceful negligence,

And without method talks us into sense,
655 Will, like a friend, familiarly convey
The truest notions in the easiest way.
He, who supreme in judgment, as in wit,
Might boldly censure, as he boldly writ,
Yet judg'd with coolness, tho' he sung with fire;
660 His Precepts teach but what his works inspire.
Our Critics take a contrary extreme,
They judge with fury, but they write with phlegm:
Nor suffers Horace more in wrong Translations
By Wits, than Critics in as wrong Quotations.
665 See Dionysius Homer's thoughts refine,
And call new beauties forth from ev'ry line!
Fancy and art in gay Petronius please,
The scholar's learning, with the courtier's ease.
In grave Quintilian's copious work, we find
670 The justest rules, and clearest method join'd:
Thus useful arms in magazines we place,
All rang'd in order, and dispos'd with grace,
But less to please the eye, than arm the hand,
Still fit for use, and ready at command.
675 Thee, bold Longinus! all the Nine inspire,
And bless their Critic with a Poet's fire.
An ardent Judge, who zealous in his trust,
With warmth gives sentence, yet is always just;
Whose own example strengthens all his laws;
680 And is himself that great Sublime he draws.
Thus long succeeding Critics justly reign'd,
Licence repress'd, and useful laws ordain'd.
Learning and Rome alike in empire grew;
And Arts still follow'd where her Eagles flew;
685 From the same foes, at last, both felt their doom,
And the same age saw Learning fall, and Rome.
With Tyranny, then Superstition join'd,
As that the body, this enslav'd the mind;
Much was believ'd, but little understood,
690 And to be dull was constru'd to be good;
A second deluge Learning thus o'er-run,
And the Monks finish'd what the Goths begun.

At length Erasmus, that great injur'd name,
(The glory of the Priesthood, and the shame!)
Stemm'd the wild torrent of a barb'rous age, 695
And drove those holy Vandals off the stage.
But see! each Muse, in LEO's golden days,
Starts from her trance, and trims her wither'd bays,
Rome's ancient Genius, o'er its ruins spread,
Shakes off the dust, and rears his rev'rend head. 700
Then Sculpture and her sister-arts revive;
Stones leap'd to form, and rocks began to live;
With sweeter notes each rising Temple rung;
A Raphael painted, and a Vida sung.
Immortal Vida: on whose honour'd brow 705
The Poet's bays and Critic's ivy grow:
Cremona now shall ever boast thy name,
As next in place to Mantua, next in fame!
But soon by impious arms from Latium chas'd,
Their ancient bounds the banish'd Muses pass'd; 710
Thence Arts o'er all the northern world advance,
But Critic-learning flourish'd most in France:
The rules a nation, born to serve, obeys;
And Boileau still in right of Horace sways.
But we, brave Britons, foreign laws despis'd, 715
And kept unconquer'd, and unciviliz'd;
Fierce for the liberties of wit, and bold,
We still defy'd the Romans, as of old.
Yet some there were, among the sounder few
Of those who less presum'd, and better knew, 720
Who durst assert the juster ancient cause,
And here restor'd Wit's fundamental laws.
Such was the Muse, whose rules and practice tell,
'Nature's chief Master-piece is writing well.'
Such was Roscommon, not more learn'd than good, 725
With manners gen'rous as his noble blood;
To him the wit of Greece and Rome was known,
And ev'ry author's merit, but his own.
Such late was Walsh—the Muse's judge and friend,
Who justly knew to blame or to commend; 730
To failings mild, but zealous for desert;

The clearest head, and the sincerest heart.
This humble praise, lamented shade! receive,
This praise at least a grateful Muse may give:
735   The Muse, whose early voice you taught to sing,
Prescrib'd her heights, and prun'd her tender wing,
(Her guide now lost) no more attempts to rise,
But in low numbers short excursions tries:
Content, if hence th' unlearn'd their wants may view,
740   The learn'd reflect on what before they knew:
Careless of censure, nor too fond of fame;
Still pleas'd to praise, yet not afraid to blame,
Averse alike to flatter, or offend;
Not free from faults, nor yet too vain to mend.

SAMUEL JOHNSON

Preface to Shakespeare

THAT praises are without reason lavished on the dead, and
that the honours due only to excellence are paid to antiquity,
is a complaint likely to be always continued by those, who,
being able to add nothing to truth, hope for eminence from the
heresies of paradox; or those, who, being forced by disappoint-   5
ment upon consolatory expedients, are willing to hope from
posterity what the present age refuses, and flatter themselves
that the regard which is yet denied by envy, will be at last
bestowed by time.

Antiquity, like every other quality that attracts the notice of   10
mankind, has undoubtedly votaries that reverence it, not from
reason, but from prejudice. Some seem to admire indiscrimi-
nately whatever has been long preserved, without considering
that time has sometimes co-operated with chance; all perhaps
arc more willing to honour past than present excellence; and   15
the mind contemplates genius through the shades of age, as the
eye surveys the sun through artificial opacity. The great contention of criticism is to find the faults of the moderns, and the
beauties of the ancients. While an author is yet living we estimate
his powers by his worst performance, and when he is dead, we   20
rate them by his best.

To works, however, of which the excellence is not absolute
and definite, but gradual and comparative; to works not raised
upon principles demonstrative and scientific, but appealing
wholly to observation and experience, no other test can be   25
applied than length of duration and continuance of esteem.
What mankind have long possessed they have often examined
and compared; and if they persist to value the possession, it
is because frequent comparisons have confirmed opinion in its
favour. As among the works of nature no man can properly call   30
a river deep, or a mountain high, without the knowledge of

many mountains, and many rivers; so in the productions of
genius, nothing can be styled excellent till it has been compared
with other works of the same kind. Demonstration immediately
35 displays its power, and has nothing to hope or fear from the
flux of years; but works tentative and experimental must be
estimated by their proportion to the general and collective
ability of man, as it is discovered in a long succession of endeavours. Of the first building that was raised, it might be with
40 certainty determined that it was round or square; but whether
it was spacious or lofty must have been referred to time. The
Pythagorean scale of numbers was at once discovered to be
perfect; but the poems of *Homer* we yet know not to transcend
the common limits of human intelligence, but by remarking,
45 that nation after nation, and century after century, has been
able to do little more than transpose his incidents, new-name his
characters, and paraphrase his sentiments.

The reverence due to writings that have long subsisted arises
therefore not from any credulous confidence in the superior
50 wisdom of past ages, or gloomy persuasion of the degeneracy of
mankind, but is the consequence of acknowledged and indubi-
table positions, that what has been longest known has been
most considered, and what is most considered is best understood.

55 The Poet, of whose works I have undertaken the revision,
may now begin to assume the dignity of an ancient, and claim
the privilege of established fame and prescriptive veneration.
He has long outlived his century, the term commonly fixed as
the test of literary merit. Whatever advantages he might once
60 derive from personal allusions, local customs, or temporary
opinions, have for many years been lost; and every topic of
merriment, or motive of sorrow, which the modes of artificial
life afforded him, now only obscure the scenes which they once
illuminated. The effects of favour and competition are at an
65 end; the tradition of his friendships and his enmities has perished; his works support no opinion with arguments, nor supply
any faction with invectives; they can neither indulge vanity nor
gratify malignity; but are read without any other reason than
the desire of pleasure, and are therefore praised only as pleasure
70 is obtained; yet, thus unassisted by interest or passion, they

have passed through variations of taste and changes of manners, and, as they devolved from one generation to another, have received new honours at every transmission.

But because human judgement, though it be gradually gaining upon certainty, never becomes infallible; and approba- 75 tion, though long continued, may yet be only the approbation of prejudice or fashion; it is proper to inquire, by what peculiarities of excellence *Shakespeare* has gained and kept the favour of his countrymen.

Nothing can please many, and please long, but just represen- 80 tations of general nature. Particular manners can be known to few, and therefore few only can judge how nearly they are copied. The irregular combinations of fanciful invention may delight awhile, by that novelty of which the common satiety of life sends us all in quest; but the pleasures of sudden wonder are 85 soon exhausted, and the mind can only repose on the stability of truth.

Shakespeare is above all writers, at least above all modern writers, the poet of nature; the poet that holds up to his readers a faithful mirror of manners and of life. His characters are not 90 modified by the customs of particular places, unpractised by the rest of the world; by the peculiarities of studies or professions, which can operate but upon small numbers; or by the accidents of transient fashions or temporary opinions: they are the genuine progeny of common humanity, such as the world will 95 always supply, and observation will always find. His persons act and speak by the influence of those general passions and principles by which all minds are agitated, and the whole system of life is continued in motion. In the writings of other poets a character is too often an individual; in those of *Shakes-* 100 *peare* it is commonly a species.

It is from this wide extension of design that so much instruction is derived. It is this which fills the plays of *Shakespeare* with practical axioms and domestic wisdom. It was said of *Euripides*, that every verse was a precept; and it may be said of *Shakes-* 105 *peare*, that from his works may be collected a system of civil and economical prudence. Yet his real power is not shown in the splendour of particular passages, but by the progress of his fable, and the tenor of his dialogue; and he that tries to

110 recommend him by select quotations, will succeed like the
pedant in *Hierocles*, who, when he offered his house to sale,
carried a brick in his pocket as a specimen.

It will not easily be imagined how much *Shakespeare* excels in
accommodating his sentiments to real life, but by comparing
115 him with other authors. It was observed of the ancient schools
of declamation, that the more diligently they were frequented,
the more was the student disqualified for the world, because he
found nothing there which he should ever meet in any other
place. The same remark may be applied to every stage but that
120 of *Shakespeare*. The theatre, when it is under any other direction,
is peopled by such characters as were never seen, conversing in a
language which was never heard, upon topics which will never
arise in the commerce of mankind. But the dialogue of this
author is often so evidently determined by the incident which
125 produces it, and is pursued with so much ease and simplicity,
that it seems scarcely to claim the merit of fiction, but to have
been gleaned by diligent selection out of common conversation,
and common occurrences.

Upon every other stage the universal agent is love, by whose
130 power all good and evil is distributed, and every action quick-
ened or retarded. To bring a lover, a lady and a rival into the
fable; to entangle them in contradictory obligations, perplex
them with oppositions of interest, and harass them with
violence of desires inconsistent with each other; to make them
135 meet in rapture and part in agony; to fill their mouths with
hyperbolical joy and outrageous sorrow; to distress them as
nothing human ever was distressed; to deliver them as nothing
human ever was delivered; is the business of a modern dramatist. For this probability is violated, life is misrepresented, and
140 language is depraved. But love is only one of many passions;
and as it has no great influence upon the sum of life, it has
little operation in the dramas of a poet, who caught his ideas
from the living world, and exhibited only what he saw before
him. He knew, that any other passion, as it was regular or
145 exorbitant, was a cause of happiness or calamity.

Characters thus ample and general were not easily discriminated and preserved, yet perhaps no poet ever kept his
personages more distinct from each other. I will not say with

Pope, that every speech may be assigned to the proper speaker, because many speeches there are which have nothing charac- 150 teristical; but perhaps, though some may be equally adapted to every person, it will be difficult to find any that can be properly transferred from the present possessor to another claimant. The choice is right, when there is reason for choice.

Other dramatists can only gain attention by hyperbolical 155 or aggravated characters, by fabulous and unexampled excellence or depravity, as the writers of barbarous romances invigorated the reader by a giant and a dwarf; and he that should form his expectations of human affairs from the play, or from the tale, would be equally deceived. *Shakespeare* has no 160 heroes; his scenes are occupied only by men, who act and speak as the reader thinks that he should himself have spoken or acted on the same occasion: Even where the agency is supernatural the dialogue is level with life. Other writers disguise the most natural passions and most frequent incidents; so that he 165 who contemplates them in the book will not know them in the world: *Shakespeare* approximates the remote, and familiarizes the wonderful; the event which he represents will not happen, but if it were possible, its effects would probably be such as he has assigned; and it may be said, that he has not only shown 170 human nature as it acts in real exigencies, but as it would be found in trials, to which it cannot be exposed.

This therefore is the praise of *Shakespeare*, that his drama is the mirror of life; that he who has mazed his imagination, in following the phantoms which other writers raise up before 175 him, may here be cured of his delirious ecstasies, by reading human sentiments in human language, by scenes from which a hermit may estimate the transactions of the world, and a confessor predict the progress of the passions.

His adherence to general nature has exposed him to the 180 censure of critics, who form their judgements upon narrower principles. *Dennis* and *Rhymer* think his *Romans* not sufficiently *Roman*; and *Voltaire* censures his kings as not completely royal. *Dennis* is offended, that *Menenius*, a senator of *Rome*, should play the buffoon; and *Voltaire* perhaps thinks decency violated 185 when the *Danish* Usurper is represented as a drunkard. But *Shakespeare* always makes nature predominate over accident;

and if he preserves the essential character, is not very careful
of distinctions superinduced and adventitious. His story requires
190 Romans or kings, but he thinks only on men. He knew that
Rome, like every other city, had men of all dispositions; and
wanting a buffoon, he went into the senate-house for that
which the senate-house would certainly have afforded him.
He was inclined to show a usurper and a murderer not only
195 odious but despicable, he therefore added drunkenness to his
other qualities, knowing that kings love wine like other men,
and that wine exerts its natural power upon kings. These are
the petty cavils of petty minds; a poet overlooks the casual
distinction of country and condition, as a painter, satisfied with
200 the figure, neglects the drapery.

The censure which he has incurred by mixing comic and
tragic scenes, as it extends to all his works, deserves more
consideration. Let the fact be first stated, and then examined.

Shakespeare's plays are not in the rigorous and critical sense
205 either tragedies or comedies, but compositions of a distinct
kind; exhibiting the real state of sublunary nature, which
partakes of good and evil, joy and sorrow, mingled with endless
variety of proportion and innumerable modes of combination;
and expressing the course of the world, in which the loss of
210 one is the gain of another; in which, at the same time, the
reveller is hasting to his wine, and the mourner burying his
friend; in which the malignity of one is sometimes defeated
by the frolic of another; and many mischiefs and many benefits
are done and hindered without design.

215 Out of this chaos of mingled purposes and casualties, the
ancient poets, according to the laws which custom had prescribed, selected some the crimes of men, and some their
absurdities; some the momentous vicissitudes of life, and some
the lighter occurrences; some the terrors of distress, and some
220 the gaieties of prosperity. Thus rose the two modes of imitation, known by the names of *tragedy* and *comedy*, compositions
intended to promote different ends by contrary means, and
considered as so little allied, that I do not recollect among the
Greeks or *Romans* a single writer who attempted both.

225 *Shakespeare* has united the powers of exciting laughter and
sorrow not only in one mind, but in one composition. Almost

all his plays are divided between serious and ludicrous characters, and, in the successive evolutions of the design, sometimes
produce seriousness and sorrow, and sometimes levity and
laughter.   230

That this is a practice contrary to the rules of criticism will
be readily allowed; but there is always an appeal open from
criticism to nature. The end of writing is to instruct; the end of
poetry is to instruct by pleasing. That the mingled drama may
convey all the instruction of tragedy or comedy cannot be   235
denied, because it includes both in its alternations of exhibition
and approaches nearer than either to the appearance of life,
by showing how great machinations and slender designs may
promote or obviate one another, and the high and the low co-
operate in the general system by unavoidable concatenation.   240

It is objected, that by this change of scenes the passions
are interrupted in their progression, and that the principal
event, being not advanced by a due gradation of preparatory
incidents, wants at last the power to move, which constitutes
the perfection of dramatic poetry. This reasoning is so specious, 245
that it is received as true even by those who in daily experience
feel it to be false. The interchanges of mingled scenes seldom
fail to produce the intended vicissitudes of passion. Fiction
cannot move so much, but that the attention may be easily
transferred; and though it must be allowed that pleasing   250
melancholy be sometimes interrupted by unwelcome levity,
yet let it be considered likewise, that melancholy is often not
pleasing, and that the disturbance of one man may be the relief
of another; that different auditors have different habitudes;
and that, upon the whole, all pleasure consists in variety.   255

The players, who in their edition divided our author's works
into comedies, histories, and tragedies, seem not to have
distinguished the three kinds by any very exact or definite
ideas.

An action which ended happily to the principal persons,   260
however serious or distressful through its intermediate incidents,
in their opinion, constituted a comedy. This idea of a comedy
continued long amongst us; and plays were written, which, by
changing the catastrophe, were tragedies today, and comedies
tomorrow.   265

Tragedy was not in those times a poem of more general
dignity or elevation than comedy; it required only a calamitous
conclusion, with which the common criticism of that age was
satisfied, whatever lighter pleasure it afforded in its progress.
270 History was a series of actions, with no other than chrono-
logical succession, independent on each other, and without any
tendency to introduce or regulate the conclusion. It is not
always very nicely distinguished from tragedy. There is not
much nearer approach to unity of action in the tragedy of
275 *Antony and Cleopatra*, than in the history of *Richard the Second*.
But a history might be continued through many plays; as it
had no plan, it had no limits.

Through all these denominations of the drama, *Shakespeare's*
mode of composition is the same; an interchange of seriousness
280 and merriment, by which the mind is softened at one time, and
exhilarated at another. But whatever be his purpose, whether
to gladden or depress, or to conduct the story, without vehemence or emotion, through tracts of easy and familiar dialogue,
he never fails to attain his purpose; as he commands us, we
285 laugh or mourn, or sit silent with quiet expectation, in tranquillity without indifference.

When *Shakespeare's* plan is understood, most of the criticisms
of *Rhymer* and *Voltaire* vanish away. The play of *Hamlet* is
opened, without impropriety, by two sentinels; *Iago* bellows at
290 *Brabantio's* window, without injury to the scheme of the play,
though in terms which a modern audience would not easily
endure; the character of *Polonius* is seasonable and useful; and
the Grave-diggers themselves may be heard with applause.

Shakespeare engaged in dramatic poetry with the world open
295 before him; the rules of the ancients were yet known to few;
the public judgement was unformed; he had no example of
such fame as might force him upon imitation, nor critics of
such authority as might restrain his extravagance: He therefore
indulged his natural disposition, and his disposition, as *Rhymer*
300 has remarked, led him to comedy. In tragedy he often writes,
with great appearance of toil and study, what is written at last
with little felicity; but in his comic scenes, he seems to produce
without labour, what no labour can improve. In tragedy he is
always struggling after some occasion to be comic; but in

comedy he seems to repose, or to luxuriate, as in a mode of 305
thinking congenial to his nature. In his tragic scenes there is
always something wanting, but his comedy often surpasses expectation or desire. His comedy pleases by the thoughts and the
language, and his tragedy for the greater part by incident and
action. His tragedy seems to be skill, his comedy to be instinct. 310

The force of his comic scenes has suffered little diminution
from the changes made by a century and a half, in manners or
in words. As his personages act upon principles arising from
genuine passion, very little modified by particular forms, their
pleasures and vexations are communicable to all times and to 315
all places; they are natural, and therefore durable; the adventitious peculiarities of personal habits are only superficial dyes,
bright and pleasing for a little while, yet soon fading to a dim
tinct, without any remains of former lustre; but the discrimina-
tions of true passion are the colours of nature; they pervade 320
the whole mass, and can only perish with the body that exhibits them. The accidental compositions of heterogeneous
modes are dissolved by the chance which combined them; but
the uniform simplicity of primitive qualities neither admits
increase, nor suffers decay. The sand heaped by one flood is 325
scattered by another, but the rock always continues in its place.
The stream of time, which is continually washing the dissoluble
fabrics of other poets, passes without injury by the adamant of
Shakespeare.

If there be, what I believe there is, in every nation, a style 330
which never becomes obsolete, a certain mode of phraseology
so consonant and congenial to the analogy and principles of its
respective language as to remain settled and unaltered; this
style is probably to be sought in the common intercourse of
life, among those who speak only to be understood, without 335
ambition of elegance. The polite are always catching modish
innovations, and the learned depart from established forms of
speech, in hope of finding or making better; those who wish for
distinction forsake the vulgar, when the vulgar is right; but
there is a conversation above grossness and below refinement, 340
where propriety resides, and where this poet seems to have
gathered his comic dialogue. He is therefore more agreeable
to the ears of the present age any than other author equally

remote, and among his other excellencies deserves to be studied
345 as one of the original masters of our language.

These observations are to be considered not as unexception-
ably constant, but as containing general and predominant truth.
Shakespeare's familiar dialogue is affirmed to be smooth and
clear, yet not wholly without ruggedness or difficulty; as a
350 country may be eminently fruitful, though it has spots unfit for
cultivation: His characters are praised as natural, though their
sentiments are sometimes forced, and their actions improbable;
as the earth upon the whole is spherical, though its surface is
varied with protuberances and cavities.

355   *Shakespeare* with his excellences has likewise faults, and faults
sufficient to obscure and overwhelm any other merit. I shall
show them in the proportion in which they appear to me,
without envious malignity or superstitious veneration. No
question can be more innocently discussed than a dead poet's
360 pretensions to renown; and little regard is due to that bigotry
which sets candour higher than truth.

His first defect is that to which may be imputed most of the
evil in books or in men. He sacrifices virtue to convenience, and
is so much more careful to please than to instruct, that he seems
365 to write without any moral purpose. From his writings indeed a
system of social duty may be selected, for he that thinks reasonably must think morally; but his precepts and axioms drop
casually from him; he makes no just distribution of good or
evil, nor is always careful to show in the virtuous a disapproba-
370 tion of the wicked; he carries his persons indifferently through
right and wrong, and at the close dismisses them without further
care, and leaves their examples to operate by chance. This fault
the barbarity of his age cannot extenuate; for it is always a
writer's duty to make the world better, and justice is a virtue
375 independent on time or place.

The plots are often so loosely formed, that a very slight
consideration may improve them, and so carelessly pursued, that
he seems not always fully to comprehend his own design. He
omits opportunities of instructing or delighting which the train
380 of his story seems to force upon him, and apparently rejects
those exhibitions which would be more affecting, for the sake
of those which are more easy.

It may be observed, that in many of his plays the latter part is evidently neglected. When he found himself near the end of his work, and in view of his reward, he shortened the labour to snatch the profit. He therefore remits his efforts where he should most vigorously exert them, and his catastrophe is improbably produced or imperfectly represented.

He had no regard to distinction of time or place, but gives to one age or nation, without scruple, the customs, institutions, and opinions of another, at the expense not only of likelihood, but of possibility. These faults *Pope* has endeavoured, with more zeal than judgement, to transfer to his imagined interpolators. We need not wonder to find *Hector* quoting *Aristotle*, when we see the loves of *Theseus* and *Hippolyta* combined with the *Gothic* mythology of fairies. *Shakespeare*, indeed, was not the only violator of chronology, for in the same age *Sidney*, who wanted not the advantages of learning, has, in his *Arcadia*, confounded the pastoral with the feudal times, the days of innocence, quiet and security, with those of turbulence, violence, and adventure.

In his comic scenes he is seldom very successful when he engages his characters in reciprocations of smartness and contests of sarcasm; their jests are commonly gross, and their pleasantry licentious; neither his gentlemen nor his ladies have much delicacy, nor are sufficiently distinguished from his clowns by any appearance of refined manners. Whether he represented the real conversation of his time is not easy to determine; the reign of *Elizabeth* is commonly supposed to have been a time of stateliness, formality and reserve; yet perhaps the relaxations of that severity were not very elegant. There must, however, have been always some modes of gaiety preferable to others, and a writer ought to choose the best.

In tragedy his performance seems constantly to be worse, as his labour is more. The effusions of passion which exigence forces out are for the most part striking and energetic; but whenever he solicits his invention, or strains his faculties, the offspring of his throes is tumour, meanness, tediousness, and obscurity.

In narration he affects a disproportionate pomp of diction, and a wearisome train of circumlocution, and tells the incident

imperfectly in many words, which might have been more
plainly delivered in few. Narration in dramatic poetry is
naturally tedious, as it is unanimated and inactive, and
425 obstructs the progress of the action; it should therefore always
be rapid, and enlivened by frequent interruption. *Shakespeare*
found it an encumbrance, and instead of lightening it by
brevity, endeavoured to recommend it by dignity and
splendour.

430   His declamations or set speeches are commonly cold and
weak, for his power was the power of nature; when he endeavoured, like other tragic writers, to catch opportunities
of amplification, and instead of inquiring what the occasion
demanded, to show how much his stores of knowledge could
435 supply, he seldom escapes without the pity or resentment of
his reader.

It is incident to him to be now and then entangled with an
unwieldy sentiment, which he cannot well express, and will
not reject; he struggles with it a while, and if it continues stub-
440 born, comprises it in words such as occur, and leaves it to be
disentangled and evolved by those who have more leisure to
bestow upon it.

Not that always where the language is intricate the thought
is subtle, or the image always great where the line is bulky; the
445 equality of words to things is very often neglected, and trivial
sentiments and vulgar ideas disappoint the attention, to which
they are recommended by sonorous epithets and swelling
figures.

But the admirers of this great poet have never less reason to
450 indulge their hopes of supreme excellence, than when he seems
fully resolved to sink them in dejection, and mollify them with
tender emotions by the fall of greatness, the danger of innocence, or the crosses of love. He is not long soft and pathetic
without some idle conceit, or contemptible equivocation. He
455 no sooner begins to move, than he counteracts himself; and
terror and pity, as they are rising in the mind, are checked and
blasted by sudden frigidity.

A quibble is to *Shakespeare*, what luminous vapours are to the
traveller; he follows it at all adventures; it is sure to lead him
460 out of his way, and sure to engulf him in the mire. It has some

malignant power over his mind, and its fascinations are irresistible. Whatever be the dignity or profundity of his disquisition, whether he be enlarging knowledge or exalting affection, whether he be amusing attention with incidents, or enchaining it in suspense, let but a quibble spring up before him, and he 465 leaves his work unfinished. A quibble is the golden apple for which he will always turn aside from his career, or stoop from his elevation. A quibble, poor and barren as it is, gave him such delight, that he was content to purchase it, by the sacrifice of reason, propriety and truth. A quibble was to him the fatal 470 *Cleopatra* for which he lost the world, and was content to lose it.

It will be thought strange, that, in enumerating the defects of this writer, I have not yet mentioned his neglect of the unities; his violation of those laws which have been instituted and established by the joint authority of poets and of critics. 475

For his other deviations from the art of writing I resign him to critical justice, without making any other demand in his favour, than that which must be indulged to all human excellence: that his virtues be rated with his failings: But, from the censure which this irregularity may bring upon him, I shall, 480 with due reverence to that learning which I must oppose, adventure to try how I can defend him.

His histories, being neither tragedies nor comedies, are not subject to any of their laws; nothing more is necessary to all the praise which they expect, than that the changes of action 485 be so prepared as to be understood, that the incidents be various and affecting, and the characters consistent, natural, and distinct. No other unity is intended, and therefore none is to be sought.

In his other works he has well enough preserved the unity of 490 action. He has not, indeed, an intrigue regularly perplexed and regularly unravelled: he does not endeavour to hide his design only to discover it, for this is seldom the order of real events, and *Shakespeare* is the poet of nature: But his plan has commonly what *Aristotle* requires, a beginning, a middle, and an end; one 495 event is concatenated with another, and the conclusion follows by easy consequence. There are perhaps some incidents that might be spared, as in other poets there is much talk that only fills up time upon the stage; but the general system makes

FECT

500 gradual advances, and the end of the play is the end of expectation.

To the unities of time and place he has shown no regard; and perhaps a nearer view of the principles on which they stand will diminish their value, and withdraw from them the veneration 505 which, from the time of *Corneille*, they have very generally received, by discovering that they have given more trouble to the poet, than pleasure to the auditor.

The necessity of observing the unities of time and place arises from the supposed necessity of making the drama credible. 510 The critics hold it impossible, that an action of months or years can be possibly believed to pass in three hours; or that the spectator can suppose himself to sit in the theatre, while ambassadors go and return between distant kings, while armies are levied and towns besieged, while an exile wanders and returns, 515 or till he whom they saw courting his mistress, shall lament the untimely fall of his son. The mind revolts from evident falsehood, and fiction loses its force when it departs from the resemblance of reality.

From the narrow limitation of time necessarily arises the 520 contraction of place. The spectator, who knows that he saw the first act at *Alexandria*, cannot suppose that he sees the next at *Rome*, at a distance to which not the dragons of *Medea* could, in so short a time, have transported him; he knows with certainty that he has not changed his place, and he knows that place 525 cannot change itself; that what was a house cannot become a plain; that what was *Thebes* can never be *Persepolis*.

Such is the triumphant language with which a critic exults over the misery of an irregular poet, and exults commonly without resistance or reply. It is time therefore to tell him by 530 the authority of *Shakespeare*, that he assumes, as an unquestionable principle, a position, which, while his breath is forming it into words, his understanding pronounces to be false. It is false, that any representation is mistaken for reality; that any dramatic fable in its materiality was ever credible, or, for a single 535 moment, was ever credited.

The objection arising from the impossibility of passing the first hour at *Alexandria*, and the next at *Rome*, supposes, that when the play opens, the spectator really imagines himself

Alexandria, and believes that his walk to the theatre has been a voyage to Egypt, and that he lives in the days of *Antony* and 540 *Cleopatra*. Surely he that imagines this may imagine more. He that can take the stage at one time for the palace of the *Ptolemies*, may take it in half an hour for the promontory of *Actium*. Delusion, if delusion be admitted, has no certain limitation; if the spectator can be once persuaded, that his old 545 acquaintance are *Alexander* and *Caesar*, that a room illuminated with candles is the plain of *Pharsalia*, or the bank of *Granicus*, he is in a state of elevation above the reach of reason, or of truth, and from the heights of empyrean poetry, may despise the circumscriptions of terrestrial nature. There is no reason why 550 a mind thus wandering in ecstasy should count the clock, or why an hour should not be a century in that calenture of the brains that can make the stage a field.

The truth is, that the spectators are always in their senses, and know, from the first act to the last, that the stage is only a 555 stage, and that the players are only players. They came to hear a certain number of lines recited with just gesture and elegant modulation. The lines relate to some action, and an action must be in some place; but the different actions that complete a story may be in places very remote from each other; and 560 where is the absurdity of allowing that space to represent first *Athens*, and then *Sicily*, which was always known to be neither *Sicily* nor *Athens*, but a modern theatre?

By supposition, as place is introduced, time may be extended; the time required by the fable elapses for the most part between 565 the acts; for, of so much of the action as is represented, the real and poetical duration is the same. If, in the first act, preparations for war against *Mithridates* are represented to be made in *Rome*, the event of the war may, without absurdity, be represented, in the catastrophe, as happening in *Pontus*; we know 570 that there is neither war, nor preparation for war; we know that we are neither in *Rome* nor *Pontus*; that neither *Mithridates* nor *Lucullus* are before us. The drama exhibits successive imitations of successive actions; and why may not the second imitation represent an action that happened years after the first, if 575 it be so connected with it, that nothing but time can be supposed to intervene? Time is, of all modes of existence, most

obsequious to the imagination; a lapse of years is as easily
conceived as a passage of hours. In contemplation we easily
580 contract the time of real actions, and therefore willingly permit
it to be contracted when we only see their imitation.

It will be asked, how the drama moves, if it is not credited.
It is credited with all the credit due to a drama. It is credited,
whenever it moves, as a just picture of a real original; as repre-
585 senting to the auditor what he would himself feel, if he were
to do or suffer what is there feigned to be suffered or to be done.
The reflection that strikes the heart is not, that the evils before
us are real evils, but that they are evils to which we ourselves
may be exposed. If there be any fallacy, it is not that we fancy
590 the players, but that we fancy ourselves unhappy for a moment;
but we rather lament the possibility than suppose the presence
of misery, as a mother weeps over her babe, when she remembers that death may take it from her. The delight of tragedy
proceeds from our consciousness of fiction; if we thought
595 murders and treasons real, they would please no more.

Imitations produce pain or pleasure, not because they are
mistaken for realities, but because they bring realities to mind.
When the imagination is recreated by a painted landscape, the
trees are not supposed capable to give us shade, or the fountains
600 coolness; but we consider, how we should be pleased with such
fountains playing beside us, and such woods waving over us.
We are agitated in reading the history of *Henry* the Fifth, yet
no man takes his book for the field of *Agincourt*. A dramatic
exhibition is a book recited with concomitants that increase or
605 diminish its effect. Familiar comedy is often more powerful on
the theatre, than in the page; imperial tragedy is always less.
The humour of *Petruchio* may be heightened by grimace; but
what voice or what gesture can hope to add dignity or force to
the soliloquy of *Cato*.

610 A play read, affects the mind like a play acted. It is therefore
evident, that the action is not supposed to be real; and it follows, that between the acts a longer or shorter time may be
allowed to pass, and that no more account of space or duration
is to be taken by the auditor of a drama, than by the reader of a
615 narrative, before whom may pass in an hour the life of a hero,
or the revolutions of an empire.

Whether *Shakespeare* knew the unities, and rejected them by design, or deviated from them by happy ignorance, it is, I think, impossible to decide, and useless to inquire. We may reasonably suppose, that, when he rose to notice, he did not 620 want the counsels and admonitions of scholars and critics, and that he at last deliberately persisted in a practice, which he might have begun by chance. As nothing is essential to the fable, but unity of action, and as the unities of time and place arise evidently from false assumptions, and, by circumscribing 625 the extent of the drama, lessen its variety, I cannot think it much to be lamented, that they were not known by him, or not observed: Nor, if such another poet could arise, should I very vehemently reproach him, that his first act passed at *Venice*, and his next in *Cyprus*. Such violations of rules merely positive, 630 become the comprehensive genius of *Shakespeare*, and such censures are suitable to the minute and slender criticism of *Voltaire*:

> Non usque adeo permiscuit imis
> Longus summa dies, ut non, si voce Metelli   635
> Serventur leges, malint a Caesare tolli.

Yet when I speak thus slightly of dramatic rules, I cannot but recollect how much wit and learning may be produced against me; before such authorities I am afraid to stand, not that I think the present question one of those that are to be 640 decided by mere authority, but because it is to be suspected, that these precepts have not been so easily received but for better reasons than I have yet been able to find. The result of my inquiries, in which it would be ludicrous to boast of impartiality, is, that the unities of time and place are not 645 essential to a just drama, that though they may sometimes conduce to pleasure, they are always to be sacrificed to the nobler beauties of variety and instruction; and that a play, written with nice observation of critical rules, is to be contemplated as an elaborate curiosity, as the product of super- 650 fluous and ostentatious art, by which is shown, rather what is possible, than what is necessary.

He that, without diminution of any other excellence, shall preserve all the unities unbroken, deserves the like applause

655 with the architect, who shall display all the orders of architecture in a citadel, without any deduction from its strength; but the principal beauty of a citadel is to exclude the enemy; and the greatest graces of a play, are to copy nature and instruct life.

Perhaps, what I have here not dogmatically but deliberately 660 written, may recall the principles of the drama to a new examination. I am almost frighted at my own temerity; and when I estimate the fame and the strength of those that maintain the contrary opinion, am ready to sink down in reverential silence; as *Aeneas* withdrew from the defence of *Troy*, when he saw 665 *Neptune* shaking the wall, and *Juno* heading the besiegers.

Those whom my arguments cannot persuade to give their approbation to the judgement of *Shakespeare*, will easily, if they consider the condition of his life, make some allowance for his ignorance.

670   Every man's performances, to be rightly estimated, must be compared with the state of the age in which he lived, and with his own particular opportunities; and though to the reader a book be not worse or better for the circumstances of the author, yet as there is always a silent reference of human works to 675 human abilities, and as the inquiry, how far man may extend his designs, or how high he may rate his native force, is of far greater dignity than in what rank we shall place any particular performance, curiosity is always busy to discover the instruments, as well as to survey the workmanship, to know how 680 much is to be ascribed to original powers, and how much to casual and adventitious help. The palaces of *Peru* or *Mexico* were certainly mean and incommodious habitations, if compared to the houses of *European* monarchs; yet who could forbear to view them with astonishment, who remembered 685 that they were built without the use of iron?

The *English* nation, in the time of *Shakespeare*, was yet struggling to emerge from barbarity. The philology of *Italy* had been transplanted hither in the reign of *Henry* the Eighth; and the learned languages had been successfully cultivated by *Lily*, 690 *Linacre*, and *More*; by *Pole*, *Cheke*, and *Gardiner*; and afterwards by *Smith*, *Clerk*, *Haddon*, and *Ascham*. Greek was now taught to boys in the principal schools; and those who united elegance with learning, read, with great diligence, the *Italian* and *Spanish* poets. But literature was yet confined to professed scholars, or to men and women of high rank. The public was gross and dark; and to be able to read and write, was an accomplishment still valued for its rarity.

Nations, like individuals, have their infancy. A people newly awakened to literary curiosity, being yet unacquainted with the true state of things, knows not how to judge of that which is proposed as its resemblance. Whatever is remote from common appearances is always welcome to vulgar, as to childish credulity; and of a country unenlightened by learning, the whole people is the vulgar. The study of those who then aspired to plebeian learning was laid out upon adventures, giants, dragons, and enchantments. *The Death of Arthur* was the favourite volume.

The mind, which has feasted on the luxurious wonders of fiction, has no taste of the insipidity of truth. A play which imitated only the common occurrences of the world, would, upon the admirers of *Palmerin* and *Guy* of *Warwick*, have made little impression; he that wrote for such an audience was under the necessity of looking round for strange events and fabulous transactions, and that incredibility, by which maturer knowledge is offended, was the chief recommendation of writings, to unskilful curiosity.

Our author's plots are generally borrowed from novels, and it is reasonable to suppose, that he chose the most popular, such as were read by many, and related by more; for his audience could not have followed him through the intricacies of the drama, had they not held the thread of the story in their hands.

The stories, which we now find only in remoter authors, were in his time accessible and familiar. The fable of *As You Like It*, which is supposed to be copied from *Chaucer's* Gamelyn, was a little pamphlet of those times; and old Mr. *Cibber* remembered the tale of *Hamlet* in plain *English* prose, which the critics have now to seek in *Saxo Grammaticus*.

His *English* histories he took from *English* chronicles and *English* ballads; and as the ancient writers were made known to his countrymen by versions, they supplied him with new subjects; he dilated some of *Plutarch's* lives into plays, when they had been translated by *North*.

His plots, whether historical or fabulous, are always crowded
with incidents, by which the attention of a rude people was
735 more easily caught than by sentiment or argumentation; and
such is the power of the marvellous even over those who despise
it, that every man finds his mind more strongly seized by the
tragedies of *Shakespeare* than of any other writer; others please
us by particular speeches, but he always makes us anxious for
740 the event, and has perhaps excelled all but *Homer* in securing
the first purpose of a writer, by exciting restless and unquench-
able curiosity and compelling him that reads his work to read it
through.

The shows and bustle with which his plays abound have the
745 same original. As knowledge advances, pleasure passes from the
eye to the ear, but returns, as it declines, from the ear to the eye.
Those to whom our author's labours were exhibited had more
skill in pomps or processions than in poetical language, and
perhaps wanted some visible and discriminated events, as
750 comments on the dialogue. He knew how he should most
please; and whether his practice is more agreeable to nature,
or whether his example has prejudiced the nation, we still find
that on our stage something must be done as well as said, and
inactive declamation is very coldly heard, however musical or
755 elegant, passionate or sublime.

Voltaire expresses his wonder, that our author's extravagances
are endured by a nation, which has seen the tragedy of *Cato*.
Let him be answered, that *Addison* speaks the language of poets,
and *Shakespeare*, of men. We find in *Cato* innumerable beauties
760 which enamour us of its author, but we see nothing that
acquaints us with human sentiments or human actions; we
place it with the fairest and the noblest progeny which judgement propagates by conjunction with learning, but *Othello* is
the vigorous and vivacious offspring of observation impreg-
765 nated by genius. *Cato* affords a splendid exhibition of artificial
and fictitious manners, and delivers just and noble sentiments,
in diction easy, elevated and harmonious, but its hopes and
fears communicate no vibration to the heart; the composition refers us only to the writer; we pronounce the name of
770 *Cato*, but we think on *Addison*.

The work of a correct and regular writer is a garden

accurately formed and diligently planted, varied with shades, and scented with flowers; the composition of *Shakespeare* is a forest, in which oaks extend their branches, and pines tower in the air, interspersed sometimes with weeds and brambles, and sometimes giving shelter to myrtles and to roses; filling the eye with awful pomp, and gratifying the mind with endless diversity. Other poets display cabinets of precious rarities, minutely finished, wrought into shape, and polished unto brightness. *Shakespeare* opens a mine which contains gold and diamonds in inexhaustible plenty, though clouded by incrustations, debased by impurities, and mingled with a mass of meaner minerals.

It has been much disputed, whether *Shakespeare* owed his excellence to his own native force, or whether he had the common helps of scholastic education, the precepts of critical science, and the examples of ancient authors.

There has always prevailed a tradition, that *Shakespeare* wanted learning, that he had no regular education, nor much skill in the dead languages. *Jonson*, his friend, affirms, that *he had small Latin, and no Greek*; who, besides that he had no imaginable temptation to falsehood, wrote at a time when the character and acquisitions of *Shakespeare* were known to multitudes. His evidence ought therefore to decide the controversy, unless some testimony of equal force could be opposed.

Some have imagined that they have discovered deep learning in many imitations of old writers; but the examples which I have known urged, were drawn from books translated in his time; or were such easy coincidences of thought, as will happen to all who consider the same subjects; or such remarks on life or axioms of morality as float in conversation, and are transmitted through the world in proverbial sentences.

I have found it remarked, that, in this important sentence, *Go before, I'll follow*, we read a translation of, *I prae, sequar*. I have been told, that when *Caliban*, after a pleasing dream, says, *I cry'd to sleep again*, the author imitates *Anacreon*, who had, like every other man, the same wish on the same occasion.

There are a few passages which may pass for imitations, but so few, that the exception only confirms the rule; he obtained them from accidental quotations, or by oral communication, and as he

used what he had, would have used more if he had obtained it.
The *Comedy of Errors* is confessedly taken from the *Menaechmi*
of *Plautus*; from the only play of *Plautus* which was then in
English. What can be more probable, than that he who copied
815 that, would have copied more; but that those which were not
translated were inaccessible?

Whether he knew the modern languages is uncertain. That
his plays have some *French* scenes proves but little; he might
easily procure them to be written, and probably, even though
820 he had known the language in the common degree, he could
not have written it without assistance. In the story of *Romeo
and Juliet* he is observed to have followed the *English* translation, where it deviates from the *Italian*; but this on the other
part proves nothing against his knowledge of the original.
825 He was to copy, not what he knew himself, but what was known
to his audience.

It is most likely that he had learned *Latin* sufficiently to
make him acquainted with construction, but that he never
advanced to an easy perusal of the *Roman* authors. Concerning
830 his skill in modern languages, I can find no sufficient ground
of determination; but as no imitations of *French* or *Italian*
authors have been discovered, though the *Italian* poetry was
then high in esteem, I am inclined to believe, that he read little
more than *English*, and chose for his fables only such tales as he
835 found translated.

That much knowledge is scattered over his works is very
justly observed by *Pope*, but it is often such knowledge as books
did not supply. He that will understand *Shakespeare*, must not
be content to study him in the closet, he must look for his
840 meaning sometimes among the sports of the field, and sometimes among the manufactures of the shop.

There is however proof enough that he was a very diligent
reader, nor was our language then so indigent of books, but
that he might very liberally indulge his curiosity without
845 excursion into foreign literature. Many of the *Roman* authors
were translated, and some of the *Greek*; the reformation had
filled the kingdom with theological learning; most of the topics
of human disquisition had found *English* writers; and poetry
had been cultivated, not only with diligence, but success.

This was a stock of knowledge sufficient for a mind so capable 850
of appropriating and improving it.

But the greater part of his excellence was the product of his
own genius. He found the *English* stage in a state of the utmost
rudeness; no essays either in tragedy or comedy had appeared,
from which it could be discovered to what degree of delight 855
either one or other might be carried. Neither character nor
dialogue were yet understood. *Shakespeare* may be truly said to
have introduced them both amongst us, and in some of his
happier scenes to have carried them both to the utmost height.

By what gradations of improvement he proceeded, is not 860
easily known; for the chronology of his works is yet unsettled.
Rowe is of opinion, that *perhaps we are not to look for his beginning,
like those of other writers, in his least perfect works; art had so little,
and nature so large a share in what he did, that for ought I know,* says
he, *the performances of his youth, as they were the most vigorous, were* 865
the best. But the power of nature is only the power of using to
any certain purpose the materials which diligence procures, or
opportunity supplies. Nature gives no man knowledge, and
when images are collected by study and experience, can only
assist in combining or applying them. *Shakespeare,* however 870
favoured by nature, could impart only what he had learned;
and as he must increase his ideas, like other mortals, by gradual
acquisition, he, like them, grew wiser as he grew older, could
display life better, as he knew it more, and instruct with more
efficacy, as he was himself more amply instructed.   875

There is a vigilance of observation and accuracy of distinction which books and precepts cannot confer; from this almost
all original and native excellence proceeds. *Shakespeare* must
have looked upon mankind with perspicacity, in the highest
degree curious and attentive. Other writers borrow their 880
characters from preceding writers, and diversify them only
by the accidental appendages of present manners; the dress is a
little varied, but the body is the same. Our author had both
matter and form to provide; for except the characters of
Chaucer, to whom I think he is not much indebted, there were 885
no writers in *English,* and perhaps not many in other modern
languages, which showed life in its native colours.

The contest about the original benevolence or malignity of

man had not yet commenced. Speculation had not yet at-
890 tempted to analyse the mind, to trace the passions to their
sources, to unfold the seminal principles of vice and virtue, or
sound the depths of the heart for the motives of action. All
those inquiries, which from that time that human nature
became the fashionable study, have been made sometimes with
895 nice discernment, but often with idle subtlety, were yet un-
attempted. The tales, with which the infancy of learning was
satisfied, exhibited only the superficial appearances of action,
related the events but omitted the causes, and were formed for
such as delighted in wonders rather than in truth. Mankind
900 was not then to be studied in the closet; he that would know the
world, was under the necessity of gleaning his own remarks,
by mingling as he could in its business and amusements.

Boyle congratulated himself upon his high birth, because it
favoured his curiosity, by facilitating his access. *Shakespeare* had
905 no such advantage; he came to *London* a needy adventurer,
and lived for a time by very mean employments. Many works
of genius and learning have been performed in states of life,
that appear very little favourable to thought or to inquiry; so
many, that he who considers them is inclined to think that he
910 sees enterprise and perseverance predominating over all
external agency, and bidding help and hindrance vanish
before them. The genius of *Shakespeare* was not to be depressed
by the weight of poverty, nor limited by the narrow conversation to which men in want are inevitably condemned; the
915 encumbrances of his fortune were shaken from his mind, *as
dewdrops from a lion's mane.*

Though he had so many difficulties to encounter, and so
little assistance to surmount them, he has been able to obtain
an exact knowledge of many modes of life, and many casts of
920 native dispositions; to vary them with great multiplicity; to
mark them by nice distinctions; and to show them in full view
by proper combinations. In this part of his performances he
had none to imitate, but has himself been imitated by all
succeeding writers; and it may be doubted, whether from all
925 his successors more maxims of theoretical knowledge, or more
rules of practical prudence, can be collected, than he alone
has given to his country.

Nor was his attention confined to the actions of men; he was an exact surveyor of the inanimate world; his descriptions have always some peculiarities, gathered by contemplating ₉₃₀ things as they really exist. It may be observed, that the oldest poets of many nations preserve their reputation, and that the following generations of wit, after a short celebrity, sink into oblivion. The first, whoever they be, must take their sentiments and descriptions immediately from knowledge; the resemblance ₉₃₅ is therefore just, their descriptions are verified by every eye, and their sentiments acknowledged by every breast. Those whom their fame invites to the same studies, copy partly them, and partly nature, till the books of one age gain such authority, as to stand in the place of nature to another, and imitation, ₉₄₀ always deviating a little, becomes at last capricious and casual. *Shakespeare*, whether life or nature be his subject, shows plainly, that he has seen with his own eyes; he gives the image which he receives, not weakened or distorted by the intervention of any other mind; the ignorant feel his representations to be just, ₉₄₅ and the learned see that they are complete.

Perhaps it would not be easy to find any author, except *Homer*, who invented so much as *Shakespeare*, who so much advanced the studies which he cultivated, or effused so much novelty upon his age or country. The form, the characters, the ₉₅₀ language, and the shows of the *English* drama are his. *He seems, says Dennis, to have been the very original of our English tragical harmony, that is, the harmony of blank verse, diversified often by dissyllable and trissyllable terminations. For the diversity distinguishes it from heroic harmony, and by bringing it nearer to common use makes it ₉₅₅ more proper to gain attention, and more fit for action and dialogue. Such verse we make when we are writing prose; we make such verse in common conversation.*

I know not whether this praise is rigorously just. The dissyllable termination, which the critic rightly appropriates to ₉₆₀ the drama, is to be found, though, I think, not in *Gorboduc* which is confessedly before our author; yet in *Hieronimo*, of which the date is not certain, but which there is reason to believe at least as old as his earliest plays. This however is certain, that he is the first who taught either tragedy or comedy ₉₆₅ to please, there being no theatrical piece of any older writer, of which the name is known, except to antiquaries and collectors of books, which are sought because they are scarce, and would not have been scarce, had they been much esteemed.

970   To him we must ascribe the praise, unless *Spenser* may divide it with him, of having first discovered to how much smoothness and harmony the *English* language could be softened. He has speeches, perhaps sometimes scenes, which have all the delicacy of *Rowe*, without his effeminacy. He endeavours indeed com-
975 monly to strike by the force and vigour of his dialogue, but he never executes his purpose better than when he tries to soothe by softness.

   Yet it must be at last confessed, that as we owe every thing to him, he owes something to us; that, if much of his praise is paid
980 by perception and judgement, much is likewise given by custom and veneration. We fix our eyes upon his graces, and turn them from his deformities, and endure in him what we should in another loathe or despise. If we endured without praising, respect for the father of our drama might excuse us; but I have
985 seen, in the book of some modern critic, a collection of ano-malies, which show that he has corrupted language by every mode of depravation, but which his admirer has accumulated as a monument of honour.

   He has scenes of undoubted and perpetual excellence, but
990 perhaps not one play, which, if it were now exhibited as the work of a contemporary writer, would be heard to the con-clusion. I am indeed far from thinking, that his works were wrought to his own ideas of perfection; when they were such as would satisfy the audience, they satisfied the writer. It is seldom
995 that authors, though more studious of fame than *Shakespeare*, rise much above the standard of their own age; to add a little of what is best will always be sufficient for present praise, and those who find themselves exalted into fame, are willing to credit their encomiasts, and to spare the labour of contending
1000 with themselves.

   It does not appear, that *Shakespeare* thought his works worthy of posterity, that he levied any ideal tribute upon future times, or had any further prospect, than of present popularity and present profit. When his plays had been acted, his hope was at
1005 an end; he solicited no addition of honour from the reader. He

therefore made no scruple to repeat the same jests in many dialogues, or to entangle different plots by the same knot of perplexity, which may be at least forgiven him, by those who recollect, that of *Congreve's* four comedies, two are concluded by a marriage in a mask, by a deception, which perhaps never 1010 happened, and which, whether likely or not, he did not invent.

So careless was this great poet of future fame, that, though he retired to ease and plenty, while he was yet little *declined into the vale of years*, before he could be disgusted with fatigue, or disabled by infirmity, he made no collection of his works, nor 1015 desired to rescue those that had been already published from the depravations that obscured them, or secure to the rest a better destiny, by giving them to the world in their genuine state.

Of the plays which bear the name of *Shakespeare* in the late editions, the greater part were not published till about seven 1020 years after his death, and the few which appeared in his life are apparently thrust into the world without the care of the author, and therefore probably without his knowledge.

Of all the publishers, clandestine or professed, their negligence and unskilfulness has by the late revisers been sufficiently 1025 shown. The faults of all are indeed numerous and gross, and have not only corrupted many passages perhaps beyond recovery, but have brought others into suspicion, which are only obscured by obsolete phraseology, or by the writer's unskilfulness and affectation. To alter is more easy than to explain, 1030 and temerity is a more common quality than diligence. Those who saw that they must employ conjecture to a certain degree, were willing to indulge it a little further. Had the author published his own works, we should have sat quietly down to disentangle his intricacies, and clear his obscurities; but now 1035 we tear what we cannot loose, and eject what we happen not to understand.

The faults are more than could have happened without the concurrence of many causes. The style of *Shakespeare* was in itself ungrammatical, perplexed and obscure; his works were 1040 transcribed for the players by those who may be supposed to have seldom understood them; they were transmitted by copyers equally unskilful, who still multiplied errors; they were perhaps sometimes mutilated by the actors, for the sake of

1045 shortening the speeches; and were at last printed without correction of the press.

In this state they remained, not as Dr. *Warburton* supposes, because they were unregarded, but because the editor's art was not yet applied to modern languages, and our ancestors were
1050 accustomed to so much negligence of *English* printers, that they could very patiently endure it. At last an edition was undertaken by *Rowe* ...

[Johnson then comments on the work of his predecessors in the editing of Shakespeare. In the last pages of the Preface he speaks of his own practice and of the duties of an editor. From these pages we have extracted passages which seem of permanent interest. Editors' Note.]

After the labours of all the editors, I found many passages which appeared to me likely to obstruct the greater number of
1055 readers, and thought it my duty to facilitate their passage. It is impossible for an expositor not to write too little for some, and too much for others. He can only judge what is necessary by his own experience; and how long soever he may deliberate, will at last explain many lines which the learned will think impossible
1060 to be mistaken, and omit many for which the ignorant will want his help. These are censures merely relative, and must be quietly endured. I have endeavoured to be neither superfluously copious, nor scrupulously reserved, and hope that I have made my author's meaning accessible to many who
1065 before were frightened from perusing him, and contributed something to the public, by diffusing innocent and rational pleasure.

*   *   *   *   *

The poetical beauties or defects I have not been very diligent to observe. Some plays have more, and some fewer judicial
1070 observations, not in proportion to their difference of merit, but because I gave this part of my design to chance and to caprice. The reader, I believe, is seldom pleased to find his opinion anticipated; it is natural to delight more in what we find or make, than in what we receive. Judgement, like other
1075 faculties, is improved by practice, and its advancement is hindered by submission to dictatorial decisions, as the memory

grows torpid by the use of a table book. Some initiation is
however necessary; of all skill, part is infused by precept, and
part is obtained by habit; I have therefore shown so much as
may enable the candidate of criticism to discover the rest.   1080

*   *   *   *   *

The part of criticism in which the whole succession of editors
has laboured with the greatest diligence, which has occasioned
the most arrogant ostentation, and excited the keenest acrimony, is the emendation of corrupted passages . . .
Conjecture, though it be sometimes unavoidable, I have not   1085
wantonly nor licentiously indulged. It has been my settled
principle, that the reading of the ancient books is probably
true, and therefore is not to be disturbed for the sake of elegance, perspicuity, or mere improvement of the sense. For
though much credit is not due to the fidelity, nor any to the   1090
judgement of the first publishers, yet they who had the copy
before their eyes were more likely to read it right, than we who
read it only by imagination. But it is evident that they have
often made strange mistakes by ignorance or negligence, and that
therefore something may be properly attempted by criticism,   1095
keeping the middle way between presumption and timidity.
Such criticism I have attempted to practise, and where any
passage appeared inextricably perplexed, have endeavoured to
discover how it may be recalled to sense, with least violence.
But my first labour is, always to turn the old text on every side,   1100
and try if there be any interstice, through which light can find
its way; nor would *Huetius* himself condemn me, as refusing
the trouble of research, for the ambition of alteration. In this
modest industry I have not been unsuccessful. I have rescued
many lines from the violations of temerity, and secured many   1105
scenes from the inroads of correction. I have adopted the *Roman*
sentiment, that it is more honourable to save a citizen, than to
kill an enemy, and have been more careful to protect than to
attack.
I have preserved the common distribution of the plays into   1110
acts, though I believe it to be in almost all the plays void of
authority. Some of those which are divided in the later editions
have no division in the first folio, and some that are divided

in the folio have no division in the preceding copies. The
1115 settled mode of the theatre requires four intervals in the play,
but few, if any, of our author's compositions can be properly
distributed in that manner. An act is so much of the drama as
passes without intervention of time or change of place. A pause
makes a new act. In every real, and therefore in every imitative
1120 action, the intervals may be more or fewer, the restriction of
five acts being accidental and arbitrary. This *Shakespeare* knew,
and this he practised; his plays were written, and at first
printed in one unbroken continuity, and ought now to be
exhibited with short pauses, interposed as often as the scene is
1125 changed, or any considerable time is required to pass. This
method would at once quell a thousand absurdities.

* * * * *

Notes are often necessary, but they are necessary evils. Let
him, that is yet unacquainted with the powers of *Shakespeare*,
and who desires to feel the highest pleasure that the drama can
1130 give, read every play from the first scene to the last, with utter
negligence of all his commentators. When his fancy is once on
the wing, let it not stoop at correction or explanation. When his
attention is strongly engaged, let it disdain alike to turn aside
to the name of *Theobald* and of *Pope*. Let him read on through
1135 brightness and obscurity, through integrity and corruption;
let him preserve his comprehension of the dialogue and his
interest in the fable. And when the pleasures of novelty have
ceased, let him attempt exactness, and read the commentators.
Particular passages are cleared by notes, but the general
1140 effect of the work is weakened. The mind is refrigerated by
interruption; the thoughts are diverted from the principal
subject; the reader is weary, he suspects not why; and at last
throws away the book, which he has too diligently studied.
Parts are not to be examined till the whole has been sur-
1145 veyed; there is a kind of intellectual remoteness necessary for
the comprehension of any great work in its full design and its
true proportions; a close approach shows the smaller niceties,
but the beauty of the whole is discerned no longer.
It is not very grateful to consider how little the succession of
1150 editors has added to this author's power of pleasing. He was

read, admired, studied, and imitated, while he was yet deformed with all the improprieties which ignorance and neglect
could accumulate upon him; while the reading was yet not
rectified, nor his allusions understood; yet then did *Dryden*
pronounce 'that *Shakespeare* was the man, who, of all modern 1155
and perhaps ancient poets, had the largest and most comprehensive soul. All the images of nature were still present to him,
and he drew them not laboriously, but luckily: When he
describes any thing, you more than see it, you feel it too.
Those who accuse him to have wanted learning, give him the 1160
greater commendation: he was naturally learned: he needed
not the spectacles of books to read nature; he looked inwards,
and found her there. I cannot say he is every where alike; were
he so, I should do him injury to compare him with the greatest
of mankind. He is many times flat and insipid; his comic wit 1165
degenerating into clenches, his serious swelling into bombast.
But he is always great, when some great occasion is presented to
him: No man can say, he ever had a fit subject for his wit, and
did not then raise himself as high above the rest of poets,

Quantum lenta solent inter viburna cupressi.'   1170

It is to be lamented, that such a writer should want a commentary; that his language should become obsolete, or his
sentiments obscure. But it is vain to carry wishes beyond the
condition of human things; that which must happen to all, has
happened to *Shakespeare*, by accident and time; and more than 1175
has been suffered by any other writer since the use of types, has
been suffered by him through his own negligence of fame, or perhaps by that superiority of mind, which despised its own performances, when it compared them with its powers, and judged
those works unworthy to be preserved, which the critics of follow- 1180
ing ages were to contend for the fame of restoring and explaining.
Among these candidates of inferior fame, I am now to stand
the judgement of the public; and wish that I could confidently
produce my commentary as equal to the encouragement which
I have had the honour of receiving. Every work of this kind is 1185
by its nature deficient, and I should feel little solicitude about
the sentence, were it to be pronounced only by the skilful and
the learned.

WILLIAM WORDSWORTH
Preface to Lyrical Ballads

THE first Volume of these Poems has already been submitted to general perusal. It was published, as an experiment, which, I hoped, might be of some use to ascertain, how far, by fitting to metrical arrangement a selection of the real language of men in a
5 state of vivid sensation, that sort of pleasure and that quantity of pleasure may be imparted, which a Poet may rationally endeavour to impart.

I had formed no very inaccurate estimate of the probable effect of those Poems: I flattered myself that they who should
10 be pleased with them would read them with more than common pleasure: and, on the other hand, I was well aware, that by those who should dislike them, they would be read with more than common dislike. The result has differed from my expectation in this only, that a greater number have been
15 pleased than I ventured to hope I should please.

*   *   *   *   *

Several of my Friends are anxious for the success of these Poems, from a belief, that, if the views with which they were composed were indeed realised, a class of Poetry would be produced, well adapted to interest mankind permanently, and
20 not unimportant in the quality, and in the multiplicity of its moral relations: and on this account they have advised me to prefix a systematic defence of the theory upon which the Poems were written. But I was unwilling to undertake the task, knowing that on this occasion the Reader would look coldly
25 upon my arguments, since I might be suspected of having been principally influenced by the selfish and foolish hope of *reasoning* him into an approbation of these particular Poems: and I was still more unwilling to undertake the task, because, adequately to display the opinions, and fully to enforce the arguments,

would require a space wholly disproportionate to a preface. For, 30
to treat the subject with the clearness and coherence of which
it is susceptible, it would be necessary to give a full account of
the present state of the public taste in this country, and to
determine how far this taste is healthy or depraved; which,
again, could not be determined, without pointing out in what 35
manner language and the human mind act and re-act on each
other, and without retracing the revolutions, not of literature
alone, but likewise of society itself. I have therefore altogether
declined to enter regularly upon this defence; yet I am sensible,
that there would be something like impropriety in abruptly 40
obtruding upon the Public, without a few words of introduction,
Poems so materially different from those upon which general
approbation is at present bestowed.

It is supposed, that by the act of writing in verse an Author
makes a formal engagement that he will gratify certain known 45
habits of association; that he not only thus apprises the Reader
that certain classes of ideas and expressions will be found in his
book, but that others will be carefully excluded. This exponent
or symbol held forth by metrical language must in different
eras of literature have excited very different expectations: for 50
example, in the age of Catullus, Terence, and Lucretius, and
that of Statius or Claudian; and in our own country, in the age
of Shakespeare and Beaumont and Fletcher, and that of Donne
and Cowley, or Dryden, or Pope. I will not take upon me to
determine the exact import of the promise which, by the act of 55
writing in verse, an Author, in the present day makes to his
reader: but it will undoubtedly appear to many persons that I
have not fulfilled the terms of an engagement thus voluntarily
contracted. They who have been accustomed to the gaudiness
and inane phraseology of many modern writers, if they persist 60
in reading this book to its conclusion, will, no doubt, frequently
have to struggle with feelings of strangeness and awkwardness:
they will look round for poetry, and will be induced to inquire
by what species of courtesy these attempts can be permitted to
assume that title. I hope therefore the reader will not censure 65
me for attempting to state what I have proposed to myself to
perform; and also (as far as the limits of a preface will permit)
to explain some of the chief reasons which have determined me

in the choice of my purpose: that at least he may be spared any
70 unpleasant feeling of disappointment, and that I myself may
be protected from one of the most dishonourable accusations
which can be brought against an Author; namely, that of an
indolence which prevents him from endeavouring to ascertain
what is his duty, or, when his duty is ascertained, prevents him
75 from performing it.

The principal object, then, proposed in these Poems was to
choose incidents and situations from common life, and to
relate or describe them, throughout, as far as was possible in
a selection of language really used by men, and, at the same
80 time, to throw over them a certain colouring of imagination,
whereby ordinary things should be presented to the mind in an
unusual aspect; and, further, and above all, to make these
incidents and situations interesting by tracing in them, truly
though not ostentatiously, the primary laws of our nature:
85 chiefly, as far as regards the manner in which we associate ideas
in a state of excitement. Humble and rustic life was generally
chosen, because, in that condition, the essential passions of the
heart find a better soil in which they can attain their maturity,
are less under restraint, and speak a plainer and more emphatic
90 language; because in that condition of life our elementary
feelings co-exist in a state of greater simplicity, and, consequently, may be more accurately contemplated, and more
forcibly communicated; because the manners of rural life
germinate from those elementary feelings, and, from the neces-
95 sary character of rural occupations, are more easily comprehended, and are more durable; and, lastly, because in that
condition the passions of men are incorporated with the
beautiful and permanent forms of nature. The language, too,
of these men has been adopted (purified indeed from what
100 appear to be its real defects, from all lasting and rational
causes of dislike or disgust) because such men hourly communicate with the best objects from which the best part of
language is originally derived; and because, from their rank
in society and the sameness and narrow circle of their inter-
105 course, being less under the influence of social vanity, they
convey their feelings and notions in simple and unelaborated
expressions. Accordingly, such a language, arising out of

repeated experience and regular feelings, is a more permanent, and a far more philosophical language, than that which is frequently substituted for it by Poets, who think that they are 110 conferring honour upon themselves and their art, in proportion as they separate themselves from the sympathies of men, and indulge in arbitrary and capricious habits of expression, in order to furnish food for fickle tastes, and fickle appetites, of their own creation.[1]   115

I cannot, however, be insensible to the present outcry against the triviality and meanness, both of thought and language, which some of my contemporaries have occasionally introduced into their metrical compositions; and I acknow-ledge that this defect, where it exists, is more dishonourable to 120 the Writer's own character than false refinement or arbitrary innovation, though I should contend at the same time, that it is far less pernicious in the sum of its consequences. From such verses the Poems in these volumes will be found distinguished at least by one mark of difference, that each of them has a worthy 125 *purpose*. Not that I always began to write with a distinct purpose formally conceived; but habits of meditation have, I trust, so prompted and regulated my feelings, that my descriptions of such objects as strongly excite those feelings, will be found to carry along with them a *purpose*. If this opinion be erroneous, 130 I can have little right to the name of a Poet. For all good poetry is the spontaneous overflow of powerful feelings: and though this be true, Poems to which any value can be attached were never produced on any variety of subjects but by a man who, being possessed of more than usual organic sensibility, had 135 also thought long and deeply. For our continued influxes of feeling are modified and directed by our thoughts, which are indeed the representatives of all our past feelings; and, as by contemplating the relation of these general representatives to each other, we discover what is really important to men, so, 140 by the repetition and continuance of this act, our feelings will be connected with important subjects, till at length, if we be originally possessed of much sensibility, such habits of mind

---

[1] It is worth while here to observe, that the affecting parts of Chaucer are almost always expressed in language pure and universally intelligible even to this day.

will be produced, that, by obeying blindly and mechanically
145 the impulses of those habits, we shall describe objects, and utter
sentiments, of such a nature, and in such connection with each
other, that the understanding of the Reader must necessarily
be in some degree enlightened, and his affections strengthened
and purified.

150   It has been said that each of these poems has a purpose.
Another circumstance must be mentioned which distinguishes
these Poems from the popular Poetry of the day; it is this, that
the feeling therein developed gives importance to the action
and situation, and not the action and situation to the feeling.
155   A sense of false modesty shall not prevent me from asserting,
that the Reader's attention is pointed to this mark of distinction,
far less for the sake of these particular Poems than from the
general importance of the subject. The subject is indeed important! For the human mind is capable of being excited with-
160 out the application of gross and violent stimulants; and he must
have a very faint perception of its beauty and dignity who
does not know this, and who does not further know, that one
being is elevated above another, in proportion as he possesses
this capability. It has therefore appeared to me, that to endeav-
165 our to produce or enlarge this capability is one of the best ser-
vices in which, at any period, a Writer can be engaged; but this
service, excellent at all times, is especially so at the present day.
For a multitude of causes, unknown to former times, are now
acting with a combined force to blunt the discriminating powers
170 of the mind, and, unfitting it for all voluntary exertion, to
reduce it to a state of almost savage torpor. The most effective
of these causes are the great national events which are daily
taking place, and the increasing accumulation of men in cities,
where the uniformity of their occupations produces a craving
175 for extraordinary incident, which the rapid communication of
intelligence hourly gratifies. To this tendency of life and manners the literature and theatrical exhibitions of the country
have conformed themselves. The invaluable works of our elder
writers, I had almost said the works of Shakespeare and Milton,
180 are driven into neglect by frantic novels, sickly and stupid
German Tragedies, and deluges of idle and extravagant
stories in verse.—When I think upon this degrading thirst after

outrageous stimulation, I am almost ashamed to have spoken
of the feeble endeavour made in these volumes to counteract it;
and, reflecting upon the magnitude of the general evil, I should 185
be oppressed with no dishonourable melancholy, had I not a
deep impression of certain inherent and indestructible qualities
of the human mind, and likewise of certain powers in the great
and permanent objects that act upon it, which are equally
inherent and indestructible; and were there not added to this 190
impression a belief, that the time is approaching when the evil
will be systematically opposed, by men of greater powers, and
with far more distinguished success.

Having dwelt thus long on the subjects and aim of these
Poems, I shall request the Reader's permission to apprise him 195
of a few circumstances relating to their *style*, in order, among
other reasons, that he may not censure me for not having
performed what I never attempted. The Reader will find that
personifications of abstract ideas rarely occur in these volumes;
and are utterly rejected, as an ordinary device to elevate the 200
style, and raise it above prose. My purpose was to imitate,
and, as far as is possible, to adopt the very language of men;
and assuredly such personifications do not make any natural
or regular part of that language. They are, indeed, a figure of
speech occasionally prompted by passion, and I have made use 205
of them as such; but have endeavoured utterly to reject them
as a mechanical device of style, or as a family language which
Writers in metre seem to lay claim to by prescription. I have
wished to keep the Reader in the company of flesh and blood,
persuaded that by so doing I shall interest him. Others who 210
pursue a different track will interest him likewise; I do not
interfere with their claim, but wish to prefer a claim of my own.
There will also be found in these volumes little of what is
usually called poetic diction; as much pains has been taken to
avoid it as is ordinarily taken to produce it; this has been done 215
for the reason already alleged, to bring my language near to
the language of men; and further, because the pleasure which
I have proposed to myself to impart, is of a kind very different
from that which is supposed by many persons to be the proper
object of poetry. Without being culpably particular, I do not 220
know how to give my Reader a more exact notion of the style

in which it was my wish and intention to write, than by informing him that I have at all times endeavoured to look
steadily at my subject; consequently, there is I hope in these
225 Poems little falsehood of description, and my ideas are expressed
in language fitted to their respective importance. Something
must have been gained by this practice, as it is friendly to one
property of all good poetry, namely, good sense: but it has
necessarily cut me off from a large portion of phrases and figures
230 of speech which from father to son have long been regarded as
the common inheritance of Poets. I have also thought it expedient to restrict myself still further, having abstained from
the use of many expressions, in themselves proper and beautiful,
but which have been foolishly repeated by bad Poets, till such
235 feelings of disgust are connected with them as it is scarcely
possible by any art of association to overpower.

If in a poem there should be found a series of lines, or even
a single line, in which the language, though naturally arranged,
and according to the strict laws of metre, does not differ from
240 that of prose, there is a numerous class of critics, who, when
they stumble upon these prosaisms, as they call them, imagine
that they have made a notable discovery, and exult over the
Poet as over a man ignorant of his own profession. Now these
men would establish a canon of criticism which the Reader will
245 conclude he must utterly reject, if he wishes to be pleased with
these volumes. And it would be a most easy task to prove to
him, that not only the language of a large portion of every
good poem, even of the most elevated character, must necessarily, except with reference to the metre, in no respect differ
250 from that of good prose, but likewise that some of the most
interesting parts of the best poems will be found to be strictly
the language of prose when prose is well written. The truth of
this assertion might be demonstrated by innumerable passages
from almost all the poetical writings, even of Milton himself.
255 To illustrate the subject in a general manner, I will here adduce
a short composition of Gray, who was at the head of those
who, by their reasonings, have attempted to widen the space
of separation betwixt Prose and Metrical composition, and
was more than any other man curiously elaborate in the
260 structure of his own poetic diction.

'In vain to me the smiling mornings shine,
And reddening Phoebus lifts his golden fire:
The birds in vain their amorous descant join,
Or cheerful fields resume their green attire.
These ears, alas! for other notes repine;   265
A different object do these eyes require;
My lonely anguish melts no heart but mine;
And in my breast the imperfect joys expire;
Yet morning smiles the busy race to cheer,
And new-born pleasure brings to happier men;   270
The fields to all their wonted tribute bear;
To warm their little loves the birds complain.
I fruitless mourn to him that cannot hear,
And weep the more because I weep in vain.'

It will easily be perceived, that the only part of this Sonnet 275
which is of any value is the lines printed in Italics; it is equally
obvious, that, except in the rhyme, and in the use of the single
word 'fruitless' for fruitlessly, which is so far a defect, the
language of these lines does in no respect differ from that of
prose.   280

By the foregoing quotation it has been shown that the
language of Prose may yet be well adapted to Poetry; and it
was previously asserted, that a large portion of the language
of every good poem can in no respect differ from that of good
Prose. We will go further. It may be safely affirmed, that there 285
neither is, nor can be, any *essential* difference between the
language of prose and metrical composition. We are fond of
tracing the resemblance between Poetry and Painting, and,
accordingly, we call them Sisters: but where shall we find
bonds of connection sufficiently strict to typify the affinity 290
betwixt metrical and prose composition? They both speak by
and to the same organs; the bodies in which both of them are
clothed may be said to be of the same substance, their affections
are kindred, and almost identical, not necessarily differing
even in degree; Poetry[1] sheds no tears 'such as Angels weep,' 295
but natural and human tears; she can boast of no celestial

---

[1] I here use the word 'Poetry' (though against my own judgement) as
opposed to the word Prose, and synonymous with metrical composition.
But much confusion has been introduced into criticism by this contradis-
tinction of Poetry and Prose, instead of the more philosophical one of
Poetry and Matter of Fact, or Science. The only strict antithesis to Prose

ichor that distinguishes her vital juices from those of prose; the same human blood circulates through the veins of them both.

300   If it be affirmed that rhyme and metrical arrangement of themselves constitute a distinction which overturns what has just been said on the strict affinity of metrical language with that of prose, and paves the way for other artificial distinctions which the mind voluntarily admits, I answer that the language 305 of such Poetry as is here recommended is, as far as is possible, a selection of the language really spoken by men; that this selection, wherever it is made with true taste and feeling, will of itself form a distinction far greater than would at first be imagined, and will entirely separate the composition from the 310 vulgarity and meanness of ordinary life; and, if metre be superadded thereto, I believe that a dissimilitude will be produced altogether sufficient for the gratification of a rational mind. What other distinction would we have? Whence is it to come? And where is it to exist? Not, surely, where the Poet 315 speaks through the mouths of his characters: it cannot be necessary here, either for elevation of style, or any of its supposed ornaments: for, if the Poet's subject be judiciously chosen, it will naturally, and upon fit occasion, lead him to passions the language of which, if selected truly and judici- 320 ously, must necessarily be dignified and variegated, and alive with metaphors and figures. I forbear to speak of an incongruity which would shock the intelligent Reader, should the Poet interweave any foreign splendour of his own with that which the passion naturally suggests: it is sufficient to say that 325 such addition is unnecessary. And, surely, it is more probable that those passages, which with propriety abound with metaphors and figures, will have their due effect, if, upon other occasions where the passions are of a milder character, the style also be subdued and temperate.

330   But, as the pleasure which I hope to give by the Poems now presented to the Reader must depend entirely on just notions upon this subject, and, as it is in itself of high importance to

---

is Metre; nor is this, in truth, a *strict* antithesis, because lines and passages of metre so naturally occur in writing prose, that it would be scarcely possible to avoid them, even were it desirable.

our taste and moral feelings, I cannot content myself with these detached remarks. And if, in what I am about to say, it shall appear to some that my labour is unnecessary, and that I am 335 like a man fighting a battle without enemies, such persons may be reminded, that, whatever be the language outwardly holden by men, a practical faith in the opinions which I am wishing to establish is almost unknown. If my conclusions are admitted, and carried as far as they must be carried if admitted 340 at all, our judgements concerning the works of the greatest Poets both ancient and modern will be far different from what they are at present, both when we praise, and when we censure: and our moral feelings influencing and influenced by these judgments will, I believe, be corrected and purified. 345

Taking up the subject, then, upon general grounds, let me ask, what is meant by the word Poet? What is a Poet? To whom does he address himself? And what language is to be expected from him?—He is a man speaking to men: a man, it is true, endowed with more lively sensibility, more en- 350 thusiasm and tenderness, who has a greater knowledge of human nature, and a more comprehensive soul, than are supposed to be common among mankind; a man pleased with his own passions and volitions, and who rejoices more than other men in the spirit of life that is in him; delighting to 355 contemplate similar volitions and passions as manifested in the goings-on of the Universe, and habitually impelled to create them where he does not find them. To these qualities he has added a disposition to be affected more than other men by absent things as if they were present; an ability of conjuring up 360 in himself passions, which are indeed far from being the same as those produced by real events, yet (especially in those parts of the general sympathy which are pleasing and delightful) do more nearly resemble the passions produced by real events, than anything which, from the motions of their own minds 365 merely, other men are accustomed to feel in themselves:— whence, and from practice, he has acquired a greater readiness and power in expressing what he thinks and feels, and especially those thoughts and feelings which, by his own choice, or from the structure of his own mind, arise in him without immediate 370 external excitement.

But whatever portion of this faculty we may suppose even the greatest Poet to possess, there cannot be a doubt that the language which it will suggest to him, must often, in liveliness
375 and truth, fall short of that which is uttered by men in real life, under the actual pressure of those passions, certain shadows of which the Poet thus produces, or feels to be produced, in himself.

However exalted a notion we would wish to cherish of the
380 character of a Poet, it is obvious, that while he describes and imitates passions, his employment is in some degree mechanical, compared with the freedom and power of real and substantial action and suffering. So that it will be the wish of the Poet to bring his feelings near to those of the persons whose feelings he
385 describes, nay, for short spaces of time, perhaps, to let himself slip into an entire delusion, and even confound and identify his own feelings with theirs; modifying only the language which is thus suggested to him by a consideration that he describes for a particular purpose, that of giving pleasure. Here, then, he will
390 apply the principle of selection which has been already insisted upon. He will depend upon this for removing what would otherwise be painful or disgusting in the passion; he will feel that there is no necessity to trick out or to elevate nature: and, the more industriously he applies this principle, the deeper will
395 be his faith that no words, which *his* fancy or imagination can suggest, will be to be compared with those which are the emanations of reality and truth.

But it may be said by those who do not object to the general spirit of these remarks, that, as it is impossible for the Poet to
400 produce upon all occasions language as exquisitely fitted for the passion as that which the real passion itself suggests, it is proper that he should consider himself as in the situation of a translator, who does not scruple to substitute excellences of another kind for those which are unattainable by him; and
405 endeavours occasionally to surpass his original, in order to make some amends for the general inferiority to which he feels that he must submit. But this would be to encourage idleness and unmanly despair. Further, it is the language of men who speak of what they do not understand; who talk of Poetry as of
410 a matter of amusement and idle pleasure; who will converse

with us as gravely about a *taste* for Poetry, as they express it, as if it were a thing as indifferent as a taste for rope-dancing, or Frontiniac or Sherry. Aristotle, I have been told, has said, that Poetry is the most philosophic of all writing: it is so: its object is truth, not individual and local, but general, and operative; 415 not standing upon external testimony, but carried alive into the heart by passion; truth which is its own testimony, which gives competence and confidence to the tribunal to which it appeals, and receives them from the same tribunal. Poetry is the image of man and nature. The obstacles which stand in the 420 way of the fidelity of the Biographer and Historian, and of their consequent utility, are incalculably greater than those which are to be encountered by the Poet who comprehends the dignity of his art. The Poet writes under one restriction only, namely, the necessity of giving immediate pleasure to a human Being 425 possessed of that information which may be expected from him, not as a lawyer, a physician, a mariner, an astronomer, or a natural philosopher, but as a Man. Except this one restriction, there is no object standing between the Poet and the image of things; between this, and the Biographer and Historian, there 430 are a thousand.

Nor let this necessity of producing immediate pleasure be considered as a degradation of the Poet's art. It is far otherwise. It is an acknowledgement of the beauty of the universe, an acknowledgement the more sincere, because not formal, but 435 indirect; it is a task light and easy to him who looks at the world in the spirit of love: further, it is a homage paid to the native and naked dignity of man, to the grand elementary principle of pleasure, by which he knows, and feels, and lives, and moves. We have no sympathy but what is propagated by 440 pleasure: I would not be misunderstood; but wherever we sympathise with pain, it will be found that the sympathy is produced and carried on by subtle combinations with pleasure. We have no knowledge, that is, no general principles drawn from the contemplation of particular facts, but what has been 445 built up by pleasure, and exists in us by pleasure alone. The Man of science, the Chemist and Mathematician, whatever difficulties and disgusts they may have had to struggle with, know and feel this. However painful may be the objects with

450 which the Anatomist's knowledge is connected, he feels that his
knowledge is pleasure; and where he has no pleasure he has
no knowledge. What then does the Poet? He considers man
and the objects that surround him as acting and re-acting upon
each other, so as to produce an infinite complexity of pain and
455 pleasure; he considers man in his own nature and in his ordinary
life as contemplating this with a certain quantity of immediate
knowledge, with certain convictions, intuitions, and deductions,
which from habit acquire the quality of intuitions; he considers
him as looking upon this complex scene of ideas and sensations,
460 and finding every where objects that immediately excite in
him sympathies which, from the necessities of his nature, are
accompanied by an overbalance of enjoyment.

To this knowledge which all men carry about with them,
and to these sympathies in which, without any other discipline
465 than that of our daily life, we are fitted to take delight, the Poet
principally directs his attention. He considers man and nature
as essentially adapted to each other, and the mind of man as
naturally the mirror of the fairest and most interesting properties of nature. And thus the Poet, prompted by this feeling
470 of pleasure, which accompanies him through the whole course
of his studies, converses with general nature, with affections
akin to those, which, through labour and length of time, the
Man of science has raised up in himself, by conversing with
those particular parts of nature which are the objects of his
475 studies. The knowledge both of the Poet and the Man of
science is pleasure; but the knowledge of the one cleaves to us
as a necessary part of our existence, our natural and unalien-
able inheritance; the other is a personal and individual
acquisition, slow to come to us, and by no habitual and direct
480 sympathy connecting us with our fellow-beings. The Man of
science seeks truth as a remote and unknown benefactor; he
cherishes and loves it in his solitude: the Poet, singing a song
in which all human beings join with him, rejoices in the
presence of truth as our visible friend and hourly companion.
485 Poetry is the breath and finer spirit of all knowledge; it is the
impassioned expression which is in the countenance of all
Science. Emphatically may it be said of the Poet, as Shakespeare
hath said of man, 'that he looks before and after.' He is the

rock of defence for human nature; an upholder and preserver, carrying everywhere with him relationship and love. In spite 490 of difference of soil and climate, of language and manners, of laws and customs: in spite of things silently gone out of mind, and things violently destroyed; the Poet binds together by passion and knowledge the vast empire of human society, as it is spread over the whole earth, and over all time. The objects 495 of the Poet's thoughts are every where; though the eyes and senses of man are, it is true, his favourite guides, yet he will follow wheresoever he can find an atmosphere of sensation in which to move his wings. Poetry is the first and last of all knowledge—it is as immortal as the heart of man. If the labours 500 of Men of science should ever create any material revolution, direct or indirect, in our condition, and in the impressions which we habitually receive, the Poet will sleep then no more than at present; he will be ready to follow the steps of the Man of science, not only in those general indirect effects, but 505 he will be at his side, carrying sensation into the midst of the objects of the science itself. The remotest discoveries of the Chemist, the Botanist, or Mineralogist, will be as proper objects of the Poet's art as any upon which it can be employed, if the time should ever come when these things shall be familiar 510 to us, and the relations under which they are contemplated by the followers of these respective sciences shall be manifestly and palpably material to us as enjoying and suffering beings. If the time should ever come when what is now called science, thus familiarised to men, shall be ready to put on, as it were, a form 515 of flesh and blood, the Poet will lend his divine spirit to aid the transfiguration, and will welcome the Being thus produced, as a dear and genuine inmate of the household of man.—It is not, then, to be supposed that any one, who holds that sublime notion of Poetry which I have attempted to convey, will break 520 in upon the sanctity and truth of his pictures by transitory and accidental ornaments, and endeavour to excite admiration of himself by arts, the necessity of which must manifestly depend upon the assumed meanness of his subject.

What has been thus far said applies to Poetry in general; but 525 especially to those parts of composition where the Poet speaks through the mouths of his characters; and upon this point it

GECT

appears to authorise the conclusion that there are few persons of good sense, who would not allow that the dramatic parts of
530 composition are defective, in proportion as they deviate from the real language of nature, and are coloured by a diction of the Poet's own, either peculiar to him as an individual Poet or belonging simply to Poets in general; to a body of men who, from the circumstance of their compositions being in metre, it
535 is expected will employ a particular language.

It is not, then, in the dramatic parts of composition that we look for this distinction of language; but still it may be proper and necessary where the Poet speaks to us in his own person and character. To this I answer by referring the Reader to the
540 description before given of a Poet. Among the qualities there enumerated as principally conducing to form a Poet, is implied nothing differing in kind from other men, but only in degree. The sum of what was said is, that the Poet is chiefly distinguished from other men by a greater promptness to think and
545 feel without immediate external excitement, and a greater power in expressing such thoughts and feelings as are produced in him in that manner. But these passions and thoughts and feelings are the general passions and thoughts and feelings of men. And with what are they connected? Undoubtedly with
550 our moral sentiments and animal sensations, and with the causes which excite these; with the operations of the elements, and the appearances of the visible universe; with storm and sunshine, with the revolutions of the seasons, with cold and heat, with loss of friends and kindred, with injuries and resentments,
555 gratitude and hope, with fear and sorrow. These, and the like, are the sensations and objects which the Poet describes, as they are the sensations of other men, and the objects which interest them. The Poet thinks and feels in the spirit of human passions. How, then, can his language differ in any material
560 degree from that of all other men who feel vividly and see clearly? It might be *proved* that it is impossible. But supposing that this were not the case, the Poet might then be allowed to use a peculiar language when expressing his feelings for his own gratification, or that of men like himself. But Poets do not
565 write for Poets alone, but for men. Unless therefore we are advocates for that admiration which subsists upon ignorance,

and that pleasure which arises from hearing what we do not understand, the Poet must descend from this supposed height; and, in order to excite rational sympathy, he must express himself as other men express themselves. To this it may be 570 added, that while he is only selecting from the real language of men, or, which amounts to the same thing, composing accurately in the spirit of such selection, he is treading upon safe ground, and we know what we are to expect from him. Our feelings are the same with respect to metre; for, as it may be 575 proper to remind the Reader, the distinction of metre is regular and uniform, and not, like that which is produced by what is usually called POETIC DICTION, arbitrary, and subject to infinite caprices upon which no calculation whatever can be made. In the one case, the Reader is utterly at the mercy of the Poet, 580 respecting what imagery or diction he may choose to connect with the passion; whereas, in the other, the metre obeys certain laws, to which the Poet and Reader both willingly submit because they are certain, and because no interference is made by them with the passion, but such as the concurring testimony 585 of ages has shown to heighten and improve the pleasure which co-exists with it.

It will now be proper to answer an obvious question, namely, Why, professing these opinions, have I written in verse? To this, in addition to such answer as is included in what has been 590 already said, I reply, in the first place, Because, however I may have restricted myself, there is still left open to me what confessedly constitutes the most valuable object of all writing, whether in prose or verse; the great and universal passions of men, the most general and interesting of their occupations, and 595 the entire world of nature before me—to supply endless combinations of forms and imagery. Now, supposing for a moment that whatever is interesting in these objects may be as vividly described in prose, why should I be condemned for attempting to superadd to such description, the charm which, by the con- 600 sent of all nations, is acknowledged to exist in metrical language? To this, by such as are yet unconvinced, it may be answered that a very small part of the pleasure given by Poetry depends upon the metre, and that it is injudicious to write in metre, unless it be accompanied with the other artificial 605

distinctions of style with which metre is usually accompanied, and that, by such deviation, more will be lost from the shock which will thereby be given to the Reader's associations than will be counterbalanced by any pleasure which he can derive
610 from the general power of numbers. In answer to those who still contend for the necessity of accompanying metre with certain appropriate colours of style in order to the accomplishment of its appropriate end, and who also, in my opinion, greatly under-rate the power of metre in itself, it might, perhaps, as
615 far as relates to these Volumes, have been almost sufficient to observe, that poems are extant, written upon more humble subjects, and in a still more naked and simple style, which have continued to give pleasure from generation to generation. Now, if nakedness and simplicity be a defect, the fact here mentioned
620 affords a strong presumption that poems somewhat less naked and simple are capable of affording pleasure at the present day; and, what I wished *chiefly* to attempt, at present, was to justify myself for having written under the impression of this belief.
625 But various causes might be pointed out why, when the style is manly, and the subject of some importance, words metrically arranged will long continue to impart such a pleasure to mankind as he who proves the extent of that pleasure will be desirous to impart. The end of Poetry is to produce excitement
630 in co-existence with an overbalance of pleasure; but, by the supposition, excitement is an unusual and irregular state of the mind; ideas and feelings do not, in that state, succeed each other in accustomed order. If the words, however, by which this excitement is produced be in themselves powerful, or the images
635 and feelings have an undue proportion of pain connected with them, there is some danger that the excitement may be carried beyond its proper bounds. Now the co-presence of something regular, something to which the mind has been accustomed in various moods and in a less excited state, cannot but have
640 great efficacy in tempering and restraining the passion by an intertexture of ordinary feeling, and of feeling not strictly and necessarily connected with the passion. This is unquestionably true; and hence, though the opinion will at first appear paradoxical, from the tendency of metre to divest language, in a

certain degree, of its reality, and thus to throw a sort of half- 645
consciousness of unsubstantial existence over the whole composition, there can be little doubt but that more pathetic
situations and sentiments, that is, those which have a greater
proportion of pain connected with them, may be endured in
metrical composition, especially in rhyme, than in prose. The 650
metre of the old ballads is very artless; yet they contain many
passages which would illustrate this opinion; and, I hope, if
the following Poems be attentively perused, similar instances
will be found in them. This opinion may be further illustrated
by appealing to the Reader's own experience of the reluctance 655
with which he comes to the re-perusal of the distressful parts of
Clarissa Harlowe, or *The Gamester*; while Shakespeare's writings,
in the most pathetic scenes, never act upon us, as pathetic,
beyond the bounds of pleasure—an effect which, in a much
greater degree than might at first be imagined, is to be ascribed 660
to small, but continual and regular impulses of pleasurable
surprise from the metrical arrangement.—On the other hand
(what it must be allowed will much more frequently happen)
if the Poet's words should be incommensurate with the passion,
and inadequate to raise the Reader to a height of desirable 665
excitement, then, (unless the Poet's choice of his metre has been
grossly injudicious) in the feelings of pleasure which the Reader
has been accustomed to connect with metre in general, and in
the feeling, whether cheerful or melancholy, which he has been
accustomed to connect with that particular movement of metre, 670
there will be found something which will greatly contribute to
impart passion to the words, and to effect the complex end
which the Poet proposes to himself.

   If I had undertaken a SYSTEMATIC defence of the theory here
maintained, it would have been my duty to develop the various 675
causes upon which the pleasure received from metrical language depends. Among the chief of these causes is to be
reckoned a principle which must be well known to those who
have made any of the Arts the object of accurate reflection:
namely, the pleasure which the mind derives from the percep- 680
tion of similitude in dissimilitude. This principle is the great
spring of the activity of our minds, and their chief feeder.
From this principle the direction of the sexual appetite, and all

the passions connected with it, take their origin: it is the life of
685 our ordinary conversation; and upon the accuracy with which
similitude in dissimilitude, and dissimilitude in similitude are
perceived, depend our taste and our moral feelings. It would
not be a useless employment to apply this principle to the consideration of metre, and to show that metre is hence enabled to
690 afford much pleasure, and to point out in what manner that
pleasure is produced. But my limits will not permit me to enter
upon this subject, and I must content myself with a general
summary.

I have said that poetry is the spontaneous overflow of power-
695 ful feelings: it takes its origin from emotion recollected in
tranquillity: the emotion is contemplated till, by a species of
re-action, the tranquillity gradually disappears, and an emotion, kindred to that which was before the subject of contemplation, is gradually produced, and does itself actually exist in the
700 mind. In this mood successful composition generally begins,
and in a mood similar to this it is carried on; but the emotion,
of whatever kind, and in whatever degree, from various causes,
is qualified by various pleasures, so that in describing any
passions whatsoever, which are voluntarily described, the mind
705 will, upon the whole, be in a state of enjoyment. If Nature be
thus cautious to preserve in a state of enjoyment a being so
employed, the Poet ought to profit by the lesson held forth to
him, and ought especially to take care, that, whatever passions
he communicates to his Reader, those passions, if his Reader's
710 mind be sound and vigorous, should always be accompanied
with an overbalance of pleasure. Now the music of harmonious
metrical language, the sense of difficulty overcome, and the
blind association of pleasure which has been previously received
from works of rhyme or metre of the same or similar construc-
715 tion, an indistinct perception perpetually renewed of language
closely resembling that of real life, and yet, in the circumstance
of metre, differing from it so widely—all these imperceptibly
make up a complex feeling of delight, which is of the most
important use in tempering the painful feeling always found
720 intermingled with powerful descriptions of the deeper passions.
This effect is always produced in pathetic and impassioned
poetry; while, in lighter compositions, the ease and graceful-

ness with which the Poet manages his numbers are themselves confessedly a principal source of the gratification of the Reader. All that it is *necessary* to say, however, upon this subject, may be 725 effected by affirming, what few persons will deny, that, of two descriptions, either of passions, manners, or characters, each of them equally well executed, the one in prose and the other in verse, the verse will be read a hundred times where the prose is read once. 730

Having thus explained a few of my reasons for writing in verse, and why I have chosen subjects from common life, and endeavoured to bring my language near to the real language of men, if I have been too minute in pleading my own cause, I have at the same time been treating a subject of general 735 interest; and for this reason a few words shall be added with reference solely to these particular poems, and to some defects which will probably be found in them. I am sensible that my associations must have sometimes been particular instead of general, and that, consequently, giving to things a false impor- 740 tance, I may have sometimes written upon unworthy subjects; but I am less apprehensive on this account, than that my language may frequently have suffered from those arbitrary connections of feelings and ideas with particular words and phrases, from which no man can altogether protect himself. 745 Hence I have no doubt, that, in some instances, feelings, even of the ludicrous, may be given to my Readers by expressions which appeared to me tender and pathetic. Such faulty expressions, were I convinced they were faulty at present, and that they must necessarily continue to be so, I would willingly 750 take all reasonable pains to correct. But it is dangerous to make these alterations on the simple authority of a few individuals, or even of certain classes of men; for where the understanding of an Author is not convinced, or his feelings altered, this cannot be done without great injury to himself: for his own 755 feelings are his stay and support; and, if he set them aside in one instance, he may be induced to repeat this act till his mind shall lose all confidence in itself, and become utterly debili- tated. To this it may be added, that the critic ought never to forget that he is himself exposed to the same errors as the Poet, 760 and, perhaps, in a much greater degree: for there can be no

presumption in saying of most readers, that it is not probable they will be so well acquainted with the various stages of meaning through which words have passed, or with the fickle-
765 ness or stability of the relations of particular ideas to each other; and, above all, since they are so much less interested in the subject, they may decide lightly and carelessly.

Long as the Reader has been detained, I hope he will permit me to caution him against a mode of false criticism
770 which has been applied to Poetry, in which the language closely resembles that of life and nature. Such verses have been triumphed over in parodies, of which Dr. Johnson's stanza is a fair specimen:—

> 'I put my hat upon my head
775 > And walked into the Strand,
> And there I met another man
> Whose hat was in his hand.'

Immediately under these lines let us place one of the most justly-admired stanzas of the 'Babes in the Wood.'

780 > 'These pretty Babes with hand in hand
> Went wandering up and down;
> But never more they saw the Man
> Approaching from the Town.'

In both these stanzas the words, and the order of the words,
785 in no respect differ from the most unimpassioned conversation. There are words in both, for example, 'the Strand,' and 'the Town,' connected with none but the most familiar ideas; yet the one stanza we admit as admirable, and the other as a fair example of the superlatively contemptible. Whence arises this
790 difference? Not from the metre, not from the language, not from the order of the words; but the *matter* expressed in Dr. Johnson's stanza is contemptible. The proper method of treating trivial and simple verses, to which Dr. Johnson's stanza would be a fair parallelism, is not to say, this is a bad kind of
795 poetry, or, this is not poetry; but, this wants sense; it is neither interesting in itself, nor can *lead* to any thing interesting; the images neither originate in that sane state of feeling which arises out of thought, nor can excite thought or feeling in the Reader.

This is the only sensible manner of dealing with such verses. Why trouble yourself about the species till you have previously 800 decided upon the genus? Why take pains to prove that an ape is not a Newton, when it is self-evident that he is not a man?

One request I must make of my reader, which is, that in judging these Poems he would decide by his own feelings 805 genuinely, and not by reflection upon what will probably be the judgement of others. How common is it to hear a person say, I myself do not object to this style of composition, or this or that expression, but, to such and such classes of people it will appear mean or ludicrous! This mode of criticism, so 810 destructive of all sound unadulterated judgement, is almost universal: let the Reader then abide, independently, by his own feelings, and, if he finds himself affected, let him not suffer such conjectures to interfere with his pleasure.

If an Author, by any single composition, has impressed us 815 with respect for his talents, it is useful to consider this as affording a presumption, that on other occasions where we have been displeased, he, nevertheless, may not have written ill or absurdly; and further, to give him so much credit for this one composition as may induce us to review what has displeased us, 820 with more care than we should otherwise have bestowed upon it. This is not only an act of justice, but, in our decisions upon poetry especially, may conduce, in a high degree, to the improvement of our own taste; for an *accurate* taste in poetry, and in all the other arts, as Sir Joshua Reynolds has observed, 825 is an *acquired* talent, which can only be produced by thought and a long-continued intercourse with the best models of composition. This is mentioned, not with so ridiculous a purpose as to prevent the most inexperienced Reader from judging for himself, (I have already said that I wish him to judge for 830 himself;) but merely to temper the rashness of decision, and to suggest, that, if Poetry be a subject on which much time has not been bestowed, the judgement may be erroneous; and that, in many cases, it necessarily will be so.

Nothing would, I know, have so effectually contributed to 835 further the end which I have in view, as to have shown of what kind the pleasure is, and how that pleasure is produced, which

is confessedly produced by metrical composition essentially
different from that which I have here endeavoured to recom-
840 mend: for the Reader will say that he has been pleased by such
composition; and what more can be done for him? The power
of any art is limited; and he will suspect, that, if it be proposed
to furnish him with new friends, that can be only upon condition of his abandoning his old friends. Besides, as I have said,
845 the Reader is himself conscious of the pleasure which he has
received from such composition, composition to which he has
peculiarly attached the endearing name of Poetry; and all men
feel an habitual gratitude, and something of an honourable
bigotry, for the objects which have long continued to please
850 them: we not only wish to be pleased, but to be pleased in the
particular way in which we have been accustomed to be
pleased. There is in these feelings enough to resist a host of
arguments; and I should be the less able to combat them successfully, as I am willing to allow, that, in order entirely to
855 enjoy the Poetry which I am recommending, it would be
necessary to give up much of what is ordinarily enjoyed. But,
would my limits have permitted me to point out how this
pleasure is produced, many obstacles might have been removed,
and the Reader assisted in perceiving that the powers of lan-
860 guage are not so limited as he may suppose; and that it is
possible for poetry to give other enjoyments, of a purer, more
lasting, and more exquisite nature. This part of the subject has
not been altogether neglected, but it has not been so much
my present aim to prove, that the interest excited by some other
865 kinds of poetry is less vivid, and less worthy of the nobler
powers of the mind, as to offer reasons for presuming, that if my
purpose were fulfilled, a species of poetry would be produced,
which is genuine poetry; in its nature well adapted to interest
mankind permanently, and likewise important in the multi-
870 plicity and quality of its moral relations.

From what has been said, and from a perusal of the Poems,
the Reader will be able clearly to perceive the object which
I had in view: he will determine how far it has been attained;
and, what is a much more important question, whether it be
875 worth attaining: and upon the decision of these two questions
will rest my claim to the approbation of the Public.

Appendix

Perhaps, as I have no right to expect that attentive perusal,
without which, confined, as I have been, to the narrow limits
of a preface, my meaning cannot be thoroughly understood, I
am anxious to give an exact notion of the sense in which the 880
phrase poetic diction has been used; and for this purpose, a few
words shall here be added, concerning the origin and characteristics of the phraseology, which I have condemned under that
name.

The earliest poets of all nations generally wrote from passion 885
excited by real events; they wrote naturally, and as men: feeling
powerfully as they did, their language was daring, and figurative. In succeeding times, Poets, and Men ambitious of the
fame of Poets, perceiving the influence of such language, and
desirous of producing the same effect without being animated 890
by the same passion, set themselves to a mechanical adoption
of these figures of speech, and made use of them, sometimes
with propriety, but much more frequently applied them to
feelings and thoughts with which they had no natural connection whatsoever. A language was thus insensibly produced, 895
differing materially from the real language of men in *any situation*. The Reader or Hearer of this distorted language found
himself in a perturbed and unusual state of mind: when
affected by the genuine language of passion he had been in a
perturbed and unusual state of mind also: in both cases he was 900
willing that his common judgement and understanding should
be laid asleep, and he had no instinctive and infallible perception of the true to make him reject the false; the one served as a
passport for the other. The emotion was in both cases delightful, and no wonder if he confounded the one with the other, 905
and believed them both to be produced by the same, or similar
causes. Besides, the Poet spoke to him in the character of a man
to be looked up to, a man of genius and authority. Thus, and
from a variety of other causes, this distorted language was
received with admiration; and Poets, it is probable, who had 910
before contented themselves for the most part with misapplying
only expressions which at first had been dictated by real passion, carried the abuse still further, and introduced phrase

composed apparently in the spirit of the original figurative
915 language of passion, yet altogether of their own invention, and
characterised by various degrees of wanton deviation from good
sense and nature.

It is indeed true, that the language of the earliest Poets was
felt to differ materially from ordinary language, because it
920 was the language of extraordinary occasions; but it was really
spoken by men, language which the Poet himself had uttered
when he had been affected by the events which he described,
or which he had heard uttered by those around him. To this
language it is probable that metre of some sort or other was
925 early superadded. This separated the genuine language of
Poetry still further from common life, so that whoever read or
heard the poems of these earliest Poets felt himself moved in a
way in which he had not been accustomed to be moved in real
life, and by causes manifestly different from those which acted
930 upon him in real life. This was the great temptation to all the
corruptions which have followed: under the protection of this
feeling succeeding Poets constructed a phraseology which had
one thing, it is true, in common with the genuine language of
poetry, namely, that it was not heard in ordinary conversation;
935 that it was unusual. But the first Poets, as I have said, spoke a
language which, though unusual, was still the language of men.
This circumstance, however, was disregarded by their successors; they found that they could please by easier means:
they became proud of modes of expression which they them-
940 selves had invented, and which were uttered only by themselves.
In process of time metre became a symbol or promise of this
unusual language, and whoever took upon him to write in
metre, according as he possessed more or less of true poetic
genius, introduced less or more of this adulterated phraseology
945 into his compositions, and the true and the false were insepar-
ably interwoven until, the taste of men becoming gradually
perverted, this language was received as a natural language:
and at length, by the influence of books upon men, did to a
certain degree really become so. Abuses of this kind were
950 imported from one nation to another, and with the progress of
refinement this diction became daily more and more corrupt,
thrusting out of sight the plain humanities of nature by a motley

masquerade of tricks, quaintnesses, hieroglyphics, and enigmas.

It would not be uninteresting to point out the causes of the pleasure given by this extravagant and absurd diction. It 955 depends upon a great variety of causes, but upon none, perhaps, more than its influence in impressing a notion of the peculiarity and exaltation of the Poet's character, and in flattering the Reader's self-love by bringing him nearer to a sympathy with that character; an effect which is accomplished 960 by unsettling ordinary habits of thinking, and thus assisting the Reader to approach to that perturbed and dizzy state of mind in which if he does not find himself, he imagines that he is *balked* of a peculiar enjoyment which poetry can and ought to bestow.   965

The sonnet quoted from Gray, in the Preface, except the lines printed in Italics, consists of little else but this diction, though not of the worst kind; and indeed, if one may be permitted to say so, it is far too common in the best writers both ancient and modern. Perhaps in no way, by positive example, 970 could more easily be given a notion of what I mean by the phrase *poetic diction* than by referring to a comparison between the metrical paraphrases which we have of passages in the Old and New Testament, and those passages as they exist in our common Translation. See Pope's 'Messiah' throughout; 975 Prior's 'Did sweeter sounds adorn my flowing tongue,' &c. &c. 'Though I speak with the tongues of men and of angels,' &c. &c. 1st Corinthians, chap. xiii. By way of immediate example, take the following of Dr. Johnson:

> 'Turn on the prudent Ant thy heedless eyes,   980
> Observe her labours, Sluggard, and be wise;
> No stern command, no monitory voice,
> Prescribes her duties, or directs her choice;
> Yet, timely provident, she hastes away
> To snatch the blessings of a plenteous day;   985
> When fruitful Summer loads the teeming plain,
> She crops the harvest, and she stores the grain.
> How long shall sloth usurp thy useless hours,
> Unnerve thy vigour, and enchain thy powers?
> While artful shades thy downy couch enclose,   990
> And soft solicitation courts repose,
> Amidst the drowsy charms of dull delight,

Year chases year with unremitted flight,
Till Want now following, fraudulent and slow,
995   Shall spring to seize thee, like an ambush'd foe.'

From this hubbub of words pass to the original. 'Go to the Ant, thou Sluggard, consider her ways, and be wise: which having no guide, overseer, or ruler, provideth her meat in the summer, and gathereth her food in the harvest. How long wilt 1000 thou sleep, O Sluggard? when wilt thou arise out of thy sleep? Yet a little sleep, a little slumber, a little folding of the hands to sleep. So shall thy poverty come as one that travelleth, and thy want as an armed man.' Proverbs, chap. vi.

One more quotation, and I have done. It is from Cowper's 1005 Verses supposed to be written by Alexander Selkirk:—

'Religion! what treasure untold
Resides in that heavenly word!
More precious than silver and gold,
Or all that this earth can afford.
1010   But the sound of the church-going bell
These valleys and rocks never heard,
Ne'er sighed at the sound of a knell,
Or smiled when a sabbath appeared.

Ye winds, that have made me your sport,
1015   Convey to this desolate shore
Some cordial endearing report
Of a land I must visit no more.
My Friends, do they now and then send
A wish or a thought after me?
1020   O tell me I yet have a friend,
Though a friend I am never to see.'

This passage is quoted as an instance of three different styles of composition. The first four lines are poorly expressed; some Critics would call the language prosaic; the fact is, it would be 1025 bad prose, so bad, that it is scarcely worse in metre. The epithet 'church-going' applied to a bell, and that by so chaste a writer as Cowper, is an instance of the strange abuses which Poets have introduced into their language, till they and their Readers take them as matters of course, if they do not single 1030 them out expressly as objects of admiration. The two lines 'Ne'er sighed at the sound,' &c., are, in my opinion, an instance of the language of passion wrested from its proper use, and, from the mere circumstance of the composition being in metre, applied upon an occasion that does not justify such violent expressions; and I should condemn the passage, though perhaps 1035 few Readers will agree with me, as vicious poetic diction. The last stanza is throughout admirably expressed: it would be equally good whether in prose or verse, except that the Reader has an exquisite pleasure in seeing such natural language so naturally connected with metre. The beauty of this stanza 1040 tempts me to conclude with a principle which ought never to be lost sight of, and which has been my chief guide in all I have said,—namely, that in works *of imagination and sentiment*, for of these only have I been treating, in proportion as ideas and feelings are valuable, whether the composition be in prose or 1045 in verse, they require and exact one and the same language. Metre is but adventitious to composition, and the phraseology for which that passport is necessary, even where it may be graceful at all, will be little valued by the judicious.

S. T. COLERIDGE

Biographia Literaria

CHAPTER XIV

Occasion of the Lyrical Ballads, and the objects originally proposed
—Preface to the second edition—The ensuing controversy, its
causes and acrimony—Philosophic definitions of a poem and
poetry with scholia.

DURING the first year that Mr. Wordsworth and I were neighbours, our conversations turned frequently on the two cardinal
points of poetry, the power of exciting the sympathy of the
reader by a faithful adherence to the truth of nature, and the
5 power of giving the interest of novelty by the modifying colours
of imagination. The sudden charm, which accidents of light
and shade, which moon-light or sun-set diffused over a known
and familiar landscape, appeared to represent the practicability
of combining both. These are the poetry of nature. The thought
10 suggested itself (to which of us I do not recollect) that a series
of poems might be composed of two sorts. In the one, the
incidents and agents were to be, in part at least, supernatural;
and the excellence aimed at was to consist in the interesting
of the affections by the dramatic truth of such emotions, as
15 would naturally accompany such situations, supposing them
real. And real in *this* sense they have been to every human
being who, from whatever source of delusion, has at any time
believed himself under supernatural agency. For the second
class, subjects were to be chosen from ordinary life; the charac-
20 ters and incidents were to be such, as will be found in every
village and its vicinity, where there is a meditative and feeling
mind to seek after them, or to notice them, when they present
themselves.

In this idea originated the plan of the *Lyrical Ballads*; in
25 which it was agreed, that my endeavours should be directed

to persons and characters supernatural, or at least romantic; yet so as to transfer from our inward nature a human interest and a semblance of truth sufficient to procure for these shadows of imagination that willing suspension of disbelief for the moment, which constitutes poetic faith. Mr. Wordsworth, on 30 the other hand, was to propose to himself as his object, to give the charm of novelty to things of every day, and to excite a feeling analogous to the supernatural, by awakening the mind's attention from the lethargy of custom, and directing it to the loveliness and the wonders of the world before us; an inex- 35 haustible treasure, but for which, in consequence of the film of familiarity and selfish solicitude, we have eyes, yet see not, ears that hear not, and hearts that neither feel nor understand.

With this view I wrote 'The Ancient Mariner,' and was preparing among other poems, 'The Dark Ladie,' and the 40 'Christabel,' in which I should have more nearly realized my ideal, than I had done in my first attempt. But Mr. Words-worth's industry had proved so much more successful, and the number of his poems so much greater, that my compositions, instead of forming a balance, appeared rather an interpolation 45 of heterogeneous matter. Mr. Wordsworth added two or three poems written in his own character, in the impassioned, lofty, and sustained diction, which is characteristic of his genius. In this form the 'Lyrical Ballads' were published; and were presented by him, as an *experiment*, whether subjects, which 50 from their nature rejected the usual ornaments and extra-colloquial style of poems in general, might not be so managed in the language of ordinary life as to produce the pleasurable interest, which it is the peculiar business of poetry to impart. To the second edition he added a preface of considerable 55 length; in which, notwithstanding some passages of apparently a contrary import, he was understood to contend for the extension of this style to poetry of all kinds, and to reject as vicious and indefensible all phrases and forms of style that were not included in what he (unfortunately, I think, adopting an 60 equivocal expression) called the language of *real* life. From this preface, prefixed to poems in which it was impossible to deny the presence of original genius, however mistaken its direction might be deemed, arose the whole long-continued controversy.

65 For from the conjunction of perceived power with supposed
heresy I explain the inveteracy and in some instances, I grieve
to say, the acrimonious passions, with which the controversy
has been conducted by the assailants.

Had Mr. Wordsworth's poems been the silly, the childish
70 things, which they were for a long time described as being;
had they been really distinguished from the compositions of
other poets merely by meanness of language and inanity of
thought; had they indeed contained nothing more than what
is found in the parodies and pretended imitations of them; they
75 must have sunk at once, a dead weight, into the slough of
oblivion, and have dragged the preface along with them. But
year after year increased the number of Mr. Wordsworth's
admirers. They were found too not in the lower classes of the
reading public, but chiefly among young men of strong sensi-
80 bility and meditative minds; and their admiration (inflamed
perhaps in some degree by opposition) was distinguished by its
intensity, I might almost say, by its *religious* fervour. These
facts, and the intellectual energy of the author, which was more
or less consciously felt, where it was outwardly and even
85 boisterously denied, meeting with sentiments of aversion to his
opinions, and of alarm at their consequences, produced an
eddy of criticism, which would of itself have borne up the poems
by the violence with which it whirled them round and round.
With many parts of this preface, in the sense attributed to
90 them, and which the words undoubtedly seem to authorize, I
never concurred; but on the contrary objected to them as
erroneous in principle, and as contradictory (in appearance at
least) both to other parts of the same preface, and to the
author's own practice in the greater number of the poems
95 themselves. Mr. Wordsworth in his recent collection has, I
find, degraded this prefatory disquisition to the end of his
second volume, to be read or not at the reader's choice. But he
has not, as far as I can discover, announced any change in his
poetic creed. At all events, considering it as the source of a
100 controversy, in which I have been honoured more than I
deserve by the frequent conjunction of my name with his,
I think it expedient to declare once for all, in what points I
coincide with his opinions, and in what points I altogether

differ. But in order to render myself intelligible I must previously, in as few words as possible, explain my ideas, first, of a 105 POEM; and secondly, of POETRY itself, in *kind*, and in *essence*.

The office of philosophical *disquisition* consists in just *distinction*; while it is the privilege of the philosopher to preserve himself constantly aware, that distinction is not division. In order to obtain adequate notions of any truth, we must intel- 110 lectually separate its distinguishable parts; and this is the technical *process* of philosophy. But having so done, we must then restore them in our conceptions to the unity, in which they actually co-exist; and this is the *result* of philosophy. A poem contains the same elements as a prose composition; the 115 difference therefore must consist in a different combination of them, in consequence of a different object being proposed. According to the difference of the object will be the difference of the combination. It is possible, that the object may be merely to facilitate the recollection of any given facts or observations 120 by artificial arrangement; and the composition will be a poem, merely because it is distinguished from prose by metre, or by rhyme, or by both conjointly. In this, the lowest sense, a man might attribute the name of a poem to the well-known enumeration of the days in the several months; 125

'Thirty days hath September,
April, June, and November,' &c.

and others of the same class and purpose. And as a particular pleasure is found in anticipating the recurrence of sounds and quantities, all compositions that have this charm superadded, 130 whatever be their contents, *may* be entitled poems.

So much for the superficial *form*. A difference of object and contents supplies an additional ground of distinction. The immediate purpose may be the communication of truths; either of truth absolute and demonstrable, as in works of science; or 135 of facts experienced and recorded, as in history. Pleasure, and that of the highest and most permanent kind, may *result* from the *attainment* of the end; but it is not itself the immediate end. In other works the communication of pleasure may be the immediate purpose; and though truth, either moral or intel- 140 lectual, ought to be the *ultimate* end, yet this will distinguish

the character of the author, not the class to which the work belongs. Blest indeed is that state of society, in which the immediate purpose would be baffled by the perversion of the
145 proper ultimate end; in which no charm of diction or imagery could exempt the Bathyllus even of an Anacreon, or the Alexis of Virgil, from disgust and aversion!

But the communication of pleasure may be the immediate object of a work not metrically composed; and that object may
150 have been in a high degree attained, as in novels and romances. Would then the mere superaddition of metre, with or without rhyme, entitle *these* to the name of poems? The answer is, that nothing can permanently please, which does not contain in itself the reason why it is so, and not otherwise. If metre be
155 superadded, all other parts must be made consonant with it. They must be such, as to justify the perpetual and distinct attention to each part, which an exact correspondent recurrence of accent and sound are calculated to excite. The final definition then, so deduced, may be thus worded. A poem is that species
160 of composition, which is opposed to works of science, by proposing for its *immediate* object pleasure, not truth; and from all other species (having *this* object in common with it) it is discriminated by proposing to itself such delight from the *whole*, as is compatible with a distinct gratification from each com-
165 ponent *part*.

Controversy is not seldom excited in consequence of the disputants attaching each a different meaning to the same word; and in few instances has this been more striking, than in disputes concerning the present subject. If a man chooses to
170 call every composition a poem, which is rhyme, or measure, or both, I must leave his opinion uncontroverted. The distinction is at least competent to characterize the writer's intention. If it were subjoined, that the whole is likewise entertaining or affecting, as a tale, or as a series of interesting reflections, I of course
175 admit this as another fit ingredient of a poem, and an additional merit. But if the definition sought for be that of a *legitimate* poem, I answer, it must be one, the parts of which mutually support and explain each other; all in their proportion harmonizing with, and supporting the purpose and known
180 influences of metrical arrangement. The philosophic critics of

all ages coincide with the ultimate judgement of all countries, in equally denying the praises of a just poem, on the one hand, to a series of striking lines or distiches, each of which, absorbing the whole attention of the reader to itself, disjoins it from its context, and makes it a separate whole, instead of a harmoniz- 185 ing part; and on the other hand, to an unsustained composition, from which the reader collects rapidly the general result, unattracted by the component parts. The reader should be carried forward, not merely or chiefly by the mechanical impulse of curiosity, or by a restless desire to arrive at the final 190 solution; but by the pleasurable activity of mind excited by the attractions of the journey itself. Like the motion of a serpent, which the Egyptians made the emblem of intellectual power; or like the path of sound through the air; at every step he pauses and half recedes, and from the retrogressive movement 195 collects the force which again carries him onward. 'Praeci-pitandus est *liber* spiritus,' says Petronius Arbiter most happily. The epithet, *liber*, here balances the preceding verb; and it is not easy to conceive more meaning condensed in fewer words.

But if this should be admitted as a satisfactory character of a 200 poem, we have still to seek for a definition of poetry. The writings of PLATO, and Bishop TAYLOR, and the 'Theoria Sacra' of BURNET, furnish undeniable proofs that poetry of the highest kind may exist without metre, and even without the contra-distinguishing objects of a poem. The first chapter of 205 Isaiah (indeed a very large portion of the whole book) is poetry in the most emphatic sense; yet it would be not less irrational than strange to assert, that pleasure, and not truth, was the immediate object of the prophet. In short, whatever *specific* import we attach to the word, poetry, there will be found in- 210 volved in it, as a necessary consequence, that a poem of any length neither can be, nor ought to be, all poetry. Yet if a harmonious whole is to be produced, the remaining parts must be preserved *in keeping* with the poetry; and this can be no otherwise effected than by such a studied selection and arti- 215 ficial arrangement, as will partake of *one*, though not a *peculiar* property of poetry. And this again can be no other than the property of exciting a more continuous and equal attention than the language of prose aims at, whether colloquial or written.

220   My own conclusions on the nature of poetry, in the strict use of the word, have been in part anticipated in the preceding disquisition on the fancy and imagination. What is poetry? is so nearly the same question with, what is a poet? that the answer to the one is involved in the solution of the other. For
225 it is a distinction resulting from the poetic genius itself, which sustains and modifies the images, thoughts, and emotions of the poet's own mind.

   The poet, described in *ideal* perfection, brings the whole soul of man into activity, with the subordination of its faculties to
230 each other, according to their relative worth and dignity. He diffuses a tone and spirit of unity, that blends, and (as it were) *fuses*, each into each, by that synthetic and magical power, to which we have exclusively appropriated the name of imagination. This power, first put in action by the will and understand-
235 ing, and retained under their irremissive, though gentle and unnoticed, control (*laxis effertur habenis*) reveals itself in the balance or reconciliation of opposite or discordant qualities: of sameness, with difference; of the general, with the concrete; the idea, with the image; the individual, with the representa-
240 tive; the sense of novelty and freshness, with old and familiar objects; a more than usual state of emotion, with more than usual order; judgment ever awake and steady self-possession, with enthusiasm and feeling profound or vehement; and while it blends and harmonizes the natural and the artificial, still
245 subordinates art to nature; the manner to the matter; and our admiration of the poet to our sympathy with the poetry. 'Doubtless,' as Sir John Davies observes of the soul (and his words may with slight alteration be applied, and even more appropriately, to the poetic IMAGINATION)

250   'Doubtless this could not be, but that she turns
        Bodies to spirit by sublimation strange,
      As fire converts to fire the things it burns,
        As we our food into our nature change.

      From their gross matter she abstracts their forms,
255   And draws a kind of quintessence from things;
      Which to her proper nature she transforms,
        To bear them light on her celestial wings.

Thus does she, when from individual states
She doth abstract the universal kinds;
Which then re-clothed in divers names and fates   260
Steal access through our senses to our minds.'

Finally, GOOD SENSE is the BODY of poetic genius, FANCY its
DRAPERY, MOTION its LIFE, and IMAGINATION the SOUL that is
everywhere, and in each; and forms all into one graceful and
intelligent whole.   265

CHAPTER XVII

Examination of the tenets peculiar to Mr. Wordsworth—Rustic
life (above all, *low* and rustic life) especially unfavourable to the
formation of a human diction—The *best* parts of language the
product of philosophers, not of clowns or shepherds—Poetry
essentially ideal and generic—The language of Milton as much
the language of *real* life, yea, incomparably more so than that of
the cottager.

As far then as Mr. Wordsworth in his preface contended, and
most ably contended, for a reformation in our poetic diction,
as far as he has evinced the truth of passion, and the *dramatic*
propriety of those figures and metaphors in the original poets,
which, stripped of their justifying reasons, and converted into 270
mere artifices of connection or ornament, constitute the characteristic falsity in the poetic style of the moderns; and as far as he
has, with equal acuteness and clearness, pointed out the process
by which this change was effected, and the resemblances between that state into which the reader's mind is thrown by the 275
pleasurable confusion of thought from an unaccustomed train
of words and images; and that state which is induced by the
natural language of impassioned feeling; he undertook a useful
task, and deserves all praise, both for the attempt and for the
execution. The provocations to this remonstrance in behalf of 280
truth and nature were still of perpetual recurrence before and
after the publication of this preface. I cannot likewise but add,
that the comparison of such poems of merit, as have been given
to the public within the last ten or twelve years, with the
majority of those produced previously to the appearance of 285

that preface, leave no doubt on my mind, that Mr. Wordsworth is fully justified in believing his efforts to have been by
no means ineffectual. Not only in the verses of those who have
professed their admiration of his genius, but even of those who
290 have distinguished themselves by hostility to his theory, and
depreciation of his writings, are the impressions of his principles
plainly visible. It is possible, that with these principles others
may have been blended, which are not equally evident; and
some which are unsteady and subvertible from the narrowness
295 or imperfection of their basis. But it is more than possible, that
these errors of defect or exaggeration, by kindling and feeding
the controversy, may have conduced not only to the wider
propagation of the accompanying truths, but that, by their
frequent presentation to the mind in an excited state, they may
300 have won for them a more permanent and practical result.
A man will borrow a part from his opponent the more easily,
if he feels himself justified in continuing to reject a part. While
there remain important points in which he can still feel himself
in the right, in which he still finds firm footing for continued
305 resistance, he will gradually adopt those opinions, which were
the least remote from his own convictions, as not less congruous with his own theory than with that which he reprobates.
In like manner with a kind of instinctive prudence, he will
abandon by little and little his weakest posts, till at length he
310 seems to forget that they had ever belonged to him, or affects to
consider them at most as accidental and 'petty annexments,'
the removal of which leaves the citadel unhurt and unen-
dangered.

My own differences from certain supposed parts of Mr.
315 Wordsworth's theory ground themselves on the assumption,
that his words had been rightly interpreted, as purporting that
the proper diction for poetry in general consists altogether in a
language taken, with due exceptions, from the mouths of men
in real life, a language which actually constitutes the natural
320 conversation of men under the influence of natural feelings.
My objection is, first, that in *any* sense this rule is applicable
only to *certain* classes of poetry; secondly, that even to these
classes it is not applicable, except in such a sense, as hath
never by any one (as far as I know or have read) been denied

or doubted; and lastly, that as far as, and in that degree in 325
which it is *practicable,* yet as a *rule* it is useless, if not injurious,
and therefore either need not, or ought not to be practised.
The poet informs his reader, that he had generally chosen *low
and rustic* life; but not *as* low and rustic, or in order to repeat
that pleasure of doubtful moral effect, which persons of 330
elevated rank and of superior refinement oftentimes derive from
a happy *imitation* of the rude unpolished manners and discourse
of their inferiors. For the pleasure so derived may be traced to
three exciting causes. The first is the naturalness, in *fact,* of the
things represented. The second is the apparent naturalness of 335
the *representation,* as raised and qualified by an imperceptible
infusion of the author's own knowledge and talent, which
infusion does, indeed, constitute it an *imitation* as distinguished
from a mere *copy.* The third cause may be found in the reader's
conscious feeling of his superiority awakened by the contrast 340
presented to him; even as for the same purpose the kings and
great barons of yore retained sometimes *actual* clowns and fools,
but more frequently shrewd and witty fellows in that *character.*
These, however, were not Mr. Wordsworth's objects. *He* chose
low and rustic life, 'because in that condition the essential pas- 345
sions of the heart find a better soil, in which they can attain
their maturity, are less under restraint, and speak a plainer and
more emphatic language; because in that condition of life our
elementary feelings coexist in a state of greater simplicity, and
consequently may be more accurately contemplated, and 350
more forcibly communicated; because the manners of rural life
germinate from those elementary feelings; and from the necessary character of rural occupations are more easily comprehended, and are more durable; and lastly, because in that
condition the passions of men are incorporated with the beauti- 355
ful and permanent forms of nature.'

Now it is clear to me, that in the most interesting of the
poems, in which the author is more or less dramatic, as 'the
Brothers,' 'Michael,' 'Ruth,' 'the Mad Mother,' &c., the
persons introduced are by no means taken *from low or rustic life* 360
in the common acceptation of those words; and it is not less
clear, that the sentiments and language, as far as they can be
conceived to have been really transferred from the minds and

conversation of such persons, are attributable to causes and
365 circumstances not necessarily connected with 'their occupations
and abode.' The thoughts, feelings, language, and manners of
the shepherd-farmers in the vales of Cumberland and West-
moreland, as far as they are actually adopted in those poems,
may be accounted for from causes, which will and do produce
370 the same results in *every* state of life, whether in town or country.
As the two principal I rank that INDEPENDENCE, which raises a
man above servitude, or daily toil for the profit of others, yet
not above the necessity of industry and a frugal simplicity of
domestic life; and the accompanying unambitious, but solid
375 and religious, EDUCATION, which has rendered few books
familiar, but the Bible, and the liturgy or hymn book. To this
latter cause, indeed, which is so far *accidental*, that it is the
blessing of particular countries and a particular age, not the
product of particular places or employments, the poet owes
380 the show of probability, that his personages might really feel,
think, and talk with any tolerable resemblance to his representation. It is an excellent remark of Dr. Henry More's, (*Enthusias-
mus Triumphatus*, Sec. XXXV.), that 'a man of confined education, but of good parts, by constant reading of the Bible will
385 naturally form a more winning and commanding rhetoric
than those that are learned; the intermixture of tongues and of
artificial phrases debasing *their* style.'

It is, moreover, to be considered that to the formation of
healthy feelings, and a reflecting mind, *negations* involve im-
390 pediments not less formidable than sophistication and vicious
intermixture. I am convinced, that for the human soul to
prosper in rustic life a certain vantage-ground is pre-requisite.
It is not every man that is likely to be improved by a country
life or by country labours. Education, or original sensibility,
395 or both, must pre-exist, if the changes, forms, and incidents of
nature are to prove a sufficient stimulant. And where these are
not sufficient, the mind contracts and hardens by want of
stimulants: and the man becomes selfish, sensual, gross, and
hard-hearted. Let the management of the POOR LAWS in
400 Liverpool, Manchester, or Bristol be compared with the
ordinary dispensation of the poor rates in agricultural villages,
where the *farmers* are the overseers and guardians of the poor.

If my own experience have not been particularly unfortunate, as well as that of the many respectable country clergymen with whom I have conversed on the subject, the result would 405 engender more than scepticism concerning the desirable influences of low and rustic life in and for itself. Whatever may be concluded on the other side, from the stronger local attachments and enterprising spirit of the Swiss, and other mountaineers, applies to a particular mode of pastoral life, under 410 forms of property that permit and beget manners truly republican, not to rustic life in general, or to the absence of artificial cultivation. On the contrary the mountaineers, whose manners have been so often eulogized, are in general better educated and greater readers than men of equal rank elsewhere. But 415 where this is not the case, as among the peasantry of North Wales, the ancient mountains, with all their terrors and all their glories, are pictures to the blind, and music to the deaf.

I should not have entered so much into detail upon this passage, but here seems to be the point, to which all the lines 420 of difference converge as to their source and centre. (I mean, as far as, and in whatever respect, my poetic creed *does* differ from the doctrines promulged in this preface.) I adopt with full faith the principle of Aristotle, that poetry as poetry is essentially[1] *ideal*, that it avoids and excludes all *accident*; that its 425

---

[1] Say not that I am recommending abstractions; for these class-characteristics which constitute the instructiveness of a character, are so modified and particularized in each person of the Shakespearean Drama, that life itself does not excite more distinctly that sense of individuality which belongs to real existence. Paradoxical as it may sound, one of the essential properties of Geometry is not less essential to dramatic excellence; and Aristotle has accordingly required of the poet an involution of the universal in the individual. The chief differences are, that in Geometry it is the universal truth, which is uppermost in the consciousness; in poetry the individual form, in which the truth is clothed. With the ancients, and not less with the elder dramatists of England and France, both comedy and tragedy were considered as kinds of poetry. They neither sought in comedy to make us laugh merely; much less to make us laugh by wry faces, accidents of jargon, *slang* phrases for the day, or the clothing of commonplace morals drawn from the shops or mechanic occupations of their characters. Nor did they condescend in tragedy to wheedle away the applause of the spectators, by representing before them facsimiles of their own mean selves in all their existing meanness, or to work on the sluggish sympathies by a pathos not a whit more respectable than the maudlin tears of drunkenness.

apparent individualities of rank, character, or occupation must
be *representative* of a class; and that the *persons* of poetry must be
clothed with *generic* attributes, with the *common* attributes of the
class: not with such as one gifted individual might *possibly*
430 possess, but such as from his situation it is most probable
beforehand that he *would* possess. If my premises are right and
my deductions legitimate, it follows that there can be no *poetic*
medium between the swains of Theocritus and those of an
imaginary golden age.

435   The characters of the vicar and the shepherd-mariner in the
poem of 'THE BROTHERS,' that of the shepherd of Greenhead
Ghyll in the 'MICHAEL,' have all the verisimilitude and representative quality, that the purposes of poetry can require.
They are persons of a known and abiding class, and their
440 manners and sentiments the natural product of circumstances
common to the class. Take 'MICHAEL' for instance:

       'An old man stout of heart, and strong of limb:
       His bodily frame had been from youth to age
       Of an unusual strength: his mind was keen,
445   Intense, and frugal, apt for all affairs,
       And in his shepherd's calling he was prompt
       And watchful more than ordinary men.
       Hence he had learnt the meaning of all winds,
       Of blasts of every tone; and oftentimes
450   When others heeded not, he heard the South
       Make subterraneous music, like the noise
       Of bagpipers on distant Highland hills.
       The shepherd, at such warning, of his flock
       Bethought him, and he to himself would say,
455   The winds are now devising work for me!
       And truly at all times the storm, that drives
       The traveller to a shelter, summon'd him
       Up to the mountains. He had been alone
       Amid the heart of many thousand mists,

Their tragic scenes were meant to *affect* us indeed; but yet within the
bounds of pleasure, and in union with the activity both of our understanding
and imagination. They wished to transport the mind to a sense of its
possible greatness, and to implant the germs of that greatness, during the
temporary oblivion of the worthless 'thing we are,' and of the peculiar state
in which each man *happens* to be, suspending our individual recollections
and lulling them to sleep amid the music of nobler thoughts.

FRIEND, Pages 251, 252.

That came to him and left him on the heights. 460
So liv'd he, till his eightieth year was pass'd.
And grossly that man errs, who should suppose
That the green valleys, and the streams and rocks,
Were things indifferent to the shepherd's thoughts.
Fields, where with cheerful spirits he had breath'd 465
The common air; the hills, which he so oft
Had climb'd with vigorous steps; which had impress'd
So many incidents upon his mind
Of hardship, skill or courage, joy or fear;
Which, like a book, preserved the memory 470
Of the dumb animals, whom he had sav'd,
Had fed or shelter'd, linking to such acts,
So grateful in themselves, the certainty
Of honourable gain; these fields, these hills
Which were his living being, even more 475
Than his own blood—what could they less? had laid
Strong hold on his affections, were to him
A pleasurable feeling of blind love,
The pleasure which there is in life itself.'

On the other hand, in the poems which are pitched at a lower 480
note, as the 'HARRY GILL,' 'IDIOT BOY,' the *feelings* are those of
human nature in general; though the poet has judiciously laid
the *scene* in the country, in order to place *himself* in the vicinity
of interesting images, without the necessity of ascribing a sentimental perception of their beauty to the persons of his drama. 485
In the 'Idiot Boy,' indeed, the mother's character is not so
much a real and native product of a 'situation where the
essential passions of the heart find a better soil, in which they
can attain their maturity and speak a plainer and more
emphatic language,' as it is an impersonation of an instinct 490
abandoned by judgement. Hence the two following charges
seem to me not wholly groundless: at least, they are the only
plausible objections, which I have heard to that fine poem.
The one is, that the author has not, in the poem itself, taken
sufficient care to preclude from the reader's fancy the disgusting 495
images of *ordinary morbid idiocy*, which yet it was by no means
his intention to represent. He has even by the 'burr, burr, burr,'
uncounteracted by any preceding description of the boy's
beauty, assisted in recalling them. The other is, that the idiocy
of the *boy* is so evenly balanced by the folly of the *mother*, as to 500

present to the general reader rather a laughable burlesque on
the blindness of anile dotage, than an analytic display of
maternal affection in its ordinary workings.

In the "Thorn" the poet himself acknowledges in a note the
505 necessity of an introductory poem, in which he should have
portrayed the character of the person from whom the words
of the poem are supposed to proceed: a superstitious man
moderately imaginative, of slow faculties and deep feelings,
'a captain of a small trading vessel, for example, who, being
510 past the middle age of life, had retired upon an annuity, or
small independent income, to some village or country town of
which he was not a native, or in which he had not been
accustomed to live. Such men having nothing to do become
credulous and talkative from indolence.' But in a poem, still
515 more in a lyric poem (and the NURSE in Shakespeare's *Romeo
and Juliet* alone prevents me from extending the remark even to
dramatic *poetry*, if indeed the Nurse itself can be deemed altogether a case in point) it is not possible to imitate truly a dull
and garrulous discourser, without repeating the effects of dull-
520 ness and garrulity. However this may be, I dare assert, that the
parts (and these form the far larger portion of the whole) which
might as well or still better have proceeded from the poet's own
imagination, and have been spoken in his own character, are
those which have given, and which will continue to give,
525 universal delight; and that the passages exclusively appropriate
to the supposed narrator, such as the last couplet of the third
stanza;[1] the seven last lines of the tenth;[2] and the five following

---

[1] 'I've measured it from side to side;
'Tis three feet long, and two feet wide.'

[2] 'Nay, rack your brain—'tis all in vain,
I'll tell you every thing I know;
But to the Thorn, and to the Pond
Which is a little step beyond,
I wish that you would go:
Perhaps when you are at the place,
You something of her tale may trace.

I'll give you the best help I can:
Before you up the mountain go,
Up to the dreary mountain-top,
I'll tell you all I know.

stanzas, with the exception of the four admirable lines at the
commencement of the fourteenth, are felt by many unpre-
judiced and unsophisticated hearts, as sudden and unpleasant 530
sinkings from the height to which the poet had previously

'Tis now some two-and-twenty years
Since she (her name is Martha Ray)
Gave, with a maiden's true good will,
Her company to Stephen Hill;
And she was blithe and gay,
And she was happy, happy still
Whene'er she thought of Stephen Hill.

And they had fix'd the wedding-day,
The morning that must wed them both;
But Stephen to another maid
Had sworn another oath;
And, with this other maid, to church
Unthinking Stephen went—
Poor Martha! on that woeful day
A pang of pitiless dismay
Into her soul was sent;
A fire was kindled in her breast,
Which might not burn itself to rest.

They say, full six months after this,
While yet the summer leaves were green,
She to the mountain-top would go,
And there was often seen.
'Tis said a child was in her womb,
As now to any eye was plain;
She was with child, and she was mad;
Yet often she was sober sad
From her exceeding pain.
Oh me! ten thousand times I'd rather
That he had died, that cruel father!

*   *   *   *   *
*   *   *   *   *
*   *   *   *   *
*   *   *   *   *

Last Christmas when we talked of this,
Old farmer Simpson did maintain,
That in her womb the infant wrought
About its mother's heart, and brought
Her senses back again:
And, when at last her time drew near,
Her looks were calm, her senses clear.

lifted them, and to which he again re-elevates both himself
and his reader.

If then I am compelled to doubt the theory, by which the
535 choice of *characters* was to be directed, not only *a priori*, from
grounds of reason, but both from the few instances in which the
poet himself *need* be supposed to have been governed by it,
and from the comparative inferiority of those instances; still
more must I hesitate in my assent to the sentence which im-
540 mediately follows the former citation; and which I can neither
admit as particular fact, or as general rule. 'The language too
of these men is adopted (purified indeed from what appear to
be its real defects, from all lasting and rational causes of dislike
or disgust) because such men hourly communicate with the
545 best objects from which the best part of language is originally
derived; and because, from their rank in society and the sameness and narrow circle of their intercourse, being less under
the action of social vanity, they convey their feelings and notions
in simple and unelaborated expressions.' To this I reply; that
550 a rustic's language, purified from all provincialism and grossness, and so far reconstructed as to be made consistent with
the rules of grammar (which are in essence no other than the
laws of universal logic, applied to psychological materials)
will not differ from the language of any other man of common
555 sense, however learned or refined he may be, except as far as
the notions, which the rustic has to convey, are fewer and more
indiscriminate. This will become still clearer, if we add the
consideration (equally important though less obvious) that the
rustic, from the more imperfect development of his faculties,
560 and from the lower state of their cultivation, aims almost solely

---

No more I know, I wish I did,
And I would tell it all to you:
For what became of this poor child
    There's none that ever knew:
And if a child was born or no,
There's no one that could ever tell;
And if 'twas born alive or dead,
There's no one knows, as I have said:
But some remember well,
That Martha Ray about this time
Would up the mountain often climb.'

to convey *insulated facts*, either those of his scanty experience or his traditional belief; while the educated man chiefly seeks to discover and express those *connections* of things, or those relative *bearings* of fact to fact, from which some more or less general law is deducible. For *facts* are valuable to a wise man, chiefly 565 as they lead to the discovery of the indwelling *law*, which is the true *being* of things, the sole solution of their modes of existence, and in the knowledge of which consists our dignity and our power.

As little can I agree with the assertion, that from the objects with 570 which the rustic hourly communicates the best part of language is formed. For first, if to communicate with an object implies such an acquaintance with it, as renders it capable of being discriminately reflected on; the distinct knowledge of an uneducated rustic would furnish a very scanty vocabulary. 575 The few things, and modes of action, requisite for his bodily conveniences, would alone be individualized; while all the rest of nature would be expressed by a small number of confused general terms. Secondly, I deny that the words and combinations of words derived from the objects, with which 580 the rustic is familiar, whether with distinct or confused knowledge, can be justly said to form the *best* part of language. It is more than probable, that many classes of the brute creation possess discriminating sounds, by which they can convey to each other notices of such objects as concern their food, shelter, 585 or safety. Yet we hesitate to call the aggregate of such sounds a language, otherwise than metaphorically. The best part of human language, properly so called, is derived from reflection on the acts of the mind itself. It is formed by a voluntary appropriation of fixed symbols to internal acts, to processes 590 and results of imagination, the greater part of which have no place in the consciousness of uneducated man; though in civilized society, by imitation and passive remembrance of what they hear from their religious instructors and other superiors, the most uneducated share in the harvest which they 595 neither sowed or reaped. If the history of the phrases in hourly currency among our peasants were traced, a person not previously aware of the fact would be surprised at finding so large a number, which three or four centuries ago were the exclusive

HECT

600 property of the universities and the schools; and, at the commencement of the Reformation, had been transferred from the school to the pulpit, and thus gradually passed into common life. The extreme difficulty, and often the impossibility, of finding words for the simplest moral and intellectual processes 605 of the languages of uncivilized tribes has proved perhaps the weightiest obstacle to the progress of our most zealous and adroit missionaries. Yet these tribes are surrounded by the same nature as our peasants are; but in still more impressive forms; and they are, moreover, obliged to *particularize* many 610 more of them. When, therefore, Mr. Wordsworth adds, 'accordingly, such a language' (meaning, as before, the language of rustic life purified from provincialism) 'arising out of repeated experience and regular feelings, is a more permanent, and a far more philosophical language, than that which is 615 frequently substituted for it by poets, who think they are conferring honour upon themselves and their art in proportion as they indulge in arbitrary and capricious habits of expression:' it may be answered, that the language, which he has in view, can be attributed to rustics with no greater right, than 620 the style of Hooker or Bacon to Tom Brown or Sir Roger L'Estrange. Doubtless, if what is peculiar to each were omitted in each, the result must needs be the same. Further, that the poet, who uses an illogical diction, or a style fitted to excite only the low and changeable pleasure of wonder by means of 625 groundless novelty, substitutes a language of *folly* and *vanity*, not for that of the *rustic*, but for that of *good sense* and *natural feeling*.

Here let me be permitted to remind the reader, that the positions, which I controvert, are contained in the sentences— 630 '*a selection of the* REAL *language of men;*'—'*the language of these men*' (i.e. men in low and rustic life) *has been adopted.*' '*I propose to myself to imitate, and, as far as is possible, to adopt the very language of men.*' '*Between the language of prose and that of metrical composition, there neither is, nor can be any essential difference.*' It is against these 635 exclusively that my opposition is directed.

I object, in the very first instance, to an equivocation in the use of the word 'real'. Every man's language varies, according to the extent of his knowledge, the activity of his faculties, and the depth or quickness of his feelings. Every man's language has, first, its *individualities*; secondly, the common properties 640 of the *class* to which he belongs; and thirdly, words and phrases of *universal* use. The language of Hooker, Bacon, Bishop Taylor, and Burke differs from the common language of the learned class only by the superior number and novelty of the thoughts and relations which they had to convey. The language of 645 Algernon Sidney differs not at all from that, which every well-educated gentleman would wish to write, and (with due allowances for the undeliberateness, and less connected train, of thinking natural and proper to conversation) such as he would wish to talk. Neither one nor the other differ half so much 650 from the general language of cultivated society, as the language of Mr. Wordsworth's homeliest composition differs from that of a common peasant. For 'real' therefore, we must substitute *ordinary*, or *lingua communis*. And this, we have proved, is no more to be found in the phraseology of low and rustic life than 655 in that of any other class. Omit the peculiarities of each, and the result of course must be common to all. And assuredly the omissions and changes to be made in the language of rustics, before it could be transferred to any species of poem, except the drama or other professed imitation, are at least as numerous 660 and weighty, as would be required in adapting to the same purpose the ordinary language of tradesmen and manufacturers. Not to mention, that the language so highly extolled by Mr. Wordsworth varies in every county, nay in every village, according to the accidental character of the clergyman, the 665 existence or non-existence of schools; or even, perhaps, as the exciseman, publican, or barber, happen to be, or not to be, zealous politicians, and readers of the weekly newspaper *pro bono publico*. Anterior to cultivation, the *lingua communis* of every country, as Dante has well observed, exists everywhere in 670 parts, and no where as a whole.

Neither is the case rendered at all more tenable by the addition of the words, *in a state of excitement*. For the nature of a man's words, where he is strongly affected by joy, grief, or anger, must necessarily depend on the number and quality of 675 the general truths, conceptions and images, and of the words expressing them, with which his mind had been previously

stored. For the property of passion is not to *create*; but to set in
increased activity. At least, whatever new connections of
680 thoughts or images, or (which is equally, if not more than
equally, the appropriate effect of strong excitement) whatever
generalizations of truth or experience, the heat of passion may
produce; yet the terms of their conveyance must have pre-existed
in his former conversations, and are only collected and crowded
685 together by the unusual stimulation. It is indeed very possible
to adopt in a poem the unmeaning repetitions, habitual
phrases, and other blank counters, which an unfurnished or
confused understanding interposes at short intervals, in order
to keep hold of his subject, which is still slipping from him, and
690 to give him time for recollection; or in mere aid of vacancy, as
in the scanty companies of a country stage the same player
pops backwards and forwards, in order to prevent the appearance of empty spaces, in the procession of Macbeth, or Henry
VIIIth. But what assistance to the poet, or ornament to the
695 poem, these can supply, I am at a loss to conjecture. Nothing
assuredly can differ either in origin or in mode more widely
from the *apparent* tautologies of intense and turbulent feeling, in
which the passion is greater and of longer endurance than to
be exhausted or satisfied by a single representation of the
700 image or incident exciting it. Such repetitions I admit to be a
beauty of the highest kind; as illustrated by Mr. Wordsworth
himself from the song of Deborah. '*At her feet he bowed, he fell,
he lay down; at her feet he bowed, he fell; where he bowed, there he fell
down dead.*'

CHAPTER XVIII

Language of metrical composition, why and wherein essentially
different from that of prose—Origin and elements of metre—
Its necessary consequences, and the conditions thereby imposed
on the metrical writer in the choice of his diction.

705 I CONCLUDE, therefore, that the attempt is impracticable;
and that, were it not impracticable, it would still be useless.
For the very power of making the selection implies the previous
possession of the language selected. Or where can the poet have
lived? And by what rules could he direct his choice, which

would not have enabled him to select and arrange his words by 710
the light of his own judgement? We do not adopt the language
of a class by the mere adoption of such words exclusively, as
that class would use, or at least understand; but likewise by
following the *order*, in which the words of such men are wont to
succeed each other. Now this order, in the intercourse of un- 715
educated men, is distinguished from the diction of their
superiors in knowledge and power, by the greater *disjunction*
and *separation* in the component parts of that, whatever it be,
which they wish to communicate. There is a want of that
prospectiveness of mind, that *surview*, which enables a man to 720
foresee the whole of what he is to convey, appertaining to any
one point; and by this means so to subordinate and arrange
the different parts according to their relative importance, as to
convey it at once, and as an organized whole.

Now I will take the first stanza, on which I have chanced to 725
open, in the Lyrical Ballads. It is one the most simple and
the least peculiar in its language.

> 'In distant countries have I been,
> And yet I have not often seen
> A healthy man, a man full grown,   730
> Weep in the public roads alone.
> But such a one, on English ground,
> And in the broad highway, I met;
> Along the broad highway he came,
> His cheeks with tears were wet: 735
> Sturdy he seem'd, though he was sad;
> And in his arms a lamb he had.'

The words here are doubtless such as are current in all ranks
of life; and of course not less so in the hamlet and cottage than
in the shop, manufactory, college, or palace. But is this the 740
order, in which the rustic would have placed the words? I am
grievously deceived, if the following less *compact* mode of com-
mencing the same tale be not a far more faithful copy. 'I
have been in many parts, far and near, and I don't know
that I ever saw before a man crying by himself in the public 745
road; a grown man I mean, that was neither sick nor hurt,'
&c., &c. But when I turn to the following stanza in 'The
Thorn':

'At all times of the day and night
750   This wretched woman thither goes,
And she is known to every star,
And every wind that blows:
And there, beside the thorn, she sits,
When the blue day-light's in the skies;
755   And when the whirlwind's on the hill,
Or frosty air is keen and still;
And to herself she cries,
Oh misery! Oh misery!
Oh woe is me! Oh misery!'

760 and compare this with the language of ordinary men; or with that which I can conceive at all likely to proceed, in *real* life, from *such* a narrator, as is supposed in the note to the poem; compare it either in the succession of the images or of the sentences; I am reminded of the sublime prayer and hymn of 765 praise, which MILTON, in opposition to an established liturgy, presents as a fair *specimen* of common extemporary devotion, and such as we might expect to hear from every self-inspired minister of a conventicle! And I reflect with delight, how little a mere theory, though of his own workmanship, interferes with 770 the processes of genuine imagination in a man of true poetic genius, who possesses, as Mr. Wordsworth, if ever man did, most assuredly does possess,

'THE VISION AND THE FACULTY DIVINE.'

One point then alone remains, but that the most important; 775 its examination having been, indeed, my chief inducement for the preceding inquisition. '*There neither is nor can be any essential difference between the language of prose and metrical composition.*' Such is Mr. Wordsworth's assertion. Now prose itself, at least in all argumentative and consecutive works, differs, and 780 ought to differ, from the language of conversation; even as[1]

---

[1] It is no less an error in teachers, than a torment to the poor children, to enforce the necessity of reading as they would talk. In order to cure them of *singing* as it is called, that is, of too great a difference, the child is made to repeat the words with his eyes from off the book; and then, indeed, his tones resemble talking, as far as his fears, tears and trembling will permit. But as soon as his eye is again directed to the printed page, the spell begins anew; for an instinctive sense tells the child's feelings, that to utter its own momentary thoughts, and to recite the written thoughts of another, as of

reading ought to differ from talking. Unless therefore the difference denied be that of the mere *words*, as materials common to all styles of writing, and not of the *style* itself in the universally admitted sense of the term, it might be naturally presumed that there must exist a still greater between the 785 ordonnance of poetic composition and that of prose, than is expected to distinguish prose from ordinary conversation.

There are not, indeed, examples wanting in the history of literature, of apparent paradoxes that have summoned the public wonder as new and startling truths, but which on 790 examination have shrunk into tame and harmless *truisms*; as the eyes of a cat, seen in the dark, have been mistaken for flames of fire. But Mr. Wordsworth is among the last men, to whom a delusion of this kind would be attributed by anyone, who had enjoyed the slightest opportunity of understanding his mind and 795 character. Where an objection has been anticipated by such an author as natural, his answer to it must needs be interpreted in some sense which either is, or has been, or is capable of being controverted. My object then must be to discover some other meaning for the term '*essential difference*' in this 800 place, exclusive of the indistinction and community of the words themselves. For whether there ought to exist a class of words in the English, in any degree resembling the poetic dialect of the Greek and Italian, is a question of very subordinate importance. The number of such words would be small indeed, in 805

---

another, and a far wiser than himself, are two widely different things; and as the two acts are accompanied with widely different feelings, so must they justify different modes of enunciation. Joseph Lancaster, among his other sophistications of the excellent Dr. Bell's invaluable system, cures this fault of *singing*, by hanging fetters and chains on the child, to the music of which one of his school-fellows, who walks before, dolefully chants out the child's last speech and confession, birth, parentage, and education. And this soul-benumbing ignominy, this unholy and heart-hardening burlesque on the last fearful infliction of outraged law, in pronouncing the sentence to which the stern and familiarized judge not seldom bursts into tears, has been extolled as a happy and ingenious method of remedying —what? and how?—why, one extreme in order to introduce another, scarce less distant from good sense, and certainly likely to have worse moral effects, by enforcing a semblance of petulant ease and self-sufficiency, in repression, and possible after-perversion of the natural feelings. I have to beg Dr. Bell's pardon for this connection of the two names, but he knows that contrast is no less powerful a cause of association than likeness.

our language; and even in the Italian and Greek, they consist
not so much of different words, as of slight differences in the
forms of declining and conjugating the same words; forms,
doubtless, which having been, at some period more or less
810 remote, the common grammatic flexions of some tribe or
province, had been accidentally appropriated to poetry by the
general admiration of certain master intellects, the first established lights of inspiration, to whom that dialect happened to
be native.

815   Essence, in its primary signification, means the principle of
individuation, the inmost principle of the possibility of any thing,
as that particular thing. It is equivalent to the *idea* of a thing,
when ever we use the word, idea, with philosophic precision.
Existence, on the other hand, is distinguished from essence, by
820 the superinduction of *reality*. Thus we speak of the essence, and
essential properties of a circle; but we do not therefore assert,
that any thing, which really exists, is mathematically circular.
Thus too, without any tautology we contend for the *existence* of
the Supreme Being; that is, for a reality correspondent to the
825 idea. There is, next, a *secondary* use of the word essence, in which
it signifies the point or ground of contra-distinction between
two modifications of the same substance or subject. Thus we
should be allowed to say, that the style of architecture of
Westminster Abbey is *essentially* different from that of St. Paul's,
830 even though both had been built with blocks cut into the same
form, and from the same quarry. Only in this latter sense of the
term must it have been *denied* by Mr. Wordsworth (for in this
sense alone is it *affirmed* by the general opinion) that the language of poetry (i.e. the formal construction, or architecture, of
835 the words and phrases) is *essentially* different from that of prose.
Now the burthen of the proof lies with the oppugner, not with
the supporters of the common belief. Mr. Wordsworth, in
consequence, assigns as the proof of his position, 'that not only
the language of a large portion of every good poem, even of the
840 most elevated character, must necessarily, except with reference
to the metre, in no respect differ from that of good prose, but
likewise that some of the most interesting parts of the best
poems will be found to be strictly the language of prose, when
prose is well written. The truth of this assertion might be

demonstrated by innumerable passages from almost all the 845
poetical writings even of Milton himself.' He then quotes
Gray's sonnet—

'In vain to me the smiling mornings shine,
And reddening Phoebus lifts his golden fire;
The birds in vain their amorous descant join, 850
Or cheerful fields resume their green attire.
These ears, alas! for other notes repine;
A different object do these eyes require;
My lonely anguish melts no heart but mine;
And in my breast the imperfect joys expire. 855
Yet morning smiles the busy race to cheer,
And newborn pleasure brings to happier men:
The fields to all their wonted tribute bear,
To warm their little loves the birds complain.
I fruitless mourn to him that cannot hear, 860
And weep the more because I weep in vain,'

and adds the following remark:—'It will easily be perceived,
that the only part of this Sonnet, which is of any value, is the
lines printed in italics. It is equally obvious, that, except in
the rhyme, and in the use of the single word "fruitless" for 865
"fruitlessly", which is so far a defect, the language of these
lines does in no respect differ from that of prose.'

An idealist defending his system by the fact, that when asleep
we often believe ourselves awake, was well answered by his
plain neighbour, 'Ah, but when awake do we ever believe 870
ourselves asleep?'—Things identical must be convertible.
The preceding passage seems to rest on a similar sophism. For
the question is not, whether there may not occur in prose an
order of words, which would be equally proper in a poem; nor
whether there are not beautiful lines and sentences of frequent 875
occurrence in good poems, which would be equally becoming
as well as beautiful in good prose; for neither the one nor the
other has ever been either denied or doubted by any one. The
true question must be, whether there are not modes of expression, a *construction*, and an *order* of sentences, which are in their 880
fit and natural place in a serious prose composition, but would
be disproportionate and heterogeneous in metrical poetry;
and, vice versa, whether in the language of a serious poem
there may not be an arrangement both of words and sentences,

885 and a use and selection of (what are called) *figures of speech*, both
as to their kind, their frequency, and their occasions, which on
a subject of equal weight would be vicious and alien in correct
and manly prose. I contend that in both cases this unfitness of
each for the place of the other frequently will and ought to
890 exist.

And first from the *origin* of metre. This I would trace to the
balance in the mind effected by that spontaneous effort which
strives to hold in check the workings of passion. It might be
easily explained likewise in what manner this salutary antagon-
895 ism is assisted by the very state, which it counteracts; and how
this balance of antagonists became organized into *metre* (in the
usual acceptation of that term) by a supervening act of the will
and judgement, consciously and for the foreseen purpose of
pleasure. Assuming these principles, as the data of our argu-
900 ment, we deduce from them two legitimate conditions, which
the critic is entitled to expect in every metrical work. First, that,
as the *elements* of metre owe their existence to a state of increased
excitement, so the metre itself should be accompanied by the
natural language of excitement. Secondly, that as these ele-
905 ments are formed into metre *artificially*, by a *voluntary* act, with
the design and for the purpose of blending *delight* with emotion,
so the traces of present *volition* should throughout the metrical
language be proportionately discernible. Now these two conditions must be reconciled and co-present. There must be not
910 only a partnership, but a union; an interpenetration of passion
and of will, of *spontaneous* impulse and of *voluntary* purpose.
Again, this union can be manifested only in a frequency of
forms and figures of speech (originally the offspring of passion,
but now the adopted children of power) greater than would be
915 desired or endured, where the emotion is not voluntarily encouraged and kept up for the sake of that pleasure, which such
emotion, so tempered and mastered by the will, is found capable
of communciating. It not only dictates, but of itself tends to
produce, a more frequent employment of picturesque and
920 vivifying language, than would be natural in any other case,
in which there did not exist, as there does in the present, a
previous and well understood, though tacit, *compact* between the
poet and his reader, that the latter is entitled to expect, and the

former bound to supply, this species and degree of pleasurable excitement. We may in some measure apply to this union the 925 answer of POLIXENES, in *The Winter's Tale*, to PERDITA's neglect of the streaked gilly-flowers, because she had heard it said,

> 'There is an art which, in their piedness, shares
> With great creating nature.
>   *Pol*: Say there be;   930
> Yet nature is made better by no mean,
> But nature makes that mean; so, ev'n that art,
> Which, you say, adds to nature, is an art,
> That nature makes. You see, sweet maid, we marry
> *A gentler scion to the wildest stock*;   935
> And make conceive a bark of ruder kind
> By bud of nobler race. This is an art,
> Which does mend nature—change it rather; but
> The art itself is nature.'

Secondly, I argue from the EFFECTS of metre. As far as metre 940 acts in and for itself, it tends to increase the vivacity and susceptibility both of the general feelings and of the attention. This effect it produces by the continued excitement of surprise, and by the quick reciprocations of curiosity still gratified and still re-excited, which are too slight indeed to be at any one moment 945 objects of distinct consciousness, yet become considerable in their aggregate influence. As a medicated atmosphere, or as wine during animated conversation; they act powerfully, though themselves unnoticed. Where, therefore, correspondent food and appropriate matter are not provided for the attention 950 and feelings thus roused, there must needs be a disappointment felt; like that of leaping in the dark from the last step of a staircase, when we had prepared our muscles for a leap of three or four.

The discussion on the powers of metre in the preface is highly ingenious and touches at all points on truth. But I cannot 955 find any statement of its powers considered abstractly and separately. On the contrary Mr. Wordsworth seems always to estimate metre by the powers, which it exerts during (and, as I think, in *consequence of*) its combination with other elements of poetry. Thus the previous difficulty is left unanswered, *what* 960 the elements are, with which it must be combined in order to produce its own effects to any pleasurable purpose. Double and tri-syllable rhymes, indeed, form a lower species of wit, and,

attended to exclusively for their own sake, may become a
965 source of momentary amusement; as in poor Smart's distich to
the Welsh Squire who had promised him a hare:

'Tell me, thou son of great Cadwallader!
Hast sent the hare? or hast thou swallow'd her?'

But for any *poetic* purposes, metre resembles (if the aptness of
970 the simile may excuse its meanness) yeast, worthless or dis-
agreeable by itself, but giving vivacity and spirit to the liquor
with which it is proportionally combined.

The reference to the 'Children in the Wood,' by no means
satisfies my judgement. We all willingly throw ourselves back
975 for awhile into the feelings of our childhood. This ballad, therefore, we read under such recollections of our own childish
feelings, as would equally endear to us poems, which Mr.
Wordsworth himself would regard as faulty in the opposite
extreme of gaudy and technical ornament. Before the invention
980 of printing, and in a still greater degree, before the introduction
of writing, metre, especially *alliterative* metre (whether alliterative at the beginning of the words, as in 'Piers Plowman,' or at
the end as in rhymes) possessed an independent value as assisting the recollection, and consequently the preservation, of *any*
985 series of truths or incidents. But I am not convinced by the
collation of facts, that the 'Children in the Wood' owes either
its preservation, or its popularity, to its metrical form. Mr.
Marshal's repository affords a number of tales in prose inferior
in pathos and general merit, some of as old a date, and many as
990 widely popular. 'TOM HICKATHRIFT,' 'JACK THE GIANT-KILLER,'
'GOODY TWO-SHOES,' and 'LITTLE RED RIDING-HOOD' are formidable rivals. And that they have continued in prose, cannot be
fairly explained by the assumption, that the comparative meanness of their thoughts and images precluded even the humblest
995 forms of metre. The scene of GOODY TWO-SHOES in the church
is perfectly susceptible of metrical narration; and, among the
θαύματα θαυμαστότατα even of the present age, I do not recollect a more astonishing image than that of the '*whole rookery,
that flew out of the giant's beard*,' scared by the tremendous voice,
1000 with which this monster answered the challenge of the heroic
TOM HICKATHRIFT!

If from these we turn to compositions universally, and independently of all early associations, beloved and admired; would 'THE MARIA,' 'THE MONK,' or 'THE POOR MAN'S ASS' of Sterne, be read with more delight, or have a better chance of immortality, had they without any change in the diction been composed in rhyme, than in their present state? If I am not grossly mistaken, the general reply would be in the negative. Nay, I will confess, that, in Mr. Wordworth's own volumes, the 'ANECDOTE FOR FATHERS,' 'SIMON LEE,' 'ALICE FELL,' 'THE BEGGARS,' and 'THE SAILOR'S MOTHER,' notwithstanding the beauties which are to be found in each of them where the poet interposes the music of his own thoughts, would have been more delightful to me in prose, told and managed, as by Mr. Wordsworth they would have been, in a moral essay, or pedestrian tour.

Metre in itself is simply a stimulant of the attention, and therefore excites the question: Why is the attention to be thus stimulated? Now the question cannot be answered by the pleasure of the metre itself: for this we have shown to be *conditional*, and dependent on the appropriateness of the thoughts and expressions, to which the metrical form is superadded. Neither can I conceive any other answer that can be rationally given, short of this: I write in metre, because I am about to use a language different from that of prose. Besides, where the language is not such, how interesting soever the reflections are, that are capable of being drawn by a philosophic mind from the thoughts or incidents of the poem, the metre itself must often become feeble. Take the last three stanzas of 'THE SAILOR'S MOTHER,' for instance. If I could for a moment abstract from the effect produced on the author's feelings, as a man, by the incident at the time of its real occurrence, I would dare appeal to his own judgement, whether in the *metre* itself he found a sufficient reason for *their* being written *metrically*?

'And, thus continuing, she said,
I had a son, who many a day
Sailed on the seas; but he is dead;
In Denmark he was cast away:
And I have travelled far as Hull, to see
What clothes he might have left, or other property.

The bird and cage they both were his:
'Twas my son's bird; and neat and trim
He kept it: many voyages
This singing-bird hath gone with him;
1045   When last he sailed he left the bird behind;
As it might be, perhaps, from bodings of his mind.

He to a fellow-lodger's care
Had left it, to be watched and fed,
Till he came back again; and there
1050   I found it when my son was dead;
And how, God help me for my little wit!
I trail it with me, Sir! he took so much delight in it.'

If disproportioning the emphasis we read these stanzas so as
to make the rhymes perceptible, even *tri-syllable* rhymes could
1055 scarcely produce an equal sense of oddity and strangeness, as
we feel here in finding *rhymes at all* in sentences so exclusively
colloquial. I would further ask whether, but for that visionary
state, into which the figure of the woman and the susceptibility
of his own genius had placed the poet's imagination, (a state,
1060 which spreads its influence and colouring over all, that co-exists
with the exciting cause, and in which

'The simplest, and the most familiar things
Gain a strange power of spreading awe around[1] them,')

I would ask the poet whether he would not have felt an abrupt
1065 downfall in these verses from the preceding stanza?

'The ancient spirit is not dead;
Old times, thought I, are breathing there;
Proud was I that my country bred
Such strength, a dignity so fair:
1070   She begged an alms, like one in poor estate;
I looked at her again, nor did my pride abate.'

[1] Altered from the description of Night-Mair in the 'Remorse.'
'Oh Heaven! 'twas frightful! Now run down and stared at
By hideous shapes that cannot be remembered;
Now seeing nothing and imagining nothing;
But only being afraid—stifled with fear!
While every goodly or familiar form
Had a strange power of spreading terror round me!'
N.B. Though Shakespeare has, for his own *all-justifying* purposes, intro-
duced the Night-*Mare* with her own foals, yet Mair means a Sister, or
perhaps a Hag.

It must not be omitted, and is besides worthy of notice, that those stanzas furnish the only fair instance that I have been able to discover in all Mr. Wordsworth's writings, of an *actual* adoption, or true imitation, of the *real* and *very* language of 1075 *low and rustic life*, freed from provincialisms.

Thirdly, I deduce the position from all the causes elsewhere assigned, which render metre the proper form of poetry, and poetry imperfect and defective without metre. Metre therefore having been connected with *poetry* most often and by a peculiar 1080 fitness, whatever else is combined with *metre* must, though it be not itself *essentially* poetic, have nevertheless some property in common with poetry, as an intermedium of affinity, a sort (if I may dare borrow a well-known phrase from technical chemistry) of *mordant* between it and the superadded metre. 1085 Now poetry, Mr. Wordsworth truly affirms, does always imply PASSION: which word must be here understood in its general sense, as an excited state of the feelings and faculties. And as every passion has its proper pulse, so will it likewise have its characteristic modes of expression. But where there exists that 1090 degree of genius and talent which entitles a writer to aim at the honours of a poet, the very *act* of poetic composition *itself* is, and is *allowed* to imply and to produce, an unusual state of excitement, which of course justifies and demands a correspondent difference of language, as truly, though not perhaps in 1095 as marked a degree, as the excitement of love, fear, rage, or jealousy. The vividness of the descriptions or declamations in DONNE or DRYDEN is as much and as often derived from the force and fervour of the describer, as from the reflections, forms or incidents, which constitute their subject and materials. The 1100 wheels take fire from the mere rapidity of their motion. To what extent, and under what modifications, this may be admitted to act, I shall attempt to define in an after remark on Mr. Wordsworth's reply to this objection, or rather on his objection to this reply, as already anticipated in his preface.   1105

Fourthly, and as intimately connected with this, if not the same argument in a more general form, I adduce the high spiritual instinct of the human being impelling us to seek unity by harmonious adjustment, and thus establishing the principle, that *all* the parts of an organized whole must be assimilated to 1110

the more *important* and *essential* parts. This and the preceding arguments may be strengthened by the reflection, that the composition of a poem is among the *imitative* arts; and that imitation, as opposed to copying, consists either in the inter-
1115 fusion of the SAME throughout the radically DIFFERENT, or of the different throughout a base radically the same.

Lastly, I appeal to the practice of the best poets, of all countries and in all ages, as *authorizing* the opinion (*deduced* from all the foregoing) that in every import of the word
1120 ESSENTIAL, which would not here involve a mere truism, there may be, is, and ought to be an *essential* difference between the language of prose and of metrical composition.

In Mr. Wordsworth's criticism of GRAY's Sonnet, the readers' sympathy with his praise or blame of the different parts is
1125 taken for granted rather perhaps too easily. He has not, at least, attempted to win or compel it by argumentative analysis. In *my* conception at least, the lines rejected as of no value do, with the exception of the two first, differ as much and as little from the language of common life, as those which he has
1130 printed in italics as possessing genuine excellence. Of the five lines thus honourably distinguished, two of them differ from prose, even more widely than the lines which either precede or follow, in the *position* of the words.

> '*A different object do these eyes require;*
1135 > My lonely anguish melts no heart but mine;
> *And in my breast the imperfect joys expire.*'

But were it otherwise, what would this prove, but a truth, of which no man ever doubted? Videlicet, that there are sentences, which would be equally in their place both in verse
1140 and prose. Assuredly it does not prove the point, which alone requires proof; namely, that there are not passages, which would suit the one and not suit the other. The first line of this sonnet is distinguished from the ordinary language of men by the epithet to morning. (For we will set aside, at present, the
1145 consideration, that the particular word '*smiling*' is hackneyed and (as it involves a sort of personification) not quite congruous with the common and material attribute of *shining*.) And, doubtless, this adjunction of epithets for the purpose of

additional description, where no particular attention is demanded for the quality of the thing, would be noticed as giving 1150 a poetic cast to a man's conversation. Should the sportsman exclaim, '*Come boys! the rosy morning calls you up,*' he will be supposed to have some song in his head. But no one suspects this, when he says, 'A wet morning shall not confine us to our beds.' This then is either a defect in poetry, or it is not. Who- 1155 ever should decide in the *affirmative*, I would request him to reperuse any one poem of any confessedly great poet from Homer to Milton, or from Aeschylus to Shakespeare; and to strike out (in thought I mean) every instance of this kind. If the number of these fancied erasures did not startle him; or if he 1160 continued to deem the work improved by their total omission; he must advance reasons of no ordinary strength and evidence, reasons grounded in the essence of human nature. Otherwise, I should not hesitate to consider him as a man not so much *proof against* all authority, as *dead to* it. 1165

The second line,

'And reddening Phoebus lifts his golden fire;'

has indeed almost as many faults as words. But then it is a bad line, not because the language is distinct from that of prose; but because it conveys incongruous images, because it con- 1170 founds the cause and the effect, the real *thing* with the personified *representative* of the thing; in short, because it differs from the language of GOOD SENSE! That the 'Phoebus' is hackneyed, and a school-boy image, is an *accidental* fault, dependent on the age in which the author wrote, and not deduced from the nature 1175 of the thing. That it is part of an exploded mythology, is an objection more deeply grounded. Yet when the torch of ancient learning was re-kindled, so cheering were its beams, that our eldest poets, cut off by Christianity from all *accredited* machinery, and deprived of all *acknowledged* guardians and symbols of 1180 the great objects of nature,[1] were naturally induced to adopt, as a *poetic* language, those fabulous personages, those forms of

---

[1] But still more by the mechanical system of philosophy which has needlessly infected our theological opinions, and teaching us to consider the world in its relation to God, as of a building to its mason, leaves the idea of omnipresence a mere abstract notion in the state-room of our reason.

the supernatural in nature, which had given them such dear delight in the poems of their great masters. Nay, even at this 1185 day what scholar of genial taste will not so far sympathize with them, as to read with pleasure in PETRARCH, CHAUCER, or SPENSER, what he would perhaps condemn as puerile in a modern poet?

*   *   *   *   *

To sum up the whole in one sentence. When a poem, or a part 1190 of a poem, shall be adduced, which is evidently vicious in the figures and contexture of its style, yet for the condemnation oi which no reason can be assigned, except that it differs from the style in which men actually converse, then, and not till then, can I hold this theory to be either plausible, or practicable, or 1195 capable of furnishing either rule, guidance, or precaution, that might not, more easily and more safely, as well as more naturally, have been deduced in the author's own mind from considerations of grammar, logic, and the truth and nature of things, confirmed by the authority of works, whose fame is 1200 not of ONE country nor of ONE age.

PERCY BYSSHE SHELLEY

A Defence of Poetry

ACCORDING to one mode of regarding those two classes of mental action, which are called reason and imagination, the former may be considered as mind contemplating the relations borne by one thought to another, however produced; and the latter, as mind acting upon those thoughts so as to colour them 5 with its own light, and composing from them, as from elements, other thoughts, each containing within itself the principle of its own integrity. The one is the τὸ ποιεῖν, or the principle of synthesis, and has for its object those forms which are common to universal nature and existence itself; the other is the τὸ 10 λογίζειν, or principle of analysis, and its action regards the relations of things, simply as relations; considering thoughts, not in their integral unity, but as the algebraical representations which conduct to certain general results. Reason is the enumeration of quantities already known; imagination is the 15 perception of the value of those quantities, both separately and as a whole. Reason respects the differences, and imagination the similitudes of things. Reason is to imagination as the instrument to the agent, as the body to the spirit, as the shadow to the substance.   20

Poetry, in a general sense, may be defined to be 'the expression of the imagination': and poetry is connate with the origin of man. Man is an instrument over which a series of external and internal impressions are driven, like the alternations of an ever-changing wind over an Aeolian lyre, which move it by 25 their motion to ever-changing melody. But there is a principle within the human being, and perhaps within all sentient beings, which acts otherwise than in a lyre, and produces not melody alone, but harmony, by an internal adjustment of the sounds and motions thus excited to the impressions which excite them. 30 It is as if the lyre could accommodate its chords to the motions

225

of that which strikes them, in a determined proportion of
sound; even as the musician can accommodate his voice to the
sound of the lyre. A child at play by itself will express its delight
35 by its voice and motions; and every inflection of tone and every
gesture will bear exact relation to a corresponding antitype in
the pleasurable impressions which awakened it; it will be the
reflected image of that impression; and as the lyre trembles and
sounds after the wind has died away, so the child seeks, by
40 prolonging in its voice and motions the duration of the effect,
to prolong also a consciousness of the cause. In relation to the
objects which delight a child, these expressions are what poetry
is to higher objects. The savage (for the savage is to ages what
the child is to years) expresses the emotions produced in him by
45 surrounding objects in a similar manner; and language and
gesture, together with plastic or pictorial imitation, become
the image of the combined effect of those objects and his apprehension of them. Man in society, with all his passions and his
pleasures, next becomes the object of the passions and pleasures
50 of man; an additional class of emotions produces an augmented
treasure of expression; and language, gesture, and the imitative
arts, become at once the representation and the medium, the
pencil and the picture, the chisel and the statue, the chord and
the harmony. The social sympathies, or those laws from which,
55 as from its elements, society results, begin to develop themselves
from the moment that two human beings co-exist; the future is
contained within the present as the plant within the seed; and
equality, diversity, unity, contrast, mutual dependence, become
the principles alone capable of affording the motives according
60 to which the will of a social being is determined to action,
inasmuch as he is social; and constitute pleasure in sensation,
virtue in sentiment, beauty in art, truth in reasoning, and love
in the intercourse of kind. Hence men, even in the infancy of
society, observe a certain order of their words and actions,
65 distinct from that of the objects and the impressions represented
by them, all expression being subject to the laws of that from
which it proceeds. But let us dismiss those more general considerations which might involve an inquiry into the principles
of society itself, and restrict our view to the manner in which
70 the imagination is expressed upon its forms.

In the youth of the world, men dance and sing and imitate
natural objects, observing in these actions, as in all others, a
certain rhythm or order. And, although all men observe a
similar, they observe not the same order in the motions of the
dance, in the melody of the song, in the combinations of lan- 75
guage, in the series of their imitations of natural objects. For
there is a certain order or rhythm belonging to each of these
classes of mimetic representation, from which the hearer and the
spectator receive an intenser and purer pleasure than from any
other: the sense of an approximation to this order has been 80
called taste by modern writers. Every man in the infancy of art,
observes an order which approximates more or less closely to
that from which this highest delight results: but the diversity
is not sufficiently marked, as that its gradations should be
sensible, except in those instances where the predominance of 85
this faculty of approximation to the beautiful (for so we may be
permitted to name the relation between this highest pleasure
and its cause) is very great. Those in whom it exists to excess are
poets, in the most universal sense of the word; and the pleasure
resulting from the manner in which they express the influence 90
of society or nature upon their own minds, communicates
itself to others, and gathers a sort of reduplication from the
community. Their language is vitally metaphorical; that is,
it marks the before unapprehended relations of things and
perpetuates their apprehension, until words, which represent 95
them, become, through time, signs for portions or classes of
thoughts instead of pictures of integral thoughts; and then, if
no new poets should arise to create afresh the associations which
have been thus disorganized, language will be dead to all the
nobler purposes of human intercourse. These similitudes or 100
relations are finely said by Lord Bacon to be 'the same footsteps of nature impressed upon the various subjects of the
world'—and he considers the faculty which perceives them as
the storehouse of axioms common to all knowledge. In the
infancy of society every author is necessarily a poet, because 105
language itself is poetry; and to be a poet is to apprehend the
true and the beautiful, in a word, the good which exists in the
relation, subsisting, first between existence and perception, and
secondly between perception and expression. Every original

110 language near to its source is in itself the chaos of a cyclic poem: the copiousness of lexicography and the distinctions of grammar are the works of a later age, and are merely the catalogue and the form of the creations of poetry.

But poets, or those who imagine and express this indestruc-
115 tible order, are not only the authors of language and of music, of the dance, and architecture, and statuary, and painting; they are the institutors of laws, and the founders of civil society, and the inventors of the arts of life, and the teachers, who draw into a certain propinquity with the beautiful and the true, that
120 partial apprehension of the agencies of the invisible world which is called religion. Hence all original religions are allegorical, or susceptible of allegory, and, like Janus, have a double face of false and true. Poets, according to the circumstances of the age and nation in which they appeared, were called, in the
125 earlier epochs of the world, legislators or prophets: a poet essentially comprises and unites both these characters. For he not only beholds intensely the present as it is, and discovers those laws according to which present things ought to be ordered, but he beholds the future in the present, and his
130 thoughts are the germs of the flower and the fruit of latest time. Not that I assert poets to be prophets in the gross sense of the word, or that they can foretell the form as surely as they foreknow the spirit of events: such is the pretence of superstition, which would make poetry an attribute of prophecy, rather
135 than prophecy an attribute of poetry. A poet participates in the eternal, the infinite, and the one; as far as relates to his conceptions, time and place and number are not. The grammatical forms which express the moods of time, and the difference of persons, and the distinction of place, are convert-
140 ible with respect to the highest poetry without injuring it as poetry; and the choruses of Aeschylus, and the *Book of Job*, and Dante's *Paradise*, would afford, more than any other writings, examples of this fact, if the limits of this essay did not forbid citation. The creations of sculpture, painting, and music, are
145 illustrations still more decisive.

Language, colour, form, and religious and civil habits of action, are all the instruments and materials of poetry; they may be called poetry by that figure of speech which considers

the effect as a synonym of the cause. But poetry in a more
restricted sense expresses those arrangements of language, and 150
especially metrical language, which are created by that imperial faculty, whose throne is curtained within the invisible
nature of man. And this springs from the nature itself of
language, which is a more direct representation of the actions
and passions of our internal being, and is susceptible of more 155
various and delicate combinations, than colour, form, or
motion, and is more plastic and obedient to the control of that
faculty of which it is the creation. For language is arbitrarily
produced by the imagination, and has relation to thoughts
alone; but all other materials, instruments, and conditions of 160
art, have relations among each other, which limit and inter-
pose between conception and expression. The former is as a
mirror which reflects, the latter as a cloud which enfeebles, the
light of which both are mediums of communication. Hence
the fame of sculptors, painters, and musicians, although the 165
intrinsic powers of the great masters of these arts may yield in
no degree to that of those who have employed language as the
hieroglyphic of their thoughts, has never equalled that of poets
in the restricted sense of the term; as two performers of equal
skill will produce unequal effects from a guitar and a harp. 170
The fame of legislators and founders of religions, so long as
their institutions last, alone seems to exceed that of poets in the
restricted sense; but it can scarcely be a question, whether, if
we deduct the celebrity which their flattery of the gross opinions
of the vulgar usually conciliates, together with that which be- 175
longed to them in their higher character of poets, any excess
will remain.

We have thus circumscribed the word poetry within the
limits of that art which is the most familiar and the most
perfect expression of the faculty itself. It is necessary, however, 180
to make the circle still narrower, and to determine the distinction between measured and unmeasured language; for the
popular division into prose and verse is inadmissible in accurate
philosophy.

Sounds as well as thoughts have relation both between each 185
other and towards that which they represent, and a perception
of the order of those relations has always been found connected

with a perception of the order of the relations of thoughts. Hence the language of poets has ever affected a sort of uniform
190 and harmonious recurrence of sound, without which it were not poetry, and which is scarcely less indispensable to the communication of its influence, than the words themselves, without reference to that peculiar order. Hence the vanity of translation; it were as wise to cast a violet into a crucible that
195 you might discover the formal principles of its colour and odour, as seek to transfuse from one language into another the creations of a poet. The plant must spring again from its seed, or it will bear no flower—and this is the burthen of the curse of Babel.

200   An observation of the regular mode of the recurrence of harmony in the language of poetical minds, together with its relation to music, produced metre, or a certain system of traditional forms of harmony and language. Yet it is by no means essential that a poet should accommodate his language to this
205 traditional form, so that the harmony, which is its spirit, be observed. The practice is indeed convenient and popular, and to be preferred, especially in such composition as includes much action: but every great poet must inevitably innovate upon the example of his predecessors in the exact structure of his peculiar
210 versification. The distinction between poets and prose writers is a vulgar error. The distinction between philosophers and poets has been anticipated. Plato was essentially a poet—the truth and splendour of his imagery, and the melody of his language, are the most intense that it is possible to conceive. He
215 rejected the harmony of the epic, dramatic, and lyrical forms, because he sought to kindle a harmony in thoughts divested of shape and action, and he forbore to invent any regular plan of rhythm which would include, under determinate forms, the varied pauses of his style. Cicero sought to imitate the cadence
220 of his periods, but with little success. Lord Bacon was a poet. His language has a sweet and majestic rhythm, which satisfies the sense, no less than the almost superhuman wisdom of his philosophy satisfies the intellect; it is a strain which distends, and then bursts the circumference of the reader's mind, and
225 pours itself forth together with it into the universal element with which it has perpetual sympathy. All the authors of

revolutions in opinion are not only necessarily poets as they are inventors, nor even as their words unveil the permanent analogy of things by images which participate in the life of truth; but as their periods are harmonious and rhythmical, and contain 230 in themselves the elements of verse; being the echo of the eternal music. Nor are those supreme poets, who have employed traditional forms of rhythm on account of the form and action of their subjects, less capable of perceiving and teaching the truth of things, than those who have omitted that form. 235 Shakespeare, Dante, and Milton (to confine ourselves to modern writers) are philosophers of the very loftiest power.

A poem is the very image of life expressed in its eternal truth. There is this difference between a story and a poem, that a story is a catalogue of detached facts, which have no 240 other connection than time, place, circumstance, cause and effect; the other is the creation of actions according to the unchangeable forms of human nature, as existing in the mind of the Creator, which is itself the image of all other minds. The one is partial, and applies only to a definite period of time, and 245 a certain combination of events which can never again recur; the other is universal, and contains within itself the germ of a relation to whatever motives or actions have place in the possible varieties of human nature. Time, which destroys the beauty and the use of the story of particular facts, stripped of 250 the poetry which should invest them, augments that of poetry, and for ever develops new and wonderful applications of the eternal truth which it contains. Hence epitomes have been called the moths of just history; they eat out the poetry of it. A story of particular facts is as a mirror which obscures and 255 distorts that which should be beautiful: poetry is a mirror which makes beautiful that which is distorted.

The parts of a composition may be poetical, without the composition as a whole being a poem. A single sentence may be considered as a whole, though it may be found in the midst of a 260 series of unassimilated portions; a single word even may be a spark of inextinguishable thought. And thus all the great historians, Herodotus, Plutarch, Livy, were poets; and although the plan of these writers, especially that of Livy, restrained them from developing this faculty in its highest degree, they 265 made copious and ample amends for their subjection, by filling all the interstices of their subjects with living images.

Having determined what is poetry, and who are poets, let us proceed to estimate its effects upon society.

270 Poetry is ever accompanied with pleasure: all spirits on which it falls open themselves to receive the wisdom which is mingled with its delight. In the infancy of the world, neither poets themselves nor their auditors are fully aware of the excellence of poetry: for it acts in a divine and unapprehended manner,
275 beyond and above consciousness; and it is reserved for future generations to contemplate and measure the mighty cause and effect in all the strength and splendour of their union. Even in modern times, no living poet ever arrived at the fulness of his fame; the jury which sits in judgement upon a poet, belonging
280 as he does to all time, must be composed of his peers: it must be impanelled by Time from the selectest of the wise of many generations. A poet is a nightingale, who sits in darkness and sings to cheer its own solitude with sweet sounds; his auditors are as men entranced by the melody of an unseen musician,
285 who feel that they are moved and softened, yet know not whence or why. The poems of Homer and his contemporaries were the delight of infant Greece; they were the elements of that social system which is the column upon which all succeeding civilization has reposed. Homer embodied the ideal per-
290 fection of his age in human character; nor can we doubt that those who read his verses were awakened to an ambition of becoming like to Achilles, Hector, and Ulysses: the truth and beauty of friendship, patriotism, and persevering devotion to an object, were unveiled to their depths in these immortal
295 creations: the sentiments of the auditors must have been refined and enlarged by a sympathy with such great and lovely impersonations, until from admiring they imitated, and from imitation they identified themselves with the objects of their admiration. Nor let it be objected, that these characters are
300 remote from moral perfection, and that they are by no means to be considered as edifying patterns for general imitation. Every epoch, under names more or less specious, has deified its peculiar errors; Revenge is the naked idol of the worship of a semi-barbarous age; and Self-deceit is the veiled image of

unknown evil, before which luxury and satiety lie prostrate. 305
But a poet considers the vices of his contemporaries as the temporary dress in which his creations must be arrayed, and which
cover without concealing the eternal proportions of their
beauty. An epic or dramatic personage is understood to wear
them around his soul, as he may the ancient armour or modern 310
uniform around his body; whilst it is easy to conceive a dress
more graceful than either. The beauty of the internal nature
cannot be so far concealed by its accidental vesture, but that
the spirit of its form shall communicate itself to the very
disguise, and indicate the shape it hides from the manner in 315
which it is worn. A majestic form and graceful motions will
express themselves through the most barbarous and tasteless
costume. Few poets of the highest class have chosen to exhibit
the beauty of their conceptions in its naked truth and splendour;
and it is doubtful whether the alloy of costume, habit, &c., be 320
not necessary to temper this planetary music for mortal ears.

The whole objection, however, of the immorality of poetry
rests upon a misconception of the manner in which poetry acts
to produce the moral improvement of man. Ethical science
arranges the elements which poetry has created, and propounds 325
schemes and proposes examples of civil and domestic life:
nor is it for want of admirable doctrines that men hate, and
despise, and censure, and deceive, and subjugate one another.
But poetry acts in another and diviner manner. It awakens and
enlarges the mind itself by rendering it the receptacle of a 330
thousand unapprehended combinations of thought. Poetry
lifts the veil from the hidden beauty of the world, and makes
familiar objects be as if they were not familiar; it reproduces all
that it represents, and the impersonations clothed in its Elysian
light stand thenceforward in the minds of those who have once 335
contemplated them, as memorials of that gentle and exalted
content which extends itself over all thoughts and actions with
which it co-exists. The great secret of morals is love; or a going
out of our own nature, and an identification of ourselves with
the beautiful which exists in thought, action, or person, not our 340
own. A man, to be greatly good, must imagine intensely and
comprehensively; he must put himself in the place of another
and of many others; the pains and pleasures of his species must

become his own. The great instrument of moral good is the
345 imagination; and poetry administers to the effect by acting
upon the cause. Poetry enlarges the circumference of the
imagination by replenishing it with thoughts of ever new
delight, which have the power of attracting and assimilating
to their own nature all other thoughts, and which form new
350 intervals and interstices whose void for ever craves fresh food.
Poetry strengthens the faculty which is the organ of the moral
nature of man, in the same manner as exercise strengthens a
limb. A poet therefore would do ill to embody his own conceptions of right and wrong, which are usually those of his
355 place and time, in his poetical creations, which participate in
neither. By this assumption of the inferior office of interpreting
the effect, in which perhaps after all he might acquit himself
but imperfectly, he would resign a glory in the participation of
the cause. There was little danger that Homer, or any of the
360 eternal poets, should have so far misunderstood themselves as
to have abdicated this throne of their widest dominion. Those
in whom the poetical faculty, though great, is less intense, as
Euripides, Lucan, Tasso, Spenser, have frequently affected a
moral aim, and the effect of their poetry is diminished in exact
365 proportion to the degree in which they compel us to advert to
this purpose.

Homer and the cyclic poets were followed at a certain
interval by the dramatic and lyrical poets of Athens, who flourished contemporaneously with all that is most perfect in the
370 kindred expressions of the poetical faculty; architecture,
painting, music, the dance, sculpture, philosophy, and we may
add, the forms of civil life. For although the scheme of Athenian
society was deformed by many imperfections which the poetry
existing in chivalry and Christianity has erased from the habits
375 and institutions of modern Europe; yet never at any other
period has so much energy, beauty, and virtue been developed;
never was blind strength and stubborn form so disciplined and
rendered subject to the will of man, or that will less repugnant
to the dictates of the beautiful and the true, as during the cen-
380 tury which preceded the death of Socrates. Of no other epoch
in the history of our species have we records and fragments
stamped so visibly with the image of the divinity in man. But

it is poetry alone, in form, in action, and in language, which has rendered this epoch memorable above all others, and the store-house of examples to everlasting time. For written poetry 385 existed at that epoch simultaneously with the other arts, and it is an idle inquiry to demand which gave and which received the light, which all, as from a common focus, have scattered over the darkest periods of succeeding time. We know no more of cause and effect than a constant conjunction of events: 390 poetry is ever found to co-exist with whatever other arts con-tribute to the happiness and perfection of man. I appeal to what has already been established to distinguish between the cause and the effect.

It was at the period here adverted to, that the drama had 395 its birth; and however a succeeding writer may have equalled or surpassed those few great specimens of the Athenian drama which have been preserved to us, it is indisputable that the art itself never was understood or practised according to the true philosophy of it, as at Athens. For the Athenians employed 400 language, action, music, painting, the dance, and religious institutions, to produce a common effect in the representation of the highest idealisms of passion and of power; each division in the art was made perfect in its kind by artists of the most consummate skill, and was disciplined into a beautiful propor- 405 tion and unity one towards the other. On the modern stage a few only of the elements capable of expressing the image of the poet's conception are employed at once. We have tragedy without music and dancing; and music and dancing without the highest impersonations of which they are the fit accompani- 410 ment, and both without religion and solemnity. Religious institution has indeed been usually banished from the stage. Our system of divesting the actor's face of a mask, on which the many expressions appropriated to his dramatic character might be moulded into one permanent and unchanging expres- 415 sion, is favourable only to a partial and inharmonious effect; it is fit for nothing but a monologue, where all the attention may be directed to some great master of ideal mimicry. The modern practice of blending comedy with tragedy, though liable to great abuse in point of practice, is undoubtedly an 420 extension of the dramatic circle; but the comedy should be as in

King Lear, universal, ideal, and sublime. It is perhaps the
intervention of this principle which determines the balance in
favour of *King Lear* against the *Oedipus Tyrannus* or the *Aga-*
425 *memnon*, or, if you will, the trilogies with which they are connected; unless the intense power of the choral poetry, especially
that of the latter, should be considered as restoring the equili-
brium. *King Lear*, if it can sustain this comparison, may be
judged to be the most perfect specimen of the dramatic art
430 existing in the world; in spite of the narrow conditions to which
the poet was subjected by the ignorance of the philosophy of
the drama which has prevailed in modern Europe. Calderon,
in his religious Autos, has attempted to fulfil some of the high
conditions of dramatic representation neglected by Shakes-
435 peare; such as the establishing a relation between the drama
and religion, and the accommodating them to music and dancing; but he omits the observation of conditions still more
important, and more is lost than gained by the substitution of
the rigidly-defined and ever-repeated idealisms of a distorted
440 superstition for the living impersonations of the truth of human
passion.

But I digress.—The connection of scenic exhibitions with the
improvement or corruption of the manners of men has been
universally recognised: in other words, the presence or absence
445 of poetry in its most perfect and universal form, has been found
to be connected with good and evil in conduct or habit. The
corruption which has been imputed to the drama as an effect,
begins, when the poetry employed in its constitution ends: I
appeal to the history of manners whether the periods of the
450 growth of the one and the decline of the other have not corresponded with an exactness equal to any example of moral
cause and effect.

The drama at Athens, or wheresoever else it may have
approached to its perfection, ever co-existed with the moral
455 and intellectual greatness of the age. The tragedies of the Athenian poets are as mirrors in which the spectator beholds himself,
under a thin disguise of circumstance, stripped of all but that
ideal perfection and energy which every one feels to be the
internal type of all that he loves, admires, and would become.
460 The imagination is enlarged by a sympathy with pains and

passions so mighty, that they distend in their conception the capacity of that by which they are conceived; the good affections are strengthened by pity, indignation, terror and sorrow; and an exalted calm is prolonged from the satiety of this high exercise of them into the tumult of familiar life: even crime is 465 disarmed of half its horror and all its contagion by being represented as the fatal consequence of the unfathomable agencies of nature; error is thus divested of its wilfulness; men can no longer cherish it as the creation of their choice. In the drama of the highest order there is little food for censure or 470 hatred; it teaches rather self-knowledge and self-respect. Neither the eye nor the mind can see itself, unless reflected upon that which it resembles. The drama, so long as it continues to express poetry, is a prismatic and many-sided mirror, which collects the brightest rays of human nature and divides and 475 reproduces them from the simplicity of their elementary forms, and touches them with majesty and beauty, and multiplies all that it reflects, and endows it with the power of propagating its like wherever it may fall.

But in periods of the decay of social life, the drama sym- 480 pathizes with that decay. Tragedy becomes a cold imitation of the form of the great masterpieces of antiquity, divested of all harmonious accompaniment of the kindred arts; and often the very form misunderstood, or a weak attempt to teach certain doctrines, which the writer considers as moral truths; and which 485 are usually no more than specious flatteries of some gross vice or weakness, with which the author, in common with his auditors, are infected. Hence what has been called the classical and domestic drama. Addison's *Cato* is a specimen of the one; and would it were not superfluous to cite examples of the other! 490 To such purposes poetry cannot be made subservient. Poetry is a sword of lightning, ever unsheathed, which consumes the scabbard that would contain it. And thus we observe that all dramatic writings of this nature are unimaginative in a singular degree; they affect sentiment and passion, which, divested of 495 imagination, are other names for caprice and appetite. The period in our own history of the grossest degradation of the drama is the reign of Charles II, when all forms in which poetry had been accustomed to be expressed became hymns to the

500 triumph of kingly power over liberty and virtue. Milton stood
alone illuminating an age unworthy of him. At such periods the
calculating principle pervades all the forms of dramatic exhibition, and poetry ceases to be expressed upon them. Comedy
loses its ideal universality: wit succeeds to humour; we laugh
505 from self-complacency and triumph, instead of pleasure;
malignity, sarcasm, and contempt, succeed to sympathetic
merriment; we hardly laugh, but we smile. Obscenity, which is
ever blasphemy against the divine beauty in life, becomes, from
the very veil which it assumes, more active if less disgusting: it
510 is a monster for which the corruption of society for ever brings
forth new food, which it devours in secret.

The drama being that form under which a greater number of
modes of expression of poetry are susceptible of being combined
than any other, the connection of poetry and social good is
515 more observable in the drama than in whatever other form.
And it is indisputable that the highest perfection of human
society has ever corresponded with the highest dramatic excellence; and that the corruption or the extinction of the drama
in a nation where it has once flourished, is a mark of a corrup-
520 tion of manners, and an extinction of the energies which sustain
the soul of social life. But, as Machiavelli says of political
institutions, that life may be preserved and renewed, if men
should arise capable of bringing back the drama to its principles. And this is true with respect to poetry in its most
525 extended sense: all language, institution and form, require not
only to be produced but to be sustained: the office and character of a poet participates in the divine nature as regards
providence, no less than as regards creation.

Civil war, the spoils of Asia, and the fatal predominance first
530 of the Macedonian, and then of the Roman arms, were so many
symbols of the extinction or suspension of the creative faculty
in Greece. The bucolic writers, who found patronage under the
lettered tyrants of Sicily and Egypt, were the latest representatives of its most glorious reign. Their poetry is intensely melodi-
535 ous; like the odour of the tuberose, it overcomes and sickens the
spirit with excess of sweetness; whilst the poetry of the preceding age was as a meadow-gale of June, which mingles the frag-
rance of all the flowers of the field, and adds a quickening and

harmonizing spirit of its own which endows the sense with a
power of sustaining its extreme delight. The bucolic and erotic 540
delicacy in written poetry is correlative with that softness in
statuary, music, and the kindred arts, and even in manners and
institutions, which distinguished the epoch to which I now refer.
Nor is it the poetical faculty itself, or any misapplication of it,
to which this want of harmony is to be imputed. An equal 545
sensibility to the influence of the senses and the affections is to
be found in the writings of Homer and Sophocles: the former,
especially, has clothed sensual and pathetic images with irresistible attractions. Their superiority over these succeeding writers
consists in the presence of those thoughts which belong to the 550
inner faculties of our nature, not in the absence of those which
are connected with the external: their incomparable perfection
consists in a harmony of the union of all. It is not what the
erotic poets have, but what they have not, in which their
imperfection consists. It is not inasmuch as they were poets, but 555
inasmuch as they were not poets, that they can be considered
with any plausibility as connected with the corruption of their
age. Had that corruption availed so as to extinguish in them
the sensibility to pleasure, passion, and natural scenery, which
is imputed to them as an imperfection, the last triumph of 560
evil would have been achieved. For the end of social corruption
is to destroy all sensibility to pleasure; and, therefore, it is
corruption. It begins at the imagination and the intellect as at
the core, and distributes itself thence as a paralysing venom,
through the affections into the very appetites, until all become a 565
torpid mass in which hardly sense survives. At the approach of
such a period, poetry ever addresses itself to those faculties
which are the last to be destroyed, and its voice is heard, like
the footsteps of Astraea, departing from the world. Poetry ever
communicates all the pleasure which men are capable of 570
receiving: it is ever still the light of life; the source of whatever
of beautiful or generous or true can have place in an evil time. It
will readily be confessed that those among the luxurious citizens
of Syracuse and Alexandria, who were delighted with the poems
of Theocritus, were less cold, cruel, and sensual than the rem- 575
nant of their tribe. But corruption must utterly have destroyed
the fabric of human society before poetry can ever cease. The

IECT

sacred links of that chain have never been entirely disjoined,
which descending through the minds of many men is attached
580 to those great minds, whence as from a magnet the invisible
effluence is sent forth, which at once connects, animates, and
sustains the life of all. It is the faculty which contains within
itself the seeds at once of its own and of social renovation. And
let us not circumscribe the effects of the bucolic and erotic
585 poetry within the limits of the sensibility of those to whom it
was addressed. They may have perceived the beauty of those
immortal compositions, simply as fragments and isolated
portions: those who are more finely organized, or born in a
happier age, may recognise them as episodes to that great
590 poem, which all poets, like the co-operating thoughts of one
great mind, have built up since the beginning of the world.

The same revolution within a narrower sphere had place in
ancient Rome; but the actions and forms of its social life never
seem to have been perfectly saturated with the poetical element.
595 The Romans appear to have considered the Greeks as the
selectest treasuries of the selectest forms of manners and of
nature, and to have abstained from creating in measured
language, sculpture, music, or architecture, anything which
might bear a particular relation to their own condition, whilst
600 it should bear a general one to the universal constitution of the
world. But we judge from partial evidence, and we judge perhaps partially. Ennius, Varro, Pacuvius, and Accius, all great
poets, have been lost. Lucretius is in the highest, and Virgil
in a very high sense, a creator. The chosen delicacy of expres-
605 sions of the latter, are as a mist of light which conceal from us
the intense and exceeding truth of his conceptions of nature.

Livy is instinct with poetry. Yet Horace, Catullus, Ovid,
and generally the other great writers of the Virgilian age, saw
man and nature in the mirror of Greece. The institutions also,
610 and the religion of Rome, were less poetical than those of
Greece, as the shadow is less vivid than the substance. Hence
poetry in Rome seemed to follow, rather than accompany, the
perfection of political and domestic society. The true poetry of
Rome lived in its institutions; for whatever of beautiful, true
615 and majestic, they contained, could have sprung only from
the faculty which creates the order in which they consist. The

life of Camillus, the death of Regulus; the expectation of the senators, in their godlike state, of the victorious Gauls; the refusal of the republic to make peace with Hannibal, after the battle of Cannae, were not the consequences of a refined calculation of the probable personal advantage to result from such a rhythm and order in the shows of life, to those who were at once the poets and the actors of these immortal dramas. The imagination beholding the beauty of this order, created it out of itself according to its own idea; the consequence was empire, and the reward everlasting fame. These things are not the less poetry *quia carent vate sacro*. They are the episodes of that cyclic poem written by Time upon the memories of men. The Past, like an inspired rhapsodist, fills the theatre of everlasting generations with their harmony.

At length the ancient system of religion and manners had fulfilled the circle of its evolutions. And the world would have fallen into utter anarchy and darkness, but that there were found poets among the authors of the Christian and chivalric systems of manners and religion, who created forms of opinion and action never before conceived; which, copied into the imaginations of men, became as generals to the bewildered armies of their thoughts. It is foreign to the present purpose to touch upon the evil produced by these systems: except that we protest, on the ground of the principles already established, that no portion of it can be attributed to the poetry they contain.

It is probable that the poetry of Moses, Job, David, Solomon, and Isaiah, had produced a great effect upon the mind of Jesus and his disciples. The scattered fragments preserved to us by the biographers of this extraordinary person, are all instinct with the most vivid poetry. But his doctrines seem to have been quickly distorted. At a certain period after the prevalence of a system of opinions founded upon those promulgated by him, the three forms into which Plato had distributed the faculties of mind underwent a sort of apotheosis, and became the object of the worship of the civilized world. Here it is to be confessed that 'Light' seems to 'thicken',

> And the crow makes wing to the rooky wood;
> Good things of day begin to droop and drowse,
> Whiles night's black agents to their preys do rouse.

But mark how beautiful an order has sprung from the dust and
blood of this fierce chaos! how the world, as from a resurrection,
balancing itself on the golden wings of knowledge and of hope,
has reassumed its yet unwearied flight into the heaven of time.
660 Listen to the music, unheard by outward ears, which is as a
ceaseless and invisible wind, nourishing its everlasting course
with strength and swiftness.

The poetry in the doctrines of Jesus Christ, and the mythology and institutions of the Celtic conquerors of the Roman
665 empire, outlived the darkness and the convulsions connected
with their growth and victory, and blended themselves in a
new fabric of manners and opinion. It is an error to impute the
ignorance of the dark ages to the Christian doctrines or the
predominance of the Celtic nations. Whatever of evil their
670 agencies may have contained sprang from the extinction of the
poetical principle, connected with the progress of despotism
and superstition. Men, from causes too intricate to be here
discussed, had become insensible and selfish: their own will
had become feeble, and yet they were its slaves, and thence the
675 slaves of the will of others: lust, fear, avarice, cruelty, and
fraud, characterized a race amongst whom no one was to be
found capable of *creating* in form, language, or institution. The
moral anomalies of such a state of society are not justly to be
charged upon any class of events immediately connected with
680 them, and those events are most entitled to our approbation
which could dissolve it most expeditiously. It is unfortunate
for those who cannot distinguish words from thoughts, that
many of these anomalies have been incorporated into our
popular religion.
685   It was not until the eleventh century that the effects of the
poetry of the Christian and chivalric systems began to manifest
themselves. The principle of equality had been discovered and
applied by Plato in his *Republic*, as the theoretical rule of the
mode in which the materials of pleasure and of power produced
690 by the common skill and labour of human beings ought to be
distributed among them. The limitations of this rule were
asserted by him to be determined only by the sensibility of
each, or the utility to result to all. Plato, following the doctrines
of Timaeus and Pythagoras, taught also a moral and intellectual

system of doctrine, comprehending at once the past, the present, 695
and the future condition of man. Jesus Christ divulged the
sacred and eternal truths contained in these views to mankind,
and Christianity, in its abstract purity, became the exoteric
expression of the esoteric doctrines of the poetry and wisdom
of antiquity. The incorporation of the Celtic nations with the 700
exhausted population of the south, impressed upon it the
figure of the poetry existing in their mythology and institutions.
The result was a sum of the action and reaction of all the
causes included in it; for it may be assumed as a maxim that
no nation or religion can supersede any other without incorpor- 705
ating into itself a portion of that which it supersedes. The
abolition of personal and domestic slavery, and the emancipa-
tion of women from a great part of the degrading restraints of
antiquity, were among the consequences of these events.

The abolition of personal slavery is the basis of the highest 710
political hope that it can enter into the mind of man to conceive. The freedom of women produced the poetry of sexual
love. Love became a religion, the idols of whose worship were
ever present. It was as if the statues of Apollo and the Muses
had been endowed with life and motion, and had walked forth 715
among their worshippers; so that earth became peopled by the
inhabitants of a diviner world. The familiar appearances and
proceedings of life became wonderful and heavenly, and a
paradise was created as out of the wrecks of Eden. And as this
creation itself is poetry, so its creators were poets; and language 720
was the instrument of their art: 'Galeotto fù il libro, e chi lo
scrisse.' The Provençal Trouveurs, or inventors, preceded
Petrarch, whose verses are as spells which unseal the inmost
enchanted fountains of the delight which is in the grief of love.
It is impossible to feel them without becoming a portion of that 725
beauty which we contemplate: it were superfluous to explain
how the gentleness and elevation of mind connected with these
sacred emotions can render men more amiable, more generous
and wise, and lift them out of the dull vapours of the little
world of self. Dante understood the secret things of love even 730
more than Petrarch. His *Vita Nuova* is an inexhaustible fountain
of purity of sentiment and language: it is the idealized history
of that period and those intervals of his life which were

dedicated to love. His apotheosis of Beatrice in Paradise, and
735 the gradations of his own love and her loveliness, by which
as by steps he feigns himself to have ascended to the throne of
the Supreme Cause, is the most glorious imagination of
modern poetry. The acutest critics have justly reversed the
judgement of the vulgar, and the order of the great acts of the
740 *Divina Commedia*, in the measure of the admiration which they
accord to the Hell, Purgatory, and Paradise. The latter is a
perpetual hymn of everlasting love. Love, which found a
worthy poet in Plato alone of all the ancients, has been celebrated by a chorus of the greatest writers of the renovated
745 world; and the music has penetrated the caverns of society, and
its echoes still drown the dissonance of arms and superstition.
At successive intervals, Ariosto, Tasso, Shakespeare, Spenser,
Calderon, Rousseau, and the great writers of our own age,
have celebrated the dominion of love, planting as it were
750 trophies in the human mind of that sublimest victory over
sensuality and force. The true relation borne to each other by
the sexes into which human kind is distributed has become less
misunderstood; and if the error which confounded diversity
with inequality of the powers of the two sexes has been partially
755 recognised in the opinions and institutions of modern Europe,
we owe this great benefit to the worship of which chivalry
was the law, and poets the prophets.

The poetry of Dante may be considered as the bridge thrown
over the stream of time, which unites the modern and ancient
760 world. The distorted notions of invisible things which Dante
and his rival Milton have idealized, are merely the mask
and the mantle in which these great poets walk through
eternity enveloped and disguised. It is a difficult question to
determine how far they were conscious of the distinction
765 which must have subsisted in their minds between their own
creeds and that of the people. Dante at least appears to wish to
mark the full extent of it by placing Riphaeus, whom Virgil
calls *justissimus unus*, in Paradise, and observing a most here-
tical caprice in his distribution of rewards and punishments.
770 And Milton's poem contains within itself a philosophical refutation of that system, of which, by a strange and natural antithesis,
it has been a chief popular support. Nothing can exceed the

energy and magnificence of the character of Satan as expressed
in *Paradise Lost*. It is a mistake to suppose that he could ever
have been intended for the popular personification of evil. 775
Implacable hate, patient cunning, and a sleepless refinement of
device to inflict the extremest anguish on an enemy, these
things are evil; and, although venial in a slave, are not to be
forgiven in a tyrant; although redeemed by much that ennobles
his defeat in one subdued, are marked by all that dishonours his 780
conquest in the victor. Milton's Devil as a moral being is as far
superior to his God, as one who perseveres in some purpose
which he has conceived to be excellent, in spite of adversity
and torture, is to one who in the cold security of undoubted
triumph inflicts the most horrible revenge upon his enemy, not 785
from any mistaken notion of inducing him to repent of a per-
severence in enmity, but with the alleged design of exasperating
him to deserve new torments. Milton has so far violated the
popular creed (if this shall be judged to be a violation) as to
have alleged no superiority of moral virtue to his God over his 790
Devil. And this bold neglect of a direct moral purpose is the
most decisive proof of the supremacy of Milton's genius. He
mingled as it were the elements of human nature as colours
upon a single pallet, and arranged them in the composition of
his great picture according to the laws of epic truth, that is, 795
according to the laws of that principle by which a series of
actions of the external universe and of intelligent and ethical
beings is calculated to excite the sympathy of succeeding generations of mankind. The *Divina Commedia* and *Paradise Lost* have
conferred upon modern mythology a systematic form; and 800
when change and time shall have added one more superstition
to the mass of those which have arisen and decayed upon the
earth, commentators will be learnedly employed in elucidating
the religion of ancestral Europe, only not utterly forgotten
because it will have been stamped with the eternity of genius. 805
 Homer was the first and Dante the second epic poet: that is,
the second poet, the series of whose creations bore a defined
and intelligible relation to the knowledge and sentiment and
religion of the age in which he lived, and of the ages which
followed it: developing itself in correspondence with their 810
development. For Lucretius had limed the wings of his swift

spirit in the dregs of the sensible world; and Virgil, with a
modesty that ill became his genius, had affected the fame of an
imitator, even whilst he created anew all that he copied; and
815 none among the flock of mock-birds, though their notes are
sweet, Apollonius Rhodius, Quintus (Calaber) Smyrnaeus,
Nonnus, Lucan, Statius, or Claudian, have sought even to
fulfil a single condition of epic truth. Milton was the third
epic poet. For if the title of epic in its highest sense be refused
820 to the *Aeneid*, still less can it be conceded to the *Orlando Furioso*,
the *Gerusalemme Liberata*, the *Lusiad*, or the *Faerie Queene*.

Dante and Milton were both deeply penetrated with the
ancient religion of the civilized world; and its spirit exists in
their poetry probably in the same proportion as its forms sur-
825 vived in the unreformed worship of modern Europe. The one
preceded and the other followed the Reformation at almost
equal intervals. Dante was the first religious reformer, and
Luther surpassed him rather in the rudeness and acrimony,
than in the boldness of his censures of papal usurpation. Dante
830 was the first awakener of entranced Europe; he created a
language, in itself music and persuasion, out of a chaos of
inharmonious barbarisms. He was the congregator of those
great spirits who presided over the resurrection of learning; the
Lucifer of that starry flock which in the thirteenth century
835 shone forth from republican Italy, as from a heaven, into the
darkness of the benighted world. His very words are instinct
with spirit; each is as a spark, a burning atom of inextinguishable thought; and many yet lie covered in the ashes of their
birth, and pregnant with a lightning which has yet found no
840 conductor. All high poetry is infinite; it is as the first acorn,
which contained all oaks potentially. Veil after veil may be
undrawn, and the inmost naked beauty of the meaning never
exposed. A great poem is a fountain for ever overflowing with
the waters of wisdom and delight; and after one person and one
845 age has exhausted all its divine effluence which their peculiar
relations enable them to share, another and yet another
succeeds, and new relations are ever developed, the source of
an unforeseen and an unconceived delight.

The age immediately succeeding to that of Dante, Petrarch,
850 and Boccaccio, was characterized by a revival of painting,

sculpture, and architecture. Chaucer caught the sacred inspiration, and the superstructure of English literature is based upon
the materials of Italian invention.

But let us not be betrayed from a defence into a critical
history of poetry and its influence on society. Be it enough to   855
have pointed out the effects of poets, in the large and true
sense of the word, upon their own and all succeeding times.

But poets have been challenged to resign the civic crown to
reasoners and mechanists, on another plea. It is admitted that
the exercise of the imagination is most delightful, but it is   860
alleged that that of reason is more useful. Let us examine, as
the grounds of this distinction, what is here meant by utility.
Pleasure or good, in a general sense, is that which the consciousness of a sensitive and intelligent being seeks, and in which, when
found, it acquiesces. There are two kinds of pleasure, one   865
durable, universal, and permanent; the other transitory and particular. Utility may either express the means of producing the
former or the latter. In the former sense, whatever strengthens
and purifies the affections, enlarges the imagination, and adds
spirit to sense, is useful. But a narrower meaning may be   870
assigned to the word utility, confining it to express that which
banishes the importunity of the wants of our animal nature,
the surrounding men with security of life, the dispersing the
grosser delusions of superstition, and the conciliating such a
degree of mutual forbearance among men as may consist with   875
the motives of personal advantage.

Undoubtedly the promoters of utility, in this limited sense,
have their appointed office in society. They follow the footsteps
of poets, and copy the sketches of their creations into the book of
common life. They make space and give time. Their exertions   880
are of the highest value, so long as they confine their adminis-
tration of the concerns of the inferior powers of our nature
within the limits due to the superior ones. But whilst the sceptic
destroys gross superstitions, let him spare to deface, as some of
the French writers have defaced, the eternal truths charactered   885
upon the imaginations of men. Whilst the mechanist abridges,
and the political economist combines labour, let them beware
that their speculations, for want of correspondence with those
first principles which belong to the imagination, do not tend,

890 as they have in modern England, to exasperate at once the
extremes of luxury and of want. They have exemplified the
saying, 'To him that hath, more shall be given; and from him
that hath not, the little that he hath shall be taken away.' The
rich have become richer, and the poor have become poorer; and
895 the vessel of the state is driven between the Scylla and Charybdis
of anarchy and despotism. Such are the effects which must ever
flow from an unmitigated exercise of the calculating faculty.

It is difficult to define pleasure in its highest sense; the
definition involving a number of apparent paradoxes. For, from
900 an inexplicable defect of harmony in the constitution of human
nature, the pain of the inferior is frequently connected with the
pleasures of the superior portions of our being. Sorrow, terror,
anguish, despair itself, are often the chosen expressions of an
approximation to the highest good. Our sympathy in tragic
905 fiction depends on this principle; tragedy delights by affording
a shadow of that pleasure which exists in pain. This is the
source also of the melancholy which is inseparable from the
sweetest melody. The pleasure that is in sorrow is sweeter than
the pleasure of pleasure itself. And hence the saying, 'It is
910 better to go to the house of mourning than to the house of
mirth.' Not that this highest species of pleasure is necessarily
linked with pain. The delight of love and friendship, the ecstasy
of the admiration of nature, the joy of the perception and still
more of the creation of poetry, is often wholly unalloyed.

915   The production and assurance of pleasure in this highest
sense is true utility. Those who produce and preserve this
pleasure are poets or poetical philosophers.

The exertions of Locke, Hume, Gibbon, Voltaire, Rousseau,
and their disciples, in favour of oppressed and deluded human-
920 ity, are entitled to the gratitude of mankind. Yet it is easy to
calculate the degree of moral and intellectual improvement
which the world would have exhibited, had they never lived.
A little more nonsense would have been talked for a century
or two; and perhaps a few more men, women, and children,
925 burnt as heretics. We might not at this moment have been
congratulating each other on the abolition of the Inquisition in
Spain. But it exceeds all imagination to conceive what would
have been the moral condition of the world if neither Dante,

Petrarch, Boccaccio, Chaucer, Shakespeare, Calderon, Lord
Bacon, nor Milton, had ever existed; if Raphael and Michael 930
Angelo had never been born; if the Hebrew poetry had never
been translated; if a revival of the study of Greek literature had
never taken place; if no monuments of ancient sculpture had
been handed down to us; and if the poetry of the religion of the
ancient world had been extinguished together with its belief. 935
The human mind could never, except by the intervention of
these excitements, have been awakened to the invention of the
grosser sciences, and that application of analytical reasoning to
the aberrations of society which it is now attempted to exalt over
the direct expression of the inventive and creative faculty itself. 940
    We have more moral, political, and historical wisdom than
we know how to reduce into practice; we have more scientific
and economical knowledge than can be accommodated to the
just distribution of the produce which it multiplies. The poetry
in these systems of thought is concealed by the accumulation of 945
facts and calculating processes. There is no want of knowledge
respecting what is wisest and best in morals, government, and
political economy, or at least what is wiser and better than
what men now practise and endure. But we let '*I dare not*
wait upon *I would*, like the poor cat in the adage.' We want 950
the creative faculty to imagine that which we know; we
want the generous impulse to act that which we imagine; we
want the poetry of life: our calculations have outrun conception;
we have eaten more than we can digest. The cultivation of those
sciences which have enlarged the limits of the empire of man 955
over the external world, has, for want of the poetical faculty,
proportionally circumscribed those of the internal world; and
man, having enslaved the elements, remains himself a slave.
To what but a cultivation of the mechanical arts in a degree
disproportioned to the presence of the creative faculty, which is 960
the basis of all knowledge, is to be attributed the abuse of all
invention for abridging and combining labour, to the exaspera-
tion of the inequality of mankind? From what other cause has it
arisen that the discoveries which should have lightened, have
added a weight to the curse imposed on Adam? Poetry, and the 965
principle of Self of which money is the visible incarnation, are
the God and Mammon of the world.

The functions of the poetical faculty are twofold; by one it creates new materials of knowledge, and power, and pleasure; 970 by the other it engenders in the mind a desire to reproduce and arrange them according to a certain rhythm and order which may be called the beautiful and the good. The cultivation of poetry is never more to be desired than at periods when, from an excess of the selfish and calculating principle, the ac975 cumulation of the materials of external life exceed the quantity of the power of assimilating them to the internal laws of human nature. The body has then become too unwieldy for that which animates it.

Poetry is indeed something divine. It is at once the centre and 980 circumference of knowledge; it is that which comprehends all science, and that to which all science must be referred. It is at the same time the root and blossom of all other systems of thought; it is that from which all spring, and that which adorns all; and that which, if blighted, denies the fruit and the 985 seed, and withholds from the barren world the nourishment and the succession of the scions of the tree of life. It is the perfect and consummate surface and bloom of all things; it is as the odour and the colour of the rose to the texture of the elements which compose it, as the form and splendour of unfaded beauty 990 to the secrets of anatomy and corruption. What were virtue, love, patriotism, friendship—what were the scenery of this beautiful universe which we inhabit; what were our consolations on this side of the grave—and what were our aspirations beyond it, if poetry did not ascend to bring light and fire from 995 those eternal regions where the owl-winged faculty of calculation dare not ever soar? Poetry is not like reasoning, a power to be exerted acording to the determination of the will. A man cannot say, 'I will compose poetry.' The greatest poet even cannot say it; for the mind in creation is as a fading coal, which 1000 some invisible influence, like an inconstant wind, awakens to transitory brightness; this power arises from within, like the colour of a flower which fades and changes as it is developed, and the conscious portions of our natures are unprophetic either of its approach or its departure. Could this influence be 1005 durable in its original purity and force, it is impossible to predict the greatness of the results; but when composition

begins, inspiration is already on the decline, and the most
glorious poetry that has ever been communicated to the world
is probably a feeble shadow of the original conceptions of the
poet. I appeal to the greatest poets of the present day, whether 1010
it is not an error to assert that the finest passages of poetry are
produced by labour and study. The toil and the delay recommended by critics, can be justly interpreted to mean no more
than a careful observation of the inspired moments, and an
artificial connexion of the spaces between their suggestions by 1015
the intertexture of conventional expressions; a necessity only
imposed by the limitedness of the poetical faculty itself; for
Milton conceived the *Paradise Lost* as a whole before he executed
it in portions. We have his own authority also for the muse
having 'dictated' to him the 'unpremeditated song.' And let 1020
this be an answer to those who would allege the fifty-six various
readings of the first line of the *Orlando Furioso*. Compositions so
produced are to poetry what mosaic is to painting. The
instinct and intuition of the poetical faculty is still more observable in the plastic and pictorial arts: a great statue or 1025
picture grows under the power of the artist as a child in the
mother's womb; and the very mind which directs the hands in
formation, is incapable of accounting to itself for the origin,
the gradations, or the media of the process.

Poetry is the record of the best and happiest moments of the 1030
happiest and best minds. We are aware of evanescent visitations
of thought and feeling, sometimes associated with place or
person, sometimes regarding our own mind alone, and always
arising unforeseen and departing unbidden, but elevating and
delightful beyond all expression: so that even in the desire and 1035
the regret they leave, there cannot but be pleasure, participating
as it does in the nature of its object. It is as it were the interpenetration of a diviner nature through our own; but its footsteps are like those of a wind over the sea, which the morning
calm erases, and whose traces remain only, as on the wrinkled 1040
sand which paves it. These and corresponding conditions of
being are experienced principally by those of the most delicate
sensibility and the most enlarged imagination; and the state
of mind produced by them is at war with every base desire.
The enthusiasm of virtue, love, patriotism, and friendship is 1045

essentially linked with such emotions; and whilst they last, self
appears as what it is, an atom to a universe. Poets are not only
subject to these experiences as spirits of the most refined organization, but they can colour all that they combine with the
1050 evanescent hues of this ethereal world; a word, a trait in the
representation of a scene or a passion will touch the enchanted
chord, and reanimate, in those who have ever experienced
these emotions, the sleeping, the cold, the buried image of the
past. Poetry thus makes immortal all that is best and most
1055 beautiful in the world; it arrests the vanishing apparitions
which haunt the interlunations of life, and veiling them or in
language or in form, sends them forth among mankind, bearing
sweet news of kindred joy to those with whom their sisters abide
—abide, because there is no portal of expression from the caverns
1060 of the spirit which they inhabit into the universe of things. Poetry
redeems from decay the visitations of the divinity in man.

Poetry turns all things to loveliness; it exalts the beauty of
that which is most beautiful, and it adds beauty to that which
is most deformed; it marries exultation and horror, grief and
1065 pleasure, eternity and change; it subdues to union under its
light yoke all irreconcilable things. It transmutes all that it
touches, and every form moving within the radiance of its
presence is changed by wondrous sympathy to an incarnation
of the spirit which it breathes: its secret alchemy turns to pot-
1070 able gold the poisonous waters which flow from death through
life; it strips the veil of familiarity from the world, and lays bare
the naked and sleeping beauty which is the spirit of its forms.

All things exist as they are perceived; at least in relation to
the percipient. 'The mind is its own place, and in itself can
1075 make a Heaven of Hell, a Hell of Heaven.' But poetry defeats
the curse which binds us to be subjected to the accident of
surrounding impressions. And whether it spreads its own figured
curtain, or withdraws life's dark veil from before the scene of
things, it equally creates for us a being within our being. It
1080 makes us the inhabitant of a world to which the familiar world
is a chaos. It reproduces the common universe of which we are
portions and percipients, and it purges from our inward sight
the film of familiarity which obscures from us the wonder of
our being. It compels us to feel that which we perceive, and to

imagine that which we know. It creates anew the universe, after 1085
it has been annihilated in our minds by the recurrence of impressions blunted by reiteration. It justifies the bold and true
word of Tasso: *Non merita nome di creatore, se non Iddio ed il Poeta.*

A poet, as he is the author to others of the highest wisdom,
pleasure, virtue, and glory, so he ought personally to be the 1090
happiest, the best, the wisest, and the most illustrious of men.
As to his glory, let time be challenged to declare whether the
fame of any other institutor of human life be comparable to
that of a poet. That he is the wisest, the happiest, and the best,
inasmuch as he is a poet, is equally incontrovertible: the 1095
greatest poets have been men of the most spotless virtue, of
the most consummate prudence, and, if we would look into the
interior of their lives, the most fortunate of men: and the exceptions, as they regard those who possessed the poetic faculty in
a high yet inferior degree, will be found on consideration to 1100
confirm rather than destroy the rule. Let us for a moment stoop
to the arbitration of popular breath, and usurping and uniting
in our own persons the incompatible characters of accuser,
witness, judge, and executioner, let us decide without trial,
testimony, or form, that certain motives of those who are 'there 1105
sitting where we dare not soar,' are reprehensible. Let us
assume that Homer was a drunkard, that Virgil was a flatterer,
that Horace was a coward, that Tasso was a madman, that
Lord Bacon was a peculator, that Raphael was a libertine, that
Spenser was a poet laureate. It is inconsistent with this division 1110
of our subject to cite living poets, but posterity has done ample
justice to the great names now referred to. Their errors have
been weighed and found to have been dust in the balance; if
their sins 'were as scarlet, they are now white as snow': they
have been washed in the blood of the mediator and redeemer, 1115
Time. Observe in what a ludicrous chaos the imputations of
real or fictitious crime have been confused in the contemporary
calumnies against poetry and poets; consider how little is, as it
appears—or appears, as it is; look to your own motives, and
judge not, lest ye be judged.   1120

Poetry, as has been said, differs in this respect from logic, that
it is not subject to the control of the active powers of the mind,
and that its birth and recurrence have no necessary connection

with the consciousness or will. It is presumptuous to determine
1125 that these are the necessary conditions of all mental causation,
when mental effects are experienced insusceptible of being
referred to them. The frequent recurrence of the poetical power,
it is obvious to suppose, may produce in the mind a habit of
order and [harmony correlative with its own nature and with
1130 its effects upon other minds. But in the intervals of inspiration,
and they may be frequent without being durable, a poet becomes a man, and is abandoned to the sudden reflux of the
influences under which others habitually live. But as he is more
delicately organized than other men, and sensible to pain and
1135 pleasure, both his own and that of others, in a degree unknown
to them, he will avoid the one and pursue the other with an
ardour proportioned to this difference. And he renders himself
obnoxious to calumny when he neglects to observe the circumstances under which these objects of universal pursuit and
1140 flight have disguised themselves in one another's garments.

But there is nothing necessarily evil in this error, and thus
cruelty, envy, revenge, avarice, and the passions purely evil,
have never formed any portion of the popular imputations on
the lives of poets.

1145 I have thought it most favourable to the cause of truth to
set down these remarks according to the order in which they
were suggested to my mind, by a consideration of the subject
itself, instead of observing the formality of a polemical reply;
but if the view which they contain be just, they will be found
1150 to involve a refutation of the arguers against poetry, so far at
least as regards the first division of the subject. I can readily
conjecture what should have moved the gall of some learned
and intelligent writers who quarrel with certain versifiers; I,
like them, confess myself unwilling to be stunned by the
1155 Theseids of the hoarse Codri of the day. Bavius and Maevius
undoubtedly are, as they ever were, insufferable persons. But it
belongs to a philosophical critic to distinguish rather than
confound.

The first part of these remarks has related to poetry in its
1160 elements and principles; and it has been shown, as well as the
narrow limits assigned them would permit, that what is called
poetry in a restricted sense, has a common source with all other

forms of order and of beauty, according to which the materials of human life are susceptible of being arranged, and which is poetry in a universal sense.   1165

The second part will have for its object an application of these principles to the present state of the cultivation of poetry, and a defence of the attempt to idealize the modern forms of manners and opinions, and compel them into a subordination to the imaginative and creative faculty. For the literature of 1170 England, an energetic development of which has ever preceded or accompanied a great and free development of the national will, has arisen as it were from a new birth. In spite of the low-thoughted envy which would undervalue contemporary merit, our own will be a memorable age in intellectual achievements, 1175 and we live among such philosophers and poets as surpass beyond comparison any who have appeared since the last national struggle for civil and religious liberty. The most un-failing herald, companion, and follower of the awakening of a great people to work a beneficial change in opinion or institu- 1180 tion, is poetry. At such periods there is an accumulation of the power of communicating and receiving intense and impassioned conceptions respecting man and nature. The persons in whom this power resides, may often, as far as regards many portions of their nature, have little apparent correspondence with that 1185 spirit of good of which they are the ministers. But even whilst they deny and abjure, they are yet compelled to serve the power which is seated on the throne of their own soul. It is impossible to read the compositions of the most celebrated writers of the present day without being startled with the 1190 electric life which burns within their words. They measure the circumference and sound the depths of human nature with a comprehensive and all-penetrating spirit, and they are them-selves perhaps the most sincerely astonished at its manifesta-tions; for it is less their spirit than the spirit of the age. Poets 1195 are the hierophants of an unapprehended inspiration; the mirrors of the gigantic shadows which futurity casts upon the present; the words which express what they understand not; the trumpets which sing to battle and feel not what they inspire; the influence which is moved not, but moves. Poets 1200 are the unacknowledged legislators of the world.

JOHN KEATS

From the Letters

From Letter to Benjamin Bailey, 22 November 1817:
I AM certain of nothing but of the holiness of the Heart's
affections and the truth of Imagination. What the imagination
seizes as Beauty must be truth—whether it existed before or not
—for I have the same Idea of all our Passions as of Love:
5 they are all, in their sublime, creative of essential Beauty. In a
word, you may know my favourite speculation by my first Book
and the little song I sent in my last—which is a representation
from the fancy of the probable mode of operating in these
Matters. The Imagination may be compared to Adam's dream,
10 —he awoke and found it truth. I am the more zealous in this
affair, because I have never yet been able to perceive how any
thing can be known for truth by consecutive reasoning—and
yet it must be. Can it be that even the greatest Philosopher
ever arrived at his goal without putting aside numerous
15 objections? However it may be, O for a life of Sensations rather
than of Thoughts! It is 'a Vision in the form of Youth', a
Shadow of reality to come—and this consideration has further
convinced me, for it has come as auxiliary to another favourite
speculation of mine—that we shall enjoy ourselves hereafter
20 by having what we called happiness on Earth repeated in a
finer tone and so repeated. And yet such a fate can only befall
those who delight in Sensation, rather than hunger as you do
after Truth. Adam's dream will do here, and seems to be a
conviction that Imagination and its empyreal reflection is the
25 same as human Life and its Spiritual repetition. But as I was
saying—the simple imaginative Mind may have its rewards in
the repetition of its own silent Working coming continually on
the Spirit with a fine Suddenness—to compare great things
with small, have you never by being surprised with an old
30 Melody, in a delicious place, by a delicious voice, felt over

again your very speculations and surmises at the time it first
operated on your soul?—do you not remember forming to
yourself the singer's face more beautiful than it was possible,
and yet with the elevation of the Moment you did not think so?
—even then you were mounted on the Wings of Imagination 35
so high—that the Prototype must be hereafter—that delicious
face you will see. What a time! I am continually running away
from the subject—sure this cannot be exactly the case with a
complex Mind—one that is imaginative and at the same time
careful of its fruits—who would exist partly on Sensation, 40
partly on thought—to whom it is necessary that years should
bring the philosophic Mind?—Such a one I consider yours,
and therefore it is necessary to your eternal Happiness that you
not only drink this old Wine of Heaven, which I shall call the
redigestion of our most ethereal Musings on Earth, but also 45
increase in knowledge and know all things.

From Letter to George and Thomas Keats, 21 December 1817:
    I had not a dispute but a disquisition with Dilke, on various
subjects; several things dovetailed in my mind, and at once it
struck me what quality went to form a Man of Achievement,
especially in Literature, and which Shakespeare possessed so 50
enormously—I mean *Negative Capability*, that is, when man is
capable of being in uncertainties, mysteries, doubts, without
any irritable reaching after fact and reason.—Coleridge, for
instance, would let go by a fine isolated verisimilitude caught
from the Penetralium of mystery, from being incapable of 55
remaining content with half-knowledge. This pursued through
volumes would perhaps take us no further than this, that with
a great poet the sense of Beauty overcomes every other consideration, or rather obliterates all consideration.

From Letter to John Hamilton Reynolds, 3 February 1818:
    We hate poetry that has a palpable design upon us—and, 60
if we do not agree, seems to put its hand in its breeches pocket.
Poetry should be great and unobtrusive, a thing which enters
into one's soul, and does not startle it or amaze it with itself,
but with its subject.—How beautiful are the retired flowers!
How would they lose their beauty were they to throng into 65

the highway crying out, 'Admire me, I am a violet!—Dote upon me, I am a primrose!"

From Letter to John Taylor, 27 February 1818:
In Poetry I have a few axioms, and you will see how far I am from their centre. First, I think Poetry should surprise by
70 a fine excess and not by singularity—it should strike the reader as a wording of his own highest thoughts, and appear almost a remembrance. Second, its touches of Beauty should never be half-way, thereby making the reader breathless instead of content: the rise, the progress, the setting of imagery should,
75 like the sun, come natural to him—shine over him, and set soberly although in magnificence, leaving him in the luxury of twilight. But it is easier to think what Poetry should be than to write it—and this leads me on to another axiom. That if Poetry comes not as naturally as the leaves to a tree, it had
80 better not come at all.

From Letter to Richard Woodhouse, 27 October 1818:
As to the poetical Character itself (I mean that sort of which, if I am anything, I am a member; that sort distinguished from the Wordsworthian or egotistical sublime, which is a thing *per se* and stands alone), it is not itself—it has no self—it is every
85 thing and nothing.—It has no character—it enjoys light and shade; it lives in gusto, be it foul or fair, high or low, rich or poor, mean or elevated.—It has as much delight in conceiving an Iago as an Imogen. What shocks the virtuous philosopher, delights the chameleon Poet. It does no harm from its relish
90 of the dark side of things any more than from its taste for the bright one, because they both end in speculation. A Poet is the most unpoetical of any thing in existence, because he has no Identity—he is continually in for—and filling some other body.—The sun, the moon, the sea, and men and women who
95 are creatures of impulse, are poetical and have about them an unchangeable attribute.—The poet has none, no identity—he is certainly the most unpoetical of all God's creatures. If then he has no self, and if I am a Poet, where is the wonder that I should say I would write no more? Might I not at that very
100 instant have been cogitating on the Characters of Saturn and

Ops? It is a wretched thing to confess, but is a very fact, that not one word I ever utter can be taken for granted as an opinion growing out of my identical nature—how can it, when I have no nature? When I am in a room with people, if I ever am free from speculating on creations of my own brain, then not myself 105 goes home to myself: but the identity of every one in the room begins so to press upon me that I am in a very little time annihilated—not only among men; it would be the same in a nursery of children.

From Letter to Percy Bysshe Shelley, 16 August 1820:

I received a copy of the *Cenci*, as from yourself, from Hunt. 110 There is only one part of it I am judge of: the Poetry, and dramatic effect, which by many spirits nowadays is considered the Mammon. A modern work, it is said, must have a purpose, which may be the God. *An artist* must serve Mammon—he must have 'self concentration', selfishness perhaps. You, I am 115 sure, will forgive me for sincerely remarking that you might curb your magnanimity and be more of an artist, and 'load every rift' of your subject with ore. The thought of such discipline must fall like cold chains upon you, who perhaps never sat with your wings furled for six months together. And is 120 not this extraordinary talk for the writer of *Endymion*! whose mind was like a pack of scattered cards.—I am picked up and sorted to a pip. My Imagination is a Monastery and I am its Monk. . . .

MATTHEW ARNOLD

The Study of Poetry

'THE future of poetry is immense, because in poetry, where it is worthy of its high destinies, our race, as time goes on, will find an ever surer and surer stay. There is not a creed which is not shaken, not an accredited dogma which is not shown to be
5 questionable, not a received tradition which does not threaten to dissolve. Our religion has materialised itself in the fact, in the supposed fact; it has attached its emotion to the fact, and now the fact is failing it. But for poetry the idea is everything; the rest is a world of illusion, of divine illusion. Poetry attaches its
10 emotion to the idea; the idea *is* the fact. The strongest part of our religion to-day is its unconscious poetry.'

Let me be permitted to quote these words of my own, as uttering the thought which should, in my opinion, go with us and govern us in all our study of poetry. In the present work it
15 is the course of one great contributory stream to the world-river of poetry that we are invited to follow. We are here invited to trace the stream of English poetry. But whether we set ourselves, as here, to follow only one of the several streams that make the mighty river of poetry, or whether we seek to know them all,
20 our governing thought should be the same. We should conceive of poetry worthily, and more highly than it has been the custom to conceive of it. We should conceive of it as capable of higher uses, and called to higher destinies, than those which in general men have assigned to it hitherto. More and more mankind will
25 discover that we have to turn to poetry to interpret life for us, to console us, to sustain us. Without poetry, our science will appear incomplete; and most of what now passes with us for religion and philosophy will be replaced by poetry. Science, I say, will appear incomplete without it. For finely and truly
30 does Wordsworth call poetry 'the impassioned expression which is in the countenance of all science'; and what is a countenance

without its expression? Again, Wordsworth finely and truly
calls poetry 'the breath and finer spirit of all knowledge':
our religion, parading evidences such as those on which the
popular mind relies now; our philosophy, pluming itself on its 35
reasonings about causation and finite and infinite being; what
are they but the shadows and dreams and false shows of
knowledge? The day will come when we shall wonder at ourselves for having trusted to them, for having taken them
seriously; and the more we perceive their hollowness, the more 40
we shall prize 'the breath and finer spirit of knowledge' offered
to us by poetry.

But if we conceive thus highly of the destinies of poetry, we
must also set our standard for poetry high, since poetry, to be
capable of fulfilling such high destinies, must be poetry of a 45
high order of excellence. We must accustom ourselves to a high
standard and to a strict judgement. Sainte-Beuve relates that
Napoleon one day said, when somebody was spoken of in his
presence as a charlatan: 'Charlatan as much as you please;
but where is there *not* charlatanism?'—'Yes,' answers Sainte- 50
Beuve, 'in politics, in the art of governing mankind, that is
perhaps true. But in the order of thought, in art, the glory, the
eternal honour is that charlatanism shall find no entrance;
herein lies the inviolableness of that noble portion of man's
being.' It is admirably said, and let us hold fast to it. In poetry, 55
which is thought and art in one, it is the glory, the eternal
honour, that charlatanism shall find no entrance; that this
noble sphere be kept inviolate and inviolable. Charlatanism is
for confusing or obliterating the distinctions between excellent
and inferior, sound and unsound or only half-sound, true and 60
untrue or only half-true. It is charlatanism, conscious or unconscious, whenever we confuse or obliterate these. And in
poetry, more than anywhere else, it is unpermissible to confuse
or obliterate them. For in poetry the distinction between
excellent and inferior, sound and unsound or only half-sound, 65
true and untrue or only half-true, is of paramount importance.
It is of paramount importance because of the high destinies of
poetry. In poetry, as a criticism of life under the conditions fixed
for such a criticism by the laws of poetic truth and poetic beauty,
the spirit of our race will find, we have said, as time goes on 70

and as other helps fail, its consolation and stay. But the consolation and stay will be of power in proportion to the power of the criticism of life. And the criticism of life will be of power in proportion as he poetry conveying it is excellent rather than 75 inferior, sound rather than unsound or half-sound, true rather than untrue or half-true.

The best poetry is what we want; the best poetry will be found to have a power of forming, sustaining, and delighting us, as nothing else can. A clearer, deeper sense of the best in 80 poetry, and of the strength and joy to be drawn from it, is the most precious benefit which we can gather from a poetical collection such as the present. And yet in the very nature and conduct of such a collection there is inevitably something which tends to obscure in us the consciousness of what our 85 benefit should be, and to distract us from the pursuit of it. We should therefore steadily set it before our minds at the outset, and should compel ourselves to revert constantly to the thought of it as we proceed.

Yes; constantly, in reading poetry, a sense for the best, the 90 really excellent, and of the strength and joy to be drawn from it, should be present in our minds and should govern our estimate of what we read. But this real estimate, the only true one, is liable to be superseded, if we are not watchful, by two other kinds of estimate, the historic estimate and the personal esti- 95 mate, both of which are fallacious. A poet or a poem may count to us historically, they may count to us on grounds personal to ourselves, and they may count to us really. They may count to us historically. The course of development of a nation's language, thought, and poetry, is profoundly interesting; and by 100 regarding a poet's work as a stage in this course of development we may easily bring ourselves to make it of more importance as poetry than in itself it really is, we may come to use a language of quite exaggerated praise in criticising it; in short, to overrate it. So arises in our poetic judgements the fallacy caused by the 105 estimate which we may call historic. Then, again, a poet or a poem may count to us on grounds personal to ourselves. Our personal affinities, likings, and circumstances have great power to sway our estimate of this or that poet's work, and to make us attach more importance to it as poetry than in itself it really

possesses, because to us it is, or has been, of high importance. 110
Here also we overrate the object of our interest, and apply to
it a language of praise which is quite exaggerated. And thus we
get the source of a second fallacy in our poetic judgements—
the fallacy caused by an estimate which we may call personal.

Both fallacies are natural. It is evident how naturally the 115
study of the history and development of a poetry may incline a
man to pause over reputations and works once conspicuous
but now obscure, and to quarrel with a careless public for
skipping, in obedience to mere tradition and habit, from one
famous name or work in its national poetry to another, ignorant 120
of what it misses, and of the reason for keeping what it keeps,
and of the whole process of growth in its poetry. The French
have become diligent students of their own early poetry, which
they long neglected; the study makes many of them dissatisfied
with their so-called classical poetry, the court-tragedy of the 125
seventeenth century, a poetry which Pellisson long ago reproached with its want of the true poetic stamp, with its
politesse stérile et rampante, but which nevertheless has reigned in
France as absolutely as if it had been the perfection of classical
poetry indeed. The dissatisfaction is natural; yet a lively and 130
accomplished critic, M. Charles d'Héricault, the editor of
Clément Marot, goes too far when he says that 'the cloud of
glory playing round a classic is a mist as dangerous to the
future of a literature as it is intolerable for the purposes of
history.' 'It hinders', he goes on, 'it hinders us from seeing more 135
than one single point, the culminating and exceptional point;
the summary, fictitious and arbitrary, of a thought and of a
work. It substitutes a halo for a physiognomy, it puts a statue
where there was once a man, and, hiding from us all trace of
the labour, the attempts, the weaknesses, the failures, it claims 140
not study but veneration; it does not show us how the thing is
done, it imposes upon us a model. Above all, for the historian
this creation of classic personages is inadmissible; for it withdraws the poet from his time, from his proper life, it breaks
historical relationships, it blinds criticism by conventional 145
admiration, and renders the investigation of literary origins
unacceptable. It gives us a human personage no longer, but a
God seated immovable amidst His perfect work, like Jupiter on

Olympus; and hardly will it be possible for the young student,
150 to whom such work is exhibited at such a distance from him, to
believe that it did not issue ready made from that divine head.'

All this is brilliantly and tellingly said, but we must plead
for a distinction. Everything depends on the reality of a poet's
classic character. If he is a dubious classic, let us sift him; if
155 he is a false classic, let us explode him. But if he is a real classic,
if his work belongs to the class of the very best (for this is the
true and right meaning of the word *classic, classical*), then the
great thing for us is to feel and enjoy his work as deeply as ever
we can, and to appreciate the wide difference between it and
160 all work which has not the same high character. This is what is
salutary, this is what is formative; this is the great benefit to
be got from the study of poetry. Everything which interferes
with it, which hinders it, is injurious. True, we must read our
classic with open eyes, and not with eyes blinded with super-
165 stition; we must perceive when his work comes short, when it
drops out of the class of the very best, and we must rate it, in
such cases, at its proper value. But the use of this negative
criticism is not in itself, it is entirely in its enabling us to have a
clearer sense and a deeper enjoyment of what is truly excellent.
170 To trace the labour, the attempts, the weaknesses, the failures
of a genuine classic, to acquaint oneself with his time and his
life and his historical relationships, is mere literary dilettantism
unless it has that clear sense and deeper enjoyment for its end.
It may be said that the more we know about a classic the better
175 we shall enjoy him; and, if we lived as long as Methuselah and
had all of us heads of perfect clearness and wills of perfect
steadfastness, this might be true in fact as it is plausible in
theory. But the case here is much the same as the case with the
Greek and Latin studies of our schoolboys. The elaborate
180 philological groundwork which we require them to lay is in
theory an admirable preparation for appreciating the Greek
and Latin authors worthily. The more thoroughly we lay the
groundwork, the better we shall be able, it may be said, to
enjoy the authors. True, if time were not so short, and school-
185 boys' wits not so soon tired and their power of attention exhausted; only, as it is, the elaborate philological preparation
goes on, but the authors are little known and less enjoyed. So

with the investigator of 'historic origins' in poetry. He ought to enjoy the true classic all the better for his investigations; he often is distracted from the enjoyment of the best, and with the 190 less good he overbusies himself, and is prone to overrate it in proportion to the trouble which it has cost him.

The idea of tracing historic origins and historical relationships cannot be absent from a compilation like the present. And naturally the poets to be exhibited in it will be assigned to 195 those persons for exhibition who are known to prize them highly, rather than to those who have no special inclination towards them. Moreover, the very occupation with an author, and the business of exhibiting him, disposes us to affirm and amplify his importance. In the present work, therefore, we are 200 sure of frequent temptation to adopt the historic estimate, or the personal estimate, and to forget the real estimate; which latter, nevertheless, we must employ if we are to make poetry yield us its full benefit. So high is that benefit, the benefit of clearly feeling and of deeply enjoying the really excellent, 205 the truly classic in poetry, that we do well, I say, to set it fixedly before our minds as our object in studying poets and poetry, and to make the desire of attaining it the one principle to which, as the *Imitation* says, whatever we may read or come to know, we always return. *Cum multa legeris et cognoveris, ad unum* 210 *semper oportet redire principium.*

The historic estimate is likely in especial to affect our judgement and our language when we are dealing with ancient poets; the personal estimate when we are dealing with poets our contemporaries, or at any rate modern. The exaggerations 215 due to the historic estimate are not in themselves, perhaps, of very much gravity. Their report hardly enters the general ear; probably they do not always impose even on the literary men who adopt them. But they lead to a dangerous abuse of language. So we hear Caedmon, amongst our own poets, compared 220 to Milton. I have already noticed the enthusiasm of one accomplished French critic for 'historic origins.' Another eminent French critic, M. Vitet, comments upon that famous document of the early poetry of his nation, the *Chanson de Roland*. It is indeed a most interesting document. The *joculator* or *jongleur* 225 Taillefer, who was with William the Conqueror's army at

Hastings, marched before the Norman troops, so said the
tradition, singing 'of Charlemagne and of Roland and of Oliver,
and of the vassals who died at Roncevaux'; and it is suggested
230 that in the *Chanson de Roland* by one Turoldus or Théroulde, a
poem preserved in a manuscript of the twelfth century in the
Bodleian Library at Oxford, we have certainly the matter,
perhaps even some of the words, of the chant which Taillefer
sang. The poem has vigour and freshness; it is not without
235 pathos. But M. Vitet is not satisfied with seeing in it a document of some poetic value, and of very high historic and
linguistic value; he sees in it a grand and beautiful work, a
monument of epic genius. In its general design he finds the
grandiose conception, in its details he finds the constant union
240 of simplicity with greatness, which are the marks, he truly says,
of the genuine epic, and distinguish it from the artificial epic of
literary ages. One thinks of Homer; this is the sort of praise
which is given to Homer, and justly given. Higher praise there
cannot well be, and it is the praise due to epic poetry of the
245 highest order only, and to no other. Let us try, then, the *Chanson
de Roland* at its best. Roland, mortally wounded, lays himself
down under a pine-tree, with his face turned towards Spain
and the enemy:—

'De plusurs choses à remembrer li prist,
250   De tantes teres cume li bers cunquist,
De dulce France, des humes de sun lign,
De Carlemagne sun seignor ki l'nurrit.'[1]

That is primitive work, I repeat, with an undeniable poetic
quality of its own. It deserves such praise, and such praise is
255 sufficient for it. But now turn to Homer:—

Ὣς φάτο· τοὺς δ' ἤδη κατέχεν φυσίζοος αἶα
ἐν Λακεδαίμονι αὖθι, φίλῃ ἐν πατρίδι γαίῃ.[2]

We are here in another world, another order of poetry alto-

---

[1] 'Then began he to call many things to remembrance—all the lands
which his valour conquered, and pleasant France, and the men of his
lineage, and Charlemagne his liege lord who nourished him.'—*Chanson de
Roland*, iii. 939–942.
[2] 'So said she; they long since in Earth's soft arms were reposing,
    There, in their own dear land, their fatherland, Lacedaemon.'
            Iliad, iii. 243, 244 (translated by Dr. Hawtrey).

gether; here is rightly due such supreme praise as that which M. Vitet gives to the *Chanson de Roland*. If our words are to have any meaning, if our judgements are to have any solidity, we must not heap that supreme praise upon poetry of an order immeasurably inferior.

Indeed there can be no more useful help for discovering what poetry belongs to the class of the truly excellent, and can therefore do us most good, than to have always in one's mind lines and expressions of the great masters, and to apply them as a touchstone to other poetry. Of course we are not to require this other poetry to resemble them; it may be very dissimilar. But if we have any tact we shall find them, when we have lodged them well in our minds, an infallible touchstone for detecting the presence or absence of high poetic quality, and also the degree of this quality, in all other poetry which we may place beside them. Short passages, even single lines, will serve our turn quite sufficiently. Take the two lines which I have just quoted from Homer, the poet's comment on Helen's mention of her brothers;—or take his

Ὰ δειλώ, τί σφῶϊ δόμεν Πηλῆϊ ἄνακτι
θνητῷ; ὑμεῖς δ' ἐστὸν ἀγήρω τ' ἀθανάτω τε.
ἦ ἵνα δυστήνοισι μετ' ἀνδράσιν ἄλγε' ἔχητον;[1]

the address of Zeus to the horses of Peleus;—or take finally this

καὶ σέ, γέρον, τὸ πρὶν μὲν ἀκούομεν ὄλβιον εἶναι·[2]

the words of Achilles to Priam, a suppliant before him. Take that incomparable line and a half of Dante, Ugolino's tremendous words:—

'Io no piangeva; sì dentro impietrai.
Piangevan elli . . .'[3]

take the lovely words of Beatrice to Virgil—

---

[1] 'Ah, unhappy pair, why gave we you to King Peleus, to a mortal? but ye are without old age, and immortal. Was it that with men born in misery ye might have sorrow?'—*Iliad*, xvii. 443–445.

[2] 'Nay, and thou too, old man, in former days wast, as we hear, happy.' —*Iliad*, xxiv. 543.

[3] 'I wailed not, so of stone grew I within;—*they* wailed.'—*Inferno*, xxxiii. 39, 40. (Temple Classics, 49, 50—*Ed.*)

'Io son fatta da Dio, sua mercè, tale,
290 Che la vostra miseria non mi tange,
Nè fiamma d' esto incendio non m' assale . . .'[1]

take the simple, but perfect, single line—

'In la sua volontade è nostra pacc.'[2]

Take of Shakespeare a line or two of Henry the Fourth's
295 expostulation with sleep—

'Wilt thou upon the high and giddy mast
Seal up the ship-boy's eyes, and rock his brains
In cradle of the rude imperious surge . . .'

and take, as well, Hamlet's dying request to Horatio—

300 'If thou didst ever hold me in thy heart,
Absent thee from felicity awhile,
And in this harsh world draw thy breath in pain
To tell my story . . .'

Take of Milton that Miltonic passage—

305 'Darken'd so, yet shone
Above them all the archangel; but his face
Deep scars of thunder had intrench'd, and care
Sat on his faded cheek . . .'

add two such lines as—

310 'And courage never to submit or yield
And what is else not to be overcome . . .'

and finish with the exquisite close to the loss of Proserpine,
the loss

'. . . which cost Ceres all that pain
315 To seek her through the world.'

These few lines, if we have tact and can use them, are enough
even of themselves to keep clear and sound our judgements
about poetry, to save us from fallacious estimates of it, to conduct us to a real estimate.
320 The specimens I have quoted differ widely from one another,

---

[1] 'Of such sort hath God, thanked be His mercy, made me, that your
misery toucheth me not, neither doth the flame of this fire strike me.'
—*Inferno*, ii. 91–93.
[2] 'In His will is our peace.'—*Paradiso*, iii. 85.

but they have in common this: the possession of the very highest
poetical quality. If we are thoroughly penetrated by their
power, we shall find that we have acquired a sense enabling
us, whatever poetry may be laid before us, to feel the degree in
which a high poetical quality is present or wanting there. 325
Critics give themselves great labour to draw out what in
the abstract constitutes the characters of a high quality of
poetry. It is much better simply to have recourse to concrete
examples;—to take specimens of poetry of the high, the very
highest, quality, and to say: The characters of a high quality 330
of poetry are what is expressed *there*. They are far better recognised by being felt in the verse of the master, than by being
perused in the prose of the critic. Nevertheless if we are urgently
pressed to give some critical account of them, we may safely,
perhaps, venture on laying down, not indeed how and why the 335
characters arise, but where and in what they arise. They are
in the matter and substance of the poetry, and they are in its
manner and style. Both of these, the substance and matter on
the one hand, the style and manner on the other, have a mark,
an accent, of high beauty, worth, and power. But if we are 340
asked to define this mark and accent in the abstract, our
answer must be: No, for we should thereby be darkening the
question, not clearing it. The mark and accent are as given by
the substance and matter of that poetry, by the style and
manner of that poetry, and of all other poetry which is akin to 345
it in quality.

Only one thing we may add as to the substance and matter of
poetry, guiding ourselves by Aristotle's profound observation
that the superiority of poetry over history consists in its pos-
sessing a higher truth and a higher seriousness ($\phi\iota\lambda o\sigma o\phi\omega\tau\epsilon\rho o\nu$ 350
$\kappa\alpha\grave{\iota}$ $\sigma\pi o\upsilon\delta\alpha\iota\acute{o}\tau\epsilon\rho o\nu$). Let us add, therefore, to what we have said,
this: that the substance and matter of the best poetry acquire
their special character from possessing, in an eminent degree,
truth and seriousness. We may add yet further what is in itself
evident, that to the style and manner of the best poetry their 355
special character, their accent, is given by their diction, and,
even yet more by their movement. And though we distinguish
between the two characters, the two accents, of superiority, yet
they are nevertheless vitally connected one with the other.

360 The superior character of truth and seriousness, in the matter
and substance of the best poetry, is inseparable from the superiority of diction and movement marking its style and manner.
The two superiorities are closely related, and are in steadfast
proportion one to the other. So far as high poetic truth and
365 seriousness are wanting to a poet's matter and substance, so
far also, we may be sure, will a high poetic stamp of diction
and movement be wanting to his style and manner. In proportion as this high stamp of diction and movement, again, is
absent from a poet's style and manner, we shall find, also, that
370 high poetic truth and seriousness are absent from his substance
and matter.

So stated, these are but dry generalities; their whole force
lies in their application. And I could wish every student of
poetry to make the application of them for himself. Made by
375 himself, the application would impress itself upon his mind far
more deeply than made by me. Neither will my limits allow me
to make any full application of the generalities above pro-
pounded; but in the hope of bringing out, at any rate, some
significance in them, and of establishing an important principle
380 more firmly by their means, I will, in the space which remains
to me, follow rapidly from the commencement the course of our
English poetry with them in my view.

Once more I return to the early poetry of France, with which
our own poetry, in its origins, is indissolubly connected. In the
385 twelfth and thirteenth centuries, that seed-time of all modern
language and literature, the poetry of France had a clear
predominance in Europe. Of the two divisions of that poetry,
its productions in the *langue d'oil* and its productions in the
langue d'oc, the poetry of the *langue d'oc*, of southern France, of
390 the troubadours, is of importance because of its effect on Italian
literature;—the first literature of modern Europe to strike the
true and grand note, and to bring forth, as in Dante and
Petrarch it brought forth, classics. But the predominance of
French poetry in Europe, during the twelfth and thirteenth
395 centuries, is due to its poetry of the *langue d'oil*, the poetry of
northern France and of the tongue which is now the French
language. In the twelfth century the bloom of this romance-
poetry was earlier and stronger in England, at the court of our

Anglo-Norman kings, than in France itself. But it was a bloom
of French poetry; and as our native poetry formed itself, it 400
formed itself out of this. The romance-poems which took
possession of the heart and imagination of Europe in the twelfth
and thirteenth centuries are French; 'they are,' as Southey
justly says, 'the pride of French literature, nor have we anything
which can be placed in competition with them.' Themes were 405
supplied from all quarters; but the romance-setting which was
common to them all, and which gained the ear of Europe, was
French. This constituted for the French poetry, literature, and
language, at the height of the Middle Age, an unchallenged
predominance. The Italian Brunetto Latini, the master of 410
Dante, wrote his *Treasure* in French because, he says, 'la par-
leure en est plus délitable et plus commune à toutes gens.'
In the same century, the thirteenth, the French romance-
writer, Christian of Troyes, formulates the claims, in chivalry
and letters, of France, his native country, as follows:—   415

> 'Or vous ert par ce livre apris,
> Que Gresse ot de chevalerie
> Le premier los et de clergie;
> Puis vint chevalerie à Rome,
> Et de la clergic la some,   420
> Qui ore est en France venue.
> Diex doinst qu'ele i soit retenue,
> Et que li lius li abelisse
> Tant que de France n'isse
> L'onor qui s'i est arestée!'   425

'Now by this book you will learn that first Greece had the
renown for chivalry and letters: then chivalry and the primacy
in letters passed to Rome, and now it is come to France. God
grant it may be kept there; and that the place may please it so
well, that the honour which has come to make stay in France 430
may never depart thence!'

Yet it is now all gone, this French romance-poetry, of which
the weight of substance and the power of style are not unfairly
represented by this extract from Christian of Troyes. Only
by means of the historic estimate can we persuade ourselves 435
now to think that any of it is of poetical importance.

But in the fourteenth century there comes an Englishman
KECT

nourished on this poetry, taught his trade by this poetry,
getting words, rhyme, metre from this poetry; for even of that
440 stanza which the Italians used, and which Chaucer derived
immediately from the Italians, the basis and suggestion
was probably given in France. Chaucer (I have already named
him) fascinated his contemporaries, but so too did Christian of
Troyes and Wolfram of Eschenbach. Chaucer's power of
445 fascination, however, is enduring; his poetical importance does
not need the assistance of the historic estimate; it is real. He is a
genuine source of joy and strength, which is flowing still for
us and will flow always. He will be read, as time goes on, far
more generally than he is read now. His language is a cause of
450 difficulty for us; but so also, and I think in quite as great a
degree, is the language of Burns. In Chaucer's case, as in that
of Burns, it is a difficulty to be unhesitatingly accepted and
overcome.

If we ask ourselves wherein consists the immense superiority
455 of Chaucer's poetry over the romance-poetry—why it is that in
passing from this to Chaucer we suddenly feel ourselves to be
in another world, we shall find that his superiority is both in
the substance of his poetry and in the style of his poetry. His
superiority in substance is given by his large, free, simple, clear
460 yet kindly view of human life,—so unlike the total want, in
the romance-poets, of all intelligent command of it. Chaucer
has not their helplessness; he has gained the power to survey
the world from a central, a truly human point of view. We have
only to call to mind the Prologue to *The Canterbury Tales*. The
465 right comment upon it is Dryden's: 'It is sufficient to say,
according to the proverb, that *here is God's plenty*.' And again:
'He is a perpetual fountain of good sense.' It is by a large, free,
sound representation of things, that poetry, this high criticism
of life, has truth of substance; and Chaucer's poetry has truth
470 of substance.

Of his style and manner, if we think first of the romance-
poetry and then of Chaucer's divine liquidness of diction, his
divine fluidity of movement, it is difficult to speak temperately.
They are irresistible, and justify all the rapture with which his
475 successors speak of his 'gold dew-drops of speech.' Johnson
misses the point entirely when he finds fault with Dryden for

ascribing to Chaucer the first refinement of our numbers, and says that Gower also can show smooth numbers and easy rhymes. The refinement of our numbers means something far more than this. A nation may have versifiers with smooth 480 numbers and easy rhymes, and yet may have no real poetry at all. Chaucer is the father of our splendid English poetry; he is our 'well of English undefiled', because by the lovely charm of his diction, the lovely charm of his movement, he makes an epoch and founds a tradition. In Spenser, Shakespeare, Milton, 485 Keats, we can follow the tradition of the liquid diction, the fluid movement, of Chaucer; at one time it is his liquid diction of which in these poets we feel the virtue, and at another time it is his fluid movement. And the virtue is irresistible.

Bounded as is my space, I must yet find room for an example 490 of Chaucer's virtue, as I have given examples to show the virtue of the great classics. I feel disposed to say that a single line is enough to show the charm of Chaucer's verse; that merely one line like this—

'O martyr souded[1] in virginitee!' 495

has a virtue of manner and movement such as we shall not find in all the verse of romance-poetry;—but this is saying nothing. The virtue is such as we shall not find, perhaps, in all English poetry, outside the poets whom I have named as the special inheritors of Chaucer's tradition. A single line, however, is too 500 little if we have not the strain of Chaucer's verse well in our memory; let us take a stanza. It is from *The Prioress's Tale*, the story of the Christian child murdered in a Jewry—

> 'My throte is cut unto my nekke-bone
> Saidè this child, and as by way of kinde 505
> I should have deyd, yea, longè time agone;
> But Jesu Christ, as ye in bookès finde,
> Will that his glory last and be in minde,
> And for the worship of his mother dere
> Yet may I sing O *Alma* loud and clere.' 510

Wordsworth has modernised this Tale, and to feel how delicate and evanescent is the charm of verse, we have only to read Wordsworth's first three lines of this stanza after Chaucer's—

---

[1] The French *soudé*: soldered, fixed fast.

'My throat is cut unto the bone, I trow,
515   Said this young child, and by the law of kind
I should have died, yea, many hours ago.'

The charm is departed. It is often said that the power of liquidness and fluidity in Chaucer's verse was dependent upon a free,
a licentious dealing with language, such as is now impossible;
520 upon a liberty, such as Burns too enjoyed, of making words
like *neck, bird,* into a dissyllable by adding to them, and words
like *cause, rhyme,* into a dissyllable by sounding the *e* mute. It is
true that Chaucer's fluidity is conjoined with this liberty, and
is admirably served by it; but we ought not to say that it was
525 dependent upon it. It was dependent upon his talent. Other
poets with a like liberty do not attain to the fluidity of Chaucer;
Burns himself does not attain to it. Poets, again, who have a
talent akin to Chaucer's, such as Shakespeare or Keats, have
known how to attain to his fluidity without the like liberty.
530 And yet Chaucer is not one of the great classics. His poetry
transcends and effaces, easily and without effort, all the
romance-poetry of Catholic Christendom; it transcends and
effaces all the English poetry contemporary with it; it transcends and effaces all the English poetry subsequent to it down
535 to the age of Elizabeth. Of such avail is poetic truth of substance,
in its natural and necessary union with poetic truth of style.
And yet, I say, Chaucer is not one of the great classics. He has
not their accent.

What is wanting to him is suggested by the mere mention of
540 the name of the first great classic of Christendom, the immortal
poet who died eighty years before Chaucer,—Dante. The
accent of such verse as

'In la sua volontade è nostra pace . . .'

is altogether beyond Chaucer's reach; we praise him, but we
545 feel that this accent is out of the question for him. It may be
said that it was necessarily out of the reach of any poet in the
England of that stage of growth. Possibly; but we are to adopt a
real, not a historic, estimate of poetry. However we may
account for its absence, something is wanting, then, to the
550 poetry of Chaucer, which poetry must have before it can be
placed in the glorious class of the best. And there is no doubt

what that something is. It is the σπουδαιότης, the high and
excellent seriousness, which Aristotle assigns as one of the grand
virtues of poetry. The substance of Chaucer's poetry, his view
of things and his criticism of life, has largeness, freedom, shrewd- 555
ness, benignity; but it has not this high seriousness. Homer's
criticism of life has it, Dante's has it, Shakespeare's has it. It is
this chiefly which gives to our spirits what they can rest upon;
and with the increasing demands of our modern ages upon
poetry, this virtue of giving us what we can rest upon will be 560
more and more highly esteemed. A voice from the slums of
Paris, fifty or sixty years after Chaucer, the voice of poor Villon
out of his life of riot and crime, has at its happy moments (as,
for instance, in the last stanza of *La Belle Heaulmière*[1]) more of
this important poetic virtue of seriousness than all the 565
productions of Chaucer. But its apparition in Villon, and in men
like Villon, is fitful; the greatness of the great poets, the power
of their criticism of life, is that their virtue is sustained.

To our praise, therefore, of Chaucer as a poet there must be
this limitation; he lacks the high seriousness of the great classics, 570
and therewith an important part of their virtue. Still, the main
fact for us to bear in mind about Chaucer is his sterling value
according to that real estimate which we firmly adopt for all
poets. He has poetic truth of substance, though he has not
high poetic seriousness, and corresponding to his truth of 575
substance he has an exquisite virtue of style and manner. With
him is born our real poetry.

---

[1] The name *Heaulmière* is said to be derived from a head-dress (helm)
worn as a mark by courtesans. In Villon's ballad, a poor old creature of
this class laments her days of youth and beauty. The last stanza of the
ballad runs thus—

> 'Ainsi le bon temps regretons
> Entre nous, pauvres vieilles sottes.
> Assises bas, à croppetons,
> Tout en ung tas comme pelottes;
> A petit feu de chenevottes
> Tost allumées, tost estainctes.
> Et jadis fusmes si mignottes!
> Ainsi en prend à maintz et maintes.'

'Thus amongst ourselves we regret the good time, poor silly old things,
low-seated on our heels, all in a heap like so many balls, by a little fire of
hemp-stalks, soon lighted, soon spent. And once we were such darlings! So
fares it with many and many a one.'

For my present purpose I need not dwell on our Elizabethan poetry, or on the continuation and close of this poetry in
580 Milton. We all of us profess to be agreed in the estimate of this poetry; we all of us recognise it as great poetry, our greatest, and Shakespeare and Milton as our poetical classics. The real estimate, here, has universal currency. With the next age of our poetry divergency and difficulty begin. An
585 historic estimate of that poetry has established itself; and the question is, whether it will be found to coincide with the real estimate.

The age of Dryden, together with our whole eighteenth century which followed it, sincerely believed itself to have
590 produced poetical classics of its own, and even to have made advance, in poetry, beyond all its predecessors. Dryden regards as not seriously disputable the opinion 'that the sweetness of English verse was never understood or practised by our fathers'. Cowley could see nothing at all in Chaucer's poetry.
595 Dryden heartily admired, and, as we have seen, praised its matter admirably; but of its exquisite manner and movement all he can find to say is that 'there is the rude sweetness of a Scotch tune in it, which is natural and pleasing, though not perfect.' Addison, wishing to praise Chaucer's numbers, com-
600 pares them with Dryden's own. And all through the eighteenth century, and down even into our own times, the stereotyped phrase of approbation for good verse found in our early poetry has been, that it even approached the verse of Dryden, Addison, Pope, and Johnson.
605   Are Dryden and Pope poetical classics? Is the historic estimate, which represents them as such, and which has been so long established that it cannot easily give way, the real estimate? Wordsworth and Coleridge, as is well known, denied it; but the authority of Wordsworth and Coleridge does not
610 weigh much with the young generation, and there are many signs to show that the eighteenth century and its judgements are coming into favour again. Are the favourite poets of the eighteenth century classics?

It is impossible within my present limits to discuss the ques-
615 tion fully. And what man of letters would not shrink from seeming to dispose dictatorially of the claims of two men who

are, at any rate, such masters in letters as Dryden and Pope;
two men of such admirable talent, both of them, and one of
them, Dryden, a man, on all sides, of such energetic and genial
power? And yet, if we are to gain the full benefit from poetry, 620
we must have the real estimate of it. I cast about for some mode
of arriving, in the present case, at such an estimate without
offence. And perhaps the best way is to begin, as it is easy to
begin, with cordial praise.

When we find Chapman, the Elizabethan translator of 625
Homer, expressing himself in his preface thus: 'Though truth
in her very nakedness sits in so deep a pit, that from Gades to
Aurora and Ganges few eyes can sound her, I hope yet those
few here will so discover and confirm that, the date being out
of her darkness in this morning of our poet, he shall now gird his 630
temples with the sun',—we pronounce that such a prose is
intolerable. When we find Milton writing: 'And long it was
not after, when I was confirmed in this opinion, that he, who
would not be frustrate of his hope to write well hereafter in
laudable things, ought himself to be a true poem',—we pro- 635
nounce that such a prose has its own grandeur, but that it is
obsolete and inconvenient. But when we find Dryden telling us:
'What Virgil wrote in the vigour of his age, in plenty and at
ease, I have undertaken to translate in my declining years;
struggling with wants, oppressed with sickness, curbed in my 640
genius, liable to be misconstrued in all I write,'—then we
exclaim that here at last we have the true English prose, a
prose such as we would all gladly use if we only knew how.
Yet Dryden was Milton's contemporary.

But after the Restoration the time had come when our nation 645
felt the imperious need of a fit prose. So, too, the time had
likewise come when our nation felt the imperious need of
freeing itself from the absorbing preoccupation which religion
in the Puritan age had exercised. It was impossible that this
freedom should be brought about without some negative 650
excess, without some neglect and impairment of the religious
life of the soul; and the spiritual history of the eighteenth
century shows us that the freedom was not achieved without
them. Still, the freedom was achieved; the preoccupation, an
undoubtedly baneful and retarding one if it had continued, was 655

got rid of. And as with religion amongst us at that period, so it was also with letters. A fit prose was a necessity; but it was impossible that a fit prose should establish itself amongst us without some touch of frost to the imaginative life of the soul.
660 The needful qualities for a fit prose are regularity, uniformity, precision, balance. The men of letters, whose destiny it may be to bring their nation to the attainment of a fit prose, must of necessity, whether they work in prose or in verse, give a predominating, and almost exclusive attention to the qualities of
665 regularity, uniformity, precision, balance. But an almost exclusive attention to these qualities involves some repression and silencing of poetry.

We are to regard Dryden as the puissant and glorious founder, Pope as the splendid high priest, of our age of prose
670 and reason, of our excellent and indispensable eighteenth century. For the purposes of their mission and destiny their poetry, like their prose, is admirable. Do you ask me whether Dryden's verse, take it almost where you will, is not good?

'A milk-white Hind, immortal and unchanged,
675   Fed on the lawns and in the forest ranged.'

I answer: Admirable for the purposes of the inaugurator of an age of prose and reason. Do you ask me whether Pope's verse, take it almost where you will, is not good?

'To Hounslow Heath I point, and Banstead Down;
680   Thence comes your mutton, and these chicks my own.'

I answer: Admirable for the purposes of the high priest of an age of prose and reason. But do you ask me whether such verse proceeds from men with an adequate poetic criticism of life, from men whose criticism of life has a high seriousness, or even,
685 without that high seriousness, has poetic largeness, freedom, insight, benignity? Do you ask me whether the application of ideas to life in the verse of these men, often a powerful application, no doubt, is a powerful *poetic* application? Do you ask me whether the poetry of these men has either the matter or the
690 inseparable manner of such an adequate poetic criticism whether it has the accent of

'Absent thee from felicity awhile . . .'
or of

'And what is else not to be overcome . . .'
or of   695
'O martyr souded in virginitee!'

I answer: It has not and cannot have them; it is the poetry of
the builders of an age of prose and reason. Though they may
write in verse, though they may in a certain sense be masters
of the art of versification, Dryden and Pope are not classics of 700
our poetry, they are classics of our prose.

Gray is our poetical classic of that literature and age; the
position of Gray is singular, and demands a word of notice here.
He has not the volume or the power of poets who, coming in
times more favourable, have attained to an independent 705
criticism of life. But he lived with the great poets, he lived,
above all, with the Greeks, through perpetually studying and
enjoying them; and he caught their poetic point of view
for regarding life, caught their poetic manner. The point of
view and the manner are not self-sprung in him, he caught 710
them of others; and he had not the free and abundant use of
them. But whereas Addison and Pope never had the use of
them, Gray had the use of them at times. He is the scantiest
and frailest of classics in our poetry, but he is a classic.

And now, after Gray, we are met, as we draw towards the 715
end of the eighteenth century, we are met by the great name of
Burns. We enter now on times where the personal estimate of
poets begins to be rife, and where the real estimate of them is
not reached without difficulty. But in spite of the disturbing
pressures of personal partiality, of national partiality, let us 720
try to reach a real estimate of the poetry of Burns.

By his English poetry Burns in general belongs to the
eighteenth century, and has little importance for us.

'Mark ruffian Violence, distain'd with crimes,
Rousing elate in these degenerate times;   725
View unsuspecting Innocence a prey,
As guileful Fraud points out the erring way;
While subtle Litigation's pliant tongue
The life-blood equal sucks of Right and Wrong!'

Evidently this is not the real Burns, or his name and fame 730
would have disappeared long ago. Nor is Clarinda's love-poet,

Sylvander, the real Burns either. But he tells us himself: 'These
English songs gravel me to death. I have not the command of the
language that I have of my native tongue. In fact, I think that
735 my ideas are more barren in English than in Scotch. I have
been at *Duncan Gray* to dress it in English, but all I can do is
desperately stupid.' We English turn naturally, in Burns, to the
poems in our own language, because we can read them easily;
but in those poems we have not the real Burns.

740 The real Burns is of course in his Scotch poems. Let us
boldly say that of much of this poetry, a poetry dealing
perpetually with Scotch drink, Scotch religion, and Scotch
manners, a Scotchman's estimate is apt to be personal. A
Scotchman is used to this world of Scotch drink, Scotch religion,
745 and Scotch manners; he has a tenderness for it; he meets its
poet half-way. In this tender mood he reads pieces like the
Holy Fair or *Halloween*. But this world of Scotch drink, Scotch
religion, and Scotch manners is against a poet, not for him,
when it is not a partial countryman who reads him; for in itself
750 it is not a beautiful world, and no one can deny that it is of
advantage to a poet to deal with a beautiful world. Burns's
world of Scotch drink, Scotch religion, and Scotch manners, is
often a harsh, a sordid, a repulsive world; even the world of his
Cottar's Saturday Night is not a beautiful world. No doubt a
755 poet's criticism of life may have such truth and power that it
triumphs over its world and delights us. Burns may triumph
over this world, often he does triumph over his world, but let us
observe how and where. Burns is the first case we have had
where the bias of the personal estimate tends to mislead; let us
760 look at him closely—he can bear it.

Many of his admirers will tell us that we have Burns, con-
vivial, genuine, delightful, here—

> 'Leeze me on drink! it gies us mair
> Than either school or college;
765 > It kindles wit, it waukens lair,
> It pangs us fou o' knowledge.
> Be't whisky gill or penny wheep
> Or ony stronger potion,
> It never fails, on drinking deep,
770 > To kittle up our notion
> By night or day.'

There is a great deal of that sort of thing in Burns, and it is
unsatisfactory, not because it is bacchanalian poetry, but because it has not that accent of sincerity which bacchanalian
poetry, to do it justice, very often has. There is something in it 775
of bravado, something which makes us feel that we have not
the man speaking to us with his real voice; something, therefore, poetically unsound.

With still more confidence, will his admirers tell us that we
have the genuine Burns, the great poet, when his strain asserts 780
the independence, equality, dignity, of men, as in the famous
song *For a' that and a' that*—

> 'A prince can mak' a belted knight,
>   A marquis, duke, and a' that;
> But an honest man's aboon his might,   785
>   Guid faith he mauna fa' that!
>   For a' that, and a' that,
>   Their dignities, and a' that,
>   The pith o' sense, and pride o' worth,
>   Are higher rank than a' that.'   790

Here they find his grand, genuine touches; and still more, when
this puissant genius, who so often set morality at defiance, falls
moralising—

> 'The sacred lowe o' weel-placed love
>   Luxuriantly indulge it;   795
> But never tempt th' illicit rove,
>   Tho' naething should divulge it:
> I waive the quantum o' the sin,
>   The hazard o' concealing,
> But och! it hardens a' within,   800
>   And petrifies the feeling.'

Or in a higher strain—

> 'Who made the heart, 'tis He alone
>   Decidedly can try us;
> He knows each chord, its various tone;   805
>   Each spring, its various bias.
> Then at the balance let's be mute,
>   We never can adjust it;
> What's *done* we partly may compute,
>   But know not what's resisted.'   810

Or in a better strain yet, a strain, his admirers will say, unsur-
passable—

'To make a happy fire-side clime
To weans and wife,
815   That's the true pathos and sublime
Of human life.'

There is criticism of life for you, the admirers of Burns will say
to us; there is the application of ideas to life! There is, undoubtedly. The doctrine of the last-quoted lines coincides
820 almost exactly with what was the aim and end, Xenophon tells
us, of all the teaching of Socrates. And the application is a
powerful one; made by a man of vigorous understanding, and
(need I say?) a master of language.

But for supreme poetical success more is required than the
825 powerful application of ideas to life; it must be an application
under the conditions fixed by the laws of poetic truth and poetic
beauty. Those laws fix as an essential condition, in the poet's
treatment of such matters as are here in question, high seriousness;—the high seriousness which comes from absolute sin-
830 cerity. The accent of high seriousness, born of absolute
sincerity, is what gives to such verse as

'In la sua volontade è nostra pace . . .'

to such criticism of life as Dante's, its power. Is this accent felt
in the passages which I have been quoting from Burns? Surely
835 not; surely, if our sense is quick, we must perceive that we have not
in those passages a voice from the very inmost soul of the genuine
Burns; he is not speaking to us from these depths, he is more or
less preaching. And the compensation for admiring such passages
less, from missing the perfect poetic accent in them, will be that
840 we shall admire more the poetry where that accent is found.

No; Burns, like Chaucer, comes short of the high seriousness
of the great classics, and the virtue of matter and manner which
goes with that high seriousness is wanting to his work. At
moments he touches it in a profound and passionate melan-
845 choly, as in those four immortal lines taken by Byron as a
motto for *The Bride of Abydos*, but which have in them a depth
of poetic quality such as resides in no verse of Byron's own—

'Had we never loved sae kindly,
Had we never loved sae blindly,
850   Never met, or never parted,
We had ne'er been broken-hearted.'

But a whole poem of that quality Burns cannot make; the rest, in the *Farewell to Nancy*, is verbiage.

We arrive best at the real estimate of Burns, I think, by conceiving his work as having truth of matter and truth of manner, but not the accent or the poetic virtue of the highest masters. His genuine criticism of life, when the sheer poet in him speaks, is ironic; it is not—

> 'Thou Power Supreme, whose mighty scheme
> These woes of mine fulfil,
> Here firm I rest, they must be best
> Because they are Thy will!'

It is far rather: *Whistle owre the lave o't!* Yet we may say of him as of Chaucer, that of life and the world, as they come before him, his view is large, free, shrewd, benignant,—truly poetic, therefore; and his manner of rendering what he sees is to match. But we must note, at the same time, his great difference from Chaucer. The freedom of Chaucer is heightened, in Burns, by a fiery, reckless energy; the benignity of Chaucer deepens, in Burns, into an overwhelming sense of the pathos of things;— of the pathos of human nature, the pathos, also, of non-human nature. Instead of the fluidity of Chaucer's manner, the manner of Burns has spring, bounding swiftness. Burns is by far the greater force, though he has perhaps less charm. The world of Chaucer is fairer, richer, more significant than that of Burns; but when the largeness and freedom of Burns get full sweep, as in *Tam o' Shanter*, or still more in that puissant and splendid production, *The Jolly Beggars*, his world may be what it will, his poetic genius triumphs over it. In the world of *The Jolly Beggars* there is more than hideousness and squalor, there is bestiality; yet the piece is a superb poetic success. It has a breadth, truth, and power which make the famous scene in Auerbach's Cellar, of Goethe's *Faust*, seem artificial and tame beside it, and which are only matched by Shakespeare and Aristophanes.

Here, where his largeness and freedom serve him so admirably, and also in those poems and songs where to shrewdness he adds infinite archness and wit, and to benignity infinite pathos, where his manner is flawless, and a perfect poetic whole is the result,—in things like the address to the mouse whose home

he had ruined, in things like *Duncan Gray, Tam Glen, Whistle and I'll come to you my Lad, Auld Lang Syne* (this list might be made much longer)—here we have the genuine Burns, of whom the real estimate must be high indeed. Not a classic, nor with
895 the excellent σπουδαιότης of the great classics, nor with a verse rising to a criticism of life and a virtue like theirs; but a poet with thorough truth of substance and an answering truth of style, giving us a poetry sound to the core. We all of us have a leaning towards the pathetic, and may be inclined perhaps to
900 prize Burns most for his touches of piercing, sometimes almost intolerable, pathos; for verse like—

> 'We twa hae paidl't i' the burn
> From mornin' sun till dine;
> But seas between us braid hae roar'd
905 > Sin auld lang syne . . .'

where he is as lovely as he is sound. But perhaps it is by the perfection of soundness of his lighter and archer masterpieces that he is poetically most wholesome for us. For the votary misled by a personal estimate of Shelley, as so many of us have
910 been, are, and will be,—of that beautiful spirit building his many-coloured haze of words and images

> 'Pinnacled dim in the intense inane'—

no contact can be wholesomer than the contact with Burns at his archest and soundest. Side by side with the

915 > 'On the brink of the night and the morning
> My coursers are wont to respire,
> But the Earth has just whispered a warning
> That their flight must be swifter than fire . . .'

of *Prometheus Unbound*, how salutary, how very salutary, to place
920 this from *Tam Glen*—

> 'My minnie does constantly deave me
> And bids me beware o' young men;
> They flatter, she says, to deceive me;
> But wha can think sae o' Tam Glen?'

925 But we enter on burning ground as we approach the poetry of times so near to us—poetry like that of Byron, Shelley, and Wordsworth—of which the estimates are so often not only

personal, but personal with passion. For my purpose, it is enough to have taken the single case of Burns, the first poet we come to of whose work the estimate formed is evidently apt 930 to be personal, and to have suggested how we may proceed, using the poetry of the great classics as a sort of touchstone, to correct this estimate, as we had previously corrected by the same means the historic estimate where we met with it. A collection like the present, with its succession of celebrated 935 names and celebrated poems, offers a good opportunity to us for resolutely endeavouring to make our estimates of poetry real. I have sought to point out a method which will help us in making them so, and to exhibit it in use so far as to put any one who likes in a way of applying it for himself. 940

At any rate the end to which the method and the estimate are designed to lead, and from leading to which, if they do lead to it, they get their whole value,—the benefit of being able clearly to feel and deeply to enjoy the best, the truly classic, in poetry,—is an end, let me say it once more at parting, of 945 supreme importance. We are often told that an era is opening in which we are to see multitudes of a common sort of readers, and masses of a common sort of literature; that such readers do not want and could not relish anything better than such literature, and that to provide it is becoming a vast and profitable 950 industry. Even if good literature entirely lost currency with the world, it would still be abundantly worth while to continue to enjoy it by oneself. But it never will lose currency with the world, in spite of momentary appearances; it never will lose supremacy. Currency and supremacy are insured to it, not 955 indeed by the world's deliberate and conscious choice, but by something far deeper,—by the instinct of self-preservation in humanity.

D. H. LAWRENCE

Why the Novel Matters

WE have curious ideas of ourselves. We think of ourselves as a
body with a spirit in it, or a body with a soul in it, or a body
with a mind in it. *Mens sana in corpore sano.* The years drink up
the wine, and at last throw the bottle away, the body, of course,
being the bottle.

It is a funny sort of superstition. Why should I look at my
hand, as it so cleverly writes these words, and decide that it is a
mere nothing compared to the mind that directs it? Is there
really any huge difference between my hand and my brain?
Or my mind? My hand is alive, it flickers with a life of its own.
It meets all the strange universe in touch, and learns a vast
number of things, and knows a vast number of things. My hand,
as it writes these words, slips gaily along, jumps like a grass-
hopper to dot an *i*, feels the table rather cold, gets a little bored
if I write too long, has its own rudiments of thought, and is just
as much *me* as is my brain, my mind, or my soul. Why should
I imagine that there is a *me* which is more *me* than my hand is?
Since my hand is absolutely alive, me alive.

Whereas, of course, as far as I am concerned, my pen isn't
alive at all. My pen *isn't me* alive. Me alive ends at my finger-
tips.

Whatever is me alive is me. Every tiny bit of my hands is
alive, every little freckle and hair and fold of skin. And whatever is me alive is me. Only my finger-nails, those ten little
weapons between me and an inanimate universe, they cross
the mysterious Rubicon between me alive and things like my
pen, which are not alive, in my own sense.

So, seeing my hand is all alive and me alive, wherein is it just
a bottle, or a jug, or a tin can, or a vessel of clay, or any of the
rest of that nonsense? True, if I cut it it will bleed, like a can

of cherries. But then the skin that is cut, and the veins that bleed, and the bones that should never be seen, they are all just as alive as the blood that flows. So the tin can business, or vessel of clay, is just bunk.

And that's what you learn, when you're a novelist. And that's what you are very liable *not* to know, if you're a parson, or a philosopher, or a scientist, or a stupid person. If you're a parson, you talk about souls in heaven. If you're a novelist, you know that paradise is in the palm of your hand, and on the end of your nose, because both are alive; and alive, and man alive, which is more than you can say, for certain, of paradise. Paradise is after life, and I for one am not keen on anything that is *after* life. If you are a philosopher, you talk about infinity, and the pure spirit which knows all things. But if you pick up a novel, you realize immediately that infinity is just a handle to this self-same jug of a body of mine; while as for knowing, if I find my finger in the fire, I know that fire burns with a knowledge so emphatic and vital, it leaves Nirvana merely a conjecture. Oh, yes, my body, me alive, *knows*, and knows intensely. And as for the sum of all knowledge, it can't be anything more than an accumulation of all the things I know in the body, and you, dear reader, know in the body.

These damned philosophers, they talk as if they suddenly went off in steam, and were then much more important than they are when they're in their shirts. It is nonsense. Every man, philosopher included, ends in his own finger-tips. That's the end of his man alive. As for the words and thoughts and sighs and aspirations that fly from him, they are so many tremulations in the ether, and not alive at all. But if the tremulations reach another man alive, he may receive them into his life, and his life may take on a new colour, like a chameleon creeping from a brown rock on to a green leaf. All very well and good. It still doesn't alter the fact that the so-called spirit, the message or teaching of the philosopher or the saint, isn't alive at all, but just a tremulation upon the ether, like a radio message. All this spirit stuff is just tremulations upon the ether. If you, as man alive, quiver from the tremulation of the ether into new life, that is because you are man alive, and you take sustenance and stimulation into your alive man in a myriad ways. But to

70 say that the message, or the spirit which is communicated to
you, is more important than your living body, is nonsense.
You might as well say that the potato at dinner was more
important.

Nothing is important but life. And for myself, I can absolutely
75 see life nowhere but in the living. Life with a capital L is only
man alive. Even a cabbage in the rain is cabbage alive. All
things that are alive are amazing. And all things that are dead
are subsidiary to the living. Better a live dog than a dead lion.
But better a live lion than a live dog. *C'est la vie!*

80   It seems impossible to get a saint, or a philosopher, or a
scientist, to stick to this simple truth. They are all, in a sense,
renegades. The saint wishes to offer himself up as spiritual food
for the multitude. Even Francis of Assisi turns himself into a
sort of angel-cake, of which anyone may take a slice. But an
85 angel-cake is rather less than man alive. And poor St. Francis
might well apologize to his body, when he is dying: 'Oh,
pardon me, my body, the wrong I did you through the years!'
It was no wafer, for others to eat.

The philosopher, on the other hand, because he can think,
90 decides that nothing but thoughts matter. It is as if a rabbit,
because he can make little pills, should decide that nothing but
little pills matter. As for the scientist, he has absolutely no use
for me so long as I am man alive. To the scientist, I am dead.
He puts under the microscope a bit of dead me, and calls it me.
95 He takes me to pieces, and says first one piece, and then another
piece, is me. My heart, my liver, my stomach have all been
scientifically me, according to the scientist; and nowadays I am
either a brain, or nerves, or glands, or something more up-to-
date in the tissue line.

100   Now I absolutely flatly deny that I am a soul, or a body, or a
mind, or an intelligence, or a brain, or a nervous system, or a
bunch of glands, or any of the rest of these bits of me. The
whole is greater than the part. And therefore, I, who am man
alive, am greater than my soul, or spirit, or body, or mind, or
105 consciousness, or anything else that is merely a part of me.
I am a man, and alive. I am man alive, and as long as I can,
I intend to go on being man alive.

For this reason I am a novelist. And being a novelist, I

consider myself superior to the saint, the scientist, the philosopher, and the poet, who are all great masters of different bits of 110
man alive, but never get the whole hog.

The novel is the one bright book of life. Books are not life.
They are only tremulations on the ether. But the novel as a
tremulation can make the whole man alive tremble. Which is
more than poetry, philosophy, science, or any other book- 115
tremulation can do.

The novel is the book of life. In this sense, the Bible is a great
confused novel. You may say, it is about God. But it is really
about man alive. Adam, Eve, Sarai, Abraham, Isaac, Jacob,
Samuel, David, Bath-Sheba, Ruth, Esther, Solomon, Job, 120
Isaiah, Jesus, Mark, Judas, Paul, Peter: what is it but man
alive, from start to finish? Man alive, not mere bits. Even the
Lord is another man alive, in a burning bush, throwing the
tablets of stone at Moses's head.

I do hope you begin to get my idea, why the novel is 125
supremely important, as a tremulation on the ether. Plato
makes the perfect ideal being tremble in me. But that's only a bit
of me. Perfection is only a bit, in the strange make-up of man
alive. The Sermon on the Mount makes the selfless spirit of me
quiver. But that, too, is only a bit of me. The Ten Command- 130
ments set the old Adam shivering in me, warning me that I
am a thief and a murderer, unless I watch it. But even the old
Adam is only a bit of me.

I very much like all these bits of me to be set trembling
with life and the wisdom of life. But I do ask that the whole of 135
me shall tremble in its wholeness, some time or other.

And this, of course, must happen in me, living.

But as far as it can happen from a communication, it can only
happen when a whole novel communicates itself to me. The
Bible—but *all* the Bible—and Homer, and Shakespeare: these 140
are the supreme old novels. These are all things to all men.
Which means that in their wholeness they affect the whole
man alive, which is the man himself, beyond any part of him.
They set the whole tree trembling with a new access of life,
they do not just stimulate growth in one direction.   145

I don't want to grow in any one direction any more. And, if I
can help it, I don't want to stimulate anybody else into some

particular direction. A particular direction ends in a *cul-de-sac*.
We're in a *cul-de-sac* at present.

150   I don't believe in any dazzling revelation, or in any supreme
Word. 'The grass withereth, the flower fadeth, but the Word of
the Lord shall stand for ever.' That's the kind of stuff we've
drugged ourselves with. As a matter of fact, the grass withereth,
but comes up all the greener for that reason, after the rains.
155 The flower fadeth, and therefore the bud opens. But the Word
of the Lord, being man-uttered and a mere vibration on the
ether, becomes staler and staler, more and more boring, till at
last we turn a deaf ear and it ceases to exist, far more finally
than any withered grass. It is grass that renews its youth like
160 the eagle, not any Word.

We should ask for no absolutes, or absolute. Once and for all
and for ever, let us have done with the ugly imperialism of
any absolute. There is no absolute good, there is nothing
absolutely right. All things flow and change, and even change
165 is not absolute. The whole is a strange assembly of apparently
incongruous parts, slipping past one another.

Me, man alive, I am a very curious assembly of incongruous
parts. My yea! of today is oddly different from my yea! of
yesterday. My tears of tomorrow will have nothing to do with
170 my tears of a year ago. If the one I love remains unchanged and
unchanging, I shall cease to love her. It is only because she
changes and startles me into change and defies my inertia, and
is herself staggered in her inertia by my changing, that I can
continue to love her. If she stayed put, I might as well love the
175 pepper-pot.

In all this change, I maintain a certain integrity. But woe
betide me if I try to put my finger on it. If I say of myself, I am
this, I am that!—then, if I stick to it, I turn into a stupid fixed
thing like a lamp-post. I shall never know wherein lies my
180 integrity, my individuality, my me. I *can* never know it. It is
useless to talk about my ego. That only means that I have made
up an *idea* of myself, and that I am trying to cut myself out to
pattern. Which is no good. You can cut your cloth to fit your
coat, but you can't clip bits off your living body, to trim it down
185 to your idea. True, you can put yourself into ideal corsets. But
even in ideal corsets, fashions change.

Let us learn from the novel. In the novel, the characters can do nothing but *live*. If they keep on being good, according to pattern, or bad, according to pattern, or even volatile, according to pattern, they cease to live, and the novel falls dead. A character in a novel has got to live, or it is nothing.

We, likewise, in life have got to live, or we are nothing.

What we mean by living is, of course, just as indescribable as what we mean by *being*. Men get ideas into their heads, of what they mean by Life, and they proceed to cut life out to pattern. Sometimes they go into the desert to seek God, sometimes they go into the desert to seek cash, sometimes it is wine, woman, and song, and again it is water, political reform, and votes. You never know what it will be next: from killing your neighbour with hideous bombs and gas that tears the lungs, to supporting a Foundlings Home and preaching infinite Love, and being co-respondent in a divorce.

In all this wild welter, we need some sort of guide. It's no good inventing Thou Shalt Nots!

What then? Turn truly, honourably to the novel, and see wherein you are man alive, and wherein you are dead man in life. You may love a woman as man alive, and you may be making love to a woman as sheer dead man in life. You may eat your dinner as man alive, or as a mere masticating corpse. As man alive you may have a shot at your enemy. But as a ghastly simulacrum of life you may be firing bombs into men who are neither your enemies nor your friends, but just things you are dead to. Which is criminal, when the things happen to be alive.

To be alive, to be man alive, to be whole man alive: that is the point. And at its best, the novel, and the novel supremely, can help you. It can help you not to be dead man in life. So much of a man walks about dead and a carcass in the street and house, today: so much of women is merely dead. Like a pianoforte with half the notes mute.

But in the novel you can see, plainly, when the man goes dead, the woman goes inert. You can develop an instinct for life, if you will, instead of a theory of right and wrong, good and bad.

In life, there is right and wrong, good and bad, all the time.

But what is right in one case is wrong in another. And in the novel you see one man becoming a corpse, because of his so-called goodness, another going dead because of his so-called wickedness. Right and wrong is an instinct: but an instinct of
230 the whole consciousness in a man, bodily, mental, spiritual at once. And only in the novel are *all* things given full play, or at least, they may be given full play, when we realize that life itself, and not inert safety, is the reason for living. For out of the full play of all things emerges the only thing that is any-
235 thing, the wholeness of a man, the wholeness of a woman, man alive, and live woman.

T. S. ELIOT

Tradition and the Individual Talent

I

In English writing we seldom speak of tradition, though we
occasionally apply its name in deploring its absence. We cannot refer to 'the tradition' or to 'a tradition'; at most, we
employ the adjective in saying that the poetry of So-and-so is
'traditional' or even 'too traditional'. Seldom, perhaps, does 5
the word appear except in a phrase of censure. If otherwise, it
is vaguely approbative, with the implication, as to the work
approved, of some pleasing archaeological reconstruction. You
can hardly make the word agreeable to English ears without
this comfortable reference to the reassuring science of archaeo- 10
logy.

Certainly the word is not likely to appear in our apprecia-
tions of living or dead writers. Every nation, every race, has
not only its own creative, but its own critical turn of mind;
and is even more oblivious of the shortcomings and limitations 15
of its critical habits than of those of its creative genius. We know,
or think we know, from the enormous mass of critical writing
that has appeared in the French language the critical method or
habit of the French; we only conclude (we are such unconscious
people) that the French are 'more critical' than we, and some- 20
times even plume ourselves a little with the fact, as if the French
were the less spontaneous. Perhaps they are; but we might
remind ourselves that criticism is as inevitable as breathing,
and that we should be none the worse for articulating what
passes in our minds when we read a book and feel an emotion 25
about it, for criticizing our own minds in their work of criticism.
One of the facts that might come to light in this process is our
tendency to insist, when we praise a poet, upon those aspects
of his work in which he least resembles anyone else. In these
aspects or parts of his work we pretend to find what is indivi- 30
dual, what is the peculiar essence of the man. We dwell with

satisfaction upon the poet's difference from his predecessors, especially his immediate predecessors; we endeavour to find something that can be isolated in order to be enjoyed. Whereas
35 if we approach a poet without this prejudice we shall often find that not only the best, but the most individual parts of his work may be those in which the dead poets, his ancestors, assert their immortality most vigorously. And I do not mean the impressionable period of adolescence, but the period of full maturity.
40   Yet if the only form of tradition, of handing down, consisted in following the ways of the immediate generation before us in a blind or timid adherence to its successes, 'tradition' should positively be discouraged. We have seen many such simple currents soon lost in the sand; and novelty is better than repeti-
45 tion. Tradition is a matter of much wider significance. It cannot be inherited, and if you want it you must obtain it by great labour. It involves, in the first place, the historical sense, which we may call nearly indispensable to anyone who would continue to be a poet beyond his twenty-fifth year; and the histori-
50 cal sense involves a perception, not only of the pastness of the past, but of its presence; the historical sense compels a man to write not merely with his own generation in his bones, but with a feeling that the whole of the literature of Europe from Homer and within it the whole of the literature of his own country has
55 a simultaneous existence and composes a simultaneous order. This historical sense, which is a sense of the timeless as well as of the temporal and of the timeless and of the temporal together, is what makes a writer traditional. And it is at the same time what makes a writer most acutely conscious of his place in
60 time, of his own contemporaneity.

No poet, no artist of any art, has his complete meaning alone. His significance, his appreciation is the appreciation of his relation to the dead poets and artists. You cannot value him alone; you must set him, for contrast and comparison, among
65 the dead. I mean this as a principle of aesthetic, not merely historical, criticism. The necessity that he shall conform, that he shall cohere, is not onesided; what happens when a new work of art is created is something that happens simultaneously to all the works of art which preceded it. The existing monuments
70 form an ideal order among themselves, which is modified by

the introduction of the new (the really new) work of art among them. The existing order is complete before the new work arrives; for order to persist after the supervention of novelty, the *whole* existing order must be, if ever so slightly, altered; and so the relations, proportions, values of each work of art toward 75 the whole are readjusted; and this is conformity between the old and the new. Whoever has approved this idea of order, of the form of European, of English literature will not find it preposterous that the past should be altered by the present as much as the present is directed by the past. And the poet who 80 is aware of this will be aware of great difficulties and responsibilities.

In a peculiar sense he will be aware also that he must inevitably be judged by the standards of the past. I say judged, not amputated, by them; not judged to be as good as, or worse or 85 better than, the dead; and certainly not judged by the canons of dead critics. It is a judgement, a comparison, in which two things are measured by each other. To conform merely would be for the new work not really to conform at all; it would not be new, and would therefore not be a work of art. And we do not 90 quite say that the new is more valuable because it fits in; but its fitting in is a test of its value—a test, it is true, which can only be slowly and cautiously applied, for we are none of us infallible judges of conformity. We say: it appears to conform, and is perhaps individual, or it appears individual, and may 95 conform; but we are hardly likely to find that it is one and not the other.

To proceed to a more intelligible exposition of the relation of the poet to the past: he can neither take the past as a lump, an indiscriminate bolus, nor can he form himself wholly on one 100 or two private admirations, nor can he form himself wholly upon one preferred period. The first course is inadmissible, the second is an important experience of youth, and the third is a pleasant and highly desirable supplement. The poet must be very conscious of the main current, which does not at all flow 105 invariably through the most distinguished reputations. He must be quite aware of the obvious fact that art never improves, but that the material of art is never quite the same. He must be aware that the mind of Europe—the mind of his own country—

110 a mind which he learns in time to be much more important
than his own private mind—is a mind which changes, and that
this change is a development which abandons nothing *en route*,
which does not superannuate either Shakespeare, or Homer, or
the rock drawing of the Magdalenian draughtsmen. That this
115 development, refinement perhaps, complication certainly, is
not, from the point of view of the artist, any improvement.
Perhaps not even an improvement from the point of view of the
psychologist or not to the extent which we imagine; perhaps
only in the end based upon a complication in economics and
120 machinery. But the difference between the present and the
past is that the conscious present is an awareness of the past in a
way and to an extent which the past's awareness of itself cannot
show.

Someone said: 'The dead writers are remote from us because
125 we *know* so much more than they did'. Precisely, and they are
that which we know.

I am alive to a usual objection to what is clearly part of my
programme for the *métier* of poetry. The objection is that the
doctrine requires a ridiculous amount of erudition (pedantry),
130 a claim which can be rejected by appeal to the lives of poets in
any pantheon. It will even be affirmed that much learning
deadens or perverts poetic sensibility. While, however, we persist in believing that a poet ought to know as much as will not
encroach upon his necessary receptivity and necessary laziness,
135 it is not desirable to confine knowledge to whatever can be put
into a useful shape for examinations, drawing-rooms, or the still
more pretentious modes of publicity. Some can absorb knowledge, the more tardy must sweat for it. Shakespeare acquired
more essential history from Plutarch than most men could
140 from the whole British Museum. What is to be insisted upon is
that the poet must develop or procure the consciousness of the
past and that he should continue to develop this consciousness
throughout his career.

What happens is a continual surrender of himself as he is at
145 the moment to something which is more valuable. The progress
of an artist is a continual self-sacrifice, a continual extinction of
personality.

There remains to define this process of depersonalization

and its relation to the sense of tradition. It is in this depersonalization that art may be said to approach the condition 150
of science. I therefore invite you to consider, as a suggestive
analogy, the action which takes place when a bit of finely
filiated platinum is introduced into a chamber containing
oxygen and sulphur dioxide.

II

Honest criticism and sensitive appreciation is directed not 155
upon the poet but upon the poetry. If we attend to the confused
cries of the newspaper critics and the susurrus of popular
repetition that follows, we shall hear the names of poets in
great numbers; if we seek not Blue-book knowledge but the
enjoyment of poetry, and ask for a poem, we shall seldom find 160
it. I have tried to point out the importance of the relation of
the poem to other poems by other authors, and suggested the
conception of poetry as a living whole of all the poetry that
has ever been written. The other aspect of this Impersonal
theory of poetry is the relation of the poem to its author. And 165
I hinted, by an analogy, that the mind of the mature poet differs
from that of the immature one not precisely in any valuation
of 'personality', not being necessarily more interesting, or
having 'more to say', but rather by being a more finely perfected medium in which special, or very varied, feelings are at 170
liberty to enter into new combinations.

The analogy was that of the catalyst. When the two gases
previously mentioned are mixed in the presence of a filament of
platinum, they form sulphurous acid. This combination takes
place only if the platinum is present; nevertheless the newly 175
formed acid contains no trace of platinum, and the platinum
itself is apparently unaffected: has remained inert, neutral, and
unchanged. The mind of the poet is the shred of platinum. It
may partly or exclusively operate upon the experience of the
man himself; but, the more perfect the artist, the more com- 180
pletely separate in him will be the man who suffers and the
mind which creates; the more perfectly will the mind digest
and transmute the passions which are its material.

The experience, you will notice, the elements which enter
the presence of the transforming catalyst, are of two kinds: 185

emotions and feelings. The effect of a work of art upon the person who enjoys it is an experience different in kind from any experience not of art. It may be formed out of one emotion, or may be a combination of several; and various feelings,
190 inhering for the writer in particular words or phrases or images, may be added to compose the final result. Or great poetry may be made without the direct use of any emotion whatever: composed out of feelings solely. Canto XV of the *Inferno* (Brunetto Latini) is a working up of the emotion evident in the
195 situation; but the effect, though single as that of any work of art, is obtained by considerable complexity of detail. The last quatrain gives an image, a feeling attaching to an image, which 'came', which did not develop simply out of what precedes, but which was probably in suspension in the poet's
200 mind until the proper combination arrived for it to add itself to. The poet's mind is in fact a receptacle for seizing and storing up numberless feelings, phrases, images, which remain there until all the particles which can unite to form a new compound are present together.
205   If you compare several representative passages of the greatest poetry you see how great is the variety of types of combination, and also how completely any semi-ethical criterion of 'sublimity' misses the mark. For it is not the 'greatness', the intensity, of the emotions, the components, but the intensity of the
210 artistic process, the pressure, so to speak, under which the fusion takes place, that counts. The episode of Paolo and Francesca employs a definite emotion, but the intensity of the poetry is something quite different from whatever intensity in the supposed experience it may give the impression of. It is no
215 more intense, furthermore, than Canto XXVI, the voyage of Ulysses, which has not the direct dependence upon an emotion. Great variety is possible in the process of transmutation of emotion: the murder of Agamemnon, or the agony of Othello, gives an artistic effect apparently closer to a possible original
220 than the scenes from Dante. In the *Agamemnon*, the artistic emotion approximates to the emotion of an actual spectator; in *Othello* to the emotion of the protagonist himself. But the difference between art and the event is always absolute; the combination which is the murder of Agamemnon is probably

as complex as that which is the voyage of Ulysses. In either 225
case there has been a fusion of elements. The ode of Keats
contains a number of feelings which have nothing particular
to do with the nightingale, but which the nightingale, partly
perhaps because of its attractive name, and partly because of
its reputation, served to bring together.   230

The point of view which I am struggling to attack is perhaps
related to the metaphysical theory of the substantial unity of
the soul: for my meaning is, that the poet has, not a 'personality' to express, but a particular medium, which is only a
medium and not a personality, in which impressions and experi- 235
ences combine in peculiar and unexpected ways. Impressions
and experiences which are important for the man may take no
place in the poetry, and those which become important in the
poetry may play quite a negligible part in the man, the personality.   240

I will quote a passage which is unfamiliar enough to be
regarded with fresh attention in the light—or darkness—of these
observations:

> And now methinks I could e'en chide myself
> For doating on her beauty, though her death   245
> Shall be revenged after no common action.
> Does the silkworm expend her yellow labours
> For thee? For thee does she undo herself?
> Are lordships sold to maintain ladyships
> For the poor benefit of a bewildering minute?   250
> Why does yon fellow falsify highways,
> And put his life between the judge's lips,
> To refine such a thing—keeps horse and men
> To beat their valours for her? . . .

In this passage (as is evident if it is taken in its context) there 255
is a combination of positive and negative emotions: an intensely
strong attraction towards beauty and an equally intense
fascination by the ugliness which is contrasted with it and which
destroys it. This balance of contrasted emotion is in the dramatic
situation to which the speech is pertinent, but that situation 260
alone is inadequate to it. This is, so to speak, the structural
emotion, provided by the drama. But the whole effect, the
dominant tone, is due to the fact that a number of floating

feelings, having an affinity to this emotion by no means super-
265 ficially evident, have combined with it to give us a new art
emotion.

It is not in his personal emotions, the emotions provoked by
particular events in his life, that the poet is in any way remarkable, or interesting. His particular emotions may be simple, or
270 crude, or flat. The emotion in his poetry will be a very complex
thing, but not with the complexity of the emotions of people
who have very complex or unusual emotions in life. One error,
in fact, of eccentricity in poetry is to seek for new human
emotions to express; and in this search for novelty in the wrong
275 place it discovers the perverse. The business of the poet is not
to find new emotions, but to use the ordinary ones and, in
working them up into poetry, to express feelings which are not
in actual emotions at all. And emotions which he has never
experienced will serve his turn as well as those familiar to him.
280 Consequently, we must believe that 'emotion recollected in
tranquillity' is an inexact formula. For it is neither emotion,
nor recollection, nor, without distortion of meaning, tranquillity. It is a concentration, and a new thing resulting from the
concentration, of a very great number of experiences which to
285 the practical and active person would not seem to be experiences at all; it is a concentration which does not happen
consciously or of deliberation. These experiences are not
'recollected', and they finally unite in an atmosphere which is
'tranquil' only in that it is a passive attending upon the event.
290 Of course this is not quite the whole story. There is a great
deal, in the writing of poetry, which must be conscious and
deliberate. In fact, the bad poet is usually unconscious where he
ought to be conscious, and conscious where he ought to be
unconscious. Both errors tend to make him 'personal'. Poetry
295 is not a turning loose of emotion, but an escape from emotion;
it is not the expression of personality, but an escape from
personality. But, of course, only those who have personality
and emotions know what it means to want to escape from these
things.

III

ὁ δὲ νοῦς ἴσως θειότερόν τι καὶ ἀπαθές ἐστιν.   300

This essay proposes to halt at the frontier of metaphysics or mysticism, and confine itself to such practical conclusions as can be applied by the responsible person interested in poetry. To divert interest from the poet to the poetry is a laudable aim: for it would conduce to a juster estimation of actual poetry, 305 good and bad. There are many people who appreciate the expression of sincere emotion in verse, and there is a smaller number of people who can appreciate technical excellence. But very few know when there is an expression of *significant* emotion, emotion which has its life in the poem and not in the 310 history of the poet. The emotion of art is impersonal. And the poet cannot reach this impersonality without surrendering himself wholly to the work to be done. And he is not likely to know what is to be done unless he lives in what is not merely the present, but the present moment of the past, unless he is 315 conscious, not of what is dead, but of what is already living.

T. S. ELIOT

The Metaphysical Poets

BY collecting these poems[1] from the work of a generation
more often named than read, and more often read than profit-
ably studied, Professor Grierson has rendered a service of some
importance. Certainly the reader will meet with many poems
5 already preserved in other anthologies, at the same time that he
discovers poems such as those of Aurelian Townshend or Lord
Herbert of Cherbury here included. But the function of such
an anthology as this is neither that of Professor Saintsbury's
admirable edition of Caroline poets nor that of the *Oxford Book*
10 *of English Verse*. Mr. Grierson's book is in itself a piece of criticism, and a provocation of criticism; and we think that he was
right in including so many poems of Donne, elsewhere (though
not in many editions) accessible, as documents in the case of
'metaphysical poetry'. The phrase has long done duty as a
15 term of abuse, or as the label of a quaint and pleasant taste.
The question is to what extent the so-called metaphysicals
formed a school (in our own time we should say a 'movement'),
and how far this so-called school or movement is a digression
from the main current.

20 Not only is it extremely difficult to define metaphysical
poetry, but difficult to decide what poets practise it and in
which of their verses. The poetry of Donne (to whom Marvell
and Bishop King are sometimes nearer than any of the other
authors) is late Elizabethan, its feeling often very close to that
25 of Chapman. The 'courtly' poetry is derivative from Jonson,
who borrowed liberally from the Latin; it expires in the next
century with the sentiment and witticism of Prior. There is
finally the devotional verse of Herbert, Vaughan, and Crashaw

---

[1] *Metaphysical Lyrics and Poems of the Seventeenth Century*: Donne to Butler.
Selected and edited, with an Essay, by Herbert J. C. Grierson (Oxford:
Clarendon Press. London: Milford).

(echoed long after by Christina Rossetti and Francis Thompson); Crashaw, sometimes more profound and less sectarian 30 than the others, has a quality which returns through the Elizabethan period to the early Italians. It is difficult to find any precise use of metaphor, simile, or other conceit, which is common to all the poets and at the same time important enough as an element of style to isolate these poets as a group. Donne, 35 and often Cowley, employ a device which is sometimes considered characteristically 'metaphysical'; the elaboration (contrasted with the condensation) of a figure of speech to the furthest stage to which ingenuity can carry it. Thus Cowley develops the commonplace comparison of the world to a chess- 40 board through long stanzas (*To Destiny*), and Donne, with more grace, in *A Valediction*, the comparison of two lovers to a pair of compasses. But elsewhere we find, instead of the mere explication of the content of a comparison, a development by rapid association of thought which requires considerable 45 agility on the part of the reader.

<blockquote>
On a round ball
A workeman that hath copies by, can lay
An Europe, Afrique, and an Asia,
And quickly make that, which was nothing, *All*,   50
    So doth each teare,
    Which thee doth weare,
A globe, yea world by that impression grow,
Till thy tears mixt with mine doe overflow
This world, by waters sent from thee, my heaven dissolved so.   55
</blockquote>

Here we find at least two connexions which are not implicit in the first figure, but are forced upon it by the poet: from the geographer's globe to the tear, and the tear to the deluge. On the other hand, some of Donne's most successful and characteristic effects are secured by brief words and sudden contrasts: 60

<blockquote>
A bracelet of bright hair about the bone,
</blockquote>

where the most powerful effect is produced by the sudden contrast of associations of 'bright hair' and of 'bone'. This telescoping of images and multiplied associations is characteristic of the phrase of some of the dramatists of the period which 65 Donne knew: not to mention Shakespeare, it is frequent in

LECT

Middleton, Webster, and Tourneur, and is one of the sources of the vitality of their language.

Johnson, who employed the term 'metaphysical poets',
70 apparently having Donne, Cleveland, and Cowley chiefly in mind, remarks of them that 'the most heterogeneous ideas are yoked by violence together'. The force of this impeachment lies in the failure of the conjunction, the fact that often the ideas are yoked but not united; and if we are to judge of styles of
75 poetry by their abuse, enough examples may be found in Cleveland to justify Johnson's condemnation. But a degree of heterogeneity of material compelled into unity by the operation of the poet's mind is omnipresent in poetry. We need not select for illustration such a line as:

80   Notre âme est un trois-mâts cherchant son Icarie;

we may find it in some of the best lines of Johnson himself (*The Vanity of Human Wishes*):

> His fate was destined to a barren strand,
> A petty fortress, and a dubious hand;
85 > He left a name at which the world grew pale,
> To point a moral, or adorn a tale,

where the effect is due to a contrast of ideas, different in degree but the same in principle, as that which Johnson mildly reprehended. And in one of the finest poems of the age (a
90 poem which could not have been written in any other age), the *Exequy* of Bishop King, the extended comparison is used with perfect success: the idea and the simile become one, in the passage in which the Bishop illustrates his impatience to see his dead wife, under the figure of a journey:

95 > Stay for me there; I will not faile
> To meet thee in that hollow Vale.
> And think not much of my delay;
> I am already on the way,
> And follow thee with all the speed
100 > Desire can make, or sorrows breed.
> Each minute is a short degree,
> And ev'ry houre a step towards thee.
> At night when I betake to rest,
> Next morn I rise nearer my West

Of life, almost by eight houres sail,   105
Than when sleep breath'd his drowsy gale . . .
But heark! My Pulse, like a soft Drum
Beats my approach, tells *Thee* I come;
And slow howere my marches be,
I shall at last sit down by *Thee*.   110

(In the last few lines there is that effect of terror which is several
times attained by one of Bishop King's admirers, Edgar Poe.)
Again, we may justly take these quatrains from Lord Herbert's
Ode, stanzas which would, we think, be immediately pronounced to be of the metaphysical school: 115

> So when from hence we shall be gone,
>   And be no more, nor you, nor I,
>   As one another's mystery,
> Each shall be both, yet both but one.

> This said, in her up-lifted face,   120
>   Her eyes, which did that beauty crown,
>   Were like two starrs, that having faln down,
> Look up again to find their place:

> While such a moveless silent peace
>   Did seize on their becalmed sense,   125
>   One would have thought some influence
> Their ravished spirits did possess.

There is nothing in these lines (with the possible exception of
the stars, a simile not at once grasped, but lovely and justified)
which fits Johnson's general observations on the metaphysical 130
poets in his essay on Cowley. A good deal resides in the richness
of association which is at the same time borrowed from and
given to the word 'becalmed'; but the meaning is clear,
the language simple and elegant. It is to be observed that the
language of these poets is as a rule simple and pure; in the 135
verse of George Herbert this simplicity is carried as far as it
can go—a simplicity emulated without success by numerous
modern poets. The *structure* of the sentences, on the other hand,
is sometimes far from simple, but this is not a vice; it is a fidelity
to thought and feeling. The effect, at its best, is far less arti- 140
ficial than that of an ode by Gray. And as this fidelity induces
variety of thought and feeling, so it induces variety of music.
We doubt whether, in the eighteenth century, could be found

two poems in nominally the same metre, so dissimilar as
145 Marvell's *Coy Mistress* and Crashaw's *Saint Teresa*; the one
producing an effect of great speed by the use of short syllables,
and the other an ecclesiastical solemnity by the use of long
ones:

> Love, thou art absolute sole lord
150 > Of life and death.

If so shrewd and sensitive (though so limited) a critic as
Johnson failed to define metaphysical poetry by its faults, it is
worth while to inquire whether we may not have more success
by adopting the opposite method: by assuming that the poets
155 of the seventeenth century (up to the Revolution) were the
direct and normal development of the precedent age; and,
without prejudicing their case by the adjective 'metaphysical',
consider whether their virtue was not something permanently
valuable, which subsequently disappeared, but ought not to
160 have disappeared. Johnson has hit, perhaps by accident, on one
of their peculiarities, when he observes that 'their attempts were
always analytic'; he would not agree that, after the dissociation, they put the material together again in a new unity.

It is certain that the dramatic verse of the later Elizabethan
165 and early Jacobean poets expresses a degree of development of
sensibility which is not found in any of the prose, good as it
often is. If we except Marlowe, a man of prodigious intelligence,
these dramatists were directly or indirectly (it is at least a
tenable theory) affected by Montaigne. Even if we except also
170 Jonson and Chapman, these two were notably erudite, and
were notably men who incorporated their erudition into their
sensibility: their mode of feeling was directly and freshly
altered by their reading and thought. In Chapman especially
there is a direct sensuous apprehension of thought, or a recrea-
175 tion of thought into feeling, which is exactly what we find in
Donne:

> in this one thing, all the discipline
> Of manners and of manhood is contained;
> A man to join himself with th' Universe
180 > In his main sway, and make in all things fit
> One with that All, and go on, round as it;

Not plucking from the whole his wretched part,
And into straits, or into nought revert,
Wishing the complete Universe might be
Subject to such a rag of it as he; 185
But to consider great Necessity.

We compare this with some modern passage:

No, when the fight begins within himself,
A man's worth something. God stoops o'er his head,
Satan looks up between his feet—both tug— 190
He's left, himself, i' the middle; the soul wakes
And grows. Prolong that battle through his life!

It is perhaps somewhat less fair, though very tempting (as both
poets are concerned with the perpetuation of love by offspring),
to compare with the stanzas already quoted from Lord Her- 195
bert's Ode the following from Tennyson:

One walked between his wife and child,
With measured footfall firm and mild,
And now and then he gravely smiled.

The prudent partner of his blood 200
Leaned on him, faithful, gentle, good,
Wearing the rose of womanhood.

And in their double love secure,
The little maiden walked demure,
Pacing with downward eyelids pure. 205

These three made unity so sweet,
My frozen heart began to beat,
Remembering its ancient heat.

The difference is not a simple difference of degree between
poets. It is something which had happened to the mind of 210
England between the time of Donne or Lord Herbert of
Cherbury and the time of Tennyson and Browning; it is the
difference between the intellectual poet and the reflective poet.
Tennyson and Browning are poets, and they think; but they do
not feel their thought as immediately as the odour of a rose. 215
A thought to Donne was an experience; it modified his sensibility. When a poet's mind is perfectly equipped for its work,
it is constantly amalgamating disparate experience; the ordinary man's experience is chaotic, irregular, fragmentary. The

220 latter falls in love, or reads Spinoza, and these two experiences
have nothing to do with each other, or with the noise of the
typewriter or the smell of cooking; in the mind of the poet
these experiences are always forming new wholes.

We may express the difference by the following theory: The
225 poets of the seventeenth century, the successors of the dramatists of the sixteenth, possessed a mechanism of sensibility
which could devour any kind of experience. They are simple,
artificial, difficult, or fantastic, as their predecessors were; no
less nor more than Dante, Guido Cavalcanti, Guinicelli, or
230 Cino. In the seventeenth century a dissociation of sensibility
set in, from which we have never recovered; and this dissociation, as is natural, was aggravated by the influence of the
two most powerful poets of the century, Milton and Dryden.
Each of these men performed certain poetic functions so mag-
235 nificently well that the magnitude of the effect concealed the
absence of others. The language went on and in some respects
improved; the best verse of Collins, Gray, Johnson, and even
Goldsmith satisfies some of our fastidious demands better than
that of Donne or Marvell or King. But while the language
240 became more refined, the feeling became more crude. The
feeling, the sensibility, expressed in the *Country Churchyard* (to say
nothing of Tennyson and Browning) is cruder than that in the
Coy Mistress.

The second effect of the influence of Milton and Dryden
245 followed from the first, and was therefore slow in manifestation.
The sentimental age began early in the eighteenth century,
and continued. The poets revolted against the ratiocinative,
the descriptive; they thought and felt by fits, unbalanced; they
reflected. In one or two passages of Shelley's *Triumph of Life*, in
250 the second *Hyperion*, there are traces of a struggle toward unifica-
tion of sensibility. But Keats and Shelley died, and Tennyson
and Browning ruminated.

After this brief exposition of a theory—too brief, perhaps, to
carry conviction—we may ask, what would have been the fate
255 of the 'metaphysical' had the current of poetry descended in a
direct line from them, as it descended in a direct line to them?
They would not, certainly, be classified as metaphysical. The
possible interests of a poet are unlimited; the more intelligent

he is the better; the more intelligent he is the more likely that
he will have interests: our only condition is that he turn them 260
into poetry, and not merely meditate on them poetically. A
philosophical theory which has entered into poetry is established, for its truth or falsity in one sense ceases to matter,
and its truth in another sense is proved. The poets in question
have, like other poets, various faults. But they were, at best, 265
engaged in the task of trying to find the verbal equivalent for
states of mind and feeling. And this means both that they are
more mature, and that they wear better, than later poets of
certainly not less literary ability.

It is not a permanent necessity that poets should be interested 270
in philosophy, or in any other subject. We can only say that it
appears likely that poets in our civilization, as it exists at
present, must be *difficult*. Our civilization comprehends great
variety and complexity, and this variety and complexity,
playing upon a refined sensibility, must produce various and 275
complex results. The poet must become more and more
comprehensive, more allusive, more indirect, in order to force,
to dislocate if necessary, language into !is meaning. (A brilliant
and extreme statement of this view, with which it is not
requisite to associate oneself, is that of M. Jean Epstein, *La* 280
Poésie d'aujourd'hui.) Hence we get something which looks very
much like the conceit—we get, in fact, a method curiously
similar to that of the 'metaphysical poets', similar also in its
use of obscure words and of simple phrasing.

> O géraniums diaphanes, guerroyeurs sortilèges, 285
> Sacrilèges monomanes!
> Emballages, dévergondages, douches! O pressoirs
> Des vendanges des grands soirs!
> Layettes aux abois,
> Thyrses au fond des bois! 290
> Transfusions, représailles,
> Relevailles, compresses et l'éternelle potion,
> Angélus! n'en pouvoir plus
> De débâcles nuptiales! de débâcles nuptiales!

The same poet could write also simply: 295

> Elle est bien loin, elle pleure,
> Le grand vent se lamente aussi . . .

Jules Laforgue, and Tristan Corbière in many of his poems, are
nearer to the 'school of Donne' than any modern English poet.
300 But poets more classical than they have the same essential
quality of transmuting ideas into sensations, of transforming an
observation into a state of mind.

> Pour l'enfant, amoureux de cartes et d'estampes,
> L'univers est égal à son vaste appétit.
> 305 Ah, que le monde est grand à la clarté des lampes!
> Aux yeux du souvenir que le monde est petit!

In French literature the great master of the seventeenth
century—Racine—and the great master of the nineteenth—
Baudelaire—are in some ways more like each other than they
310 are like anyone else. The greatest two masters of diction are
also the greatest two psychologists, the most curious explorers
of the soul. It is interesting to speculate whether it is not a
misfortune that two of the greatest masters of diction in our
language, Milton and Dryden, triumph with a dazzling dis-
315 regard of the soul. If we continued to produce Miltons and
Drydens it might not so much matter, but as things are it is a
pity that English poetry has remained so incomplete. Those
who object to the 'artificiality' of Milton or Dryden sometimes
tell us to 'look into our hearts and write'. But that is not looking
320 deep enough; Racine or Donne looked into a good deal more
than the heart. One must look into the cerebral cortex, the
nervous system, and the digestive tracts.

May we not conclude, then, that Donne, Crashaw, Vaughan,
Herbert and Lord Herbert, Marvell, King, Cowley at his best,
325 are in the direct current of English poetry, and that their faults
should be reprimanded by this standard rather than coddled
by antiquarian affection? They have been enough praised in
terms which are implicit limitations because they are 'metaphysical' or 'witty', 'quaint' or 'obscure', though at their best
330 they have not these attributes more than other serious poets.
On the other hand, we must not reject the criticism of Johnson
(a dangerous person to disagree with) without having mastered
it, without having assimilated the Johnsonian canons of taste.
In reading the celebrated passage in his essay on Cowley we
335 must remember that by wit he clearly means something more

serious than we usually mean to-day;[1] in his criticism of their versification we must remember in what a narrow discipline he was trained, but also how well trained; we must remember that Johnson tortures chiefly the chief offenders, Cowley and Cleveland. It would be a fruitful work, and one requiring a 340 substantial book, to break up the classification of Johnson (for there has been none since) and exhibit these poets in all their difference of kind and of degree, from the massive music of Donne to the faint, pleasing tinkle of Aurelian Townshend— whose *Dialogue between a Pilgrim and Time* is one of the few 345 regrettable omissions from the excellent anthology of Professor Grierson.

---

[1] See Mr. Eliot's definition of 'wit' in his essay *Andrew Marvell* (1921):
'With our eye still on Marvell, we can say that wit is not erudition; it is sometimes stifled by erudition, as in much of Milton. It is not cynicism, though it has a kind of toughness which may be confused with cynicism by the tender-minded. It is confused with erudition because it belongs to an educated mind, rich in generations of experience; and it is confused with cynicism because it implies a constant inspection and criticism of experience. It involves, probably, a recognition, implicit in the expression of every experience, of other kinds of experience which are possible, which we find as clearly in the greatest as in poets like Marvell.' (*Editors' Note.*)

F. R. LEAVIS

Keats

THE excuse for writing at the present day on Keats must lie
not in anything new to be said about him, but in a certain
timely obviousness. The current placing of him seems, in
essentials, likely to stand: what a critic may still propose to
5 himself is a sharper explicitness; a recall, that is, to strict
literary criticism. For Keats has become a symbolic figure, the
type of poetic genius, a hero and martyr of poetry, with claims
to a greatness such as can hardly at any time have, for the
devout, invested the symbolic Chatterton; and there is a
10 general consensus that the greatness is a matter of promise and
potentiality rather than achievement. The stress falls on the
poetry that Keats might have written and the Letters. It is
salutary then, to remind ourselves, not only that Keats's poetry,
the poetry he actually wrote, was a major influence in the nine-
15 teenth century, but that in its qualities, in what it actually is,
must reside the chief grounds for a high estimate of his potentialities.

So stated, the last proposition would seem to be axiomatic.
Yet there is a common tendency to shirk literary criticism; to
20 prefer, where creative genius is in question, some freer and
looser approach, as if relevance were an easy matter, and by
evading the chief relevant discipline one could attain to delicacy
and inwardness. Evasion, especially in a case like that of Keats,
can be comparatively subtle and plausible. Mr. Middleton
25 Murry tells us of his *Keats and Shakespeare*:

> 'It is no part of the purpose of this book to appreciate Keats's
> poems objectively as poetry; its concern is solely to elucidate the
> deep and natural movement of the poet's soul which underlies
> them.' (p. 129.)

30 Mr. Murry's purposes are his own; but even without a knowledge of the book one ought to see dangers in this sentence: the

elucidations of a poet's soul that are not controlled by the
literary critic's attention to poetry will hardly, whatever they
may be worth, turn out to be concerned wholly, or even
mainly, with the soul of the poet. And that in fact something is 35
badly wrong in Mr. Murry's book—false in its relations to
both Keats and Shakespeare—may be most simply established
by quoting a complementary sentence:

'He was twenty-three; and at the moment he wrote this letter
he was writing day after day the *Odes*, to Psyche, to the Nightingale, 40
on a Grecian Urn, on Melancholy—poems comparable to nothing
in English literature save the works of Shakespeare's maturity.'
(p. 143.)

Wrongness of this kind in criticism, such extravagant falsity in
the appreciation of 'poems objectively as poetry', clearly can- 45
not be, or go with, rightness about the poet's soul. And Keats's
genius, we find, is not really illuminated by the procedure of
Keats and Shakespeare, or, except as another of Metabiology's
cloudy trophies, exalted.

From Mr. Murry it is well to turn to a very different admirer 50
of Keats, a critic who, concerned avowedly with poetry first and
last, pronounces:[1]

'He was not troubled about his soul, or any other metaphysical
questions, to which he shows a happy indifference, or rather, a placid
unconsciousness.'
55

Mr. Symons, of course, speaks as a representative of the last
phase of the Victorian tradition that had its main poetic source
in Keats. According to Mr. Symons,

'Keats, at a time when the phrase had not yet been invented,
practised the theory of art for art's sake. He is the type, not of the 60
poet, but of the artist. He was not a great personality, his work
comes to us as a greater thing than his personality. When we read
his verse, we think of the verse, not of John Keats.'

The last sentence gets its peculiar force from the context: there
is more than one kind of impersonality in art, and what Mr. 65
Symons intends is sufficiently plain. Keats, he tells us, 'accepted
life in the spirit of art'; he is the artist 'to whom art is more
than life.'

---
[1] Arthur Symons, *The Romantic Movement in English Poetry* (1909).

Few people to-day find Mr. Symons's view of Keats accept-
70 able, yet of the poems up to the revised *Hyperion* his might
reasonably be found a more acceptable account than Mr.
Murry's. It nevertheless, we know, will not do. Mr. Symons no
doubt perceives that Keats is a greater poet than Tennyson and
Rossetti, but in what way, by what virtue, he cannot adequately
75 suggest: the essential differences between Keats's 'art' and
theirs cannot be accounted for in terms of 'art' as conceived by
the 'nineties (for the conception is none the less limiting for
being incapable of satisfactory definition). The Odes and even
The Eve of St. Agnes—the consummate works acclaimed by
80 Mr. Symons as exemplars of 'art for art's sake'—transcend the
appreciation of the 'aesthetic' taste that, with justice, finds them
congenial. To try and enforce this judgement with some particu-
larity would seem to be a promising approach to Keats.

Let us consider the *Ode to a Nightingale*, commonly placed
85 highest among the Odes, and determine in what ways, though
it is not of the supreme order to which Mr. Murry assigns it,
it is a finer and more vital thing than appreciation in terms of
'art for art's sake' can easily suggest. In memory it might at
first not seem to transcend very notably Mr. Symons's terms.
90 Indeed, it might on re-reading seem to be very fairly describ-
able as the work of a 'purely sensuous poet', one who was 'not
troubled about his soul'; for the pang in it has little to do with
moral or spiritual stress, but is, like the swooning relapse upon
death, itself a luxury. 'Luxury', in fact, is a key-word in the
95 description; 'lovely' (the beauty is of that kind), 'enchanting',
'lush' and 'exquisite' are others. One remembers the poem
both as recording, and as being for the reader, an indulgence.
Yet (unless the present critic's experience is exceptional)
memory tends to be unjust by simplifying: re-read, the poem
100 turns out to be subtler and finer than careless recollection
suggests. And to describe and discuss this fineness there is no
need to invoke the Letters; it can be discussed as a fineness of
art. In fact, using this term 'art' in a way that would seem to
Mr. Symons right and natural, one can show Keats to be in the
105 *Ode to a Nightingale* a better artist than Mr. Symons appreciates.

'With Shelley, even though he may at times seem to become
vague in thought, there is always an intellectual structure; Keats,

definite in every word, in every image, lacks intellectual structure. He saw words as things, and he saw them one at a time.'

And, we may recall, A. C. Bradley, a quite different kind of critic, appears to contemplate a serious comparison between the *Ode to a Nightingale* and Shelley's *To a Skylark*.[1] Now, if intellectual structure is what Shelley characteristically exhibits, the *Ode to a Nightingale* may freely be allowed to lack it. But the superiority of the Ode over *To a Skylark*, which beside it appears a nullity, is not merely a superiority of details ('words' and 'images' seen and felt 'one at a time'). The rich local concreteness is the local manifestation of an inclusive sureness of grasp in the whole. What the detail exhibits is not merely an extraordinary intensity of realization, but also an extraordinary rightness and delicacy of touch; a sureness of touch that is the working of a fine organization. The Ode, that is, has the structure of a fine and complex organism; whereas *To a Skylark* is a mere poetical outpouring, its ecstatic 'intensity' being a substitute for realization in the parts and for a realized whole to which the parts might be related.

The Ode, it has been said above, tends to suffer an unfair simplification in memory; the thought of its being 'rich to die' and the desire

> To cease upon the midnight with no pain,

tend to stand for more of it than they should. Actually, when we re-read it we find that it moves outwards and upwards towards life as strongly as it moves downwards towards extinction; the Ode is, in fact, an extremely subtle and varied interplay of motions, directed now positively, now negatively. Consider the opening stanza:

> My heart aches, and a drowsy numbness pains
>   My sense, as though of hemlock I had drunk,
>   Or emptied some dull opiate to the drains
>   One minute past, and Lethe-wards had sunk:
> 'Tis not through envy of thy happy lot,
>   But being too happy in thine happiness,—
> That thou, light-wingèd Dryad of the trees,
>   In some melodious plot
>   Of beechen green, and shadows numberless,
>   Singest of summer in full-throated ease.

---

[1] *Oxford Lectures* (1909), p. 228.

It starts Lethe-wards, with a heavy drugged movement ('drowsy,' 'numb,' 'dull') down to 'sunk'. The part played by the first line-division is worth noting—the difference the division
150 makes to the phrase 'a drowsy numbness pains my sense.' In the fifth and sixth lines, with the reiterated 'happy,' the direction changes, and in the next line comes the key-word, 'light-wingèd.' The stanza now moves buoyantly towards life, the fresh air and the sunlight ('shadows numberless')—the thought
155 of happy, self-sufficient vitality provides the impulse. The common medium, so to speak, in which the shift of direction takes place with such unobtrusive effectiveness, the pervasive sense of luxury, is given explicitly in the closing phrase of the stanza, 'full-throated ease.'
160   Down the throat (now the poet's) flows, in the next stanza, the 'draught of vintage,'

> Cool'd a long age in the deep-delved earth,

the coolness (having banished the drowsy fever) playing voluptuously against the warmth of 'the warm South.' The
165 sensuous luxury keeps its element of the 'light-wingèd': there are the 'beaded bubbles winking at the brim.' This second stanza reverses the movement of the first; until the last two lines it moves towards life and the stirring human world,

> Dance and Provençal song and sunburnt mirth.

170 But the optative 'O' changes direction, as if with the changing effect (now no longer excitation) of the wine, and the stanza ends on the desire to

> leave the world unseen
> And with thee fade away into the forest dim.

175   The next stanza is the only one in the poem to be completely disintoxicated and disenchanted. It is notable how at the second line the tone, the manner of reading compelled on one, alters, turning from incantatory into prosaic matter-of-fact:

> Fade far away, dissolve, and quite forget
> 180   What thou among the leaves hast never known,
> The weariness, the fever, and the fret
> Here, where men sit and hear each other groan;
> Where palsy shakes a few, sad, last gray hairs,
> Where youth grows pale, and spectre-thin, and dies . . .

—That 'spectre-thin' is a key-word, suggesting as it does, along 185
with 'gray,' the thin unreality of the disintoxicated, unbeglamoured moments that the addict dreads.

The fourth stanza takes up the 'away' again—but not the
'fade':

> Away! away! for I will fly to thee,   190
>   Not charioted by Bacchus and his pards,
> But on the viewless wings of Poesy . . .

—It points now, not to dissolution and unconsciousness but to
positive satisfactions, concretely realized in imagination: they
represent the world of 'Poesy' (for poetry was Poesy to the 195
Keats of *Endymion* and the Odes). We have now the rich evocation of enchantment and delighted senses, and here again the
touch of the consummate artist manifests itself; in the very
piling up of luxuries a sure delicacy presides:

> I cannot see what flowers are at my feet,   200
>   Nor what soft incense hangs upon the boughs,
> But, in embalmed darkness, guess each sweet
>   Wherewith the seasonable month endows
> The grass, the thicket and the fruit-tree wild;
>   White hawthorn, and the pastoral eglantine . . .   205

—the 'grass,' the 'thicket' and the cool reminders of the English
spring bring the needed note of freshness into the else too
cloying accumulation of sweets.

And now comes a stanza that, in the simplifying memory,
tends to get undue prominence: 210

> Darkling I listen; and for many a time
>   I have been half in love with easeful Death,
> Call'd him soft names in many a mused rhyme,
>   To take into the air my quiet breath;
> Now more than ever seems it rich to die,   215
> To cease upon the midnight with no pain,
>   While thou art pouring forth thy soul abroad
>   In such an ecstasy!
> Still wouldst thou sing, and I have ears in vain—
>   To thy high requiem become a sod.   220

—In the re-reading the force of that 'half' comes home to us:
Keats is strictly only half in love with death, and the positive

motion is present even in this stanza. It is present in the 'rich'
of 'rich to die,' a phrase that epitomizes the poem. The desire
225 not to die appears in the thought of becoming a sod to the
nightingale's high requiem and of having ears in vain, and it
swells into a strong revulsion against death in the opening lines
of the next stanza:

> Thou wast not born for death, immortal Bird!
230 > No hungry generations tread thee down . . .

Bridges, as a conscientious critic, solemnly points out the
fallacy here: 'the thought is fanciful or superficial—the man
being as immortal as the bird,' etc. That the thought is fallacious witnesses, of course, to the intensity of the wish that fathered
235 it. Keats entertains at one and the same time the desire to
escape into easeful death from 'the weariness, the fever and the
fret'—

> To cease upon the midnight with no pain,

and the complementary desire for a full life unattended by
240 these disadvantages. And the inappropriateness of the nightingale's song as a symbol of enduring satisfaction—

> The voice I hear this passing night was heard
> In ancient days by emperor and clown:
> Perhaps the self-same song that found a path
245 > Through the sad heart of Ruth, when, sick for home,
> She stood in tears amid the alien corn

—manifests locally the complexity of the impulsions behind the
poem. The regressive desire to 'cease upon the midnight'
slips, it will be noticed, into the positive nostalgia represented
250 by Ruth, the association of the two providing an interesting
illustration to D. W. Harding's *Note on Nostalgia*.[1]

Bridges has also a criticism to make against the opening of the
final stanza: the 'introduction,' he says, is 'artificial', by which
he would seem to suggest that Keats, having earlier in the Ode
255 got his transition, managed his development, by picking up a
word or a phrase already used, now mechanically repeats the
closing 'forlorn' of the penultimate stanza because he can think
of no better way of carrying on:

---

[1] *Determinations*, 1934 (edited by the present writer); see esp. p. 68.

The same that oft-times hath
Charm'd magic casements, opening on the foam   260
Of perilous seas, in faery lands forlorn.

VIII

Forlorn! the very word is like a bell
To toll me back from thee to my sole self!
Adieu! the fancy cannot cheat so well
As she is fam'd to do, deceiving elf.   265

Actually, that the repetition has a peculiar and appropriate
force is obvious, or would be if Keats had not here suffered the
injury incidental to becoming 'hackneyed.' In 'faery lands
forlorn'—the adjective has acquired the wrong kind of inevi-
tability; it would but for the hackneying, but for the groove in 270
one's mind, be seen to be, coming with the final emphasis at
the end of those two glamorous lines, unexpected. It is so for
Keats; he turns it over, and it becomes as he looks at it the recognition upon which the poem ends—the recognition that we,
looking back, can see to have been approaching in the passage 275
about Ruth, 'sick for home,' which gives us the sickness to
contemplate, not the home: even the illusion of a 'secure
happiness' as something to be ecstatically, if enviously, contemplated in the nightingale is recognized to be an evanescent
indulgence, belonging to the world of 'magic casements, open- 280
ing on the foam of perilous seas.' The song that fades away is no
longer an ecstasy, but a 'plaintive anthem.'

The strength of the Ode, then, is far from being merely the
strength of details—of things seen separately. In fact, the Ode
is not only incomparably better art than Mr. Symons recog- 285
nizes; it is better in a way involving a relation to life that the
prescription 'art for art's sake' (whatever it may mean) would
not tend to encourage. On the other hand, to talk of the Ode as
belonging to the same order as the work of Shakespeare's
maturity is extravagantly out. It is not for nothing that it 290
should suffer as it does in memory, or that it should not be
among the poems that bear frequent re-reading. It is as if
Keats were making major poetry out of minor—as if, that is,
the genius of a major poet were working in the material of
minor poetry. For in spite of a subtlety so far transcending the 295

powers of the not much younger poet who wrote of 'pleasant
smotherings,' the word for poetry (or Poesy) as practised by the
poet of the Ode is still 'luxury'. The pain with which his heart
aches is not that of a moral maturity, of a disenchanted wisdom
300 born of a steady contemplation of things as they are; it is itself a
luxury. The disintoxicated third stanza represents the actual
upon which the poem turns its back, seeking deception. Though
'the fancy cannot cheat so well as she is fam'd to do,' the 'sole
self,' plaintively yearning, can make of its very regret a sweet
305 anodyne.

In fact, the main impulsion of the *Ode to a Nightingale* is
essentially of the same order as that exhibited more simply by
the *Ode on a Grecian Urn*. The urn, with its 'leaf-fringed legend',
gives a firmer stay to fancy than Keats could make of his imag-
310 ined light-winged Dryad of the trees in its melodious plot of
beechen green:

> Heard melodies are sweet, but those unheard
> Are sweeter . . .

—They are less disturbing, if less intensely felt. The compensa-
315 tion for the lack of rich immediacy is the idyllic serenity of the
fourth stanza, with its 'green altar' and its 'peaceful citadel.'
But even here we are made aware of a price to be paid. The
serenity, before the end of the stanza, takes on another quality:

> Who are these coming to the sacrifice?
> 320   To what green altar, O mysterious priest,
> Lead'st thou that heifer lowing at the skies,
>   And all her silken flanks with garlands drest?
> What little town by river or sea shore,
>   Or mountain-built with peaceful citadel,
> 325   Is emptied of this folk, this pious morn?

That 'emptied' is a key-word: we end the stanza contemplating,
not the scene of ideally happy life, but the idea of streets that

> for evermore,
> Will silent be,

330 and of a town to which

> not a soul to tell
> Why thou art desolate, can e'er return.

The victory over time seems an equivocal one. The attempt to
get it both ways could, in the nature of things, have only a very
qualified success.   335
   Getting it both ways—the poem essentially *is* that. The
bargain with life and time proposed in the second stanza—

> those unheard
> Are sweeter

and   340

> Bold lover, never, never canst thou kiss,
> Though winning near the goal—yet do not grieve;
> She cannot fade, though thou hast not thy bliss,
> For ever wilt thou love and she be fair!

—the implicit bargain is within half a dozen lines of this for- 345
gotten:

> More happy love! more happy, happy love!
> For ever warm and still to be enjoyed,
> For ever panting, and for ever young;
> All breathing human passion far above,   350
> That leaves a heart high-sorrowful and cloy'd,
> A burning forehead and a parching tongue.

—In what way 'All breathing human passion far above'?
'Warm' and 'panting'—the accordant ditty would be very
decidedly to the 'sensual ear.' Clearly, the urn for Keats is the 355
incitement and support to a day-dream; the dream of a life
that, without any drawbacks, shall give him all he desires—
shall be for ever warm and still be enjoyed, remaining, 'among
the leaves,' free from all the inevitable limitations that the
nightingale, the light-winged Dryad, has never known.   360
   These observations are not offered as proof of any remarkable
percipience. The excuse for them is the puzzled, awed or
Delphic attention that, in spite of their obviousness, has been
paid to the famous concluding pronouncement of the Ode—
the subtleties and profundities it still provides occasion for. 365

> 'Beauty is truth, truth beauty'—that is all
> Ye know on earth, and all ye need to know.

This surely, in the context just examined, should cause no
metaphysical tremors of excitement or illumination, and need
no great profundity or ingenuity of any kind to elucidate it. 370

The proposition is strictly in keeping with the attitude concretely embodied in the poem. The use of the word 'truth'
corresponds strictly to the attitude towards reality analysed
above. Life, alas! is not as we would have it; but it ought to be,
375 and, with the aid of the Grecian urn, can be felt for a moment
to be: imagination, concentrating on the beauty of the urn and
ignoring the discordant and indocile facts, attains a higher
reality, compared with which actual life seems thin and unreal.
By the last stanza imagination in Keats has flagged, has relapsed
380 from its inspired dream, the enchantment has waned and the
actual has reasserted itself; but although the 'leaf-fringed
legend' is now a 'Cold Pastoral,' it remains there, a permanent
incitement to warm imaginings of an ideal life, a purely beautiful reality.

385   To show from the Letters that 'Beauty' became for Keats a
very subtle and embracing concept, and that in his use the term
takes on meanings that it could not possibly have for the un-
initiated, is gratuitous and irrelevant. However his use of the
term may have developed as he matured, 'beauty' is the term
390 he used; and in calling what seemed to him the supreme thing
in life 'beauty', he expressed a given bent—the bent everywhere
manifested in the quality of his verse, in its 'loveliness.' His
concern for beauty meant, at any rate in the first place, a concentration upon the purely delightful in experience to the
395 exclusion of 'disagreeables.' And that 'beauty' in the *Ode on a
Grecian Urn* expresses this bent is plain—that it should is the
essence of the poem, and there is nothing in the poem to suggest
otherwise.

When, then, the devotees of Art and Beauty later in the
400 century made creedal or liturgical use of Keats's

'Beauty is truth, truth beauty,'

they were not falsifying its spirit (though it is one thing for him
to say it, another thing for them to say it after him). They had
at any rate gone the way it pointed, and it is worth while
405 recalling briefly where they arrived. The pre-Raphaelite cult
of Beauty, which developed into the religion of Art (or the
aesthetic religiosity), is the completest expression of that Victorian romanticism which, in poetry, draws so much on the

Keats of *The Eve of St. Agnes*, *The Eve of St. Mark* and *La Belle
Dame sans Merci*. Victorian poetry in the central line that runs 410
from the early Tennyson through Rossetti to Mr. Symons and
his associates of the 'nineties turns its back on the actual world
and preoccupies itself with fantasies of an alternative—in a
spirit very different from Shelley's, for the Victorian poetic day-
dream does not suppose itself to have any serious relation to 415
actuality or possibility. Tennyson, of course, knows there is
something wrong about 'the Palace of Art', and aspires vaguely
(the poem named is a curious and revealing document) to
become a serious poet. But the more sophisticated (and lesser)
talent, making a virtue—or religion—of its incapacity, cherishes 420
its otherworldliness as a spiritual distinction, and invests it,
as if to make it serious, with religiose solemnity. There is a
certain unction of cult about Keats's devotion to beauty, and
in his 'temple of delight,' we remember, 'veil'd Melancholy'
has her 'sov'ran shrine' also. But in reading Rossetti, who has 425
none of Keats's magnificent vital energy, we are assisting at
devotions—aesthetic-religiose devotions. There is a sacred hush,
and an effect of candles or of light through stained glass, of
swinging censers and of rites before a veiled altar. The poetic
otherworld has been turned into a higher reality in the most 430
effectual of ways: 'Life is ritual.'

So beauty is made truth, truth beauty—for Lionel Johnson's
phrase is his equivalent for Keats's. But if life is ritual, the
beauty that Johnson and Rossetti worship has (we are moved to
frame the corollary) little to do with life—and little life in it. 435
Imputing his favourite virtues to a favourite saint (Charles I)
Johnson says, characteristically:

> And art to him was joy.

This may fairly be taken as the Aesthetic equivalent of

> A thing of beauty is a joy for ever.   440

The difference is characteristic. Keats may be an aesthete,
and he may contemplate, among other 'things of beauty,' a
Grecian urn or a Titian, but even then his joy would be better
described as being in 'life' (the word 'art' could not have been
used by Keats—or by any one of his time—in Johnson's way). 445

The difference between joy in 'art' and joy in 'life', is, of course,
not so plain as the antithetical use of the two words would
suggest; but the point just made about Keats may be enforced
by recalling that the urn, for him, becomes alive ('warm' and
450 'panting'), and that out of the Titian bursts, in *Endymion*, that
glowing triumph of Bacchus, with its irresistible rush of joyous
energy:

> Like to a moving vintage down they came,
> Crown'd with green leaves, and faces all on flame . . .

455 Keats's aestheticism, in short, does not mean any such cutting
off of the special valued order of experience from direct, vulgar
living ('Live!—our servants will do that for us') as is implied
in the aesthetic antithesis of Art and Life.

Nevertheless, a certain drawing of frontiers, a wilful delimita-
460 tion of the 'true' or 'real' in experience, a focussing of the vision
so as to shut out the uncongenial, is essentially the purpose of
Keats's worship of Beauty—a purpose such as, uncountered
and persisted in, must, we feel, necessarily result in devitaliza-
tion. Actually, we feel also that there is in the poetry of this
465 Keats, in the very richness and vitality with which he
renders his 'exquisite sense of the luxurious', an inherent
contradiction: so strong a grasping at fulness of life implies a
constitution, a being, that could not permanently refuse completeness of living.

470 Aestheticism as intensity of living was what, of course, the
Victorian devotees of Art and Beauty, of the religious cult of
the senses, were apt to preach. We remember the credo of the
religion, the 'Conclusion' to *The Renaissance* (it is through Pater
that the line passes from Rossetti to the Aesthetes of the 'nine-
475 ties):[1]

'Not the fruit of experience, but experience itself is the end. A

---

[1] 'This Chiaro dell' Erma was a young man of very honourable family in
Arezzo; where, conceiving art almost, as it were, for himself, and loving it
deeply, he endeavoured from early boyhood towards the imitation of any
objects offered in nature. The extreme longing after a visible embodiment
of his thoughts strengthened as his years increased, more even than his
sinews or the blood of his life; until he would feel faint in sunsets and at the
sight of stately persons.'—The likeness of this prose (it is the opening of
Rossetti's *Hand and Soul*) to Pater's is significant.

counted number of pulses only is given to us of a variegated, dramatic life. How may we see in them all that is to be seen in them by the finest senses? How shall we pass most swiftly from point to point, and be present always at the focus where the greatest number 480 of vital forces unite in their purest energy?

'To burn always with this hard, gemlike flame, to maintain this ecstasy, is success in life. . . . While all melts under our feet, we may well grasp at any exquisite passion . . . stirring of the sense, strange dyes, strange colours, and curious odours, or the face of one's 485 friend. . . . With this sense of the splendour of our experience and of its awful brevity, gathering all we are into one desperate effort to see and touch, we shall hardly have time to make theories about the things we see and touch.'

—'O for a life of sensations rather than of thoughts.' But the 490 contrast with Keats is as apparent as the community. Pater may talk of burning always with a hard gemlike flame, but there is nothing answering in his prose; it notably lacks all sensuous vitality. Indeed, to point to Pater's prose—cloistral, mannered, urbane, consciously subtle and sophisticated and actually 495 monotonous and irresponsive in tone, sentiment and move- ment (the eyelids always a little weary) is a way of giving force to the judgement that for the Victorian aesthete art is something that gets between him and life. (A closely related judgement is that Victorian romantic poetry is 'literary' as Keats's is not.) 500 Nevertheless, we can see why pre-Raphaelite and Aesthete should have looked to Keats as they did: we can ourselves see in Keats (if we can see more too) the great Aesthete—the one Aesthete of genius. For all his unique vitality and creative power, we can see him as related to them by those significantly 505 associated traits which Pater presents: the devotion to exquisite passion and finest senses, the religiose unction of this aesthetic- ism, the cherished pang of transience. And even in Wilde's vulgarization of Pater's prose we can be reminded that Keats's use of the Grecian urn represents a regular Aesthetic habit— 510 one that is intimately associated with the traits just mentioned:

'On that little hill, by the city of Florence, where the lovers of Giorgione are lying, it is always the solstice of noon, of noon made so languorous by summer suns that hardly can the slim naked girl dip into the marble tank the round bubble of clear glass, and 515 the long fingers of the lute-player rest idly upon the chords. It is twilight always for the dancing nymphs whom Corot set free among the silver poplars of France. In eternal twilight they move,' *etc.*

But the effect of this insisting on the Aesthete in Keats is
520 merely to bring out still more the extraordinary force of his genius. There is, for instance, the *Ode on Melancholy*, which represents one of the most obviously decadent developments of Beauty-addiction—of the cult of 'exquisite passion' and 'finest senses'. The penalties of the addiction—the 'heart high-sorrow-
525 ful and cloy'd,' the 'aching pleasure . . . turning to poison,' the besetting fret of transience—are themselves turned into a luxury, a peculiarly subtle drug. The Ode is, as it were, the prescription. The process is of the same order as that by which his Victorian successors ('world-losers and world-forsakers')
530 made of their sense of defeat and impotence a kind of religious sanction—turned it into an atmosphere of religious desiderium:

> Nothing: the autumn fall of leaves.
> The whole year sets apace

—the tone pervades the work of this line from *Mariana in the*
535 *Moated Grange* onwards. But Keats's *Ode on Melancholy*, a pre-scription for making the most of your 'sorrow's mysteries' (if you go to Lethe or make your rosary of yew-berries you drown the wakeful anguish of the soul), exhibits with peculiarly paradoxi-cal force in the inculcation of these perverse and debilitating
540 indulgences—it is his most Swinburnian mood—his character-istic vitality.

Paradoxical the manifestation of this vitality in the second stanza very plainly deserves to be called:

> But when the melancholy fit shall fall
545 >   Sudden from heaven like a weeping cloud,
> That fosters the droop-headed flowers all,
> And hides the green hill in an April shroud . . .

—the fresh touch when it comes is so welcome after the heavy drugged luxury of the first stanza that one does not immediately
550 recognize the purely formal nature of the simile, which passes only by a curious sleight or bluff. Keats's melancholy attracts no doubt both the 'weeping' and the 'cloud' quite naturally; but it is not, as the poem conveys it, at all like the sudden rain that refreshes the flowers. For the 'pale forehead' of the addict

it has no such virtue. Its quite opposite effect is given us at the 555
end of the Ode:

> His soul shall taste the sadness of her might,
> And be among her cloudy trophies hung.

The sudden burst of freshness is, as it were, the vitality behind
Keats's aestheticism breaking through. It leads on to the con- 560
trasting and very characteristic manifestation of vitality that
follows:

> Then glut thy sorrow on a morning rose,
>   Or on the rainbow of the salt sand-wave,
>   Or on the wealth of globed peonies;   565
>   Or if thy mistress some rich anger shows . . .

In the strength that makes the luxury of this more than merely
voluptuous we have that which makes Keats so much more
than a mere aesthete. That 'glut', which we can hardly imagine
Rossetti or Tennyson using in a poetical place, finds itself taken 570
up in 'globed', the sensuous concreteness of which it reinforces;
the hand is round the peony, luxuriously cupping it. Such
tactual effects are notoriously characteristic of Keats, and they
express, not merely the voluptuary's itch to be fingering, but
that strong grasp upon actualities—upon things outside himself, 575
that firm sense of the solid world, which makes Keats so
different from Shelley. Because of it Mr. Symons is able to say
of him, justly:

'Keats has a firm common sense of the imagination, seeming to
be at home in it, as if it were literally of this world, and not of 580
another.'

—It is, we may add, by virtue of this strength, which is at
once intelligence and character, that Keats never takes his
dreams for reality or (even with the Grecian urn to help him)
remains lost in them. This strength is one with that which makes 585
him put *La Belle Dame sans Merci* aside—abandoned for the
Victorian romantics to find in it the essential stuff of poetry,
and which makes him condemn *Isabella* as 'mawkish' and say:
'in my dramatic capacity I enter fully into the feeling; but in
Propria Persona I should be apt to quiz it myself. There is no 590
objection of the kind to *Lamia*—a good deal to *St. Agnes Eve*—only
not so glaring.'[1]

---

[1] Letter to Woodhouse, 21 September 1819.

The strength appears here as critical intelligence, something
intimately related to the sureness of touch and grasp that makes
595 his art in the Odes so much better than Mr. Symons recognizes.
It is the strength that is manifested in the extraordinary rapidity
with which that art developed between *Endymion* and the *Ode
to a Nightingale*.

The relation between the firmness of the art and the firm
600 grasp on the outer world appears most plainly in the Ode *To
Autumn*. Of this Mr. Middleton Murry says:

'It is the perfect and unforced utterance of the truth contained
in the magic words: "Ripeness is all".'[1]

Such talk is extravagant, and does not further the appreciation
605 of Keats. No one could have found that order of significance in
the Ode merely by inspecting the Ode itself. The ripeness with
which Keats is concerned is the physical ripeness of autumn,
and his genius manifests itself in the sensuous richness with
which he renders this in poetry, without the least touch of
610 artistic over-ripeness.

If one might justifiably call the poem Shakespearian, it
would be in emphasizing how un-Tennysonian it is—how
different from the decorative-descriptive verse to which we see
it as pointing forward. The explicit richness of detail has its life
615 in the vigour of the medium:

> To bend with apples the moss'd cottage-trees,
> And fill all fruit with ripeness to the core;
> To swell the gourd, and plump the hazel shells
> With a sweet kernel . . .

620 That 'moss'd cottage-trees' represents a strength—a native
English strength—lying beyond the scope of the poet who
aimed to make English as like Italian as possible. So too with
the unpoetical 'plump': its sensuous firmness—it introduces a
tactual image—represents a general concrete vigour such as is
625 alien to the Tennysonian habit, and such as a Tennysonian
handling of the medium cannot breed. This English strength
pervades the Ode; in another of its forms it is notably exemplified by this, from the second stanza:

---

[1] *Keats and Shakespeare*, p. 189.

And sometimes like a gleaner thou dost keep
   Steady thy laden head across a brook . . .   630

In the step from the rime-word 'keep', across (so to speak)
the pause enforced by the line-division, to 'Steady' the balancing movement of the gleaner is enacted.

The warm richness of the poem is qualified, as with the
autumnal hint of sharpness in the air, by the last stanza, 635
which, from 'the stubble plains' (appropriately unvoluptuous
in suggestion) onward, is full of the evocation of thin sounds—
the gnats 'mourn' in a 'wailful choir,' the lambs bleat, hedge-
crickets sing, the red-breast 'with treble soft' whistles, and
gathering swallows twitter in the skies.   640

If, then, in Keats's development from *Endymion* to the Ode
To Autumn we see, as we may (leaving aside for a moment the
Hyperions), the promise of greatness, it does not lie in any effec-
tive presence of the kind of seriousness aspired to in *Sleep and
Poetry*:   645

   And can I ever bid these joys farewell?
   Yes, I must pass them for a nobler life,
   Where I may find the agonies, the strife
   Of human hearts . . .

It lies rather in the marvellous vitality of the art that celebrates 650
'these joys'—in the perfection attained within a limiting
aestheticism. Remarkable intelligence and character are
implied in that attainment, especially when we consider the
starting-point and the surrounding influences: the beginning in
'pleasant smotherings', with, as the incitement towards dis- 655
cipline, such poetic models as are represented by Leigh Hunt
and the Cockney taste (at the highest level:

   Spenserian vowels that elope with ease
   And float along like birds o'er summer seas).

The achieved art itself, as has been argued, implies paradoxi- 660
cally, in the consummately kept limits of its perfection, something more serious than mere aestheticism.

'While a great deal is made of aesthetic sensibility and its refine-
ments, we hear very little about moral sensibility. It is ignored;
and the deep-seated spiritual vulgarity that lies at the heart of our 665
civilization commonly passes without notice.'

—That exquisitely sure touch which refines and lightens Keats's voluptuousness cannot, we are convinced, go with spiritual vulgarity (an argument notably relevant to the *Ode to* 670 *Psyche*, about the sensuous loveliness of which there is nothing oppressive, cloying or gross). In the place—it is the Preface to *The Root and the Flower*—from which comes the sentence just quoted, Mr. Myers also says:

'When a novelist displays an attitude of aesthetic detachment 675 from the ordinary ethical and philosophical preoccupations of humanity, something in us protests . . .'

—Something in the poet protested, we know. 'Scenery is fine', he wrote in a letter, 'but human nature is finer.' Also:

'I find cavalier days are gone by—I find that I can have no 680 enjoyment in the world but continual drinking of knowledge. I find there is no worthy pursuit but the idea of doing some good for the world. . . . The road lies through application, study, and thought. I will pursue it, and to that end purpose retiring for some years. I have been hovering for some time between an exquisite sense of 685 the luxurious, and a love for philosophy—were I calculated for the former, I should be glad. But as I am not, I shall turn all my soul to the latter. . . .'[1]

By the date of the Ode *To Autumn*, of course, this resolution, this maturer bent in Keats for which the Letters are so remark- 690 able, had taken effect in poetry: the revised *Hyperion*, in fact, had just been abandoned. It is ironical that the first result of the effort to bring his profoundest moral and philosophical concerns into poetry—to deal with

the agonies, the strife
695   Of human hearts

—should have been something deserving to be called, with a pejorative implication, 'art' as nothing does that he had written before. Mr. Middleton Murry's explanation seems reasonable: Keats, against his conscious aim, was led to cultivate an 700 'abstract' Miltonic art by the overmastering impulse to evade reality—reality made intolerable by the sufferings of his brother. In any case, Keats's own judgement upon the first *Hyperion* is clear:

[1]   24 April 1818.

'I have given up *Hyperion*—there were too many Miltonic
inversions in it—Miltonic verse cannot be written but in an artful, 705
or rather, artist's humour. I wish to give myself up to other sensations. English ought to be kept up.'[1]

This was to Reynolds. To his brother George he had written:

'I have but lately stood on my guard against Milton. Life to him
would be death to me. Miltonic verse cannot be written but in the 710
vein of art. I wish to devote myself to another sensation.'[2]

The verse of the first *Hyperion*, if not merely Miltonic, is
decidedly a verse of 'art'.

> One moon, with alternations slow, had shed
> Her silver seasons four upon the night, 715
> And still these two were postured motionless,
> Like natural sculpture in cathedral cavern;
> The frozen God still couchant on the earth,
> And the sad Goddess weeping at his feet:
> Until at length old Saturn lifted up 720
> His faded eyes, and saw his kingdom gone,
> And all the gloom and sorrow of the place,
> And that fair kneeling Goddess; and then spake,
> As with a palsied tongue, and while his beard
> Shook horrid with such aspen-malady: 725

That is a very qualified Miltonic—Miltonic as transformed by a
taste for 'Spenserian vowels that elope with ease' (the ease of
this verse is languorous and luxurious). We note, both in the
presentment of what the verse describes and in the poet's
attitude towards the verse, what may be called a decorative 730
preoccupation. The attitude towards the verse, the handling of
the medium, reminds us strongly of Tennyson:

> Until at length old Saturn lifted up
> His faded eyes, and saw his kingdom gone,
> And all the gloom and sorrow of the place, 735
> And that fair kneeling Goddess

—that is plainly very close to

---

[1] 27 September 1819.

[2] 1h-27 September 1819. Keats has said just before: 'The *Paradise Lost*,
though so fine in itself, is a corruption of our language. It should be kept as
it is, unique, a curiosity, a beautiful and grand curiosity, the most
remarkable production of the world; a northern dialect accommodating
itself to Greek and Latin inversions and intonations.'

The long day wanes: the slow moon climbs: the deep
Moans round with many voices

740 and

One seem'd all dark and red—a tract of sand,
    And some one pacing there alone,
Who paced for ever in a glimmering land,
    Lit with a low large moon.

745 *Hyperion*, in fact, offers a good way of bringing home the predominance of Milton—a Milton associated with Spenser—in
the poetry of the nineteenth century, for Tennyson represents
the Victorian main current.

If the first *Hyperion* is impersonal, it is impersonal in one of
750 the wrong ways. Keats's art does not tap the vigour either of
his aestheticism or of the more serious interests, the maturer
moral life, revealed to us in the Letters; no rich sap flows. In
the revising, his main operation was an attempt to graft the
poem on to his maturer personality—for that is what the use of
755 Moneta, in the added induction, amounts to:

'My power, which to me is still a curse,
Shall be to thee a wonder; for the scenes
Still swooning vivid through my globed brain,
With an electral changing misery,
760   Thou shalt with these dull mortal eyes behold
Free from all pain, if wonder pain thee not.'

But this mode of presentment—of introduction, rather—makes
no difference to the ensuing narrative, which remains, but for
some mechanical changes in phrasing and word-order, what it
765 was. The new life is confined to the three hundred added lines
of induction, which, however, suffice for a conclusive effect.

To talk of 'new life' in this verse may perhaps seem paradoxical, for what strikes one at once about it, compared with
the verse of the first *Hyperion*, is a kind of inertness: it lacks
770 entirely the epic (if rather languid) buoyancy, the Miltonic
wave-motion, the onward-carrying rise and fall. And it is not
merely quite without any suggestion of the Tennysonian; even
when it most suggests the Keats of the Odes it is without
poetical aura—unbeglamoured and unintoxicated:

No Asian poppy nor elixir fine   775
Of the soon-fading jealous Caliphat;
No poison gender'd in close monkish cell
To thin the scarlet conclave of old men,
Could so have rapt unwilling life away.

This exemplifies well enough the characteristic movement— 780
'inert' only by comparison and in immediate effect, while the
ear has not yet dropped the habit of expectancy brought away
from the first version. The new verse moves line by line, the
characteristic single line having, as it were, an evenly distributed weight—a settled, quite unspringy balance. It is this 785
peculiar rhythmic character that had led one to divine, as an
influence in this technical development, a study of Dante in
the Italian (Cary could hardly have had much to do with so extraordinary a change as that represented by the new verse compared with the earlier). And, at the moment of writing, that 790
guess gets something very like confirmation in a letter from
Professor Livingston Lowes to the *Times Literary Supplement*
(11 January 1936), in which he shows, in impressive detail,
that the influence of Dante (of the *Purgatorio* in especial) upon
the induction to *The Fall of Hyperion: a Vision* 'is both deeper and 795
more extensive than has apparently been observed.'

Dante, of course, for Keats was not a technical study, and
was something more than literature. What the strength of the
influence, the intensity of the effect, shows is how much the
study was part of the discipline and self-searching with which 800
Keats met the disasters, the blows of fate, that were making life
for him overwhelmingly a matter of 'the agonies, the strife of
human hearts.' The immediately personal urgency of the preoccupation with suffering and death comes out plainly in the
passage describing his nightmare race against the burning of 805
the 'gummed leaves' (ll. 106-134). But this personal urgency is
completely impersonalized; it has become the life, the informing
spirit, of the profoundest kind of impersonality. There is no
element of self-pity—nothing at all of the obliquely self-regard-
ing—about the attitude of the famous lines: 810

'None can usurp this height,' returned that shade,
'But those to whom the miseries of the world
Are misery, and will not let them rest.'

It was, in the Romantic period, the aesthete who achieved so
un-Byronic and so un-Shelleyan a note in the contemplation of
human suffering—the aesthete no longer an aesthete. There is
no afflatus here, no generous emotionality. The facts, the
objects of contemplation, absorb the poet's attention completely; he has none left for his feelings as such. As a result, his
response, his attitude, seems to us to inhere in the facts, and
to have itself the authenticity of fact. The strength that makes
the sensuous Keats's *Ode to a Nightingale* so different from the
spiritual Shelley's *To a Skylark*—the grasp of the object, the
firm sense of actuality, the character and critical intelligence
implied (we have seen) in the artist's touch and his related
command of total effect—now manifests itself in the field of
tragic experience. His own acute and inescapable distresses,
including the pain of watching helplessly the suffering of
persons dear to him, he can, without feeling them the less,
contemplate at the same time from (as it were) the outside,
as objects, as facts; and the contemplation of the inevitable and
endless human suffering to which his more immediately personal experience leads him has a like impersonal strength. This
profound tragic impersonality has its concentrated symbolic
expression in the vision of Moneta's face:

> And yet I had a terror of her robes,
> And chiefly of the veils, that from her brow
> Hung pale, and curtain'd her in mysteries,
> That made my heart too small to hold its blood.
> This saw that Goddess, and with sacred hand
> Parted the veils. Then saw I a wan face,
> Not pined by human sorrows, but bright-blanch'd
> By an immortal sickness which kills not;
> It works a constant change, which happy death
> Can put no end to; deathwards progressing
> To no death was that visage; it had past
> The lilly and the snow; and beyond these
> I must not think now, though I saw that face—
> But for her eyes I should have fled away.
> They held me back with a benignant light,
> Soft-mitigated by divinest lids
> Half-closed, and visionless entire they seem'd
> Of all external things—they saw me not,
> But in blank splendour, beam'd like the mild moon,

Who comforts those she sees not, who knows not   855
What eyes are upward cast.

The 'comfort' does not derive from any latent goodwill or
sympathy imagined to reside in the ultimate nature of things—
for Keats there are no Demogorgons; it is that paradoxical
strengthening—sense of ability to endure—which rewards 860
the full recognition of necessity. But these are empty abstract
words: the poetry is concrete in its complexity and unmistak-
able in its effect. It is clearly the expression of a rare maturity;
the attitude is the product of tragic experience, met by discipline, in a very uncommonly strong, sincere and sensitive 865
spirit.

The Ode *To Autumn* was composed immediately on the
abandonment of the revised *Hyperion*. It represents the repose—
the 'comfort'—earned. Its easy objectivity can now be seen to
be related to the tragic impersonality of the Moneta passage. 870
The moral and spiritual discipline in the background make
possible this serenity (though the Ode itself does not say, in the
sense implied by Mr. Murry, 'Ripeness is all'). And that the
Ode, being what it is, should come when it does confirms
the account given above of the relation between Keats's 875
sensuousness and his seriousness, his capacity for rapid development.

The induction to the revised *Hyperion*, then, justifies the high
estimate of Keats's potentialities. It shows the interests of the
Letters realized—become active—in technique: poet and letter- 880
writer are at last one. The verse is convincing, and the symbolism
is organic with it. The symbolic theme is extremely impressive
and, though it invites elucidation and commentary, conveys
its essential significance at once.

Keats, as has been so generally agreed, was beyond any 885
doubt gifted to become a very great poet—though no sufficient
reason appears to have been given for supposing that he might
have written great poetic plays.

NOTES

PHILIP SIDNEY:
AN APOLOGY FOR POETRY

An Apology for Poetry, or *The Defence of Poesy*, to give its alternative title, is believed to have been written about 1580. Stephen Gosson published in 1579 *The School of Abuse*, and dedicated it to Sidney: the *Apology* is Sidney's reply (*v.* note to l. 1041). The work was first published only in 1595, in two editions. The one by Ponsonby, believed to be the earlier of the two, was called *The Defence of Poesy*; the other, by Olney, *An Apology for Poetry*. Our text follows the Olney edition with, however, a few emendations from the Ponsonby. Spelling has been modernized.

5 **wit** understanding.
7 **contemplations** studies.
10 **admiration** astonishment.
17 **pedanteria** piece of useless knowledge.
39, 40 **former ... silly latter** learning ... defenceless poetry.
52 **Musaeus** legendary Greek poet, pupil of Orpheus.
66 **science** knowledge.
90 **Gyges' Ring** Plato, *Republic*, II. 359. Gyges, a shepherd, became King of Lydia with the help of a magic ring.
94 **fashion** form (as opposed to matter). **weight** persuasive or convincing power.
103 **judgements** understanding.
112 **areytos** song accompanied by dance.
127 **stand upon** rely on.
128 **but even** if only.
137 **Sortes Virgilianae** Virgilian divination. *v.* 139–42.
141 Virgil, *Aeneid*, II. 314: 'Frantic I seize arms; yet little purpose is there in arms.'
142 **in his age performed it** Albinus fulfilled this prophecy when on an impulse he took up arms against Septimus Severus and was killed in battle.
150 **conceit** fancy.
158 **Hebricians** Hebraicians, Hebrew scholars.
160 **merely** purely.
161 **changing of persons** varying the speakers.
162 **prosopopoeias** personifications.
177 **met with** agreed with.
180 **scope** purpose.

197-8   **compassed . . . matter**   limited to questions presented by the subject matter of the rhetorician and logician.

200   **metaphysic** metaphysician. **second and abstract notions** refers to distinction made in logic between first notions or primary conceptions of things, e.g. a *tree*, an *oak*, and second or 'abstract notions', e.g. *genus, species*, &c.

201   **supernatural**   metaphysical.

214   **brazen**   bronze; in reference to the gold, silver, bronze, and iron ages of the Greek and Roman poets.

219   **Theagenes**   the hero in *Aethiopica*, a Greek romance by Heliodorus (third century A.D.). *v.* 318. **Pylades**   friend of Orestes.

220   **Orlando**   hero of Ariosto's poem, *Orlando Furioso*. **Xenophon's Cyrus**   for Xenophon's flattering portrait of Cyrus *v.* his political romance *Cyropaedia* or 'Education of Cyrus'.

223   **essential**   i.e. the works of Nature 'exist'. **the other**   of the poet.

229   **by**   of.

238   **second nature**   *v. Genesis*, I. 26–30. Man is the first nature; the second nature is all the rest of the created world placed under Man.

241   **with no . . . incredulous of**   lending no small support to those who do not believe in.

242   **erected wit**   undebased understanding.

246   **name**   i.e. of poet.

248   **opening of him**   explanation of the nature of the poet.

253   **Aristotle**   *Poetics*, I. 2.

255   **a speaking picture**   cf. Horace, *Art of Poetry*, 361 (*v.* App.).

257   **three several kinds**   apparently based on the *Poetices* of J. C. Scaliger (1569).

261   **Moses**   *v. Exodus*, XV. **Deborah**   *v. Judges*, V.

262, 3   **Tremellius . . . Junius**   sixteenth-century Biblical scholars.

265   **wrong divinity** i.e. because pagan.

266   **his Hymns**   not the work of the authors of the *Iliad* and *Odyssey*, but the so-called Homeric Hymns to Apollo, Hermes, &c.

268   **St. James's counsel** *v. Epistle of St. James*, V. 13.

287   **Lucretia**   wife of Tarquinius Collatinus, who killed herself after being violated by Sextus. Paintings of this subject by Albrecht Dürer (1471–1528) and

Cranach (1472–1551) may have been known to Sidney.

295 **waited on** associated.

303 **want there not** there lack not.

306 **iambic** a piece of invective or satire in verse.

310 **numberous** consisting of 'numbers' or rhythmical periods.

312 **no cause to poetry** not the efficient cause, the producing agency.

316 **as Cicero says** *Letters*, I. i. 8. (To his brother Quintus).

317 **absolute** complete, entire.

327–8 **as in matter . . . beyond them** as poetry surpasses all else in subject matter, so should it surpass the rest in its manner of expression.

328 **table-talk fashion** in casual language.

330 **peizing** weighing.

333 **his . . . his** its . . . its.

334 **anatomies** analyses.

336 **enabling** strengthening.

337 **conceit** ideas.

362 **next end** immediate object.

368 **that** virtuous action.

375–6 **with books . . . names** *v.* Cicero, *Pro Archia Poeta*, XI: 'Why, upon the very books in which they bid us scorn ambition philosophers inscribe their names!'

386 **generalities . . . specialities** the general and specific characteristics of virtue and vice.

394 **accord** reconcile.

401 **testis temporum . . .** Cicero, *De Oratore*, II. ix. 36 (adapted): 'witness of the times, light of truth, the life of memory, the teacher of life, and messenger of the past'. [Ed.]

403 **disputative virtue** theoretical virtue, merely 'talked about'. **active** practical, as opposed to theoretical.

413 **conferring story by story** introducing story after story.

416 **their disputation** i.e. philosopher and historian. **maketh a point** comes to an end.

418 **standeth for** concerns.

430 **formidine poenae . . . virtutis amore** Horace, *Epistles*, I. XVI. 52–3 (adapted): 'from fear of punishment' . . . 'from love of virtue'.

436 **naughtiness** wickedness.

439 **manners** morals.

443 **halt** limp.

464 **who** he who. **exquisitely** carefully.
469 **true lively knowledge** that true knowledge of a thing which can only come from seeing it.
472 **judicial comprehending** such an understanding as will enable him to make a judgement.
479 **Tully** Marcus Tullius Cicero (106–43 B.C.).
489 **his** i.e. anger's. **genus** the class to which a species belongs. **difference** the characteristic by which a species is distinguished from all other species of the same genus. In 'anger is a short madness', *madness* is the genus and *short* the difference.
491 **Nisus and Euryalus** v. Virgil, *Aeneid*, IX. 176ff. **carry not an apparent shining** are not clearly depicted.
496 **Gnatho** a parasite and flatterer in Terence's *Eunuchus*.
500 **see through them** see right into them.
514 **Mediocribus . . .** Horace, *Art of Poetry*, 372–3: 'But that poets be of middling rank, neither men nor gods nor booksellers ever brooked.'
534 **formal** in respect of form.
541 **Aristotle** v. App., VIII. 1–IX. 4.
549 **in his imposed names** the names of its imagined characters.
560 **doctrinable** instructive.
561 **Justin** Justinus, *Historiarum Philippicarum Libri XLIV*, I. 4–8.
562 **Dares Phrygius** a work in Latin called *De Excidio Trojae* purporting to be a translation of an account by Dares Phrygius, a priest of Hephaestus in the *Iliad*, of the destruction of Troy.
564 **Canidia** a witch described in *Satires*, I. 8.
572 **Scipio** either Scipio Africanus the elder, the conqueror of Hannibal, or his nephew the younger Africanus, who destroyed Carthage in 146 B.C.
575 **Quintus Curtius** first century A.D., wrote a history of Alexander the Great.
576 **in universal consideration of doctrine** as regards lessons of universal application.
577–8 **doth warrant . . . follow** gives a man greater assurance as to what he should do.
581 **it hath . . . conceit** such an argument may well profit a dull imagination.
581–4 **But if . . . reasonable** but if a man recognizes that what *was* (a historical example) affords only a conjecture

AN APOLOGY FOR POETRY 343

as to what *will be*, and if he will use his reason, he must admit that the poet is superior to the historian in that the poet creates his example in accordance with reason.

588 **poetically** by using his imagination.

628 **the tragedy writer** *v.* Plutarch, *Moralia*, vol. I, p. 101; Euripides gave this reply to one who complained that his character Ixion was impious and detestable: 'But I did not remove him from the stage until I had fastened him to the wheel.'

635 **The cruel Severus** L. Septimus, Roman Emperor A.D. 193–211, died at York. **excellent Severus** M. Alexander, Roman Emperor A.D. 222–35.

639 **rebel Caesar** because he split the republic in the Civil War, 49–45 B.C.

641 **Caesar's own words** Suetonius, *Lives of the Caesars*, I. 77.

642 **put down** resign. **literas nescivit** 'Sylla did not know his ABC.'

643 **as if ... well** Sidney's point is that if Sylla had been well read in history he would have found enough examples for continuing his dictatorship.

644 **by poetry** of poetry.

646 **occidendos esse** perhaps based on Cicero, *De Officiis*, II. vii: 'that they [tyrants] are to be slain'.

652 **setting it forward** inciting it.

656 **in teaching** as regards teaching.

661 **philophilosophos** lover of philosophers. **in moving** in the power to affect the mind or feelings.

668 **Aristotle** *Nic. Ethics*, I. 3. **gnosis** knowledge. **praxis** action.

676 **painfulness** taking of pains.

684 **words of art** technical language.

685 **natural conceit** understanding based upon the innate moral feelings of mankind. **it** knowledge of good and evil.

687 **hoc opus ...** Virgil, *Aeneid*, VI. 129: 'This is the task, this the toil!'

701 **pretending no more** i.e. than to tell a tale.

705 **aloes** genus of plants with bitter juice.

714 **whereof poetry is** to which poetry belongs.

715 **Aristotle** *Poetics*, IV.

718 **Amadis de Gaule** hero of famous romance of the same name.

726–7 Virgil, *Aeneid*, XII. 645–6: 'Shall this land see [Turnus] in flight? Is death all so sad?'

344   SIDNEY

731 **well knew**   i.e. that philosophers do not move.

734 **school-name**   a matter of academic interest only.

735 **indulgere genio**   Persius, *Satires*, V. 151: 'Give your Genius a chance.'

738 **steal**   come insensibly.

743 **Menenius Agrippa**   *v.* Shakespeare's *Coriolanus*, I. i. 91 ff.

750 **learned geometry**   for Plato's views *ι Republic*, VII, 9: 'It would tend to draw the soul to truth, and would be productive of a philosophic attitude of mind.'

763 **Nathan**   *Samuel*, II. xii. 1–7.

765 **office**   in making David see the evil of his ways.

768 **ungratefully**   unkindly.

770–71 **second . . . cause**   Nathan's story is the instrument used by God, the First Cause.

772 **Psalm**   LI.

777 **end of**   its object.

778 **familiar**   usual, common.

781 **him**   poetry.

782–3 **although . . . authority**   in judging poetry its effects must carry the greatest weight.

791 **Sannazzaro**   (1458–1530) Neapolitan author of a pastoral in prose and verse called *Arcadia*.

792 **cometh . . . one**   makes no difference.

800, 802 **Meliboeus . . . Tityrus**   speakers in Virgil's *First Eclogue*; Meliboeus represents the farmers, and Tityrus may represent Virgil who appealed successfully to Augustus against the confiscation of his farm.

811–12 Virgil, *Eclogues*, VII, 69–70: 'This I remember, and how Thyrsis, vanquished, strove in vain. From that day it is Corydon, Corydon with us.'

816 **who**   the elegiac poet.

818 **painting out**   picturing.

823, 6 **Omne . . . amico; circum . . . ludit**   these words, with slight alterations, are parts of a couplet by Persius, *Satires*, I. 116–17: 'Horace, sly dog, worming his way playfully into the vitals of his laughing friend, touches up his every fault.'

827 **a passionate life**   a life under the sway of the passions.

829 Horace, *Epistles*, I. ii. 30: '[What you are seeking (happiness) is here]; it is at Ulubrae, if there fail you not a mind well balanced.' Ulubrae was a decaying town.

833 **comedy is an imitation**   Aristotle, *Poetics*, V.

842, 3 **Demea, Davus, Thraso**   characters in Terence's comedies.

849 **pistrinum** the mill; place of punishment for slaves and criminals.

859 **admiration** first introduced by Minturno (*c.* 1560), the term was accepted by Renaissance critics as describing one of the three functions of poetry; the other two being Horace's instruction and delight. Here, coupled with commiseration, it is the equivalent of Aristotle's 'pity and fear' (*v.* App., VI. 2–4).

862–3 Seneca, *Oedipus*, 705–6: 'Who harshly wields the sceptre with tyrannic sway, fears those who fear; terror recoils upon its author's head.'

864 **Plutarch** *Life of Pelopidas.*

878 **natural problems** questions dealing with our real or physical existence, as opposed to moral.

881 **old song** earlier version of *The Ballad of Chevy Chase.*

883 **crowder** fiddler.

893 **lusty** full of healthy vigour.

901 **fearful felicities** the other two, reported on the same day, were the news of a victory over the Illyrians, and the birth of his son Alexander. **fearful** because three such pieces of good fortune all at once were too good to be safe.

902 **that kind** lyric poetry.

908 **Tydeus** one of the seven heroes who fought against Thebes. *v. The Thebaid* by the Roman poet Statius.

909 **Rinaldo** the hero of Tasso's poem of that name (1562).

912 **Plato and Tully** Plato, *Phaedrus*, 250D. Tully (Cicero), *De Officiis*, I. 5.

935 **melius . . .** *Epistles,* I, ii. 4: 'Better than Chrysippus or Crantor.' Chrysippus was a Stoic philosopher, Crantor an academic philosopher.

938, 9 **his . . . him** referring to poetry. **The sum that contains him** the totality (of poetry).

980 **playing wit** one with a gift for paradox.

982 **jolly commodity** splendid advantage.

984 *Ars Amatoria,* II. 662. Sidney inverts the sense of the line.

985 **Agrippa** (1486–1533) wrote a book on the vanity of all knowledge.

998 **versing** writing in metre.

1002 **Scaliger** *v.* note on 257. Bk. II deals with metre.

1006 **his forcible quality** its convincing nature.

1008 **without** unless.

1032 Horace, *Epistles*, I. xviii. 69: 'Avoid a questioner, for he is also a tattler.'

1033   Ovid, *Remedia Amoris*, 686: 'While each of us flatters himself, we are a believing crew.'

1041   **imputations**   here Sidney is trying to answer Gosson. In *The School of Abuse* (dedicated to Sidney; and 'for his labor scorned': Spenser, *Three proper and wittie familiar letters*) and *An Apology of the School of Abuse*, Gosson called poets 'the fathers of lies, pipes of vanity, and Schools of Abuse'. [Arber Reprints, vol. I, pp. 65–6.]

1049   **field to ear**   i.e. opportunity. **Chaucer** cf. *Knight's Tale*, 28.

1055   **overshot Robin Hood**   a reference, most probably, to the proverb, 'Many a one talks of Robin Hood, who never shot in his bow.' Applied here to those who talk about matters they know little of.

1059   **petere principium**   beg the question.

1065   **first assumption**   that there are more fruitful kinds of knowledge.

1091   **before alleged**   mentioned earlier.

1101   **give the lie to**   accuse of falsehood.

1109, 10   **John a Stile . . . Noakes**   names used by lawyers for imaginary persons.

1118   **estates**   status, degree of rank.

1141, 2   **eikastikē . . . phantastikē**   terms borrowed from Plato but used here in a non-platonic sense.

1148   **ill-pleased eye**   the eye pleased by the perverse.

1153–4   **abuse . . . abused**   the wrong use of poetry should be a reproach to poetry itself.

1158   **rampire**   rampart.

1176   **Albion**   an ancient poetical name for Britain.

1178   **chain-shot**   cannon balls chained together, thus striking a larger target.

1181   **city**   Athens.

1195   Horace, *Satires*, I. i. 63 (adapted): 'I bid him be as much a fool as he pleases.' [Ed.]

1199   **quiddity**   subtlety. **ens** existence. **prima materia** the original substance of which the universe is composed.

1216, 17   **Cato . . . Fulvius . . . Ennius**   Ennius the epic poet and dramatist accompanied Fulvius on his campaign in Aetolia. Cato the elder, called Censorius on account of his severity, was displeased with ('misliked') Fulvius for this.

1219   **Cato Uticensis**   great-grandson of Cato the Censor.

1225   **Pluto**   or Hades, God of the lower world.

1227   **unmustered**   not on the pay-roll of the army.

1228 **misliked not** this does not necessarily follow, for he may have been displeased with both.

1233 **his person** Ennius as a person.

1260 **Plato . . . Dionysius** according to a common story Plato was sold as a slave by Dionysius the tyrant.

1261 **do thus** argue in this way.

1263–6 Sidney is not seriously attacking philosophy but is merely using the same unfair arguments as the opponents of poetry.

1269–70 **grew . . . wantonness** was not on account of the effeminacy caused by poetry.

1273–4 **so as . . . poetry** provided that they are not abused and that poetry is treated similarly.

1275 **twice two poets** St. Paul quotes two poets, each poet once. *v. Titus*, I. 12; *Corinthians*, I. xv. 33.

1276 **setteth . . . philosophy** utters a cautionary word to philosophy. *v. Colossians*, II. 8.

1277 **Plato** *v. Republic*, II. 377ff. and X.

1282 **induce** introduce.

1284 **very** true. **stood upon** was concerned with.

1287 **Plutarch** *v. Moralia*, V, for the first two; II, for the third.

1295 **Qua . . .** *Poetices*, I. ii: 'which authority certain barbarians and rude persons wish to abuse for the purpose of expelling poets from the republic.' [Ed.]

1298 **law** indulgence.

1317 **Heautontimoroumenos** 'Self-tormentor', title of a comedy by Terence.

1319 **Apollo** through the oracle of Delphi; *v.* Plato, *Apology*, 21A.

1320 **Aesop's Fables** *v.* Plato, *Phaedo*, 60D.

1324 **it** poetry. **Plutarch** *v. Moralia*, I: *How the young man should study Poetry*.

1325 **them** poets.

1327 **guards** ornamental trimmings or borders on a garment. Here it refers to the many quotations from poetry in Plutarch's writings.

1350 Virgil, *Aeneid*, I. 8: 'Tell me, O Muse, the cause; wherein thwarted in will . . .'

1356 **King James** I of Scotland (1394–1437), author of poem *The Kingis Quair*.

1360 **George Buchanan** (1506–82) Scots poet and scholars *v.* 1578.

1361 **Hospital of France** Michel de l'Hôpital (1505–73), statesman and poet.

1371 **over-faint quietness** twenty-five years of peace under Elizabeth.

1372 **strew** make clean.

1373 **mountebanks** quacks. Those of Venice were especially famous.

1374 **great praise** that poetry should prosper in time of war (cf. his refutation of the charge of 'effeminate wantonness', 1270). This suggests a reason why poets are not grateful to a peaceful England ('idle England', 1377) which ignores them.

1374, 6 **Venus . . . Mars . . . Vulcan** Vulcan was the husband of Venus, and Mars was her lover. The jealous husband forged a net and caught them in it.

1381 **Epaminondas** Theban general. Plutarch, *Moralia*, X. pp. 223–5, says that he gave dignity to the office of Telearch or Chief Scavenger.

1386 **post over . . . Helicon** write poetry in a hurry.

1389 Juvenal, *Satires*, XIV. 35 (adapted): 'One whose soul the Titan has fashioned . . . of a finer clay.'

1395 **Pallas** Athena, patroness of both the useful and fine arts.

1409 **Orator . . .** 'The orator is made, the poet is born.'

1413–15 **But these . . . withal** but we do not burden ourselves with either rules of art or models.

1416 **fore-backwardly** back to front.

1421 **quodlibet** what you please. The poets show no discrimination.

1421–4 **though wrongly . . . rank** i.e. they assumed that whatever they said was verse, but such was not the case as they never ordered their lines in any regular manner.

1423 *Tristia*, IV. x. 26 (adapted): 'Whatever I tried to say became verse.'

1452 **circumstances** subordinate parts.

1454 **faulty both in time and place** first appearance in English literary criticism of the idea of the unities, the three principles of dramatic composition, viz. that a play should be confined to one action, one place, and a certain time (not longer than the play takes to perform). The unities of time and place were first formulated by Castelvetro (1505–71) in his commentary on Aristotle's *Poetics*. For Aristotle, who insisted on the unity of action only, *v*. App., V. 8, VII, VIII.

1459 **inartificially** inartistically.

1462 **under-kingdoms** inferior kingdoms.

1474 **traverses** crosses, difficulties.

1479 **players in Italy** the unities were more strictly followed in Italy and France than in England.

1480 **Eunuchus** in this play the action is confined to two days.

1482 **twenty years** as in the case of the 'princes' mentioned immediately before. **played in two days** this is most probably a misunderstanding of the phrase, *bis die*, 'twice in the same day'. *v.* Suetonius, *Life of Terence*.

1495 **Pacolet's** the enchanted horse of Pacolet, in the romance *Valentine and Orson*.

1496 **Nuntius** messenger.

1499 **ab ovo** *Art of Poetry*, 147: 'from the egg'; i.e. from the beginning.

1501 **a story** the subject of Euripides' *Hecuba*.

1516 **neither right . . . comedies** like other 'classical' critics, Sidney supports the separation of Tragedy and Comedy.

1518 **head and shoulders** by force.

1521 **Apuleius** (*c.* A.D. 114) wrote *The Golden Ass*, a prose romance. It mixes comic and serious material.

1526 **daintily** sparingly.

1548–52 **We shall . . . laughter** on the other hand, we sometimes laugh at what has been said in error, even though we ought to feel sorry for the speaker. Such enforced laughter causes pain rather than delight.

1554 **Alexander's picture** perhaps a reference to Plutarch's *Life of Alexander*.

1555 **antics** clowns, buffoons.

1565 **Aristotle** *Poetics*, V.

1572–3 Juvenal, *Satires*, III. 152–3: 'Of all the woes of luckless poverty none is harder to endure than this, that it exposes men to ridicule.'

1574 **busy loving** one who loves to pry.

1575 **wry-transformed** perversely changed.

1601 **bewrayed** revealed.

1610 **coursing of a letter** alliteration.

1612 **winter-starved** withered (from constant repetition).

1619 **Nizolian paper-books** Marius Nizolius (1498–1566) published a collection of words and phrases by Cicero.

1628 **Vivit . . .** Cicero, *In Catilinam*, I. 2: 'Yet this man lives. Lives, did I say? Nay, more, he walks into the senate.'

1634 **similiter cadences** phrases containing similar sounds, commonly used by orators.

1637 **sophister** university student entitled to dispute in the schools.

1641 **fineness** subtlety.

1656 **set by it** set store by it.

1659 **knacks** devices.

1671 **pounded** impounded.

1673 **wordish consideration** consideration of the use of words.

1683 **both the other** Sidney is perhaps referring to Saxon and French as the two other languages.

1692-3 **compositions ... together** i.e. compound words.

1698 **number** each line containing an equal number of syllables. **accent** stress; *v.* 1718.

1708 **vulgar** common language of a country, the vernacular.

1710 **Dutch** including German.

1717 **rhyme** i.e. rhythm.

1730 **motion, potion** pronounced as trisyllables.

1744 **with Aristotle** mentioned nowhere in Aristotle.

1752 **quid non** what not.

1763 **libertino ...** Horace, *Satires*, I. vi. 6: 'a freedman' son'. **Herculea proles** 'a son of the house of Hercules'.

1764 Virgil, *Aeneid*, IX. 446: 'If aught my verse avail.'

1771 **mome** dolt, fool.

1772 **Momus** god of fault-finding.

1774 **Bubonax** Sidney is perhaps referring to the story of the satirical poet Hipponax and the sculptor Bupalus. The latter so annoyed Hipponax with a true-to-life statue of his ugliness that in revenge he satirized Bupalus so bitterly that he hanged himself.

1775 **to be done in Ireland** refers to the practice of rats being rhymed to death in Ireland.

JOHN DRYDEN:
AN ESSAY OF DRAMATIC POESY

First published in 1668. The present text is that of the 1684 edition, revised by Dryden. Spelling has been modernized.

1   **that memorable day**   3 June 1665.

16   **Eugenius**   Charles Sackville, Lord Buckhurst, to whom the *Essay* is dedicated. **Crites**   Sir Robert Howard.

17   **Lisideius**   Sir Charles Sedley. **Neander**   Dryden. The name which means 'new man, parvenu' is perhaps used to denote the difference in social rank between Dryden and the 'three persons of quality'.

43   **delicate**   subtle.

62   **conceit**   notion.

72   **Quem... scriberet**   Cicero (Tully), *Pro Archia*, X. 25: 'It will be remembered that once at a public meeting some poetaster from the crowd handed up to that great man a paper containing an epigram upon him, improvised in somewhat unmetrical elegiacs. Sulla immediately ordered a reward to be paid him out of the proceeds of the sale which he was then holding, but added the stipulation that he should never write again.'

79   **two poets**   the first was probably Robert Wild, the other Richard Flecknoe whom Dryden satirizes in the opening lines of *Mac Flecknoe*.

83   **clenches**   puns.

85   **Clevelandism**   in reference to the style of John Cleveland (1613–58). *v.* 683–714.

87   **un mauvais bouffon**   an unfunny clown.

102   **Leveller**   one who would level all differences of rank or position among men. The Levellers were a political party during the period of the Civil War and Commonwealth.

109   *Epigrams*, VIII. 19: 'Cinna wishes to appear poor, and he is poor.'

126   **Withers**   George Withers (1588–1667).

131   **candles' ends**   refers to practice at auction in which bids are accepted until the candle burns out.

137   **Qui Bavium ...**   Virgil, *Eclogues*, III. 90: 'Let him who hates not Bavius love your songs, Maevius.' Two bad poets satirized by Virgil and Horace.

140 **Nam . . .** author not identified: 'We despise the praises of men whom we despise.'

146 **Pace . . .** *Satyricon*, 2: 'With your permission I must tell you the truth, that you teachers more than anyone have been the ruin of true eloquence.'

159–60 *Epistles*, II. i. 76–7: 'I am impatient that any work is censured, not because it is thought to be coarse or inelegant in style, but because it is modern.'

162–3 *ib.*, 34–5: 'If poems are like wine which time improves, I should like to know what is the year that gives to writings fresh value.'

172 **moderns** those who write in modern as opposed to classical languages.

223 **humours** *v.* 1665ff.

226 **genere et fine** because it lacks 'differentiation', the definition does not enable us to distinguish drama from all other kinds of literature.

245 **the study of philosophy** science.

267 **Alit . . .** Velleius Paterculus, *History of Rome*, I. 17.

281 **go through** go through with, accomplish.

298 Περὶ τῆς Ποιητικῆς *Poetics*.

361 **Corneille** discusses this in *Discours des Trois Unités*.

374 **Ben Jonson** 'As a house consisting of divers materials, becomes one structure and one dwelling, so an action composed of divers parts may become one fable, epic or dramatic.'

389–93 *v.* Sidney, 1460–77.

401 **half-Menander** Suetonius, *Life of Terence*, V: 'Thou too, even thou, art ranked among the highest, thou half-Menander.'

414 **Macrobius** discusses Virgil in his *Saturnalia Convivia*.

432 **Father Ben** Ben Jonson.

455 **makes for** favours.

467 **Audita . . .** *History of Rome*, ii. 92: 'We are [naturally] more inclined to praise what we have heard than what has occurred before our eyes; we regard the present with envy, the past with veneration, and believe that we are eclipsed by the former, but derive instruction from the latter.'

479 **Aristotle** this division was first made by Scaliger in his *Poetices*.

505 **Neu . . .** *Art of Poetry*, 189 (adapted). *v.* App.: 'Let no play . . . five acts.'

511 **Jornadas** 'jornada' means literally a day's travel.

'Journée' in the early French drama denoted an 'act' or division of a play.

519   τῶν πραγμάτων σύνθεσις   Poetics, VII. 1: 'the arrangement of the incidents'.

520   **late writer**   probably Sir Robert Howard. *v.* his preface to *Four New Plays* (1665). For other references to his views *v.* 1040, 1919.

535   **good cheap**   advantageously.

536   **chapon bouillé**   bread soaked in broth.

546   **Juno . . .**   Terence, *Andria*, III. 424: 'Our Lady of child-birth, help me.'

549   **coming down in a machine**   *v.* Horace, App., 179–201. When a god was introduced in the ancient Greek drama, he was brought on to the stage by some mechanical device.

580   **says Scaliger**   *Poetices*, VI.

583   **in one of his tragedies**   the *Suppliants*.

595   **C'est . . .**   Corneille, *Discours des Trois Unités*: 'This is to use well a time so short.'

605   **though to others**   though he joins those already there.

636   **Medea**   of Euripides.

649   **sock and buskin**   symbols respectively of comedy and tragedy.

652   **wit**   'a propriety of thoughts and words': Dryden, Preface to *The State of Innocence* (1677).

664   **Tandem . . .**   II. 223: 'Pray, can't I go without her, if necessary, even for three days running?'

667   **Hui! . . .**   Terence, *ib.*, 224: 'Phew! Three whole days?'

674–6   *Art of Poetry*, 270–72: 'Yet our forefathers, you say, praised both the measures and the wit of Plautus. Too tolerant, not to say foolish, was their admiration of both.' [The Loeb ed. reads 'vestri'—'yours'—for 'nostri'. Ed.]

680–82   *ib.*, 70–72. *v.* App.: 'Many terms . . . rule of speech.'

687   *Eclogues*, IV. 20: '[The earth] shall pour forth the Egyptian bean blended with the smiling acanthus.'

689–91   VIII (not VII), 91–3: 'In wonder the waves, in wonder the unwonted woods view the far gleaming shields of warriors and the painted hulls floating on the stream.'

693–4   *Metamorphoses*, I.175–6: 'which, if I may make bold to say it, I would not fear to call the Palatia of high heaven'.

696   **et longas . . .**   *ib.*, 561: 'and long processions climb the Capitol'.

699   **pass**   impose.

708, 9   **one . . . other**   Donne . . . Cleveland.

713–14   Cleveland, *Rebel Scot*, 64–5.

715   **Si sic . . .**   Juvenal, *Satires*, X. 123–4: 'Had he always spoken thus.' [Ed.]

718–19   Cleveland, *Rupertismus*, 39–40.

734   **Omne genus . . .**   Ovid, *Tristia*, II. 381: 'Tragedy surpasses in seriousness all other kinds of literature.' [Ed.]

756   **anima mea;** Ζωὴ καὶ ψυχή   Juvenal, *Satires*, VI.195: 'my soul, my life'.

779   **Sum . . .**   *Aeneid*, I. 378–9: 'I am Aeneas the good, my fame is known in the heavens above.'

780   **fanfaron**   boaster.

787   **si foret . . .**   *Satires*, I. x. 68: 'had he fallen by fate upon this our day'.

794   **quos Libitina . . .**   Horace, *Epistles*, II. i. 49: 'which the goddess of funerals has hallowed'.

827   **Corneille . . . theatre**   this refers to the introduction of the three unities. Corneille's play *Le Cid* (1636) did not conform strictly to the unities, so Richelieu asked the Academy, recently founded by him (1635), for its opinion. Its judgement endorsing the rule of the unities was regarded as binding by French dramatists for nearly two centuries afterwards.

867   **Red Bull**   one of the few London theatres to keep open during the period 1640–60, it was famous for providing entertainment adapted to the taste of the groundlings.

868   Horace, *Epistles*, II. i. 185–6: 'call in the middle of a play for a bear or for boxers'.

869   **says Aristotle**   *v.* App. for Aristotle's views (VI. 2): 'through pity . . . similar emotions'.

870   **admiration**   *v.* note on Sidney, 859.

881   **Ex noto . . .**   *Art of Poetry*, 240: 'From well-known stories I shall try to shape my poetry.' [Ed.]

888–9   Horace, *ib.*, 151–2. *v.* App.: 'And so skilfully . . . the middle.'

894   **success**   issue, whether fortunate or unfortunate.

897   **Justinus**   *Historiarum Philippicarum Libri XLIV.*

898   **Xenophon**   *Cyropaedia*, VIII. 7.

911   **perspective**   telescope.

914   Horace, *Art of Poetry*, 188. *v.* App.: 'Whatever you thus show me, I discredit and abhor.'

916, 17   τὰ ἔτυμα the truth. ἐτύμοισιν ὁμοῖα the likeness of truth. Hesiod, *Theogony*, 27.

931   **plays of Calderon**   the best known is the *Adventures of*

      Five Hours (*v.* 1190), an adaptation by Sir Samuel Tuke.

936 **Rollo** subtitle of *The Bloody Brother*, ascribed to Fletcher.

947 **Golias** a comic figure in medieval literature.

977 **protatic persons** characters who appear at the beginning of a play to give the necessary information, but take no further part in the action.

979 **address** skill.

1043 **Corneille** *Discours des Trois Unités*.

1058–9 this and the two following quotations come from *Art of Poetry*, 181–7. *v.* App.: 'Less vividly . . . a snake.'

1078 **undecent** unbecoming, unfitting.

1106 **The Scornful Lady** by Beaumont and Fletcher.

1127 **Corneille** op. cit.

1141 **Sed . . .** Velleius Paterculus, *History of Rome*, I. 17: 'And as in the begining we are fired with the ambition to overtake those whom we regard as leaders, so when we have despaired of being able either to surpass or even to equal them, our zeal wanes with our hope; it ceases to follow what it cannot overtake . . . passing over that in which we cannot be pre-eminent, we seek for some new object of our effort.'

1176–7 **Corneille's . . . he tells you** *v.* *Discours du Poème Dramatique*.

1189 **Diego** comic servant in the *Adventures of Five Hours* (*v.* 931).

1236 **primum mobile** lit. 'first moving thing'. In the Ptolemaic system of astronomy it was the outermost sphere. In its revolution round the earth from east to west, it carried with it the (eight or nine) contained spheres.

1244 **Eugenius** a mistake for Crites. *v.* 381–5.

1250 **co-ordination** he is arguing that it is unnatural and dangerous for the different parts of a play to be of equal importance.

1267,8,9 **Cinna . . . Pompey . . . Polyeucte** by Corneille.

1364 **Shakespeare** perhaps a reference to the Prologue to *Every Man in His Humour*.

1461 **commending** *Miscellany*, XV.

1511 Virgil, *Eclogues*, I. 25: 'as cypresses oft do among the bending osiers'.

1527 **verses he writ** Jonson, *Epigrams*, 55.

1537 **Humour** *v.* 1665ff.

1554 **wit** 'sharpness of conceit' (Dryden, *The Dramatic Poetry of the Last Age*). *v.* 1583, where it means creative genius.

1595 **artificial one** twelve hours.

1642 τὸ γελοῖον the ludicrous. *v.* Aristotle, *Poetics*, V.

1646 **Socrates** in the *Clouds* of Aristophanes.

1653 ἦθος character. πάθος emotion.

1659 **Ex . . .** Terence, *The Eunuch*, III. 460: 'You could say that this one was born from the other.' [Ed.]

1704–6 *Epistles*, II. i. 168–70: "'Tis thought that Comedy, drawing its themes from daily life, calls for less labour; but in truth it carries a heavier burden, as the indulgence allowed is less.'

1710 **Corneille** *Discours des Trois Unités.* At 1712 Dryden by mistake says 'thrice' instead of 'four times'.

1775–6 Horace, *Art of Poetry*, 351–2: 'But when the beauties in a poem are more in number, I shall not take offence at a few blots.'

1782 **vivorum . . .** Velleius Paterculus, *History of Rome*, II. 36: 'As for living writers, while we admire them greatly, a critical list is difficult to make.'

1824 **Etiam . . .** Macrobius, *Saturnalia Convivia*, II. 7: 'Even with me on your side, you have been defeated, Laberius.' [Ed.]

1839 **Aristotle** *Poetics*, IV.

1844 **paper of verses** sonnet. *v.* 2127.

1855 **nicking of** tallying with.

1858 **Arcades . . .** Virgil, *Eclogues*, VII. 4–5: 'Arcadians all, ready in a match to sing, as well as to make reply.'

1859 **quicquid . . .** 'singing whatever I attempted'. [Ed.]. *v.* note on Sidney, 1423.

1860–61 **If they are . . . this** if they are other than born poets.

1865 **Ars. . .** 'It is an art to conceal art.' The author of this saying has not been identified.

1887 **you say** here Crites is replying not to Neander but to Dryden. *v.* his Preface to *The Rival Ladies*.

1897 **Nescivit . . .** L. Annaeus Seneca the elder (the rhetorician), *Controversiae*, IX. 5: 'He did not know how to let well alone.'

1900 **Omnia . . .** Ovid, *Metamorphoses*, I. 292. Quoted by L. Annaeus Seneca the younger (the philosopher and dramatist) in *Quaestiones Naturales*, III. 27. Seneca's point is that the force of this line is weakened by the trivialities that follow. Dryden has confused similar comments on on Ovid by the two Senecas.

1973 **perpetuo . . .** Cicero, *Orator*, VI (adapted).

2004 **Daniel** The reference to Daniel's *Defence of Rhyme* and

the words 'at least . . . antiquity' were not in the first
edition of the work.

2016   **sermo pedestris**   prose language.

2074   **tentanda** . . .   Virgil, *Georgics*, III. 8-9: 'I must essay
a path whereby I, too, may rise from earth.' For *possum*
read *possim*.

2088, 9   **Hopkins'** . . . **Sternhold's** . . . **Sandys'** . . .   refers to a
translation of the Psalms (1549) by John Hopkins and
Thomas Sternhold which was very popular in the
centuries following. George Sandys' translation (1636)
was never as popular.

2093   **Est ubi** . . .   based on Horace, *Epistles*, II. i. 63: 'At
times the public think rightly, sometimes they err.'
[Ed.]

2122-3   *Art of Poetry*, 90-91: 'likewise the feast of Thyestes scorns
to be told in strains of daily life that wellnigh befit the
comic sock'.

2125   *ib.*, 231: 'Tragedy, scorning to babble trivial verses.'

2128   **Aristotle**   *Poetics*, XXVI.

2133   **discoursive scenes**   scenes of dialogue.

2183   **quidlibet audendi**   Horace, *Art of Poetry*, 10: 'hazard-
ing anything'.

2185   **Musas** . . .   Martial, *Epigrams*, IX. xi. 17: '[who] court
muses more unbending'.

2232   **Water-poet's rhymes**   John Taylor (1580-1663), a
waterman on the Thames, was a prolific writer of
doggerel verse.

2235   **delectus** . . .   Cicero, *Brutus*, 72 (adapted): 'choice of
words is the foundation of eloquence'.

2241   *Hippolytus*, 863.

2281   **indefinitely**   vaguely.

2291   **want** . . . **within**   need other helps than that provided
by the innate ('within') judgement.

ALEXANDER POPE:
AN ESSAY ON CRITICISM (published 1711)

The present text is that of the Globe Edition, except for l. 231 ('Th' increasing prospects tire our wand'ring eyes'), where we give the generally preferred reading, and the full stop at the end of l. 416 which we have changed to a comma.

4 **sense** understanding of the work criticized.

6 **censure** here, 'judge'.

17 **wit** here, 'creative geni us'. The word occurs many time in the *Essay* and in differing senses. *v.* W. Empson, 'Wit in the *Essay on Criticism*', *The Structure of Complex Words* (1951), and E. N. Hooker, 'Pope on Wit: the *Essay on Criticism*', *Eighteenth Century English Literature: Modern Essays in Criticism*, ed. J. L. Clifford (1959).

28 **wit** intellectual ingenuity, as Johnson defined it in *Life* of Cowley: 'a kind of *discordia concors*. . . . The most heterogeneous ideas . . . yoked by violence together.'

30–31 he who can write resents rival writers, he who cannot resents all who can.

34 **Maevius** bad poet satirized by Virgil and Horace.

36 **Wits** men of letters, or perhaps brilliant talkers.

39 **mules** cross between horse and ass, neither one thing nor the other, and barren.

43 their origin or parentage is doubtful.

45 **wit** meant derogatorily here. One conceited fellow can out-talk a hundred ordinary people.

53 **pretending wit** ambitious intellect.

56–9 Pope's theory is that if the memory is strong, the intellect will be weak, and if the imaginative power is well developed, the memory will be defective.

61 **wit** *v.* 17.

68 **Nature** as opposed to the artificial or what is made by man.

76 **informing** animating.

80–81 they possess wit (imagination) but not the wit (judgement) to use it properly.

84 **'Tis more** more important. Cf. Longinus, *On the Sublime*, II (*v.* App.).

88 **Rules of old** the classical rules. Cf. Dryden, Preface to *Troilus and Cressida*: 'I will conclude with the words of

Rapin, in his reflections on Aristotle's work of poetry:
"If the rules be well considered, we shall find them to be
made only to reduce nature into method." . . .'

104 **wits** intellectuals, writers.
108 **'Pothecaries** apothecaries.
109 **bills** prescriptions.
115 **receipts** recipes.
120 **fable** plot, story.
129 read Virgil (Publius Virgilius Maro, born near Mantua)
as a commentary on Homer—for the reasons then given.
133 **but** except.
138 **Stagirite** Aristotle, born at Stagira.
142 there is the 'luck' of genius as well as painstaking obser-
vance of the rules.
159 **Great wits** poets of genius.
170 **them** the works of the ancients.
171–4 cf. Horace, *Art of Poetry*, 361–3 (*v.* App.).
180 **nods** dozes. Cf. Horace, *Art of Poetry*, 359.
183 **Flames** perhaps referring to the burning of the
Alexandrian and Palatinate libraries.
194 **must not** cannot.
199 **Wits** *v.* 45.
206 **recruits** supplies.
209 **wit** intellectual capacity.
216 **Pierian spring** Hippocrene, the Muses' well of inspiration.
220 **tempt** attempt.
233 **work of Wit** creative work.
237 **delight** i.e. in 'seeking slight faults'.
239 **in** in the case of.
240–42 cf. Horace, *Art of Poetry*, 265–8, and Longinus, *On the
Sublime*, XXXIII. 2 (*v.* App.).
259 **men of wit** writers.
261 **verbal** pedantic. **lays** lays down.
263 **subservient art** subordinate part of the whole.
265 **notions** personal eccentricities of taste.
267 **La Mancha's Knight** the incident comes from the
so-called *Second Part of Don Quixote*, a work from another
hand than Cervantes'.
270 **Dennis** John Dennis (1657–1734), a considerable
critic, and enemy of Pope. The reference is probably to
his *Advancement and Reformation of Modern Poetry* (1701).
273 **nice** discriminating.
278 **lists** fenced area in which knights met in combat.

286 **Curious not knowing** inquisitive and ingenious rather than learned. **nice** fastidious, faddy (used derogatorily).
287 **short** defective, 'half-baked'.
288 **love to parts** love of particular parts or elements rather than of the whole.
289 **Conceit** fantastic notions. *v.* note on 28.
297 **True Wit** 'a propriety of thoughts and words' (Dryden, Preface to *The State of Innocence*), as opposed to the false wit (ornateness) of 292. Johnson (*Life* of Cowley) comments, 'Pope's account of wit is undoubtedly erroneous: he depresses it below its natural dignity, and reduces it from strength of thought to happiness of language.' But E. N. Hooker suggests, 'The definition . . . presupposes the liveliness and insight of the creative mind; and it demands propriety, the perfect agreement of words, thoughts (as reshaped by the artist), and subject. The result is nature, and it is wit.' (op. cit.)
299–300 something of whose truth we are convinced at first sight; something, already known to us, which is now presented in a new light.
302 **wit** wittiness, ingenuity of imagination (as in following line).
306 **as women men** presumably, 'as women value men' (beaux), though it could be taken the other way about.
308 **upon content** on trust.
319 **decent** becoming.
328 **Fungoso** in Jonson's *Every Man out of His Humour*.
332 **as apes** i.e. as apes mimic.
337 **Numbers** metrical feet.
345 **open vowels** when a word ending with a vowel is followed by one beginning with a vowel. The line contains three examples.
346 **expletives** meaningless words which fill out the line.
347 **ten low words** as in this line itself. Cf. Dryden, 102–5.
356 **Alexandrine** a verse of six iambic feet, like the following line.
365 this passage is based on the third book of Vida's *Art of Poetry* (*v.* note on 704), which treats in detail questions of style and diction.
372 **Camilla** Volscian warrior-maiden; cf. *Aeneid*, VII. 808–11.
374 **Timotheus** musician; *v.* Dryden, *Alexander's Feast*.
376 **Libyan Jove** according to one legend, Alexander the Great was the son of Zeus Ammon, a Libyan deity.

391 **admire** wonder at, feel astonishment at. **approve** put to the test.

396 **Wit** literary genius.

400 **sublimes** refines.

415 **Quality** people of high rank.

429 i.e. their wit or 'cleverness' has led 'the schismatics' to dissent from 'the plain believers' where the latter happen to be in the right.

440 **School-divines** theologians concerned with establishment of dogma by logical demonstration.

441 **Sentences** *Book of Sentences*, a compilation (by Peter Lombard, in 1159) of passages from the Fathers of the Church, intended to settle doctrinal disputes.

444 **Scotists and Thomists** followers of the thirteenth-century theologians, Duns Scotus and Thomas Aquinas, respectively.

445 **Duck-lane** a place in London where old books were sold.

447 **Wit** learning and letters.

449 an author's wit is 'proved' by his popularity with a wide audience, i.e. the fools of the time.

456 **Wit** as in 447.

459 **Parsons, Critics, Beaux** parsons: Jeremy Collier and Luke Milbourn; critics: Sir Richard Blackmore and Thomas Shadwell, among others; beaux: George Villiers, Duke of Buckingham, and John Wilmot, Earl of Rochester.

465 **Zoilus** famous for his attack on Homer.

468 **Wit** literary genius.

479 **Patriarch-wits** the classical authors, whose fame ('second life') has lasted so long, are compared to the long-lived Patriarchs of the Old Testament.

494 **Wit** skill in writing. In these lines Pope dwells on the sorrows of being a writer: what Empson calls 'the poet-outcast idea'.

495 **Atones** compensates.

506–7 the vicious fear its satire; the virtuous shun it because they associate it with irreligion and dissoluteness; fools hate it out of envy; knaves 'undo' it perhaps through turning it to wrong purposes, perhaps (as Warburton suggested) because men who have gained power by evil means generally leave learning and letters to starve.

518 the worse the writer, the more reluctant he is to praise others.

521 **sacred** i.e. accursed.
531 **wit and art** intellectual agility together with artistry.
536 **easy Monarch** Charles II.
538 **Jilts** Charles's mistresses. **statesman** e.g. Sir George Etherege and George Villiers, Duke of Buckingham.
539 **young Lords** e.g. Buckingham, Rochester, Sir Charles Sedley (the 'Lisideius' of Dryden's *Essay of Dramatic Poesy*), Charles Sackville, Earl of Dorset (to whom Dryden dedicated his *Essay*), and John Sheffield, Earl of Mulgrave.
541 **Mask** in Charles II's reign it was customary for ladies to wear masks at the theatre. These hid their blushes more successfully than fans. **unimprov'd** ironical reference to the 'improving' entertainment offered by the Restoration stage.
542 obviously fans would not be required at the theatre if masks were used. The line may mean: hardened by their theatre-going, the ladies no longer found fans necessary for any sort of social occasion.
544 **Foreign reign** that of William III.
545 **Socinus** (1525–62), leader of the Unitarians, who rejected the Trinity, the divinity of Christ, the existence of the Devil, and the doctrine of eternal punishment.
546 **unbelieving priests** the Latitudinarians, who were often charged with being Socinians.
556–7 those, discriminating in a malicious way, who misrepresent an author as vicious.
585 **Appius** John Dennis, so called after his tragedy, *Appius and Virginia*; 'tremendous' was notoriously a favourite word of his.
588 **Honourable** of rank.
591 noblemen were at this time granted degrees without examination.
601 lashed by the critic, dull writers merely become duller, as a whipped top seems to grow motionless.
617 **Durfey** a voluminous and feeble writer.
618 **with** according to.
619 **Garth** Sir Samuel Garth, a friend of Pope, whose authorship of the mock-heroic *Dispensary* was at the time denied by some.
623 **Paul's church . . . Paul's churchyard** the body of the cathedral was earlier the resort of curiosity-mongers and idlers, and the churchyard the headquarters of the booksellers.

648 **Maeonian Star** Homer; Smyrna, in the province of Maeonia, claimed to be his birthplace.

652 Aristotle 'conquer'd Nature' in virtue of his *Natural History*, and 'should preside o'er Wit' or literary matters in virtue of his *Poetics*.

657 cf. 82.

664 i.e. than by being misquoted by critics.

665 **Dionysius** Dionysius of Halicarnassus, a critic of the last century B.C.

669 **Quintilian** a critic (A.D. 40–c. 118), celebrated for his *Institutio Oratoria*.

684 **Eagles** standards of the Roman armies.

685 **same foes** the barbarians; Alaric sacked Rome in A.D. 410.

694 as a priest himself, Erasmus was 'the glory' of the priesthood, and through his attacks on ecclesiastical abuses, 'the shame'.

697 **Leo's golden days** the papacy of Leo X, 1513–21, at the height of the Renaissance.

704 **Vida** Marco Girolamo Vida wrote both poetry and criticism (*Art of Poetry*, 1527) in Latin. He was born in Cremona.

709 Rome was sacked by the Constable of Bourbon in 1527.

714 **Boileau** poet, satirist, and critic; Pope has in mind his *Art poétique* (1674).

717 **wit** the imagination.

722 **Wit** literary work, especially perhaps as relates to the imagination.

723 **the Muse** i.e. John Sheffield, Earl of Mulgrave, later Duke of Buckinghamshire, in his *Essay on Poetry* (1682).

725 **Roscommon** Wentworth Dillon, Earl of Roscommon (c. 1633–84); his poems include *An Essay on Translated Verse* and a translation of Horace's *Art of Poetry*.

729 **Walsh** William Walsh (c. 1663–1708), a mediocre poet, but good friend to Dryden, and friend and mentor to the young Pope.

SAMUEL JOHNSON:
PREFACE TO SHAKESPEARE

Johnson's edition of *The Plays of Shakespeare* appeared in 1765. The present text of the *Preface* follows that of Walter Raleigh, *Johnson on Shakespeare* (1931), except that spelling has been modernized. Cuts are indicated in the text.

42 **Pythagorean scale of numbers** Pythagoras's discovery of the dependence of the musical intervals on certain arithmetical ratios of lengths of string at the same tension.

57 **prescriptive** prescribed by custom.

62 **modes of artificial life** manners, particularly of polite society.

82 **nearly** accurately.

111 **Hierocles** Boswell ascribed to Johnson 'A free translation of the Jests of Hierocles' (a Greek collection of comic anecdotes) which appeared in *The Gentleman's Magazine* in 1741. In speaking of 'select quotations' Johnson may have in mind William Dodd's *Beauties of Shakespeare* (1752).

148 **with Pope** in the Preface to Pope's edition of *The Works of Shakespeare* (1725).

164 **level with life** realistic.

177-9 scenes so authentic that from them a hermit could understand worldly affairs and a priest foresee the development of a passion which he has never experienced.

182 **Dennis** v. note on Pope, 270. The reference is to his *Essay on the Genius and Writings of Shakespeare* (1712). **Rhymer** in his *Short View of Tragedy* (1693).

183 **Voltaire** v. *Appel à toutes les Nations de l'Europe* and *Lettre à l'Académie française*. In *Dissertation sur la Tragédie* he objects to Hamlet, Claudius, and Gertrude drinking on the stage, and in *Lettres Philosophiques*, 18, he denounces the grossness of the grave-diggers.

233-4 cf. Dryden, Preface to *Troilus and Cressida*: 'To instruct delightfully is the general end of poetry. Philosophy instructs, but it performs its work by precept; which is not delightful, or not so delightful as example'; and Sidney, 455-8.

256 **their edition** the First Folio, 1623.

299 **Rhymer has remarked** in *A Short View of Tragedy*.

364

361 **candour**   here, 'kindliness'.

385 **in view**   within sight.

394 **Hector quoting Aristotle**   *Troilus and Cressida*, II. ii. 166.

395-6 i.e. ancient Greek and medieval Germanic myths mixed together, in *A Midsummer Night's Dream*.

418 **tumour**   tumidity, turgidity. Cf. Longinus, *On the Sublime*, III. 4: 'Tumours are bad things whether in books or in bodies, those empty inflations, void of sincerity, as likely as not producing the opposite to the effect intended.'

459 **at all adventures**   at whatever cost.

522 **dragons of Medea**   after killing Jason's new bride, Medea escaped in a chariot drawn by winged serpents.

552 **calenture**   fever.

554-63 cf. Sidney, 1096ff. Henry Home, Lord Kames, has a parallel passage in *Elements of Criticism* (1762), a work known to Johnson.

568 **Mithridates**   king of Pontus. Lucullus was a Roman general who fought against him.

598 **recreated**   refreshed.

607 **Petruchio**   in *The Taming of the Shrew*.

609 **Cato**   Addison's tragedy, 1713.

621 **want**   lack.

630 **positive**   artificial.

634-6 Lucan, *The Civil War*, III. 138: 'The course of time has not wrought such confusion that the laws would not rather be trampled on by Caesar than saved by Metellus.'

687 **philology**   i.e. study or love of literature.

704 **the vulgar**   the vulgar class.

706 **The Death of Arthur**   Malory's romance, *Morte D'Arthur*.

709 **taste of**   taste for.

711 **Palmerin**   chivalric romance translated from Spanish. **Guy of Warwick**   verse romance of early fourteenth century.

724 **Gamelyn**   found in some mss. of *The Canterbury Tales*; Chaucer may have intended to rewrite it as his 'Yeoman's Tale'.

725 **old Mr. Cibber**   Colley Cibber (d. 1757), actor, dramatist, and 'hero' of Pope's *Dunciad*; unless the reference is to his father, Caius Cibber, a sculptor of Danish origin.

726 **tale of Hamlet**   probably *The History of Hamblet* (1608), a translation of Belleforest's version in *Histoires Tragiques*. J. Dover Wilson remarks, 'Some have supposed that Shakespeare derived his plot from a lost sixteenth-century edition of the *History*; but there is no

evidence of publication before 1608' (*Hamlet*, New Shakespeare, Cambridge).

727 **Saxo Grammaticus** the story of Hamlet is first found in his *Historia Danica*.

730 **by versions** through translations.

749 **discriminated** picked out for emphasis.

756 but in one of his various references to Shakespeare and *Cato*, Voltaire admits that the cold regularity of the latter cannot equal the 'gross but engaging irregularities' of Shakespeare.

790 **Jonson affirms** in *To the Memory of my beloved, the Author*, the poem prefixed to the First Folio; the actual words are, 'small Latin, and less Greek'.

803 **important** Johnson is being ironic.

822 **English translation** Arthur Brooke's *Tragical History of Romeus and Juliet* (1562), a poem based on a French version of Bandello's romance.

825 **was to copy** would copy.

854 **essays** attempts.

862 **Rowe** in his edition of Shakespeare, 1709. Nicholas Rowe is remembered for his tragedies, *The Fair Penitent* and *Jane Shore*.

903 **Boyle** presumably Roger Boyle, Earl of Orrery, a Restoration writer of heroic drama. Robert Boyle, the physicist, was also well connected, being son of the first Earl of Cork.

904 **access** i.e. to knowledge.

913 **conversation** acquaintance.

915 **as dewdrops . . .** cf. *Troilus and Cressida*, III. iii. 222.

952 **says Dennis** *v*. note on 182.

962 **Hieronimo** i.e. Kyd's *Spanish Tragedy*, probably written 1585-7.

974 **Rowe** *v*. note on 862.

1013 **declined into the vale . . .** *Othello*, III. iii. 267.

1047 **Warburton** William Warburton, in *Preface* to his edition of Shakespeare (1747).

1077 **table book** memorandum.

1102 **Huetius** Pierre Daniel Huet (1630-1721), celebrated French scholar who published an edition of the classics 'for the use of the Dauphin'.

1134 **Theobald** Lewis Theobald's edition of Shakespeare was published in 1734.

1154 **Dryden** *Essay of Dramatic Poesy*, 1496-1511.

1176 **types** printing.

WILLIAM WORDSWORTH:
PREFACE TO LYRICAL BALLADS

The *Preface* was first published in 1800. Another version with additional matter (*v.* 304–576, and the *Appendix*) appeared in 1802. This, with minor revisions, is the basis of the standard text of 1850, which we follow.

4 **language** idiom.

48 **exponent** *v.* 55–7, 'the promise . . . reader'.

85–6 **associate . . . excitement** a statement from the associationist school of psychology, first developed by David Hartley (1705–57). 'The *general law* of association, or, more accurately, the *common condition* under which all exciting causes act . . . is this. Ideas by having been together acquire a power of recalling each other; or every partial representation awakes the total representation of which it had been a part.' Coleridge, *Biographia Literaria*, ed. J. Shawcross (1907), vol. I, p. 72.

87 **essential passions** a reference perhaps to the six primary passions of contemporary philosophy: wonder (admiration), love, hate, desire, joy, and sorrow.

90 **elementary feelings** might mean (*a*) less intense, less conscious passions; or (*b*) the same as essential passions; or (*c*) what Hartley termed *sensations*: those internal feelings of the mind which arise from the impressions made by external objects upon our bodies.

93 **manners** modes of life, rules of behaviour.

97 **incorporated** associated.

98 **nature** external nature.

109 **philosophical** precise.

172 **national events** presumably the war with France.

175 **rapid communication** the mail-coach and the telegraph had been recently introduced.

180 **frantic novels** 'Gothic' romances.

181 **German Tragedies** the best-known German dramatist was Kotzebue (1761–1819). *v.* Coleridge, *Biographia Literaria*, vol. II, p. 158: 'What (I would ask of the crowd, that press forward to the pantomimic tragedies and weeping comedies of Kotzebue and his imitators) what are you seeking?'

236   **art of association**   i.e. by re-associating the expressions with other feelings.

256   **Gray**   who said, 'The language of the age is never the language of poetry'. *v. Correspondence*, ed. Toynbee and Whibley (1935), p. 192.

261–74   *Sonnet on the Death of Richard West.*

295   **'such as Angels weep'**   *Paradise Lost*, I. 690.

304   **the language**   the additional matter of the 1802 ed. of the *Preface* begins here.

311   **dissimilitude**   i.e. a difference in effect from that given by the unselected language with its vulgarity and meanness.

337–8   **language . . . men**   whatever they may say in public.

352   **comprehensive soul**   *v.* Dryden, 1498 (on Shakespeare).

363   **sympathy**   community of feeling.

413   **Frontiniac**   a muscat wine made at Frontignan, France.

414   **philosophic**   for what Aristotle really said *v.* App., VIII. 1–IX. 4: 'For this reason . . . facts.'

462   **overbalance**   preponderance.

488   **'that he . . .'**   *Hamlet*, IV. iv. 37.

490   **relationship**   a sense of the connectedness of things.

498   **atmosphere of sensation**   climate of feeling.

524   **assumed**   presumed (by the writer).

576   **Reader**   the additional material of the 1802 version ends here.

610   **numbers**   metrical feet.

628   **proves**   knows by experience.

657   **The Gamester**   a tragedy by Edward Moore (1712–57).

779   **'Babes in the Wood'**   better known as *The Children in the Wood*. For the connection between the two versions *v.* F. W. Bateson, *Wordsworth* (1956), p. 135.

976   **'Did sweeter . . .'**   from *Charity, A Paraphrase* (of I *Corinthians* 13).

1048   **passport**   i.e. metre, which it is claimed poetic diction ('phraseology') should accompany.

S. T. COLERIDGE:
BIOGRAPHIA LITERARIA, CHAPTERS XIV, XVII, AND PART OF XVIII

In a letter to Dr. Brabant, 29 July 1815, Coleridge wrote: 'I have just finished it [*Biographia Literaria*] . . . I have given a full account (raisonné) of the controversy concerning Wordsworth's Poems and Theory, in which my name has been so constantly included. I have no doubt that Wordsworth will be displeased, but I have done my duty to myself and to the public, in, as I believe, completely subverting the theory and in proving that the poet himself has never acted on it except in particular stanzas, which are the blots of his composition.' *Biographia Literaria* was first published in 1817. Our text follows this, the only edition to appear in Coleridge's lifetime, as reprinted by J. Shawcross (Oxford, 1907).

19-23   **subjects . . . themselves**   *v.* Wordsworth, 76-86.
  61   **real**   cf. Wordsworth, 79.
  95   **recent collection**   the *Poems* of 1815.
144-5   **immediate . . . end**   i.e. which would not derive pleasure from any poetry whose ultimate aim was something other than moral or intellectual; e.g. obscene poetry.
  146   **Bathyllus**   Anacreon, *Odes*, XXIX.
  147   **Alexis**   Virgil, *Eclogues*, II.
  196   **Praecipitandus . . .**   *Satyricon*, CXVIII: 'the free spirit of genius must plunge headlong'.
  236   **laxis . . .**   probably adapted from Virgil, *Georgics*, II. 364: 'is carried onwards with loosened reins'.
250-61 *Nosce Teipsum*, IV. The third stanza here differs considerably from the original.
345-56 *v.* Wordsworth, 90-98.
  389   **negations**   qualities not present.
  424   **Aristotle**   IX. 1-4. *v.* App.: 'what we have said . . . was done to him'.   **essentially**   the footnote is an extract from *Satyrane's Letters II*, originally published in *The Friend* (1809).
432-4   **no poetic . . . age**   i.e. the persons of poetry must either be 'representative', like the swains of Theocritus, or *purely* imaginary like those of the golden age. There cannot be any intermediate alternative.

483–5 **in order . . . drama** i.e. the poet can describe the beauties in his own person instead of leaving it to his characters, in whom such descriptions might seem unlikely or sentimental.

487–90 *v.* Wordsworth, 86–90.

502 **anile** of or like an old woman.

528 **four** i.e. the passage beginning 'As now to any eye'.

541–9 *v.* Wordsworth, 98–107.

605 **of** in.

620 **Tom Brown** (1663–1704) satirist, hack writer, and translator. **Sir Roger L'Estrange** (1616–1704) journalist and writer of political pamphlets. The difference suggested is that between journalism and the 'grand style'.

630 *v.* Wordsworth, 79.

630–31 *v.* Wordsworth, 98–9.

631–3 *v.* Wordsworth, 201–2.

633–4 *v.* Wordsworth, 285–7.

646 **Algernon Sidney** (1622–83) author of *Discourses concerning Government.*

670 **Dante** in *Dᵢ Vulgari Eloquentia* (1305–9).

673 **in a state . . .** *v.* Wordsworth, 86.

702 **himself** in a note to *The Thorn.* **Deborah** *v. Judges,* V.

720 **surview** survey.

728–37 *The Last of the Flock,* i.

764 **sublime hymn** refers perhaps to *Paradise Lost,* V. 144–52.

773 *Excursion,* I. 79.

786 **ordonnance** systematic arrangement.

801–2 **exclusive . . . themselves** i.e. that would exclude the suggestion that the words are of the same class.

838–46 *v.* Wordsworth, 247–54.

862–7 *v.* Wordsworth, 275–80.

878 **denied . . . one** Wordsworth however thought differently. *v.* 237–43.

891 **origin of metre** *v.* Wordsworth, 589ff.

928–39 IV. iv. 87–97.

967–8 *To the Rev. Mr. Powell.*

973 **'Children in the Wood'** *v.* Wordsworth, 779.

997 θαύματα θαυμαστότατα wonders most wondrous.

1004 titles of chapters in *A Sentimental Journey.*

1016 **pedestrian** walking.

1063 **around** Coleridge, *Remorse,* IV. i. 68–73.

1085 **mordant** a substance used for fixing colouring matters on stuffs.

1086 **affirms** *v*. Wordsworth, 131ff.

1138 **Videlicet** namely.

1185 **genial** sympathetic.

1188 **poet** we omit the next 300 lines (p. 59, l. 7–p. 68, l. 14, Shawcross).

1189 **To sum up . . .** this is the final paragraph of Chapter XVIII.

PERCY BYSSHE SHELLEY:
A DEFENCE OF POETRY

This was written in early 1821 as an 'antidote' to Thomas Love Peacock's semi-serious essay, *The Four Ages of Poetry*, published in *Ollier's Literary Miscellany*, No. I (1820). Shelley intended to print his answer in this same magazine, but it ceased publication, and the *Defence* first appeared in 1840 in *Essays, Letters from Abroad, Translations and Fragments, by P. B. Shelley*, edited by his widow. The present text is that of the second edition (1845) which corrects minor errors in the first.

8 τὸ ποιεῖν   to make. Cf. Sidney, 176.

10 τὸ λογίζειν   to reason.

101 'the same footsteps . . .'   cf. *Advancement of Learning*, II. v. 3.

125 prophets   cf. Sidney, 129ff.

146 Language, colour, form . . .   cf. Plato, *Symposium* (205B–C), which Shelley had translated a few years before.

151 imperial faculty   imagination.

183 popular division into prose and verse   cf. Sidney, 311ff. and 999, and Wordsworth, footnote to 295.

205 so that   so long as.

212 Plato was essentially a poet   cf. Sidney, 81ff. and 1239, and Coleridge, 202ff.

244–9 *v.* Sidney, 541–51 and note.

254 moths of just history   cf. Bacon, *Advancement of Learning*, II. ii. 4.

270 accompanied with pleasure   cf. Sidney, 690ff.; Johnson, 233–4; and Wordsworth, 424ff.

286–9 cf. Sidney, 50ff.

291 an ambition   cf. Sidney, 707ff.

321 planetary music   cf. Sidney, 1768.

322 immorality of poetry   cf. Sidney, 1119ff., in answer to Gosson. Peacock had complained that poetry 'could serve only to ripen a splendid lunatic like Alexander, a puling driveller like Werther, or a morbid dreamer like Wordsworth'.

332 makes familiar objects . . .   cf. Wordsworth, 81–2.

345 **poetry administers to the effect** Peacock had written, 'as the sciences of morals and of mind advance towards perfection, as they become more enlarged and
comprehensive in their views, as reason gains the ascend-
ancy in them over imagination and feeling, poetry can
no longer accompany them in their progress, but drops
into the background, and leaves them to advance alone'.

367 **cyclic poets** Greek epic poets of Ionian school who
treated parts of the Trojan cycle not included in *Iliad* and
Odyssey.

419 **blending comedy with tragedy** cf. Sidney, 1515ff.

432 **Calderon** Spanish dramatist (1600–81), whose 'autos
sacramentales' (religious plays) Shelley much admired.

488 **classical and domestic drama** Restoration and
Augustan tragedy, and Restoration comedy, respectively.

489 **Cato** cf. Johnson, 759ff.

496 **The period** cf. Pope, 534–43.

532 **bucolic writers** Theocritus, Bion, and Moschus.

548 **sensual and pathetic** pertaining to the senses and to
the emotions, respectively.

569 **Astraea** goddess of Justice, she lived among men in the
golden age but afterwards was removed to the stars as the
constellation Virgo.

578 **sacred links** cf. Plato, *Ion*, 533D–E, 535E–536B.

617 **Camillus** a hero of the Roman Republic (447–365 B.C.),
who defeated the Gauls on several occasions. **Regulus**
captured by the Carthaginians, he accompanied their
embassy to Rome in 250 B.C. and advised the senate
against accepting their peace proposals. He kept his
promise to return to Carthage, and was there tortured
to death. **expectation of the senators . . .** when the
victorious Gauls reached Rome in 390 B.C. they found
the senators waiting in the Forum, alone, to offer themselves as sacrifices for their country.

620 **Cannae** the Carthaginians, under Hannibal, destroyed
the Roman army at Cannae in 216 B.C.

627 **quia carent . . .** Horace, *Odes*, IV. ix. 28: 'because they
lacked a sacred bard'.

649 **the three forms** the immortal soul, or reason; the
higher mortal soul, or affections of the heart; and the
lower mortal soul, or appetites. (*v. Timaeus*, 69C–72D.)
In the rest of this sentence, Shelley seems to be referring
to the doctrine of the Trinity.

652 **'Light' seems to 'thicken'** Peacock had said, 'To the

age of brass in the ancient world succeeded the dark ages, in which the light of the Gospel began to spread over Europe, and in which, by a mysterious and inscrutable dispensation, the darkness thickened with the progress of the light.'

653–5   *Macbeth*, II. ii. 50.

664   **Celtic**   mistake for 'Teutonic'; also in 669 and 700.

721   **'Galeotto fù il libro . . .'**   Dante, *Inferno*, V. 137. Francesca tells Dante how she and Paolo discovered their love while reading the story of Lancelot and Guinevere (Old French version), in which Sir Gallehault was the go-between. Thus, 'the book, and he that wrote it, was a Galeotto'.

722   **Trouveurs**   i.e. the troubadours.

743   **Plato**   cf. speech of Agathon in the *Symposium* (196E), as translated by Shelley: 'every one . . . becomes a poet as soon as he is touched by Love . . .'.

767   **Riphaeus . . . justissimus unus**   *Aeneid*, II. 426: 'foremost in justice among the Trojans'. Dante placed him in Paradise on the grounds that by divine grace he was made aware of the future redemption of mankind by Christ and so renounced paganism.

776–85   'implacable hate', &c., is exhibited both by Milton's God and by his Devil. This is mitigated by the nobility which attends Satan's defeat, but seems all the worse in God, who triumphs dishonourably (in 'cold security').

787   **alleged design**   i.e. declared design. *v. Paradise Lost*, I. 211–15 and III. 84–6.

814   **imitator**   by modelling the *Aeneid* on Homer's epics. Cf. Pope, 130–38.

834   **Lucifer**   i.e. 'light-bringer', the morning star.

858   **poets have been challenged**   cf. Peacock: poetry 'can never make a philosopher, nor a statesman, nor in any class of life a useful or rational man. It cannot claim the slightest share in any one of the comforts and utilities of life of which we have witnessed so many and so rapid advances.'

859   **mechanists**   mechanistic philosophers. Under the heading 'reasoners and mechanists' Shelley includes rationalists, social scientists, political economists—and perhaps (*v.* 886) mechanical engineers. That is, those concerned with what Peacock called 'the real business of life'.

892   **'To him that hath . . .'**   cf. *Matthew*, XIII. 12, and elsewhere in the Gospels.

909 'It is better . . .'   adapted from *Ecclesiastes*, VII. 2.

926 **abolition of the Inquisition in Spain**   in 1820.

949 'I dare not . . . .'   *Macbeth*, I. vii. 44.

950 **want**   lack; also in 952 and 953.

967 **God and Mammon**   cf. *Matthew*, VI. 24: 'Ye cannot serve God and Mammon.'

979–81 **centre and circumference** . . . cf. Wordsworth, 485–7.

1020 **'dictated'** . . . **'unpremeditated song'**   cf. *Paradise Lost*, IX. 23–4.

1021 **various readings**   Ariosto began the work *c.* 1503 and was continually revising it up to his death in 1533.

1057–60 **bearing sweet news . . . things**   bearing similar joyous news to those people in whom kindred intimations ('sisters') must abide in silence ('sleeping . . . cold . . . buried') because, not being poets, they cannot 'express' them.

1073 **All things exist as . . . perceived**   cf. Descartes and Berkeley.

1074 **'The mind is its own place . . .'**   *Paradise Lost*, I. 254–5.

1083 **film of familiarity**   cf. Coleridge, 36.

1088 **Non merita nome di creatore** . . . 'None but God and the Poet deserve the name of creator.' Reputedly a saying of Tasso.

1105 **'there sitting . . .'**   adapted from *Paradise Lost*, IV. 829.

1114 **sins 'were as scarlet . . .'**   adapted from *Isaiah*, I. 18.

1155 **Theseids . . . Codri**   referring to a dull writer satirized by Juvenal (*Satires*, I. 1–2): '. . . bored by the Theseid [*epic poem*] of the ranting Cordus'.   **Bavius and Maevius** *v.* note on Dryden, 137.

1158 **confound**   i.e. confuse.

1166 **the second part**   the *Defence* was to consist of three parts, but the second and third were never written.

1177 **last national struggle**   the Civil War, 1642- 8.

JOHN KEATS:
FROM THE LETTERS

The passages are taken from *The Letters of John Keats*, ed. Maurice Buxton Forman (4th edition, 1952). Some slight changes have been made in punctuation, spelling, and use of capital letters.

5 **sublime** sublimity.
6 **first Book** Book I of *Endymion*.
7 **little song** 'O Sorrow' (*Endymion*, IV. 146ff.), in Keats's letter to Bailey, 3 November 1817.
9 **Adam's dream** *Paradise Lost*, VIII. 460.
15 **Sensations** H. E. Rollins (*Letters of John Keats, 1814–1821*, 1958) notes W. W. Beyer's remark, *Journal of English and Germanic Philology*, LI (1952), 337n.: 'Here Keats uses "Sensations" in the sense of "intuitive perceptions through the senses" . . .' Cf. J. M. Murry, *Studies in Keats*, VI (1930): 'Abstract thinking, in the ordinary sense, was quite alien to Keats; the movement of his thought was richly imaged, and amazingly concrete—"sensations rather than thoughts".'
32–7 the punctuation is confusing, but the general tenor is fairly clear: the imagined face of the singer—more beautiful than the actuality—will be encountered (i.e. its prototype will be) in the life to come. Imagination, working on the material of present and earthly reality, prefigures the finer realities of the hereafter. (A combination of the two ideas expressed in 16–17 and 19–21.)
61 **put its hand** presumably, to pull out a bludgeon.
88 **what shocks . . .** cf. Sidney, 1078ff.
91 **speculation** probably, 'disinterested contemplation' (*v.* J. M. Murry, op. cit., VI).
93 **in for** M. B. Forman (*The Letters*, p. 227) has this note: 'Mr. G. Beaumont in *The Times Literary Supplement*, February 27 and May 1, 1930, suggests that Keats intended to write "informing". The facts are that the words "in" and "for", the last words on the page, are written closer together than other words on the same page, that they are followed by a dash which might very well be read as a hyphen, and that "informing" is in every way an improvement to an otherwise clumsy parenthesis.' For the thought of this passage, cf. Shelley, 341–4.

99 **write no more** in the letter to which this is a reply, Woodhouse had protested against Keats's statement, in conversation, that the possibilities of poetry had been exhausted and therefore he would write no more.

100 **Saturn and Ops** in *Hyperion*.

117 **'load every rift'** cf. *Faerie Queene*, II. vii. 28.

MATTHEW ARNOLD:
THE STUDY OF POETRY

First published in 1880 as the General Introduction to *The English Poets*, edited by T. H. Ward; included in *Essays in Criticism, Second Series* (1888).

475 'gold . . . speech' Lydgate, *The Life of Our Lady.* Johnson *v. Life* of Dryden.

483 'well ... undefiled' Spenser, *Faerie Queene*, IV. ii. 32.

495 *The Prioress's Tale*, 27.

504–10 *ib.*, 197–203.

553 Aristotle *v.* 350.

592 'that the sweetness . . .' Dryden, 198–200.

594 Cowley *v.* Dryden, *Preface to the Fables.*

597 'there is . . .' *v.* Dryden, *ib.*

599 Addison *An Account of the Greatest English Poets.*

608 **Wordsworth and Coleridge** for Wordsworth on *Dryden, v. Letter to Scott* (1805): 'I admire his talents and *Genius*, but he is not a poetical genius.' On *Pope, v. Essay Supplementary to the Preface* (1815). For Coleridge on *Dryden, v. Marginalia in Pepys*: 'Yet Cowley *was* a Poet, which . . . is more than (in the *strict* use of the term Poet) I can conscientiously say of Dryden.' On *Pope, v. Biographia Literaria*, ed. Shawcross, Chap. I, pp. 11ff.

632 **Milton** *v. Apology against a Pamphlet . . . against Smectymnuus.*

637 **Dryden** *v. Postscript* to his translation, *The Works of Virgil* (1697).

674–5 *The Hind and the Panther*, 1–2.

679–80 *Imitations of Horace*, II. 143–4.

724–9 *On the Death of Robert Dundas.*

731 **Clarinda's . . . Sylvander** Sylvander is the name which Burns used in his correspondence with Clarinda (Mrs. Agnes Maclehose).

732–7 **These ... stupid** *The Letters of Robert Burns*, ed. J. De L. Ferguson (Oxford 1931), Vol. II, p. 268.

763–71 from *The Holy Fair*. **Leeze me** 'commend me to'. **mair** 'more'. **waukens lear** 'awakens learning'. **pangs us fou** 'crams us full'. **Be't whisky . . . wheep** 'Be it a measure of whisky or small ale'. **ony** 'any'. **kittle** 'to tickle'.

782 **a'** 'all'.

785, 6 **aboon** 'above'. **guid** 'good'. **mauna fa'** 'must not attempt'.

794–801 *Epistle to a Young Friend*. **lowe** 'flame'.

803–10 *Address to the Unco Guid, or the Rigidly Righteous.*

813–16 *Epistle to Dr. Blacklock*. **weans** 'children'.

820 **Xenophon** *Memorabilia*, II. ii.

853 **Farewell to Nancy** Burns's title for this poem is *Ae Fond Kiss.*

859–62 *Winter: A Dirge.*
  863 **Whistle owre the lave o't!** 'Whistle over the rest of it.'
  892 **Auld Lang Syne** 'the old long-ago'.
902–5 **We twa . . . burn** 'we two have paddled in the stream'. **dine** 'noon'. **braid** 'broad'. **sin** 'since'.
  912 *Prometheus Unbound,* III. iv. 204.
915–18 II. v. 1–4.
921–4 **minnie** 'mother'. **deave** 'annoy'. **wha** 'who'. **sae** 'so'.

D. H. LAWRENCE:
WHY THE NOVEL MATTERS

First published posthumously in *Phoenix* (1936).

3   **Mens sana in corpore sano**   Juvenal, *Satires*, X. 356:
'a sound mind in a sound body'.

112   **bright book of life**   cf. *Lady Chatterley's Lover*, IX: 'It
is the way our sympathy flows and recoils that really
determines our lives. And here lies the vast importance
of the novel, properly handled. It can inform and lead
into new places the flow of our sympathetic consciousness,
and can lead our sympathy away in recoil from things
gone dead. Therefore, the novel, properly handled, can
reveal the most secret places of life: for it is in the
passional secret places of life, above all, that the tide of
sensitive awareness needs to ebb and flow, cleansing and
refreshing.'

177–81   cf. Keats, 91–104.

T. S. ELIOT:
TRADITION AND THE INDIVIDUAL TALENT

First published in *The Egoist*, VI. 4 (September–October 1919) and VI. 5 (November–December 1919). Reprinted in *The Sacred Wood* (1920) and *Selected Essays* (1932).

THE METAPHYSICAL POETS

First published in *The Times Literary Supplement*, 1031 (20 October 1921). Reprinted in *Homage to John Dryden* (1924) and *Selected Essays* (1932).

188–92   Browning, *Bishop Blougram's Apology*, 693.
197–208   from Tennyson, *The Two Voices*.
280   **La Poésie d'aujourd'hui**   pub. Paris. 1921.
285–94   Jules Laforgue (1860–87), *Derniers Vers*, X:
      'O diaphanous geraniums, war-loving sortileges,
      Sacrilegious monomaniacs!
      Packings, wantonnesses, showers! O wine-presses
      Of the vintages of the Great Days!
      Layettes at bay,
      Thyrsi in the depths of the woods!
      Transfusions, reprisals,
      Churchings, compresses and the eternal potion,
      Angelus! to be worn out
      With nuptial débâcles! with nuptial débâcles!'
296–7   *ib.*, XI:
      'She is far away, she weeps,
      The great wind also laments . . .'
303–6   Baudelaire, *Le Voyage:*
      'For the child, in love with maps and prints,
      The universe is equal to his vast appetite,
      Ah, how large the world is by the light of lamps!
      To the eyes of memory how little is the world!'
319   **'look into our hearts . . .'**   cf. Sidney, *Astrophel and Stella*, I. 14: 'Fool, said my Muse to me, look in thy heart, and write.'

F. R. LEAVIS:
KEATS

First published in *Scrutiny*, IV. 4 (March 1936). Reprinted in *Revaluation* (October 1936).

677 **'Scenery is fine . . .'** letter to Benjamin Bailey, 13 March 1818.
738–9 Tennyson, *Ulysses*.
741–4 Tennyson, *The Palace of Art*.
788 **Cary** Henry Francis Cary's translation, *The Vision of Dante*, was published in 1814.
859 **Demogorgons** the reference is to Shelley's *Prometheus Unbound*, in which Demogorgon is the eternal power or principle which prevails over the despotic Jupiter.

Classical Appendix

From

ARISTOTLE: *The Poetics*

V. 8   As regards length, tragedy tends to fall within a single revolution of the sun or slightly to exceed that, whereas epic is unlimited in point of time . . .

VI. 2–4   Tragedy is, then, a representation of an action that is heroic and complete and of a certain magnitude—by means of language enriched with all kinds of ornament, each used separately in the different parts of the play: it represents men in action and does not use narrative, and through pity and fear it effects relief to these and similar emotions. By 'language enriched' I mean that which has rhythm and tune, i.e. song, and by 'the kinds separately' I mean that some effects are produced by verse alone and some again by song.

VI. 19–21   The plot then is the first principle and as it were the soul of tragedy: character comes second. It is much the same also in painting; if a man smeared a canvas with the loveliest colours at random, it would not give as much pleasure as an outline in black and white. And it is mainly because a play is a representation of action that it also for that reason represents people.

VII. 2–7   We have laid it down that tragedy is a representation of an action that is whole and complete and of a certain magnitude, since a thing may be a whole and yet have no magnitude. A whole is what has a beginning and middle and end. A beginning is that which is not a necessary consequent of anything else but after which something else exists or happens as a natural result. An end on the contrary is that which is inevitably or, as a rule, the natural result of something else but from which nothing else follows; a middle follows something else and something follows from it. Well constructed plots must not therefore begin and end at random, but must embody the formulae we have stated.

388

CLASSICAL APPENDIX

VIII. 1–
IX. 4

A plot does not have unity, as some people think, simply because it deals with a single hero. Many and indeed innumerable things happen to an individual, some of which do not go to make up any unity, and similarly an individual is concerned in many actions which do not combine into a single piece of action. It seems therefore that all those poets are wrong who have written a *Heracleid* or *Theseid* or other such poems. They think that because Heracles was a single individual the plot must for that reason have unity. But Homer, supreme also in all other respects, was apparently well aware of this truth either by instinct or from knowledge of his art. For in writing an *Odyssey* he did not put in all that ever happened to Odysseus, his being wounded on Parnassus, for instance, or his feigned madness when the host was gathered (these being events neither of which necessarily or probably led to the other), but he constructed his *Odyssey* round a single action in our sense of the phrase. And the *Iliad* the same. As then in the other arts of representation a single representation means a representation of a single object, so too the plot being a representation of a piece of action must represent a single piece of action and the whole of it; and the component incidents must be so arranged that if one of them be transposed or removed, the unity of the whole is dislocated and destroyed. For if the presence or absence of a thing makes no visible difference, then it is not an integral part of the whole.

What we have said already makes it further clear that a poet's object is not to tell what actually happened but what could and would happen either probably or inevitably. The difference between a historian and a poet is not that one writes in prose and the other in verse —indeed the writings of Herodotus could be put into verse and yet would still be a kind of history, whether written in metre or not. The real difference is this, that one tells what happened and the other what might happen. For this reason poetry is something more scientific and serious than history, because poetry tends to give general truths while history gives particular facts.

By a 'general truth' I mean the sort of thing that a certain type of man will do or say either probably or necessarily. . . . A 'particular fact' is what Alcibiades did or what was done to him.

XIII. 1-5   Following upon what has been said above we should
next state what ought to be aimed at and what avoided
in the construction of a plot, and the means by which the
object of tragedy may be achieved. Since then the structure of the best tragedy should be not simple but complex
and one that represents incidents arousing fear and pity
—for that is peculiar to this form of art—it is obvious to
begin with that one should not show worthy men
passing from good fortune to bad. That does not arouse
fear or pity but shocks our feelings. Nor again wicked
people passing from bad fortune to good. That is the
most untragic of all, having none of the requisite qualities,
since it does not satisfy our feelings or arouse pity or fear.
Nor again the passing of a thoroughly bad man from
good fortune to bad fortune. Such a structure might
satisfy our feelings but it arouses neither pity nor fear,
the one being for the man who does not deserve his misfortune and the other for the man who is like ourselves—
pity for the undeserved misfortune, fear for the man like ourselves—so that the result will arouse neither pity nor fear.
There remains then the mean between these. This is
the sort of man who is not pre-eminently virtuous and
just, and yet it is through no badness or villainy of his
own that he falls into the misfortune, but rather through
some flaw in him, he being one of those who are in high
station and good fortune, like Oedipus and Thyestes and
the famous men of such families as those.

XIV. 1-5   Fear and pity sometimes result from the spectacle and
are sometimes aroused by the actual arrangement of the
incidents, which is preferable and the mark of a better
poet. The plot should be so constructed that even without
seeing the play anyone hearing of the incidents happening
thrills with fear and pity as a result of what occurs. So
would anyone feel who heard the story of Oedipus. To
produce this effect by means of an appeal to the eye is
inartistic and needs adventitious aid, while those who
by such means produce an effect which is not fearful but
merely monstrous have nothing in common with tragedy.
For one should not seek from tragedy all kinds of pleasure
but that which is peculiar to tragedy, and since the poet
must by 'representation' produce the pleasure which
comes from feeling pity and fear, obviously this quality
must be embodied in the incidents.

XXV. 26–
27

In general any 'impossibility' may be defended by reference to the poetic effect or to the ideal or to current opinion. For poetic effect a convincing impossibility is preferable to that which is unconvincing though possible.

(*Aristotle, Longinus, Demetrius,*
W. Hamilton Fyfe, Loeb Classical
Library, 1953)

From

HORACE: *The Art of Poetry*

38–45

Take a subject, ye writers, equal to your strength; and ponder long what your shoulders refuse, and what they are able to bear. Whoever shall choose a theme within his range, neither speech will fail him, nor clearness of order. Of order, this, if I mistake not, will be the excellence and charm that the author of the long-promised poem shall say at the moment what at that moment should be said, reserving and omitting much for the present, loving this point and scorning that.

46–72

Moreover, with a nice taste and care in weaving words together, you will express yourself most happily, if a skilful setting makes a familiar word new. . . . It has ever been, and ever will be, permitted to issue words stamped with the mint-mark of the day. As forests change their leaves with each year's decline, and the earliest drop off: so with words, the old race dies, and, like the young of human kind, the new-born bloom and thrive. . . . Many terms that have fallen out of use shall be born again, and those shall fall that are now in repute, if Usage so will it, in whose hands lies the judgement, the right and the rule of speech.

99–111

Not enough is it for poems to have beauty: they must have charm, and lead the hearer's soul where they will. As men's faces smile on those who smile, so they respond to those who weep. If you would have me weep, you must first feel grief yourself: then, O Telephus or Peleus, will your misfortunes hurt me: if the words you utter are ill suited, I shall laugh or fall asleep. Sad tones befit the face of sorrow: blustering accents that of anger; jests become the merry, solemn words the grave. For Nature first shapes us within to meet every change of fortune: she brings joy or impels to anger, or bows us to the ground and tortures us under a load of grief; then, with the tongue for interpreter, she proclaims the emotions of the soul.

119–30   Either follow tradition or invent what is self-consistent. If haply, when you write, you bring back to the stage the honouring of Achilles, let him be impatient, passionate, ruthless, fierce; let him claim that laws are not for him, let him ever make appeal to the sword. Let Medea be fierce and unyielding, Ino tearful, Ixion forsworn, Io a wanderer, Orestes sorrowful. If it is an untried theme you entrust to the stage, and if you boldly fashion a fresh character, have it kept to the end even as it came forth at the first, and have it self-consistent.

It is hard to treat in your own way what is common: and you are doing better in spinning into acts a song of Troy than if, for the first time, you were giving the world a theme unknown and unsung.

146–52   Nor does he [*the wise poet*] begin Diomede's return from the death of Meleager, or the war of Troy from the twin eggs. Ever he hastens to the issue, and hurries his hearer into the story's midst, as if already known, and what he fears he cannot make attractive with his touch he abandons; and so skilfully does he invent, so closely does he blend facts and fiction, that the middle is not discordant with the beginning, nor the end with the middle.

179–201   Either an event is acted on the stage, or the action is narrated. Less vividly is the mind stirred by what finds entrance through the ears than by what is brought before the trusty eyes, and what the spectator can see for himself. Yet you will not bring upon the stage what should be performed behind the scenes, and you will keep much from our eyes, which an actor's ready tongue will narrate anon in our presence; so that Medea is not to butcher her boys before the people, nor impious Atreus cook human flesh upon the stage, nor Procne be turned into a bird, Cadmus into a snake. Whatever you thus show me, I discredit and abhor.

Let no play be either shorter or longer than five acts, if when once seen it hopes to be called for and brought back to the stage. And let no god intervene, unless a knot come worthy of such a deliverer, nor let a fourth actor essay to speak.

Let the Chorus sustain the part and strenuous duty of an actor, and sing nothing between acts which does not advance and fitly blend into the plot. It should side with the good and give friendly counsel; sway the angry and cherish the righteous. It should praise the fare of a modest board, praise wholesome justice, law, and peace with her open gates; should keep secrets, and pray and beseech the gods that fortune may return to the unhappy, and depart from the proud.

263–9   Not every critic discerns unmusical verses, and so un-deserved indulgence has been granted our Roman poets. Am I therefore to run loose and write without restraint? Or, supposing that all will see my faults, shall I seek safety and take care to keep within hope of pardon? At the best I have escaped censure, I have earned no praise. For yourselves, handle Greek models by night, handle them by day.

309–18   Of good writing the source and fount is wisdom. Your matter the Socratic pages can set forth, and when matter is in hand words will not be loath to follow. He who has learned what he owes his country and his friends, what love is due a parent, a brother, and a guest, what is im-posed on senator and judge, what is the function of a general sent to war, he surely knows how to give each character his fitting part. I would advise one who has learned the imitative art to look to life and manners for a model, and draw from thence living words.

333–44   Poets aim either to benefit, or to amuse, or to utter words at once both pleasing and helpful to life. Whenever you instruct, be brief, so that what is quickly said the mind may readily grasp and faithfully hold: every word in excess flows away from the full mind. Fictions meant to please should be close to the real, so that your play must not ask for belief in anything it chooses . . . He has won every vote who has blended profit and pleasure, at once delighting and instructing the reader.

361–5   A poem is like a picture: one strikes your fancy more, the nearer you stand; another, the farther away. This courts the shade, that will wish to be seen in the light, and dreads not the critic insight of the judge. This pleased but once; that, though ten times called for, will always please.

408–11   Often it is asked whether a praiseworthy poem be due to Nature or to art. For my part, I do not see of what avail is either study, when not enriched by Nature's vein, or native wit, if untrained; so truly does each claim the other's aid, and make with it a friendly league.

> (Horace: *Satires, Epistles and Ars Poetica*, H. Rushton Fairclough, Loeb Classical Library, 1947)

From

LONGINUS: *On the Sublime*

I. 3–II. 3   . . . the Sublime consists in a consummate excellence and distinction of language, and that this alone gave to the greatest poets and historians their pre-eminence and clothed them with immortal fame. For the effect of genius is not to persuade the audience but rather to transport them out of themselves. Invariably what inspires wonder casts a spell upon us and is always superior to what is merely convincing and pleasing. For our convictions are usually under our own control, while such passages exercise an irresistible power of mastery and get the upper hand with every member of the audience.

Again inventive skill and the due disposal and marshalling of facts do not show themselves in one or two touches: they gradually emerge from the whole tissue of the composition, while, on the other hand, a well-timed flash of sublimity scatters everything before it like a bolt of lightning and reveals the full power of the speaker at a single stroke. . . .

We must begin now by raising the question whether there is an art of sublimity or profundity, for some think those are wholly at fault who try to bring such matters under systematic rules. Genius, it is said, is born and does not come of teaching, and the only art for producing it is nature. Works of natural genius, so people think, are spoiled and utterly demeaned by being reduced to the dry bones of rule and precept. For my part I hold that the opposite may be proved, if we consider that while in lofty emotion Nature for the most part knows no law,

yet it is not the way of Nature to work at random and
wholly without system. In all production Nature is the
prime cause, the great exemplar; but as to all questions
of degree, of the happy moment in each case, and again
of the safest rules of practice and use, such prescriptions
are the proper contribution of an art or system. We must
remember also that mere grandeur runs the greater risk,
if left to itself without the stay and ballast of scientific
method, and abandoned to the impetus of uninstructed
enterprise. For genius needs the curb as often as the spur.
Speaking of the common life of men Demosthenes de-
clares that the greatest of all blessings is good fortune,
and that next comes good judgement, which is indeed
quite as important, since the lack of it often completely
cancels the advantage of the former. We may apply this
to literature and say that Nature fills the place of good
fortune, Art that of good judgement. And above all we
must remember this: the very fact that in literature some
effects come of natural genius alone can only be learnt
from art.

VII. 2–4   For the true sublime, by some virtue of its nature,
elevates us: uplifted with a sense of proud possession, we
are filled with joyful pride, as if we had ourselves produced the very thing we heard. If, then, a man of sense,
well-versed in literature, after hearing a passage several
times finds that it does not affect him with a sense of
sublimity, and does not leave behind in his mind more
food for thought than the mere words at first suggest, but
rather that on careful consideration it sinks in his esteem,
then it cannot really be the true sublime, if its effect does
not outlast the moment of utterance. For what is truly
great gives abundant food for thought: it is irksome, nay,
impossible, to resist its effect: the memory of it is
stubborn and indelible. To speak generally, you should
consider that to be truly beautiful and sublime which
pleases all people at all times. For when men who differ
in their habits, their lives, their tastes, their ages, their
dates, all agree together in holding one and the same
view about the same writings, then the unanimous
verdict, as it were, of such discordant judges makes our
faith in the admired passage strong and indisputable.

XIV   We too, then, when we are working at some passage
that demands sublimity of thought and expression, should

do well to form in our hearts the question, 'How perchance would Homer have said this, how would Plato or
Demosthenes have made it sublime or Thucydides in his
history?' Emulation will bring those great characters
before our eyes, and like guiding stars they will lead our
thoughts to the ideal standards of perfection. Still more
will this be so, if we give our minds the further hint,
'How would Homer or Demosthenes, had either been
present, have listened to this passage of mine? How would
it have affected them?' Great indeed is the ordeal, if we
propose such a jury and audience as this to listen to our
own utterances and make believe that we are submitting
our work to the scrutiny of such superhuman witnesses
and judges. Even more stimulating would it be to add,
'If I write this, how would all posterity receive it?' But if
a man shrinks at the very thought of saying anything that
exceeds the comprehension of his own time, then must all
the conceptions of that man's nature be like some blind,
half-formed embryo, all too abortive for the life of
posthumous fame.

XXXIII.
2–4

Now I am well aware that the greatest natures are
least immaculate. Perfect precision runs the risk of
triviality, whereas in great writing as in great wealth
there must needs be something overlooked. Perhaps it is
inevitable that the humble, mediocre natures, because
they never run any risks, never aim at the heights, should
remain to a large extent safe from error, while in great
natures their very greatness spells danger. Not indeed
that I am ignorant of this second point, that whatever
men do is always inevitably regarded from the worst
side: faults make an ineradicable impression, but beauties
soon slip from our memory. I have myself noted a good
many faults in Homer and the other greatest authors, and
though these slips certainly offend my taste, yet I prefer
to call them not wilful mistakes but careless oversights,
let in casually almost and at random by the heedlessness
of genius. In spite, then, of these faults I still think that
great excellence, even if it is not sustained throughout
at the same level, should always be voted the first place,
if for nothing else, for its inherent nobility.

(*Aristotle, Longinus, Demetrius,* op. cit.)

Select Bibliography

Aristotle's Art of Poetry, W. Hamilton Fyfe (Oxford, 1940)
Aristotle's Poetics, Humphry House. Rev. by Colin Hardie (London, 1956)
Longinus and English Criticism, T. R. Henn (Cambridge, 1934)
Loci Critici, selected and arranged by George Saintsbury (Boston, 1903)
Critical Approaches to Literature, D. Daiches (London, 1956)
Prefaces to Criticism, W. J. Bate (Doubleday/Mayflower, 1960)
The Making of Literature, R. A. Scott-James (London, 1930)
A History of Criticism and Literary Taste in Europe, George Saintsbury (3 vols., Edinburgh, 1900–4)
A History of English Criticism (a revision of the English chapters of the above), George Saintsbury (Edinburgh, 1911)
Literary Criticism: A Short History, W. K. Wimsatt and Cleanth Brooks (New York, 1957)
The Poet's Defence, J. Bronowski (Cambridge, 1939)
History of Literary Criticism in the Renaissance, J. E. Spingarn (New York, 1899)
English Literary Criticism: The Renascence, J. W. H. Atkins (London, 1947)
The Use of Poetry and the Use of Criticism, T. S. Eliot (London, 1933)
Elizabethan Critical Essays, ed. G. Gregory Smith (2 vols., Oxford, 1904)
English Critical Essays: 16th to 18th Centuries, ed. Edmund D. Jones (Oxford, 1922)
'Shakespeare Criticism: from Dryden to Coleridge', T. S. Eliot (*A Companion to Shakespeare Studies*, ed. H. Granville-Barker and G. B. Harrison, Cambridge, 1934)
English Literary Criticism: 17th and 18th Centuries, J. W. H. Atkins (London, 1951)
Critical Essays of the 17th Century, ed. J. E. Spingarn (3 vols., Oxford, 1908–9)
Shakespearean Criticism, 1623–1840, ed. D. Nichol Smith (Oxford, 1916)

398   SELECT BIBLIOGRAPHY

A History of Modern Criticism, 1750–1950, R. Wellek (vols. I & II, London, 1955; III & IV to follow)

Critical Essays of the 18th Century, ed. W. H. Durham (Yale, 1915)

Taste and Criticism in the 18th Century, ed. H. A. Needham (London, 1952)

Shakespeare in the 18th Century, D. Nichol Smith (Oxford, 1928)

Samuel Johnson's Literary Criticism, J. H. Hagstrum (Minneapolis, 1952)

The Critical Opinions of Samuel Johnson, J. E. Brown (Princeton, 1926)

'Johnson and Augustanism', *The Common Pursuit*, F. R. Leavis (London, 1952)

'Johnson as Critic and Poet', *On Poetry and Poets*, T. S. Eliot (London, 1957)

Criticism and the 19th Century, G. Tillotson (London, 1951)

English Critical Essays of the 19th Century, ed. Edmund D. Jones (Oxford, 1916)

'Coleridge in Criticism', F. R. Leavis (*Scrutiny*, Vol. IX, No. 1, June 1940)

Coleridge on Imagination, I. A. Richards (London, 1934)

'Arnold as Critic', F. R. Leavis (*Scrutiny*, Vol. VII, No. 3, December 1938)

Shakespeare Criticism, 1919–1935, ed. Anne Bradby (Ridler) (Oxford, 1936)

D. H. Lawrence: Selected Literary Criticism, ed. A. Beal (London, 1955)

'The Frontiers of Criticism', *On Poetry and Poets*, T. S. Eliot (London, 1957)

Poetry and Morality, Vincent Buckley (London, 1959)